Off The Beaten Track
Britain

BRITAIN

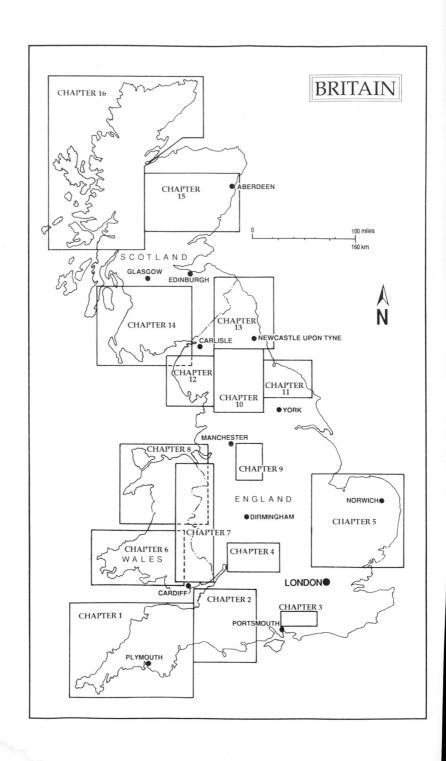

OFF
THE BEATEN TRACK
GREAT BRITAIN

HarperPerennial
A Division of HarperCollins*Publishers*

This book is published in the United Kingdom by Moorland Publishing Co Ltd.

OFF THE BEATEN TRACK: GREAT BRITAIN

© 1991 Moorland Publishing Co Ltd

First HARPERPERENNIAL edition published in 1991

ISBN 0-06-273016-9

Colour origination by:
Scantrans, Singapore

Printed in the UK by:
Butler and Tanner Ltd, Frome, Somerset

Cover photograph:
Weobley (*MPC Picture Collection*)

Black and white illustrations have been supplied as follows:

J. Barton: pp 29, 31, 33, 36; H. Brown: pp 295, 297, 307; L. Garner: pp 102, 107, 121, 125, 129; MPC Picture Collection: pp 13, 105, 118, 139, 144, 150, 159, 163, 165, 172, 209, 210; National Trust for Scotland: p 299; R. Sale: pp 9, 17, 19; Ron Scholes: pp 257, 264, 269; Bob Smith: pp 277, 279, 283; B. Spencer: pp 201, 204, 218, 221, 226; C. Tully: pp 81, 84, 86, 90; G. Wright: pp 41, 46, 49, 52, 55, 60, 63, 71, 73, 184, 186, 192, 235, 239, 245.

Colour illustrations have been supplied as follows:

J. Barton *(Bury, Petworth, Trotton Bridge)*; J. Moss *(Loch Maree)*; MPC Picture Collection *(Three Cliffs Bay, Arthur's Stone, Pembridge, Ludlow Castle, Erddig Hall, Pontcysyllte Aqueduct, Dove Valley near Hollinsclough, High Peak Trail, Rievaulx Abbey, Farm buildings at Finsthwaite)*; Ron Scholes *(Wanlockhead, MacLellan's Castle, Drumlanrig Castle)*; Bob Smith *(Loch Einich)*; B. Spencer *(Runswick Bay, Lower Eskdale)*; C. Tully *(Blakeney Quay, Denver Windmill)*; J.P. Walker *(Tobermory)*; G. Wright *(Montacute House, Dorset Coast near Swanage, Milton Abbas, Stanway House, Cotswold Lanscape, Thwaite, Semer Water, Marsden Rocks, Bamburgh Castle)*.

Contents

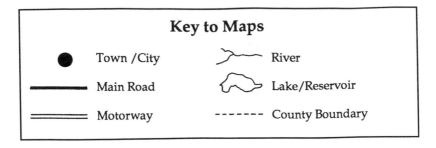

Key to Maps

● Town /City   ⌒ River

─── Main Road   ⌒ Lake/Reservoir

═══ Motorway   ------- County Boundary

Note on Maps

The maps for each chapter, while comprehensive, are not designed to be used as route maps, but rather to locate the main towns, villages and places of interest.

A Note to the Reader

We hope you have found this book informative, helpful and enjoyable. It is always our aim to make our publications as accurate and up to date as possible. With this in mind, we would appreciate any comments that you might have. If you come across any information to update this book or discover something new about the area we have covered, please let us know so that your notes may be incorporated in future editions.

As it is the publisher's principal aim to produce books that are lively and responsive to change, any information that readers provide will be a valuable asset in maintaining the highest possible standards.

Introduction

The words and images in the following pages show Britain at its best. England, Scotland and Wales combine to produce a nation of rich diversity, steeped in history and full of beautiful, varied landscapes waiting to be explored. At the same time, each of these countries exists in its own right and has a character all of its own. This book captures the essential qualities of all three countries to create a picture of the byways and quieter corners of Britain; from the green valleys of Wales, and the magnificent domain of the Scottish Highlands, to the secluded coastal coves of Cornwall.

All too often, beauty spots in Britain have become inundated with tourists, so much so that there is almost an established tour of Britain taking in honeypots such as Stratford, Oxford, York and, of course, London. Because of this, it is not always easy to find out-of-the-way places to write about. Opinions differ as to what is meant by the term 'off the beaten track'. Suffice is to say that, in a British context, the phrase describes places which are not necessarily miles from anywhere but certainly do not constitute part of the main tourist circuit.

The places described are ones which will appeal to travellers of an independent spirit who value personal discovery above prescribed experience and who would rather avoid the human conveyor belt of queues, traffic jams and packed accommodation. It is for such travellers that this guidebook has been written. In its pages, no more than passing mention is made of the famous and the well documented — other guidebooks will satisfy the appetite for such orthodox tourist information. Instead, the reader is taken if not to unknown then to relatively unvisited places. Through the specialist knowledge of the authors, visitors using this guidebook will gain insights into Britain's heartland. Occasionally the reader is urged simply to take a sideways step from a site of renowned tourist interest to discover a place less frequented but often of equivalent fascination.

From wild, scantily populated countryside whose footpaths and byways are best navigated by careful map reading, to negotiating the side streets of towns and cities, travelling 'off the beaten track' can be more demanding than following in the footsteps of countless thousands before you. The way may be less clear, but opportunities do emerge for real discovery in an age of increasing dissatisfaction with the passive predictability of conventional holidaymaking. With greater emphasis on exploring 'off the beaten track', the essence of Britain is more likely to be unearthed and its true flavours relished to the full.

John Robey
Series Editor

1 • Devon and Cornwall

Devon

Devon is a county of contrast. The south is the land of cream teas and holiday beaches that lie in shallow bays among few cliffs, while to the north there are more rugged cliffs, with sea edge villages that cling to them in a way that the visitor is more accustomed to seeing in Cornwall. Between the two lies Dartmoor, a huge brooding mass — a land of dark legend.

To the north-west of Dartmoor, and so lying between it and the sea, is the land of the 'two rivers'. The 'two rivers' are the Torridge and the Taw, famous for angling and otter-hunting, the Taw having been the 'Gentleman's River', because the inns along it were sited for the hunt's lunches. On the Torridge they were not so well defined. In this country Henry Williamson set *Tarka The Otter*, the most famous of his wild animal books. Tarka was named from the local dialect word, *Ta*, the ancient word for river which is seen in both Taw and Torridge, Tamar and Teign and several other rivers in this area. It was the waters of the Taw that closed over the heads of Tarka and Deadlock (the otter-hound) as they fought their last battle.

Between the two rivers the North Devon farmland is bleaker than the land on the southern and western sides of Dartmoor. Near Beaford and Roborough it even shows a touch of moorland. However, the wooded Torridge Valley and the sheltered Mully Brook that drains down to the Taw are splendid, perhaps not as spectacularly beautiful as other Devon rivers, but secluded and unspoilt.

To explore the local area the visitor should go to **Great Torrington** on the A386 south of Bideford, set high on the Torridge Valley side. From Castle Hill, to the east of the town, there are superb views to the river. The Norman castle that gave the hill its name was built in the twelfth century. It was not an 'official' castle, having been privately constructed by the local lord of the manor. In 1228 the Crown decided to make an example of the work and ordered it to be demolished. It was rebuilt about a century later, but demolished for good in the seventeenth century, this time not by decree, but during the Civil War. The castle walls that run along the town above the River Torridge have no connection with the real castle, having been built in Georgian times.

The obelisk that shares the hill with the visitor was erected to commemorate the Battle of Waterloo. Another battle is commemorated by the Church of St Michael's and All Angels. During the Civil War the town and area was

Great Torrington

stoutly defended by the Royalist leader Colonel Rigby, though by 1646 when Fairfax's Parliamentarian army arrived to take the town it was Lord Hopton who controlled the garrison. In the battle that followed about 200 Royalist prisoners were taken and herded into the town church which was used as a makeshift prison. The church was also used as a powder magazine until the powder exploded, killing all the prisoners, together with their guards. It seems that the incident was unfortunate rather than deliberate. Today's church was built in 1651. Near the church is the Town Hall — a fine columned building — and opposite it is the Black Horse, a few years older than the church and very elegantly set. Torrington was one of the most important market towns in North Devon during medieval times. Even today, the cattle markets are some of the most important in the South-West. Visitors to the town on the first Thursday in May can enjoy the traditional May fair celebrations.

In the town is England's famous Dartington Glass Factory where visitors are welcome to join one of the guided tours around it. Within easy reach are the Rosemoor Gardens, well worth visiting for the variety of shrubs and plants growing in this sheltered valley. Close to Great Torrington and reached along the B3220 is **Beaford**, a delightful village set above the Torridge. Beaford is home to an arts centre which offers theatre, music and poetry concerts which are staged in the summer season. Nearby are

Ashreigney and **Burrington**, two villages set on the high plateau between the two rivers. Their position means that they are frequently windswept, but the panoramic views, towards both Exmoor and Dartmoor, more than compensate for this.

North of Great Torrington the joint estuary of the Torridge and Taw rivers makes a mess of the elegant line of the South-West Peninsula Coastal Path. However, a really fine section of high cliff then offers good walking again. This is Baggy Point which lies to the north and west of Croyde. **Croyde** on the B3231 running west from Braunton is a straightforward holiday village with few pretensions. The bay is famous for its enclosing horns that channel water which rears up, offering one of the best surf runs after Cornwall's Atlantic coast.

Baggy Point sits above calmer seas, its walls a home for rock climbers who are viewed by many with the same jaundiced eye that is cast over the surfers of Croyde Bay. The point is a short and narrow thumb of land reaching out into the sea and so offers a very good walk. It is possible to return to the National Trust car park close to Croyde village along the quiet lanes near Putsborough.

Returning to Great Torrington and travelling west, you reach a strange part of Devon. Apart from places where arbitrary bureaucratic decisions have robbed it of the distinction, the River Tamar divides Cornwall from Devon. The river source is about 4 miles (7km) inland, but instead of following the line of the river to the sea, so that the border met the water near Clovelly, the boundary turns seaward, following Harsland Water to the Atlantic. At a stroke of the boundary-maker's pen a section of 'Cornish' high cliff seascape was transferred to Devon. Certainly those who associate the seascapes of Devon with the sandy beaches of Slapton, and the holiday towns to its north, will be surprised by the rugged, majestic coastline around Hartland Point, particularly the spectacular section that lies south of the lighthouse-crowned headland. On the way to Baggy Point the visitor passes an RAF station which is well sited in this secret corner.

The lighthouse at **Hartland Point** attracts many interested visitors impressed not least by the curious cement slope beside the gates. It was, until quite recently, used to catch rainwater, the lighthouse-keeper's only source of water. South of the point is **Hartland Quay** and its hotel. The quay was originally built by monks from Hartland Abbey which was built at Stoke, a village closer to the quay. A more modern mansion incorporates what little remains of the Augustinian monastery and is occasionally open to the public. The quay was destroyed by the fury of the ocean many years ago.

Stoke, reached from Hartland which lies on the B3248 but leaves the A39 close to Clovely, is a village worthy of note. Its church, with an interesting dedication to St Nectan, is quite lovely and the 130ft (40m) tower is the second highest in the county. The church below the tower was built in the thirteenth century, but it replaced an earlier one erected by Gytha, wife of the Saxon Earl Godwin. The countess built the church in thanks for the escape of her husband from a storm that threatened to destroy his ship on the Hartland rocks. The dedication is for a sixth-century Celtic monk who

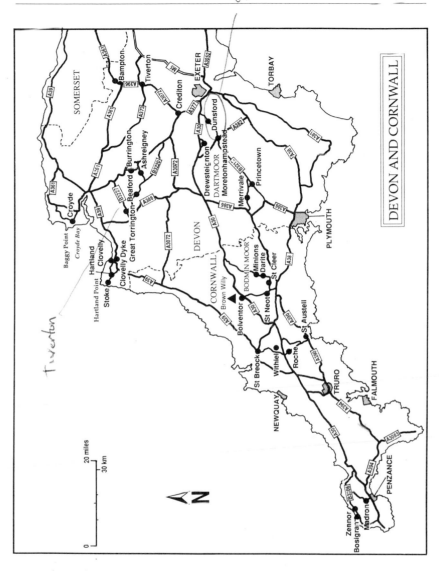

arrived near here from Ireland, setting up a hermitage in the wooded valley
of what is now called the Abbey River. The monk was set upon by local
robbers and beheaded. In time-honoured fashion, Nectan picked up his
head and carried it back to his cell where a spring of water welled up close
to stones that had been marked by droplets of the saint's blood.

Moving 3 miles (5km) north-east from Hartland, few visitors reach the
small cove that holds **Blackchurch Rock**, though the walk to it from the
nearby car park is straightforward and pleasant enough. The inverted V of
rock is remarkable, one side steep enough to keep rock climbers happy, the
other laying back enough to give the intrepid visitor a chance to reach its

top. The cove's rock pools are delightful. If you visit with children make sure they do not go too close to the steep but very loose and dangerous cliffs that lie to the east of the Blackchurch Rock.

East of Blackchurch is **Clovelly**. On a still, fine winter's day Clovelly is revealed as a charming, pretty village, blissfully free of cars. It is hard for the visitor to resist a solitary local piece of roadway called Hobby Drive, named because its construction really was the hobby of one lord of the manor. South of the village **Clovelly Dykes** is a large, 20 acre, Iron Age hillfort which was also used by the Romans. It would be interesting to know how the Roman soldiers, used to the tideless Mediterranean, viewed the Atlantic rollers crashing into Hartland Point.

Those seeking a pleasant half-day's walking should go along part of that section of the Somerset and North Devon Coastal Path that links Clovelly to Longpeak. In total there are 12 miles (19km) of marked path, but walks of any duration can be made. At any time the coast has something to offer in terms of seascape and elemental forces. The cliffs themselves are a wonderful sight, tortured grey strata, slabs and pinnacles, the vegetated flat tops often ablaze with nature's colours. Near Clovelly, on the first section west of the village, the Somerset and North Devon Coastal Path really does go past the 'No Right of Way' sign, on a permissive footpath through the Clovelly Court Estate. A little further on is Gallantry Bowers, named not for the gallants of century's past, but from *col-an-veor* or 'great ridge'.

East from the Torridge and Hartland Point are a number of small towns and large villages that are worth a visit. **Tiverton** on the A361 and **Crediton** on the A377 are the better known, the former with a fine folk museum the star attraction in which is a waterwheel, the latter with the tall-chimneyed Spurway Almshouses. These were built in the sixteenth century by a local clothier and are worth seeing not only for the magnificent chimneys, but for the Fire Mark plaque in the centre of the wall. In the nineteenth century the local fire brigade would attend houses with paid up fire insurance before those that had none. The Fire Mark was a sign that insurance had been paid.

Smaller than either Tiverton and Crediton is **Bampton**, 5 miles (8km) north of Tiverton just off the A396, a delightfully set village built on the pattern of a crossroads. At the northern end are the remains of a Norman motte-and-bailey castle, though it is not recognisable at first sight. Walk to Brook Street where the bridge over the River Batherm is a fine structure offering good views of the river itself. The old Toll House beyond once collected the levies from travellers along the Packhorse Way who used to export Bampton cloth and wool to the markets of the south. Opposite Brook Street is the aptly named Frog Street down the sides of which the Shuttern Brook runs, if the weather has been unfriendly enough to rain on the visitor. Back towards the dominating, fifteenth-century church the visitor can have a rest in The Swan, an inn of uncertain age. Many contend that its features indicate a sixteenth-century origin, while others argue that it is older.

Dartmoor can be a forbidding place to the visitor who is no great walker. **Postbridge** on the B2212 that traverses the moor is the best place to start

Granite tors are a familiar sight on Dartmoor

exploring, heading north on to the moor to visit **Sittaford Tor**, well known to readers of Agatha Christie and the one tor that is always on the route of the Ten Tors challenge walk. North beyond that, try to find the letterbox at **Cranmere Pool**. There are now many letterboxes on Dartmoor but the Cranmere Pool box is the box you must aim to reach. Years ago an intrepid walker, wondering how many others like himself reached this loneliest part of the moor, set up a box and deposited a letter addressed to himself with a note asking the next walker who arrived at the box to take the letter to the nearest village for posting — suggesting that the new man should leave a letter of his own for the next visitor to do the same. Estimates of how long the man waited vary from weeks to years, but the trend has spread

Ask anyone to name the most beautiful river in Devon and they will probably say the Dart, extolling the virtues of Dartmeet, Dittisham and Dartmouth. Ask if they know the Teign, and most are dismissive. Yet from its rise on Dartmoor near Quintin's Man (close to Cranmere Pool) the River Teign cuts a beautiful valley towards the sea, and nowhere more so than in the deeply wooded cleft that takes the river around the final eastern bastion of Dartmoor — Mardon Down.

In the wooded valley are the occasional remains of mills, evidence of the river's old industry. The whole valley in this section is now natural with trees growing right down to the water's edge, providing a protected haven for wildlife. The protection even extends, in imagination at least, to the twin hillforts that stand on each bank of the river above Fingle Bridge, a pack-horse bridge dating from the sixteenth century. Near the bridge the river valley is at its prettiest.

The Hunters' Path climbs up through the oak woods to come out above the tree line, with the spectacle of expansive views ahead to northern Dartmoor. This route provides a pleasant link to **Castle Drogo**, 1 mile (2km) north-east of the A382, built from local granite by Sir Edwin Luytens. It was designed for the local Drewe family, a twentieth-century version of an all granite medieval castle. The foundation stone was laid in 1911 but the original plans were reduced in size. Castle Drogo was built just in time for the Drewe family to move in. The castle-like form has elements which owe much to Roman, Norman and Tudor castle styles. The Drewe family gave the castle to the National Trust in 1973. Close to Castle Drogo, and on the return route, is Hunter's Tor with a superb view down the valley. From the tor the Teign is 400ft (121m) below. Be sure to visit **Dunsford**, a showpiece of thatched cottages and a real slice of old Devonshire — do not miss the Fulford memorial monument in the church. This family lived at Great Fulford which, sadly, is not open to the public.

In sharp contrast to this wooded splendour is the barren moor of **Mardon Down**, 1 mile (2km) north of Moretonhampstead. Perhaps moor is too strong a description because this is not the bleak, boggy moor but a lower, softer, grass downland, more akin to the Quantocks further north. The Headless Cross on the down is not a memorial to some foul murder, but just what its name implies. Four centuries ago such crosses, at crossroads and at the top of steep climbs, were common, but many were swept away by the wave of Puritanism that crossed England. In the case of Mardon Down only the cross was removed, so the shaft still remains. Mardon Down is a fine place to see the 'real' Dartmoor, with a panoramic view from the southern edge of the down.

Moretonhampstead, once the capital of Dartmoor, is now a small, quiet town. The almshouses are worth a visit. **Princetown** is famous for the prison, a grim looking place, the more so for the surrounding signs warning the tourist cars to keep moving. It has little to detain the traveller, but a short way to the west, at **Merrivale** on the B3357, the moor can be safely approached by anyone. There is a car park just short of the village. Heading southwards, the BBC television mast on North Hessary Tor is seen in the distance. A fine group of megaliths is soon reached. There is a double row of stones here running east-west. The most northerly row is 656ft (200m) long and finishes, at its eastern end, with a single large stone. The longer, more southerly row ends in the same way. This row has, at its centre, a small cairn set within a stone circle. About 164ft (50m) away is another cairn with another row of stones. About 492ft (150m) to the south there is also another stone circle. Elsewhere in the area there are other circles and groups of stones. Of all of these relics the only ones that are well understood are the group called the Potato or Plague Market. When Black Death struck this area of England the local folk, anxious to stay away from anyone who might be a carrier, set up a market for the buying and selling of potatoes in this out-of-the-way spot. At similar markets elsewhere the goods were left in one place to be collected by the buyer who was watched by the seller as he dropped his money into a bucket of vinegar. The sale was carried out by suspicious people who stayed at shouting distance. No record of such a vinegar bucket exists for the Merrivale site, but it is likely that something similar did take place.

For the rest of the site there are only informed guesses. The alignment of the rows suggest some ritual connected with the sun, while other astronomical interpretations have been placed on the other circles and groups. It has also been suggested that some of the circles indicate the position of huts. Perhaps this was the Bronze Age capital of Dartmoor, or an ancient monastery to some long-forgotton cult.

Cornwall

Though Bodmin Moor is both smaller and lower than Dartmoor, it is by no means the poor relation of its big brother across the Devonshire border. It too can boast the weather-worn tors, and the wonderfully barren, wild quality that characterises granite moorland. The legends of Bodmin Moor can also equal Dartmoor. There are several sites associated with King Arthur as well as the megaliths that are so frequently associated with the uplands of Cornwall.

The source of the River Fowey is in the high plateau north-east of Brown Willy, the highest place in Cornwall (1,375ft, 419m). As it flows down its shadowy valley to the sea, the Fowey civilises the moorland, its presence softening the landscape, its clear waters bubbling over small, boulder waterfalls, adding a touch of levity to the harsh moor. As the river leaves the moor, entering a delightful wooded valley section, it tumbles over the Golitha Falls, a beautiful spot and a haven for river birds.

Brown Willy can be climbed along paths that start from the main A30 near the **Jamaica Inn** at Bolventor. The inn needs no introduction to readers of Daphne du Maurier. Just south of the inn, along a narrow road, is **Dozmary Pool**, a lonely moorland pond steeped in myth. Part of the reason for its mysterious reputation is the absence of any stream feeding it, a fact viewed by ancient Cornishmen as evidence of the supernatural. The locals claimed that there was a whirlpool at the centre and that if a piece of wood was thrown in it would disappear, only to re-appear in Fowey harbour, and that it was also bottomless. Leland, the Elizabethan traveller, claimed that this part of the legend, at least, was false as his observations suggested it was 15 fathoms deep. He was clearly a poor observer because the pool is very shallow and can be comfortably waded through.

Later legends linked Dozmary Pool with King Arthur, claiming that it was into its waters that Bevidere threw Excalibur. A much older story is of John Tregeagle, a local man whose villainy was such that when he died his ghost was returned to the moor, sentenced to bail out Dozmary with a limpet shell that had a hole in it.

To the east of the Fowey is an expanse of wild moorland, not large enough or featureless enough to frighten off the walker, but covering sufficient territory to give the central region a really solitary air. The southern part of the moor is dominated by the TV mast on Caradon Hill, a useful landmark for the visitor, and by the weird rock geometry of **Cheesewring** reached from the B3254 Launceston to Liskeard road. The quarries here supplied

stone for Westminster Bridge, but thankfully closed before they had under-
mined the stone pile of the Cheesewring itself, though blasting during
quarrying operations are said to have disturbed it on many occasions. The
name does not derive from the use of the local stone in cheese making, or
from the resemblance of the pile to any part of cheese-making equipment.
The rocks look like a cider press and the apple mush that was left after the
juice had been removed was known locally as cheese. From the rocks the
views are breathtaking, taking in both the Atlantic and the Channel.

Close to the Cheesewring is **Rillaton Barrow**, a Bronze Age burial
chamber that, when excavated, was found to hold the body of a man and
several exquisite treasures, beads, a dagger and a cup which are now in the
British Museum. The gold cup has only been exhibited after a period of
being lost. Seeking to recover the cup, an archaeologist carefully searched
the records and discovered that after the excavation the cup had been given
to Queen Victoria as being part of a treasure trove. It was then re-discovered
in Buckingham Palace!

Perhaps because of this mysterious disappearance, the cup became part
of a local legend. The legend maintained that the barrow was the home of
a holy man and that the cup was his, and had the remarkable property of
refilling when it was emptied. The holy man used it to refresh passing
travellers. One day a traveller arrived and decided to scotch the reputation
of the cup by draining it dry. He drank and drank until he could hold no
more, but still the cup was full. Exasperated, but at the same time greedy to
own the cup, he threw its contents into the holy man's face, jumped on his
horse and rode off. The horse, staggering under his weight, went over the
rocks close to the Cheesewring and the man was killed.

Also close to the Cheesewring are **The Hurlers**, stones standing among
the hollow skeletons of the Bodmin's copper industry. The Hurlers are a
series of three stone circles, each 6ft (2m) in height and about 100ft (35m) in
diameter, and a pair of standing stones. The name derives from the legend
that they are a group of men turned to stone for daring to hurl a ball on the
Sabbath. The game they are said to have been playing can still be seen, a
game taking place at St Columb on Shrove Tuesday. **The Pipers** are a pair
of stones close to The Hurlers. They represent two men who played the
pipes as the game progressed. Again, the real reason for the existence of the
circles is not known, though it is obvious that the builders took enormous
trouble over their task, the individual stones having been planted into the
ground in such a way that all the tops were at the same height. One last
detail about the circle is that The Hurlers lie on the Dragon Path. This path
is known to all believers of the theory of ley lines, ancient tracks that criss-
crossed Britain as many as 5,000 years ago and beside which ancient man
built his equivalent of churches and cemeteries. The Dragon Path reputedly
links Land's End with Glastonbury Tor.

Another local prehistoric site is south of The Hurlers and close to the
village of Darite near St Cleer. **Trethevy Quoit** is one of the finest cromlechs
in England. Such cromlechs are burial chambers and there would once have
been an earth mound covering the stones. The capstone is nearly 12ft (4m)

Trethevy Quoit, believed to be a Bronze Age burial chamber

long. It is not known whether the hole in it is natural or the result of boring. Some people have suggested that it probably helped with the manoeuvring of the stone.

Near to the southern edge of Bodmin Moor are two small, but interesting villages. **St Cleer** is an ancient village famous as a centre for mining in the nineteenth century. It is calculated that ninety-five per cent of all the copper mined on Bodmin came from within the parish boundaries of St Cleer and nearby Linkinhorne. St Cleer Church chiefly dates from what might be termed the Golden Age of Cornish church building — the fifteenth century — though there are reminders of a previous Norman building. Close to the village is **King Doniert's Stone**. This is, in fact, a pair of stones, both incised with geometric patterns. One also has a Latin inscription to Doniert, a Cornish king drowned in 875.

The other village is **St Neot**, famous for the church's stained-glass rendering of the life of the saint after whom both church and village are named. There have been many theories about the exact details of the saint. Some have suggested he was only 4ft (1m) high, others that he was a healer who prayed diseases away while standing up to his neck in water. There are those who see a Glastonbury monk, others who see a brother to King Alfred.

William Cookworthy of Kingsbridge in Devon was a Quaker. He was also a chemist, and when he visited the area around **Hensbarrow** 5 miles (8km) north of St Austell he realised the potential for the porcelain industry of the kaolinised granite that lay under the poor soil. The local tin-mining was in decline and Cookworthy found no shortage of eager hands to help him found the Cornish china clay industry which is still a major employer in the country. Cookworthy made the first genuine English porcelain at his

Plymouth factory in 1768, though he failed in his attempt to keep the secret of Cornish china clay from Josiah Wedgewood.

Today the spoil from the clay mines make cones of white rock debris grouped around green pools, the water-filled remains of ancient pits. The landscape, dominated by industrial spoil heaps, may not appeal to the visitor seeking seclusion and nature in the wild. However, climb to the top of Hensbarrow Down, a mountain creeping all of 27ft (9m) past the 1,000ft (350m) contour where there are extensive views: the pyramids here may not have been artistically conceived but they do have a wild and desolate majesty.

North from Hensbarrow and visible from it, is **Roche Rock**, lying south of the village of Roche just off the A30. The rock has the remains of a chapel sculpted out of, and built on, its craggy outcrop. The visitor can climb the iron ladders and polished rock to the cell-like, fifteenth-century chapel.

North of the village of Roche is **Holy Well** where lunatics were immersed as a cure for their madness, and where a thrown pebble is said to reveal, in the bubbles that rise after it, the thrower's future. To the west is **Castle-an-Dinas**, an Iron Age hillfort set on a shallow, conical hill. According to legend, this is the hunting lodge of King Arthur.

The area close to Hensbarrow is divided by the A30. To the north of the road the countryside is quite different, though it is still dominated by the 'white pyramids'. The change to the Cornish moorland that forms the backbone of the county starts south of the main road, though the boggy mass of Goss Moor is inaccessible to all but the most stout hearted. By contrast, **St Breock Downs**, to the east of the A39 midway between Wadebridge and St Columb Major in the far north of the area, is accessible. It is a beautiful, windswept moor, a mother of Cornish rivers, with occasional curious concrete huts, doorless and windowless (but excellent windbreaks for picnic stoves). At its heart is Mene Gurta (Stone of Waiting) a Bronze Age standing stone, and from its northern edges there are superb views to the Northern Cornish Coast around Padstow Bay.

Off the down, to the south-east, is a quiet area of farmland grouped around the villages of St Wenn and Withiel, small and windswept, and the romantically named Tregonetha. **Withiel** lies on the Saints Way (Forth an Syns in Cornish), a waymarked footpath named in honour of the route followed by Celtic saints from Wales to Brittany. No evidence exists to suggest that the way is the actual route followed, but it does represent a very scenic walk from Padstow to Fowey.

The seascapes of the more secluded northern coast are as good as those to the south, and inland is some of the most mysterious scenery in Britain, littered with prehistoric stones, amazing not only for their number but for their beauty. Zennor Head and Gurnard's Head, off the B3306 south of St Ives, are excellent points from which to view the granite cliffs, each thrusting further out into the Atlantic than the local coast. The Cornish Coastal Path comes this way, but it is still possible to have a stretch of high cliff to yourself. Go when the wind and tide is bringing the sea in, to catch the best of Cornwall's sea scenery, thudding white water, and lungs full of salty air.

*Roche Rock with the remains
of its fifteenth-century chapel*

In calmer moments the caves offer excellent spots to picnic and watch the gulls or, perhaps, the rock climbers on the Great Zawn at Bosigran. The tin industry is represented at **Bosigran** on the B3306, 3 miles (5km) north of Pendeen, by twin engines houses set at right angles. The walls are solid, a chimney is still complete and nature is encroaching as ferns lodge in crevices and occasional stones loosen and fall. If you have the time, go south-west along the valley that separates Watch Croft from Carn Galver. From the rock-strewn summit, which has a magnificent view, you can survey the sea.

Inland from the coast the country is wild and ancient. Penwith District's policy of restricting building and immigration has left the landscape as depopulated as it probably was in Neolithic times, the perfect backdrop for the cromlechs (here called quoits) the standing stones and stone circles. **Zennor** has a fascinating folk museum, its displays covering both the mining and farming aspects of relatively recent local life. To complete a very good picture of the old life the museum is housed in an old mill.

South of Zennor and Bosigran is country as ancient as any in Britain. **Men-an-Tol**, close to Morvah, is as weird a site as you could visit. Here there are three stones, the outer two simple and upright, the central one circular and with a hole cut through it. Scholars have not even decided if the current alignment is original, let alone what it might truly mean. Until recent times it was said that children passed through the hole in the central stone, naked and with their backs to the sun, in order to be 'immunised' against rickets. The walk to Men-an-Tol starts from the Morvah to Madron road best taken from Penzance. Beside this lies **Lanyon Quoit**, a fine monument, though rebuilt to its present pattern after it had been carelessly knocked over. Beyond Men-an-Tol a fine walk continues, reaching **Men Scryfa**, the Written Stone. This is inscribed in ogham script and reads *Rialobranus Cunovali Fili* which could be translated as Royal Raven Son of Cunoval. It has been speculated that he died in battle as there is no evidence of a cemetery and the stone may have been a local find — a convenient Neolithic standing stone. In the early nineteenth century the stone was raised after being tipped over during the prospecting for gold said to be lying below it.

From Men Scryfa a path heads south-east to the ruined engine of the **Ding Dong Mine**. Tradition says that the famous tin mine was worked in Roman times. It re-started in 1814 but finally closed in 1928. Eastwards is the **Nine Maidens** stone circle — comprising eleven stones — and the rarely visited **Mulfra Quoit**. Beyond the latter a lane is reached; go right here and follow it to Madron. The total walk, about 8 miles (13km), is one of the finest in Cornwall, the interest at hand being frequently complimented by superb views of St Michael's Mount to the south.

Further Information
— Devon and Cornwall —

DEVON
Places of Interest

Castle Drogo
(National Trust)
Near Drewsteignton
☎ (06473) 3306
Open: April to end October, every day (including Good Friday) 11am-6pm (last admission 5.30pm).

Croyde Gem Rock and Shell Museum
Croyde
☎ (0271) 890407
Open: March to end October, daily 10am-5pm. July and August 10am-10pm. Winter opening by appointment.

Great Torrington
Dartington Glass Ltd
☎ (0805) 23797
Open: all year Monday to Friday 9.30am-10.25am, 11.45am-3.25pm. No factory tours at weekends or on Bank Holidays.

Great Torrington Museum
☎ (0805) 24324
Open: May to end September, Monday to Friday 10am-12.45pm, 2.15-4.45pm. Saturdays 10am-12.45pm.

The Plough Theatre,
Cinema and Arts Centre
☎ (0805) 22552/3
Open: all year, Tuesday to Saturday 10am-5pm.

Rosemoor Gardens
☎ (0805) 22256
Open: April to end October daily, dawn until dusk.

Dartmoor National Park
Parke, Haytor Road, Bovey Tracey
☎ (0626) 832093
Countless opportunities for walking, also guided walks. Details from the Dartmoor National Park Authority information centres or the authority's headquarters.

Hartland Abbey
Hartland, Bideford
☎ (02374) 559
Open: Easter Sunday and Monday and
Bank Holidays to August. May to
September Wednesdays 2-5.30pm.

Hartland Quay
Hartland Quay Museum
☎ Morwenstow (028883) 353
Open: daily Easter week and Whitsun to
end September 11am-5pm.

Merrivale
On Dartmoor's open land about halfway
between Tavistock and Princetown, to
south of the road. Comprehensive range
of Bronze Age antiquities: huts, stone
rows, cists, stone circles and a menhir.

Tiverton
Tiverton Castle
☎ (0884) 253200
Open: Easter to September, daily except
Fridays and Saturdays, 2.30-5.30pm.

Tiverton Museum
☎ (0884) 256295
Open: February to end December,
Monday to Saturday 10.30am-4.30pm.

Tourist Information Centres

Great Torrington
The Town Hall
☎ (0805) 24324

Tiverton
Phoenix Lane
☎ (0884) 255827

Useful Addresses

Dartmoor National Park Headquarters
Parke
Haytor Road
Bovey Tracey, Newton Abbot
☎ (0626) 832093

Devon Tourism
Devon County Council
County Hall
Exeter EX2 4QQ
☎ (0392) 273260
Operates the Tourist Information Centre
at the M5 Exeter Services, Sandygate,
and compiles several annual publications
useful to the visitor.

Devon Trust for Nature Conservation
New Bridge Street, Exeter
☎ (0392) 79244
A voluntary organisation with a small
paid staff and a shop. Manages nature
reserves throughout the county.

National Trust
(Devon Regional Office)
Killerton House, Broadclyst, Exeter
☎ (0392) 88691
Publishes a free leaflet annually giving
details of opening times of its properties
in the area. Also publishes leaflet maps
giving details of walking opportunities
in the Trust's coast and properties.

CORNWALL
Places of Interest

Bodmin
Bodmin Farm Park
Fletcher's Bridge
Off A38 Bodmin-Liskeard road at
Fletcher's Bridge signpost
☎ (0208) 20074
Open: mid-May to September, daily
(except Saturday) 10am-6pm last
admission 5pm. Nature trail, children's
activities, refreshments, gifts.

Bodmin Gaol
Cardell Road
☎ Bodmin (0208) 6292
Open: daily 10am-6pm.

The Candle Shop
Dunmere Road
☎ (0208) 3258
Ample parking.
Open: 10am-6pm weekdays and 1-6pm
Sundays, only open May to September.

Pencarrow House
Washaway 4 miles (6km) from Bodmin, 3
miles (5km) from Wadebridge, near
junction of A389 and B3266
☎ (020884) 369
Open: house and tearooms, Easter to end
of September daily, except Monday and
Saturday, 1.30-5pm (Bank Holiday
Mondays and 1 June to September,
11am-5pm). Guided tours. Self-pick soft
fruit when in season.

Castle-an-Dinas
Free access by footpath from east-south-east minor road from St Columb to A30 towards Roche.

Bodmin Moor
Colliford Lake Park Complex
☎ (020882) 335
Lakeside walks, picnic areas, rare breeds park, pets corner. Restaurant (evenings only), refreshments.

The Hurlers Stone Circles
$^1/_2$ mile north-west of Minions
(SX 255714)
Three large stone circles in a line, none of the monoliths exceeds 6ft (2m) in height. Early Bronze Age flints have been found here and the monument is considered one of the best of its type in the South-West. (English Heritage).

Trethevy Quoit
1 mile (2km) north-east of St Cleer
(SX 259688)
A closed megalithic chamber used for burials. Five standing stones supporting a huge capstone. Open any reasonable time. (English Heritage.)

Chysauster
Gulval Downs (SW 472350)
Well preserved remains of an Iron Age village with rooms arranged around an irregularly-shaped courtyard. (English Heritage.) Closed Thursday morning and Friday in winter.

Lanyon Quoit
Free access — it lies beside the minor road from Madron north-west to north coast road B3306 at Morvah.

Men-an-Tol
Bosullow Common
West Penwith
Standing stones reached by footpath from Bosullow Common.

Men Scryfa
Bosullow Common
West Penwith Inscribed stone.

Mulfra Quoit
Mulfra Hill
West Penwith
Chambered tomb reached by footpath from midway along Treen-Chyandour road.

Nine Maidens and Hangman's Barrow
Near junction of B3297 Wendron-Redruth road and B3280 Praze-an-Beeble-Redruth road. Standing stones.

St Breock Standing Stone
On St Breock Down reached from St Breock church at Wadebridge. Easily visible.

Wayside Museum
On B3306 Land's End-St Ives road at Zennor
Open: 9.30am to dusk daily May to October.
Mining, fishing, quarrying, agricultural and craft implements, domestic utensils, old mill and hearth. Admission free.

Tourist Information Centres

Bodmin
Shire House
Mount Folly
☎ (0208) 6616

Visitor Centre
Golitha Falls Centre
Between St Cleer and St Neot, slightly south-west of Siblyback Lane
Free entry.

Useful Addresses

Cornwall Birdwatching and Bird Preservation Society
13 Tregellas Road
Mullion, Cornwall
☎ (0326) 240919

National Trust
Cornwall Information Office
The Estate Office
Lanhydrock Park
Bodmin, Cornwall PL30 4DE
☎ (0208) 4281

2 • The South Downs

Southern England is so densely populated and built-up that there are very few areas quiet and remote enough to be described as 'off the beaten track'. One such area, which forms the subject of this chapter, is the western part of the South Downs in West Sussex and Hampshire and the Rother Valley bounding it on the north. Roads and railways cross this part of the country from north to south, but travel from east to west has always been difficult, the only natural route being the Rother Valley.

The area is bounded on the north by the sandy hills north of the Rother Valley, on the east by the Arun Valley, on the south by the dip slope of the South Downs and on the west by the Meon Valley, the whole area covering some 200sq miles (518sq km). There are two towns, Petersfield and Midhurst, both quite small, one or two stately homes, two museums of note and an outstanding country park (the Queen Elizabeth). Visitors who explore the area will find a countryside of small villages, each usually with an ancient parish church, an inn, a stone-built manor house and, in the Rother Valley, a mill and a medieval bridge.

Woodland once covered the whole of this region, including the downs. Much of it had been cleared by about 1000BC and by the time of the Domesday Book little natural woodland remained. Natural growth and widespread replanting since then has made Sussex the most wooded county in England.

The present landscape is a legacy of Roman and pre-Roman times, when agriculture supported a large population; the Saxons settled in a countryside that was already fully exploited. Between the eighth and twelfth centuries the typical English village with its open fields appeared on the scene; the landscape hardly changed until the Parliamentary enclosures of the eighteenth century produced the present pattern of small regular fields bounded by hedgerows.

Modern 'prairie' farming has destroyed many of these old hedgerows; the downs are now largely under crops and the famous Southdown sheep are not so common. The parks that are so much a part of the English landscape were created in the period 1500 to 1800 but at the expense of the local people who often had their villages uprooted to make way for them.

Many houses were built of local stone from the Bargate and Hythe Beds, and their Horsham stone roofs add to their charm. Many churches are small and ancient because the dwindling village population has never warranted rebuilding. Evidence of depopulation is abundant: in the downland areas many hamlets have shrunk to a farm house and a few cottages. This region retains its unspoilt appearance, free from the development that has ruined the coastal region and parts of Surrey, thanks largely to those wealthy residents who have preserved this beautiful landscape from private and public developers.

The description of this area will follow the east-west grain of the country, so that visitors will not encounter the heavy traffic on the north-south roads. From Petersfield the route follows the Rother Valley to the Arun, then from east to west along the foot of the north-facing scarp of the downs, south along the Meon Valley and then once more from west to east through the villages in the secluded combes of the downs. Mention will be made of those places where there is access to the South Downs Way, which traverses the whole length of the South Downs.

The Rother Valley

The borough of **Petersfield** was founded in the twelfth century; it was then in the parish of Buriton. The early settlement was centred on the church, and from the sixteenth century the town became increasingly important because of its markets and industries. A sheep market was held in what is now Sheep Street, and a large cattle market helped the development of a leather and cloth industry. The best houses are of the Georgian period and they show that the town was then a prosperous market centre. The Spain, said to have been named after Spanish traders, is an attractive little square, reminiscent of a village green. From it Sheep Street leads to the main square with its statue of William III, curiously dressed as a Roman. There is still a market here twice a week, when the town becomes quite busy.

St Peter's Church, founded about 1120, is one of the best Norman churches in Hampshire, retaining some of its character in spite of Victorian restoration. The chancel arch was part of the east wall of the central tower, which was never finished and was replaced by the western tower. The gravestone that stands alone in the churchyard is of John Small, the last survivor of the early Hambledon Club cricketers — his epitaph is worth reading.

A visit to the village of **Steep**, 1 mile (2km) north of Petersfield, is well worthwhile. It lies on the lower slopes of the wooded combes of this western end of the Weald and the beautiful countryside around it has been aptly named 'Little Switzerland'. The magnificent views from above the village were memorably described by the poet Edward Thomas, who lived here for a few years before his tragic death in World War I. His memorial, on Shoulder of Mutton Hill, can be reached from the end of Cockshott Lane.

At Petersfield the River Rother turns eastwards and meanders along the valley it has carved out of the Sandgate Beds, a weak zone of clays and silts in the Lower Greensand. The villages in the Rother Valley are among the oldest in Sussex, their names dating from early Saxon times. Situated on either side of the river, many consist of little more than a manor house, a

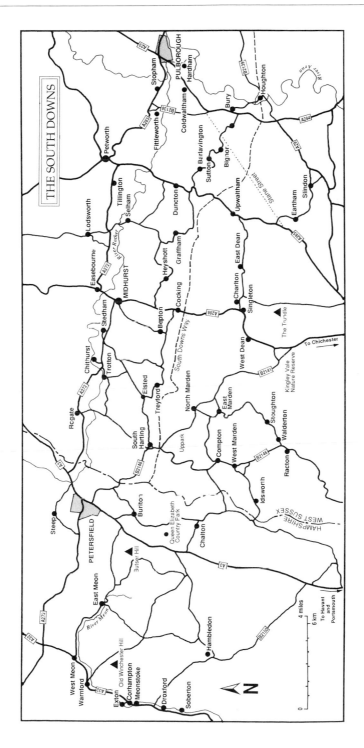

church, a medieval bridge and sometimes a mill. Most of the villages lie off the main road and are quiet and self-contained, with an ageless air about them.

Rogate is one of only three villages situated on the main road; its old houses are mostly of local yellow sandstone. St Bartholomew's Church, when restored in 1875, kept many of its old interior features, and its wooden-framed tower was moved a few feet to make way for an extra bay in the nave. One mile (2km) east is Terwick Church, a simple little Norman building alone in a field. From it there are uninterrupted views of the South Downs and the wooded hills to the north. The head of a medieval cross stands outside the west door.

At **Trotton** the main road crosses the river by a five-arched medieval bridge, one of the best along the Rother. It may have been built by Lord Camoys, whose tomb is in the church. He and his wife are commemorated on a brass (1419), one of the largest in England, and in the nave floor is the brass of Margaret de Camoys (1310), the oldest brass of a woman in England. The church is a large, barn-like building with no aisles or chancel arch and with little ornamentation. There are medieval paintings on all the walls, those on the east wall being the best preserved. The memorial tablet to Thomas Otway (1652-85), the poet and dramatist who was born in the parish, is dated 1651 because the old calendar was then in use. He died in poverty in London. The Keepers Arms inn was a blacksmith's shop until 1898, by which time it was also an alehouse called The Blue Anchor; it offers a large selection of appetising food.

This countryside was settled in the early Saxon period and much of the woodland had been removed before the Saxons came. **Chithurst** means 'Citta's wood'; Citta is an ancient Saxon personal name. The simple nave-and-chancel church perched on the bank of the Rother is the very one mentioned in the Domesday Book. It stands on an artificial mound said to be a prehistoric burial mound; this is quite possible as many churches in England were built on pagan sites to affirm the supremacy of Christianity. Many churches in this part of the Weald were built in the period just before or just after the Norman Conquest and remain little altered. The manor house near the church is a beautiful, unrestored late medieval yeoman's house with an overhanging first floor; both the church and manor house have remained unchanged for centuries.

Iping, 1 mile (2km) downstream, also has an ancient bridge; though not so compact as Chithurst, it is an attractive place. On Iping Common south of the main road, at a junction of paths a few hundred yards west of the car-park, the Roman road from Chichester to Silchester is visible as a low bank aligned north-south. Iping Common, a sandy heathland, supports heather, mosses, lichens and bracken, with patches of bog. Over 100 species of spiders have been found here.

One mile (2km) downstream is **Stedham**, the largest of the valley villages west of Midhurst. From the narrow six-arched medieval bridge there is a fine view of Stedham Hall high above the river. It has a picturesque and almost fairy-tale medieval appearance, but this is deceptive because it was largely restored in 1919. On the bridge there is a notice: 'Engine Drivers — Locomotives [ie steam traction engines] are not allowed to stand on any part of this bridge'.

Woolbeding consists of little more than a church, a large house and a farm. These tiny Rother Valley hamlets may pre-date the normal Saxon villages, which consisted of clustered farms and cottages. The countryside around here is one of scattered farms, woods and commons. The church, clearly Saxon, is tall with pilaster strips on the nave walls. It is not open but that hardly matters because interior restoration has removed everything ancient. The attractive Woolbeding Hall, with its distinctly French-looking front of about 1700, contrasts with the medieval manor houses in the other villages.

To see **Midhurst** thoroughly, one must explore the narrow streets between the busy main street and the river. The old part of the town centres on the market place where, under the old town hall, the stocks and whipping-posts have been preserved. Parts of The Spread Eagle Hotel are very old (1430 it claims); Queen Elizabeth I stayed there. It is a vast rambling place with historical mementoes in every room and passage.

The parish church was disappointingly restored in 1882-3. Church Hill leads to Knockhundred Row (derivation of the name is uncertain) where what must be the most picturesque public library in England stands, a medieval building that was once a row of tradesmen's cottages. The old Grammar School, founded in 1672, is in North Street (the main street). H.G. Wells was a junior master here; previously he had been an assistant at the present chemist's shop in Red Lion Street. Wool Lane, with its timber-framed cottages, is one of the best of the old streets. Midhurst was once served by three railway stations, with lines to Petersfield, Pulborough and Chichester; all have disappeared. There was also a canal from Pulborough; the wharf was just south of St Ann's Hill, where there was once a medieval castle. The foundations of the castle walls can be seen in the undergrowth.

At West Lavington Church, on the outskirts of Midhurst, is the grave of Richard Cobden, the free-trader and leader of the Anti-Corn-Law League, who was born at the farm where Dunford House now stands. The church, by William Butterfield, is a simple and restrained design in marked contrast to the majority of over-elaborate Victorian Gothic churches.

The romantic ruins of **Cowdray**, on the north side of the town, are open to visitors in summer. The house was built in the early sixteenth century on the site of an earlier house by Sir David Owen. After his death the house was completed by Sir William FitzWilliam, a favourite of King Henry VIII. The three-storeyed gatehouse and the remains of the east range, with hall, chapel and kitchen, give an idea of its former magnificence. Cowdray was burned down in 1793, only a week after its owner, the eighth Viscount Montague, died in Germany. The house was left to rot for many years afterwards.

Easebourne, north of the river, is as old as Midhurst and was once just as important. A neat and tidy village, most of it belongs to the Cowdray estate; houses rented from the estate have yellow woodwork. The parish church was rebuilt in 1876 but retains its twelfth-century tower. The monument to Sir Anthony Browne, first Viscount Montague, was removed from Midhurst Church. Adjoining the church is Easebourne Priory, formerly a nunnery; the building is partly medieval. The abbesses here were often in trouble for extravagant living and the priory was dissolved in 1535. Note the old cattle-grid opposite the church: 'Private byepass bridge'.

Car-parks and footpaths facilitate public access to Cowdray Park, which is well known for its polo games. North of the A272 is **Lodsworth**, a beautiful village on the slopes of the Lod Valley in the greensand hills. The Hollist Arms inn stands at the centre of the village and a long winding street runs down to the half-hidden parish church, which though of little architectural interest is well cared-for; from the churchyard there is a good view across the valley.

On the opposite side of the River Rother is **Selham**, a scattered village of stone and brick houses with a curiously named inn, The Three Moles. Its tiny church could be Saxon or Norman — there are details of both periods. The chancel arch has carvings that must be Saxon; they depict two snakes and a monster eating its own tail, a Saxon symbol of eternity.

The handsome stone-built village of **Tillington** lies on the west side of Petworth Park. The novelist A.E.W. Mason lived at Tillington Hill House on the road to Upperton, and the essayist E.V. Lucas lived at Tillington Cottage on the main road. The Horse Guards inn was named after the regiment that was stationed in Petworth Park during the Napoleonic Wars. The church tower is one of the most distinctive in Sussex; the four flying buttresses supporting its weather-vane resemble a crown or corona. Inside the church there are several memorials to the local Mitford family, and a strange object to find in a church — a 1928 horse-plough.

Petworth comes as a surprise to visitors; there are few straggling suburbs to signal its presence. Though officially only a village, it really deserves to be called a town. The buildings in its streets are of all dates and styles but they blend so harmoniously that hardly any seem out of place. The streets run off from the corners of the market square; all are worth exploring at leisure, perhaps the most attractive being the narrow Lombard Street on the north side. The best feature of the parish church is the tower, the lower part medieval and the top part added by Sir Charles Barry in 1827.

The town is dominated by Petworth House which, most unusually for an English mansion, stands very close to the town, separated from it by a high wall ('with its elbow to the town' as Daniel Defoe described it). Rebuilt in 1688-96 by the sixth Duke of Somerset, it is owned by the National Trust and is open in summer. Its magnificent west front of twenty-one bays faces the beautiful park created by the famous 'Capability' Brown. The chapel, part of the thirteenth-century house, is embellished with seventeenth-century wood panelling, ceiling and gallery; it is one of the finest chapel interiors in England. However, the house is probably best known for its great collection of paintings. A whole room is devoted to J.M.W. Turner's works, and other rooms contain many by Van Dyck and Lely.

One mile (2km) south of Petworth, at Coultershaw Bridge, a beam-

Middle Street, Petworth

pump dating from about 1790 is open to visitors on certain Sundays in summer. The first left turn beyond the Badger and Honeyjar inn passes Burton Mill Pond nature reserve, where fishing is available by permit. The old mill is in working order but is not open to visitors at the time of writing. Further on, a left fork passes the isolated Church of Coates, a small simple building, its plain round chancel arch evidence of its early Norman date.

Fittleworth, at the junction of the A283 and the B2138, was once the haunt of artists such as John Constable, when The Swan inn near the river had a sign board spanning the road. The village has not changed much since then; an attractive water-mill of 1742 stands near the ancient bridge over the Rother. The church has a good early English tower and chancel but an inferior Victorian nave.

The tiny village of **Stopham**, off the A283, the last in the Rother Valley, has another small ancient church. It probably dates from just after the Conquest but has some Saxon characteristics, such as the two nave door-ways with very high inner arches. The Barttelot family — local squires — are commemorated by thirteen mural tablets and four brasses.

The old bridge here over the Arun is the finest medieval bridge in Sussex. All the arches are original except the centre one, which had to be raised for the Wey and Arun Canal. First built in 1442, the bridge has been constantly restored, and has now been superseded by a concrete bridge a few yards upstream. Although no doubt necessary to cope with modern traffic, this has destroyed the beautiful setting of the old bridge. From the terrace of The White Hart inn, visitors can view the old bridge and contemplate the price of progress.

The Arun to the Meon

The route now follows the Arun Valley for a few miles. One mile (2km) south of Pulborough via the A29 is **Hardham**, a very small village that is mercifully by-passed. There was a Roman posting station here, on Stane Street, which was cut through by the Midhurst branch railway. The Norman Church of St Botolph has some of the earliest and best-preserved wall-paintings in England. They date from the early twelfth century and provide a remarkable and almost unique picture of the typical interior of a medieval parish church. Those depicting the legends of St George may be the earliest representations of him in the country. Half a mile (1km) further south, a footpath to the left passes the ruins of Hardham Priory (incorporated in a farmhouse) and the derelict bed of the Wey and Arun Canal, disused since 1871. The water-filled south entrance to the canal tunnel is an eerie sight. Opened in 1816, this canal was the only one ever to link London with the South Coast; it traversed the heart of Surrey and Sussex and played a useful part in local trade.

Coldwaltham's church has a Norman tower; a notice in the churchyard states that its yew tree is one of the twelve oldest in the country, a rash claim because yew trees are very difficult to date. The Old Priest House opposite the church is supposed to date from about 1220.

Bury is a beautiful village between the A29 and the river; the large houses in the sunken lane leading down to the river are mostly hidden by the high banks and trees. There was once a ferry across the Arun to Amberley. Bury House (near the crossroads) was the home of John Galsworthy for the last 7 years of his life; the house opposite is named Forsytes after his novel sequence *The Forsyte Saga*. Note the grotesque carvings on the post office and adjoining house. The medieval parish church near the river has a Norman tower with a broach spire.

The route now turns west along the foot of the downland scarp to follow the narrow zone that separates the South Downs from the Weald. The varied soils along this belt have proved good for agriculture, as shown by the large farms and houses and prosperous villages. **West Burton** is a typical village of mainly stone-built houses, some with brick-nogging (infilling of bricks between the timber frames).

Bignor Roman villa, a short distance from the Roman Stane Street, enjoys a splendid view of the downs. Its mosaic floors, discovered in 1811, are among the finest in Britain; the one in the north corridor is the longest on display anywhere, measuring 80ft (24m). The museum contains artefacts found on the site. The quiet and charming village of **Bignor** forms a square; the fifteenth-century brick, flint and timber house on the east side was once a shop and has never been restored, a rare example of a house of that period in original condition. The parish church is spacious but rather bare inside.

From the village visitors can drive up to Bignor Hill, where the South Downs Way crosses the Roman Stane Street. **Sutton** is another attractive village of brick and flint houses with a Norman church, and at **Barlavington**

Fifteenth-century house in Bignor

the ancient little church stands virtually in a farmyard, as it must have done in Saxon and Norman times.

The route crosses the main road from Petworth to Chichester at **Duncton**; there is little of interest in the village but it does enjoy splendid views. An old Sussex custom known as 'wassailing the apple trees' survived here until the 1920s; the locals visit orchards, blow horns and sing to drive away evil spirits. A side road under Duncton Down leads to East Lavington Church, now the chapel of Seaford College. In the churchyard is the grave of Bishop Wilberforce of Winchester, who owned an estate here.

The short walk from Duncton to Burton Church in Burton Park is well worth the effort. The completely unrestored interior, with its old screen and pews, is reminiscent of a centuries-old Welsh border church. It has the only brass in England of a woman wearing a tabard (a short coat emblazoned with the family arms) and a Royal Arms of 1636 painted on the wall. Royal Arms of this date are very rare as most were destroyed during the Commonwealth.

A long detour must be taken to reach **Graffham**, the next village, which consists of a very long, winding uphill street ending at the parish church right under the downs (this is handy for the South Downs Way). The well preserved houses in the village are built of a variety of materials: flint, brick, clunch, sandstone and timber. The church was restored in 1875 by G.E. Street as a memorial to Bishop Wilberforce. There is a curious fifteenth-century lock on the vestry door. **Heyshott's** houses border a large green, with a smaller green near the church, which has a memorial to Richard Cobden, who was born in the parish and worshipped here.

Cocking, on the A286 between Midhurst and Chichester, just north of a gap in the downs, is a neat Cowdray estate village. The church stands above a small stream and appears to be nineteenth-century with a medieval tower, but the interior reveals an eleventh-century church mentioned in the Domesday Book. There are some unusual memorials in the chancel and strange iron headstones in the churchyard.

A quiet, winding road below the steep scarp of the downs connects a line of small villages. **Bepton's** houses are of sandstone and timber. The church was drastically restored in 1878 but kept its squat Norman tower. There is a medieval tombstone in the chancel and a mass grave for Black Death victims outside near the porch. From the village it is a short but steep walk to the South Downs Way and Linch Down, from where there are splendid views of the coast.

There can be few churches in England so remote, unspoilt and charged with atmosphere as the simple 'shepherds' church, at **Didling**. At the end of a lane right under the downs, it has not changed much since it was rebuilt about 1220. There is no electric light; the fifteenth-century pews have holes for candles. Many things have been stolen from this remote church but, in true Christian spirit, it remains open to visitors.

Treyford has a manor house with a striking front, and two churchyards but no church. The early medieval church is a ruin in the grounds of the manor house, and the Victorian church was blown up in 1951 because it was unsafe. The nearest church, at **Elsted** 1 mile (2km) north-west, was itself ruinous until a restoration in 1951 preserved some of its ancient features, such as the eleventh-century herring-bone masonry. Treyford is also handy for the South Downs Way; on Treyford Hill the Way passes the Devil's Jumps, six Bronze Age barrows.

South Harting, the largest of the three Hartings, is a charming and unspoilt village at the foot of the downs. W.H. Hudson, whose opinions are always worth noting, thought it the most attractive of the downland villages. From any direction the church with its copper spire (the only one in Sussex) dominates the scene. Its interior wooden chancel roof is noteworthy and the war memorial outside was designed by Eric Gill. The village school, built in 1865, is said to have been the first to serve school dinners, during World War I.

Uppark, the late seventeenth-century country house on the crest of the downs, was badly damaged by fire in 1989, the upper floor being destroyed. It is owned by the National Trust, who hope one day to see it restored to its former glory; meanwhile the grounds are open to visitors on Sundays in summer. H.G. Wells spent part of his youth here; his mother was the housekeeper.

The route now takes visitors into Hampshire, to **Buriton**, where the manor house, parish church and village pond with weeping willows present as charming a picture as anywhere in the county. Buriton Manor House was the home, in his youth, of Edward Gibbon, the famous historian; after his father's death he sold the house and went to live in London.

A quintessential English scene: cottages clustered around the village church at Bury, South Downs

Lombard Street, Petworth, South Downs

Trotton Bridge, South Downs

Montacute House, Somerset, Wessex

South Harting, one of the most beautiful villages in southern England

The Meon Valley

The Meon Valley does not mark the western limit of the South Downs, but it is the first natural north-south route across the downs west of the Arun Valley and so forms a convenient boundary to the area described in this chapter.

The River Meon rises south of the village of East Meon, flows north then west and finally south to the sea through one of the most attractive valleys in Hampshire. The names Warnford and Droxford indicate where the river was once crossed by ancient trackways. The Meon Valley was once used by a railway from Alton to Fareham.

East Meon, which can be reached directly from Buriton by minor roads or from the Winchester-Petersfield road (the A272), is sheltered on the north by the steep slopes of Park Hill, at the very foot of which stands the parish church. The embryo River Meon flows along High Street where, before the bridges were improved, there were sometimes floods after heavy rain. High Street is attractive with its old houses, and so is Church Street, with The George inn and the old almshouses. All Saints Church is one of the best Norman churches in the south of England; the tower with its broach spire is particularly impressive. The font is one of the seven in England made of black marble from Tournai in Belgium; its bold and expressive carvings include the *Creation of Adam* and *Expulsion from Paradise*. The stained glass in the east window depicts the patron saints of all the Allied countries of World War I.

West Meon is situated where the river turns to the south. In Station Road the remains of the old Meon Valley Railway station, disused since 1955, make a sad sight. The platforms are covered in weeds, and trees arch across the old track. The line was designed in 1903 as a through route from London to Gosport and this station, like the others on the line, was built to a high standard.

The cross in the village centre commemorates Dr George Rogers, for over 40 years a doctor in West Meon. One of his sons was James Thorold Rogers, the nineteenth-century writer and economist. St John's Church, rebuilt between 1843 and 1846 in what was called the 'second pointed' style of the Gothic Revival, was George Gilbert Scott's first church in Hampshire. In the churchyard is the grave of Thomas Lord, founder of Lord's cricket ground, and of Guy Burgess, the British diplomat who defected to Russia.

Warnford village lies near the river but its parish church is in the park on the east side of the main road. The park was once part of the Belmont estate and may have been landscaped by the famous 'Capability' Brown. The church has an aisleless early English nave and chancel and a massive Norman tower; above the south door there is a rare Saxon sundial. Inside is the remarkable Neale monument, with effigies of Sir Thomas and his two wives and the figures of nine of their children, four of them carrying skulls to show that they died in infancy. Behind the church is King John's House, which was built probably in the early thirteenth century and has been a ruin for hundreds of years.

A by-road from Warnford leads to Old Winchester Hill, the site of a National Nature Reserve and an impressive Iron Age hill-fort. It is not known how it got its name, for it has no connection with Winchester. Typical chalk downland flora and fauna survive here because the landscape is carefully maintained by rotational grazing. Many species of orchids can be found and the area is rich in butterflies. Two of the three native British conifers (yew and juniper) grow here naturally. The hill-fort dates from the second century BC and may have been the tribal capital of this region.

Two miles (3km) south of Warnford, three villages stand close together at a bend in the river. **Exton's** name means 'East Saxons' farm', ie settlers from Essex. It has a riverside inn (The Shoe) and a medieval church, where the headstone of Richard Pratt depicts the Angel of Death summoning a scholar from his books.

The simple Saxon church at **Corhampton** was built about 1035 and has important twelfth-century wall-paintings in the chancel. On the nave wall is a rare Saxon sundial, which as usual for that period divides the day into 3-hour 'tides'. **Meonstoke** is an attractive village on the east side of the river where the church, mainly early English, has a Norman font.

Droxford owes its attractiveness to the small Georgian houses in its sloping main street, mostly built of local bricks and tiles. The Malt House, Old Bakery and Old Post House are reminders of former village trades. Izaak Walton, author of *The Compleat Angler*, often came here to visit his son-in-law, the rector. The church has curious dormer windows in the nave roof and an odd stair-turret in the tower. The former railway station, across the river near The Hurdles inn, was the scene in June 1944 of a historic meeting in a train, when Churchill, Smuts, De Gaulle, Eisenhower and other Allied leaders made plans for the invasion of Europe (see the plaque on the letter-box). **Soberton** was the home of Admiral Anson, the famous eighteenth-century seaman, who lived at the manor house, which is now demolished. The church has some fourteenth-century wall-paintings.

A by-road from Soberton through pleasant countryside leads to **Hambledon**, once a more important place than it is now. Tidy and at-tractive, with many interesting old houses, it retains its old village at-mosphere. The church could well serve as a textbook example of the enlargement of a parish church through successive centuries. The famous Hambledon Cricket Club played its matches on Broadhalfpenny Down; a memorial opposite The Bat and Ball inn marks the site of the cricket ground. The club flourished from 1750 to 1796, and in 1777 beat All-England by an innings and 168 runs.

The South Downs

From Hambledon it is only a short drive to Butser Hill, the highest point of the South Downs, 888ft (271m) above sea-level. Here, as one would expect, there are superb views over Hampshire and West Sussex. The hill is grazed by a large flock of sheep and in summer visitors can watch demonstrations of sheep husbandry. Iron Age field boundaries and defensive dykes are evidence of prehistoric man's activities.

Queen Elizabeth Country Park (entrance on the east side of the A3) comprises 1,400 acres of woods and downs. Beech trees predominate on the chalky soil, but yews, thorns and junipers can also be found. Constant grazing by rabbits and sheep has made the downland a habitat for a wide range of flowers and insects. Roe-deer and many smaller animals are often to be seen. The Park Centre provides all the necessary information about the footpaths, nature trails, picnic areas and car-parks. At the Ancient Farm, a reconstruction of an Iron Age farm, there are barns, houses, animals and crops that resemble, as far as possible, those existing in the Iron Age. The animals are descendants of ancient species and the crops are those iden-tified by carbonised seeds.

South of the park, a turn off the A3 leads to **Chalton**, a tiny village in the downs where the Red Lion, a genuine old thatched inn, faces the early medieval church. East of Chalton the road joins the old coach road from Buriton to Havant, which was the main road from London to Portsmouth before the turnpike road of 1710 (the modern A3). Alone in a field at Idsworth stands St Hubert's Chapel, a small Norman building; its early fourteenth-century wall-paintings are the best in Hampshire after those in Winchester Cathedral.

The route now enters West Sussex and the remotest part of the South Downs, where narrow winding by-roads connect small villages, hamlets and lonely farms. **Compton** is the largest of these small communities; its miniature square with the village stores and inn is on the B2146 between South Harting and Emsworth. The church, though restored in 1849, has

The reconstructed Iron Age farm at the Queen Elizabeth Country Park

early medieval features, and the squire's pew is as large as a small room. The road from Compton to Up Marden passes Bevis's Thumb, a large neolithic long barrow, 210ft (64m) long, one of the three in West Sussex. A bungalow on Telegraph Hill, a short walk from the barrow, was one of the semaphore telegraph stations that connected London with Portsmouth in the early nineteenth century.

South of Compton are **West Marden**, the largest of the four Mardens but the only one without a church, and **Racton**. The church at Racton is early medieval, its chancel separated from the nave by a tie-beam and tympanum. It has two contrasting monuments, the table-tomb of John Gunter, who died in 1557, and the coloured kneeling effigies of Sir George Gunter and his wife (1624). High above the village is Racton Tower, an 80ft (24m) high folly erected about 1772, now in a dangerous state and better viewed from a distance.

North-east of Racton lie Stoughton and Walderton, in a valley of the downs, with beautiful scenery all around them accessible by numerous footpaths. Stoughton's church has the high narrow proportions that suggest a Saxon origin, and its chancel arch is thought to date from 1040-65. Its plain exterior belies the richness of its interior. From the car-park on Stoughton Down a long walk through woodlands leads to Kingley Vale National Nature Reserve, famous for its yew wood, said to be about the best in Europe. Old gnarled yews and young straight yews, with ash and oak, make up a beautiful and mysterious forest. Nothing grows beneath the yews, but outside the forest scrubland supports a rich flora. Deer are found here, also a great variety of birds and butterflies. From the memorial at the head of the vale there is a superb view of the coastal plain.

Up Marden consists of only a farm and a church, but the church is perhaps the most memorable of this whole area. It dates from the fifteenth century and, other than the provision of pews and pulpit, has not been altered since then. It is not used for services but visitors would be unaware of this for there is no sign of neglect; it has plastered walls and roof and brick floors, and is without electricity.

North Marden's church also adjoins a farmyard and is even smaller. It is one of the only four single-cell apsidal churches in England, and its semi-circular apse and narrow lancet windows make the interior dark and mysterious.

East Marden, though small, is more of a village, but remote and peaceful. At its triangular road junction stands a picturesque thatched well-head with rusting machinery, and nearby is a cottage dated 1728. At Battine House the philosopher Bertrand Russell started a school in about 1928. The church is thirteenth century but has lost some of its character through restoration. The splendid organ was once at St James's Palace and belonged to Prince Albert.

The route follows the B2141 south and then the A286 north to **West Dean** in the valley of the River Lavant, which rises at Singleton. At West Dean College, built in 1804, where arts and crafts and conservation are taught, the gardens are open to visitors and include a wild garden and a walled garden with an exhibition of garden history. The parish church was rebuilt in 1934 after a fire. At **Singleton** old railway station, where Goodwood racegoers once alighted, there is now a winery and vineyard; the station building of 1880 remains intact.

Singleton is a most attractive downland village, with charming small flint houses in the lanes off the main road. It was once a very busy place on race-days, entertaining visitors to Goodwood, which was opened in 1801. The parish church has many interesting features, including a Saxon tower, west gallery, rood-loft stairs and medieval pews. The memorial to Thomas Johnson (1744) is worth reading. The Weald and Downland Open Air Museum is one of the most unusual museums in England. Re-erected here are many old houses, cottages, barns and public buildings, from Sussex and adjoining counties, that were threatened with destruction. Visitors can enter buildings dating back to the Middle Ages and see the living conditions and of people's way of life in past centuries.

From Singleton there is a road up to The Trundle, a hill commanding extensive views over the downs and coast, though spoilt by the radio masts on top. Within the ramparts of the Iron Age hill-fort are the faint remains of a much earlier Neolithic causewayed camp.

The Singleton and East Dean Women's Institute, the first in England, held its first meeting at The Fox inn at **Charlton** in 1915; a plaque in the bar records the fact. The inn was renamed when fox-hunting became popular in the district — it was formerly called The Pig and Whistle.

East Dean, a secluded village in the downs with a long street of old cottages, has a pond which is often crowded with ducks. One of the flint houses opposite The Hurdlemakers inn bears the date 1788 and the Duke of Richmond's coat of arms. The late Norman parish church has a fine south doorway.

From East Dean the narrow valley road goes on to meet the A285 at **Upwaltham**, which consists only of two farms and a church high up on the downs. The Norman church is unrestored and is one of the four in Sussex with an apse; it stands in a field with no road to it.

Many hamlets on the downs have never consisted of more than a farm and one or two cottages. The great Saxon estates that covered the downs had no large central villages, only dispersed hamlets; the importance of the hamlet in English rural history is clearly evident in Sussex. The downs are now largely covered by large farms growing cereals and rearing cattle and sheep. Much woodland has been destroyed in the post-war years, and with it hundreds of acres of prehistoric fields and other evidence of human settlement.

The route follows the A285 south before turning off to **Eartham**. In Eartham Wood (there is a convenient car-park) the Roman road known as Stane Street can be seen; it continues as a terrace-way up and over the downs to Bignor. Here in the wood it is particularly well-preserved, the agger 4ft (1m) high and 85ft (26m) wide between its ditches. Constructed by about AD70, Stane Street ran from the east gate of Chichester (*Noviomagus*) to London.

Eartham village is quiet and unspoilt; its church has a fine Norman chancel arch. Near the church is Eartham House, built by Lutyens in 1905. The poet William Hayley (1745-1820), who wrote a life of Cowper, lived at the previous house on the site. The statesman William Huskisson (1770-1830) also lived here. He was the first man to be killed by a train, at the opening of the Liverpool and Manchester Railway — his memorial can be seen in the church.

At **Slindon**, an unexpectedly large village to find on the slopes of the downs, lanes converge from all directions. Unspoilt, with attractive flint and brick houses, it is best seen by taking a circular walk past the church, village pond and inn. Slindon House, now a school, originated as a palace of the Archbishops of Canterbury; one of them, Stephen Langton, died here in 1228. The parish church, restored in 1866, has eleventh-century nave arcade walls and the only wooden effigy in Sussex, probably of Sir Anthony St Leger who died in 1539. A footpath north of the village leads uphill to The Folly, a strange flint archway whose origin is rather obscure.

The A29 and B2139 lead to **Houghton** in the Arun Valley, where the best houses are in the lane leading down to the river. At the quaint George and Dragon inn on the main road, Charles II is said to have stopped for refreshment during his escape to France. The heavy traffic on the road through the village suggests that visitors are no longer off the beaten track and brings to an end their exploration of the downs.

Further Information

— The South Downs —

Places of Interest

Bignor
Bignor Roman Villa
☎ 079 87 259
Cafeteria, picnic area, gift shop.
Open: 1 March to 31 May, October daily
except Monday 10am-5pm; 1 June to 31
September daily, 10am-6pm.

Buriton
Queen Elizabeth Country Park
☎ 0705 595040
Café, picnic areas, gift shop.
Open: Park Centre March to October
daily 10am-6pm, November to February,
Sunday 10am-dusk. Ancient Farm April
to September, Sunday to Friday 10am-
5.30pm, Saturday 2-5.30pm.

Midhurst
Cowdray
☎ 0730 812423
Open: April to September, Friday to
Tuesday 1-6pm.

Petersfield
Bear Museum
Dragon Street
☎ 0730 65108/66962
Open: Monday, Tuesday, Thursday,
Friday 10am-1pm, 2-5pm, Wednesday,
Saturday 10am-1pm.

Doll Museum
☎ 0730 63438
16a Chapel Street
Open: Monday to Saturday 9am-5.30pm.

Petworth
Coultershaw Beam Pump
☎ 0798 43491
Open: April to September, first and third
Sundays in month 11am-4pm.

Petworth House
(National Trust)
☎ 0798 42207

Restaurant, gift shop.
Open: April to October, Tuesday to
Thursday, Saturday, Sunday 1-5pm.
Gardens 12.30-5pm. Park 9am-sunset.

Singleton
Weald and Downland
Open Air Museum
☎ 024 363 348
Tea-room (April to October), shop.
Open: daily, November to January 10am-
4pm, February to October 10am-5pm,
March 10am-6pm, April to September
10am-7pm.

South Harting
Uppark (National Trust)
☎ 0730 825317/825458
Open: Grounds only April to October,
Sunday 11am-5.30pm.

West Dean
Chilsdown Vineyard
☎ 024 363 398
The Old Station House
Open: 1 May to 30 September daily
10am-5pm.

West Dean Gardens
☎ 024 363 301
Refreshments, garden shop.
Open: 1 March to 31 October daily 11am-
6pm.

Tourist Information Centres

Arundel
61 High Street
☎ 0903 882268

Chichester
St Peter's Market
West Street
☎ 0243 775888

Petersfield
27 The Square
☎ 0730 68829

3 • Wessex

W essex only has a definite border where it meets the sea. Historically, in centuries before the Conquest, it was the Kingdom of the West Saxons, with boundaries that varied according to the strength of its kings compared to that of its neighbours. King Alfred's Wessex extended across Southern England from Cornwall to Sussex, from the Valley of the Upper Thames to the Channel Coast.

For almost 1,000 years the name ceased to exist, except to historians. It was revived in the 1870s with the publication of Thomas Hardy's novel, *Far From the Madding Crowd* in serial form in a popular magazine. Hardy, who was born in Dorset, near Dorchester, in 1840, and lived in the town or nearby for 72 of his 87 years, wrote most of his novels there, and all of his later poetry. Hardy captured rural life and landscape as well as any other writer in the English language, and his novels present a unique portrait of nineteenth-century Wessex which, for him, was centred on Dorchester. The present county of Dorset was his South Wessex. However, for the purposes of this chapter, the area covered will extend a little eastwards into Hampshire ('Upper Wessex'), much of Wiltshire ('Mid Wessex'), and to the west, a narrow strip of Somerset ('Outer Wessex'). Today's maps show proper county names, and not the literary ones.

Hardy recognised the historical and physical unity of his Wessex: its softly rounded landscapes of chalk downland and clear, gentle rivers flowing east or south; its small towns, villages and countless farms; its language and certain forms of speech; all blending together in a rich and unique culture. Hardy's Wessex is part fantasy, part reality, with a timelessness that can still be felt. Most of those who visit his Wessex today do so as tourists, and never become part of it, as he undoubtedly did. However, by journeying slowly, and with senses alert, it is possible to approach its character.

While it is possible to approach Wessex by sea, from Cherbourg to Poole or Weymouth, most visitors are more likely to come by road. From London, the M3 (easily reached from Heathrow) provides the most direct route south-west. At Basingstoke there are two choices. The A303, much of it dual-carriageway, takes the more northerly course, by Amesbury and Salisbury Plain, aiming for Honiton in Devon. The M3 swings more to the south, by-passing Winchester, continuing as the A33 to Southampton. North of that city, the M27 points westwards, becoming the A31. This, in

Hardy's birthplace at Higher Bockhampton

turn, cuts across the New Forest to Ringwood and Wimborne Minster, joining the A35 to Dorchester and hence following a much more southward route to Honiton.

A compromise route by way of **Winchester** offers an historical hors d'oeuvre, and presents no problems, as the city is conveniently close to the M3. Winchester is one of England's smaller cities, and its heart is easily explored on foot. High Street and Broadway form an east-west spine, between Westgate, one of two surviving medieval gateways, and King Alfred's statue near the Victorian-Gothic Town Hall, which houses the city art gallery and an excellent Tourist Information Centre. Nearby is Europe's longest cathedral which is 556ft (195m) long. Building began soon after the Conquest, and it was completed, after various additions and remodelling, in about 1528. Lying, like the city, in a hollow, and having no strong vertical accents, it is better appreciated from the inside. Mortuary chests of Anglo-Saxon kings and bishops around the chancel screen mark its deep historical roots, and among many monuments is one to Jane Austen.

The city has a wealth of historic buildings, and a self-guiding Town Trail leaflet, available from the Tourist Information Centre, outlines a convenient way of incorporating these in an easy walk. With a variety of guest houses and hotels Winchester is a tempting place to stay, but it is poorly placed for a Wessex tour.

Salisbury is about 22 miles (35km) away, via the A272 and the A30. Sited where five chalk-born rivers meet to mingle in the waters of the Avon, Salisbury is larger than Winchester, has more industry, and is 1,000 years older. Two miles (3km) north of the present city, **Old Sarum** was occupied as an Iron Age hill-fort, a Roman town, a Saxon town, and a Norman city with a cathedral; each of these has left its prominent mark. In 1220 Bishop Poore led his people from Old Sarum to a new site by the river meadows, where he started his cathedral and laid out to its north-east the grid-iron pattern of the town of New Sarum, the origins of present Salisbury. The cathedral was consecrated in 1258, the tower and spire, 404ft (141m) high, added between 1300 and 1340 — it is the soaring spire that is Salisbury's town-mark.

Although most main roads by-pass the city, it is focal point for all roads in this part of Wiltshire, with markets on Tuesdays and Saturdays. A busy, lively place with excellent hotels and shops, many occupying timber-framed buildings dating from the fifteenth to seventeenth centuries, Salisbury formerly had a flourishing cloth trade. Street names give clues to other trades: Fish Row, Butcher Row (with its beautiful fifteenth-century Poultry Cross), Silver Street, Ox Row, Oatmeal Row and the Cheese Market. Public parkland on the riverside meadows north-west of the cathedral provide the most rewarding views of the graceful building, differing only slightly from the famous picture painted by Constable early last century.

By taking the A354 from Salisbury you nearly bisect the angle between the A303, crossing Salisbury Plain to the north, and the A31, coming across the New Forest to the south. The A354 is the Blandford road, it crosses the little River Ebble at Coombe Bissett, and does not pass any more villages until it reaches **Blandford Forum**. Broad, corn-growing chalk downlands stretch away on both sides, and to the east at Handley roundabout the great raised agger of Ackling Dyke, a Roman road, is easily identified.

Blandford now has a ring road around it. At the time of Domesday it was one of five small farming settlements close together on the River Stour. However, being at a major crossing-point, it was sufficiently important to have gained a market in medieval times, adding 'Forum' (similar meaning to 'Chipping') to its name. The town was partly destroyed by fire in 1713, and almost completely levelled by another fire in 1731 — a tragedy which afflicted many timber-built places in the seventeenth and early eighteenth centuries. A prosperous place, with many great estates and good farmland all around, it was speedily and handsomely rebuilt, mainly by two local builder-architects, John and William Bastard, who kept the original street layout. Using brick throughout has ensured a rare degree of unity, and Blandford remains a remarkably attractive example of an eighteenth-century market town. The best buildings command the market place; they are the parish church, dating from 1739 and completely Classical, and the Town Hall, dating from 1734 and of Portland stone.

Bastard's new houses were designed for different social classes. Their size varied accordingly and they were also zoned, with the larger ones, having symmetrical elevations, on the outskirts, smaller houses for shop-keepers and lesser merchants, often with side passages, and paired houses sharing a common central entrance passage, for artisans and other labourers.

From Blandford head south-eastwards along the A350, down the vale of

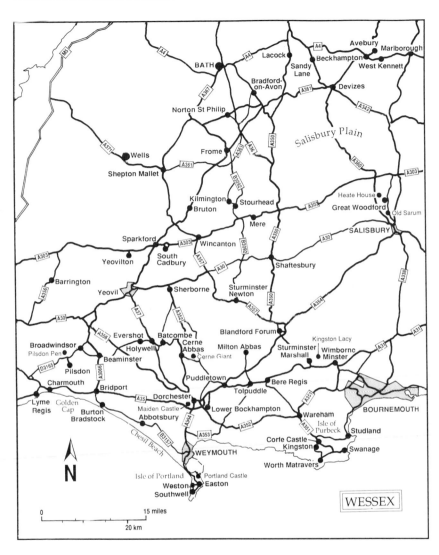

the River Stour, diverting at **Sturminster Marshall** to cross a noteworthy medieval bridge spanning the river. Turn right on the B3082 heading for Wimborne Minster. The road passes the entrance to the wooded parklands and gracious mansion of **Kingston Lacy** (National Trust). The house was built between 1663 and 1665 for Sir Ralph Bankes, but was extensively altered in early Victorian times by Sir Charles Barry, designer of the Houses of Parliament which were being rebuilt at about the same time. Kingston Lacy is noted for its collection of Italian and English paintings.

Three miles (5km) to the east, **Wimborne Minster** is a friendly, intimate small town centred on its twin-towered, brown-and-grey chequered church which displays most architectural styles from Norman to Gothic, and has a 'quarter-jack' clock on the west tower. Old inns, hotels, tree-lined corners, and small shops add to Wimborne's appeal, and there is a good local history museum in the sixteenth-century Priest's House in High Street.

Leave Wimborne by the A31, continue past the A350 roundabout and in another 3 miles (5km) turn south on the B3075 to **Wareham**. This small town was founded during King Alfred's reign as a *burh*, or stronghold, which quickly developed as a small trading port. Its Saxon ramparts enclose the town on three sides and St Martin's Church, just within them at the end of North Street, retains many pre-Conquest features, as well as an impressive effigy of T.E. Lawrence (of Arabia) by Eric Kennington. **Clouds Hill** (National Trust), the small cottage he bought when he rejoined the RAF in 1924, lies 5 miles (8km) north-west of Wareham, on the now afforested heaths near Bovington Camp. Its spare, almost crude simplicity partly captures the character of this very remarkable man. He is buried in the cemetery at **Moreton**, a nearby village, whose church alone makes a detour to this area so worthwhile. This eighteenth-century gem contains clear glass windows superbly engraved by Lawrence Whistler in 1958; they are delicate, detailed, elegant and quite beautiful.

Wareham is the obvious gateway to the **Isle of Purbeck**, which is not an island in the geographical sense, but more in a geological one. Cross the Stour and take the A351 to Swanage. Soon the low-lying heaths are left behind, and the road passes through the only gap in the long chalk ridge separating Purbeck from the rest of Dorset. The small town of **Corfe Castle** occupies this gap, and the gaunt ruins of the medieval castle (National Trust) command the town and the skyline.

Purbeck prospered through the quarrying of its limestone, which forms a ridge above the coastline. Villages like **Worth Matravers, Langton Matravers** and **Kingston** developed as quarrying settlements. Some stone was shipped from the medieval fishing village of **Swanage** which, with the coming of the railway in 1881, grew into a small fashionable resort, though never reaching the status of Lyme Regis and Weymouth farther west.

The coast turns a right angle here, and the official Dorset Coast Path is the best way of exploring it. Northwards are the chalk cliffs of Ballard Point and the Foreland, with the wide sandy sweep of Studland Bay beyond, backed by the National Nature Reserve of Studland Heath, and the minor road to the Sandbanks Ferry behind that. **Studland** is a rarity, an undeveloped little seaside resort, with an almost wholly Norman village church. The B3351 leads back to Corfe Castle, with occasional glimpses northwards over heaths and woodland, where Britain's largest onshore oilfield, Wych Farm, is situated, to the wide expanse of Poole Harbour and the vast sprawl of Bournemouth to the east.

From Wareham take the minor road north-westwards across Bloxworth Heath to **Bere Regis**, a former market town, and now little more than a large village, whose outstanding church has the finest timbered roof in Dorset. Constructed in about 1500, its colourful and glorious detail, which includes whole carved figures, thoroughly justifies the small fee needed to activate the special lighting, which is controlled by a time-switch.

The A35 westwards to Dorchester passes through **Tolpuddle**, where the desperate working conditions in agriculture in the 1830s were such that six local farm labourers sought to join the Grand National Consolidated Trades Union, which had recently been founded by Robert Owen. Union officials instructed them to form a lodge, to which they had to swear an oath of secrecy. This contravened an Act of 1797 forbidding 'unlawful oaths', and the labourers were arrested, tried, found guilty and sentenced to 7 years' hard labour in Australia in 1835. Public resentment was so great that they were reprieved, but slow communications and transport meant that they did not return until 1838. Near the church, a shelter of 1934 commemorates the six 'Tolpuddle Martyrs', and the row of Trades Union Congress Memorial Cottages at the west end of the village is a more practical way of remembering these Dorset labourers.

Many Dorset villages take their name from that of the river whose vale they grace. **Puddletown** is the main settlement in the Piddle Valley; it was the village Hardy knew best as a boy, and in *Far From the Madding Crowd* he called it Weatherbury. The best of the village lies north of the main road, together with the church, probably the finest example in Wessex of a medieval church ignored by Victorian restorers, so that it retains its high box pews, musicians' gallery and seventeenth-century furnishings. Book-lovers may appreciate the homely atmosphere and good selection of secondhand books and old maps in the Puddletown Map and Bookshop.

A mile ($1^1/_2$ km) east of Puddletown is **Athelhampton House**, built for Sir William Martyn at the end of the fifteenth century and added to 50 years later. It is a delight of grey and gold stone, the perfect medieval manor house, with a tall oriel window, decorated porch, and battlements. Inside, the great hall and gallery has an open timber roof, and a circular, early sixteenth-century dovecote graces the beautiful, wooded gardens which back onto the River Stour.

Beyond Puddletown the A35 sweeps on towards Dorchester. Afforestation now covers the bare, bleak heaths south of the road and regrettably encroaches on Hardy's birthplace at **Higher Bockhampton**. This is reached by a side road and then only by a short walk through woodland. It is owned by the National Trust but the interior is open only by appointment with the custodian. The cottage, built by Hardy's grandfather around 1800, is easily appreciated from the end of its garden. He lived there from his birth in 1840 until his move to London in 1862, and again, still with his parents, from 1867 until 1874. He wrote most of his first five novels here including *Under the Greenwood Tree* and *Far From the Madding Crowd*. After his marriage to Emma Gifford in 1874 he was only a visitor to his birthplace, having lived at Sturminster Newton, South London and Wimborne. He finally moved to Dorchester in 1883, building his own home, Max Gate, in 1885, where he lived until his death in 1928.

The A35 now by-passes **Dorchester**, a lively market and county town of 15,000 people at the heart of Hardy's Wessex, and an excellent centre for exploring Dorset. The Dorset County Museum displays many aspects of

Athelhampton House, a fine example of fifteenth-century architecture

local history, including finds from nearby Maiden Castle, while its Thomas Hardy Memorial Collection includes some original manuscripts, personal possessions and first editions of all the novels, housed in a faithful reconstruction of his study.

Outside, in spite of some new façades to some buildings, and all aspects of street life in a country town today, it is difficult not to feel a strong sense of the Victorian town which was the novelist's Casterbridge. If time permits, visit Maumbury Rings on the town's southern edge, a Stone Age circle adapted by the Romans into a vast amphitheatre.

Two miles (3km) south-west are the enormous earthworks of **Maiden Castle**. Excavations here in 1934-7, and again more recently, prove an almost continuous use from early Stone Age times (3000 BC) to Roman days when the then hilltop town was attacked. Its defenders were massacred, its inhabitants subjugated, and by AD70 they had moved down into the new Roman town of *Durnovaria*, the present Dorchester.

The **Isle of Portland**, much nearer to being an island than Purbeck, thrusts its great headland out into the English Channel. It is linked by road to the mainland only by a narrow causeway running along the eastward end of Chesil Beach. From the seventeenth century onwards, quarries have yielded thousands of tons of fine limestone, much of it going to London. St Paul's Cathedral and Buckingham Palace are among many famous buildings using Portland stone. Easton, Weston and Southwell are largely quarrymen's villages, and at the northern end of the island, Portland Castle was built by Henry VIII in 1520 as one of his chain of South Coast forts.

From Portland the view embraces another great arc of coastline westwards to Lyme Regis, over 20 miles (30km) away. The famous **Chesil Beach** extends for 16 miles (26km), for half of which it separates the sea from the tidal waters of the Fleet, breached only at Small Mouth, crossed by the Weymouth to Portland road. The pebbles comprising Chesil Beach, mainly of flint, are graded from pea size at West Bay to fist-size at Portland, and this unique beach is over 40ft (14m) high in places. No completely satisfactory explanation has been agreed upon as to how or when the beach was formed, but it has been the graveyard of many sailing ships when gales have swept across Lyme Bay.

By taking the B3157 from Weymouth to Portland, through Portesham, Abbotsbury and Burton Bradstock to Bridport, the coast is in view for most of the way. **Abbotsbury** has rows of golden stone, thatched-roof cottages, a fifteenth-century tithe barn, a hilltop chapel, and the only nesting colony of mute swans in Britain, where up to 400 or 500 may be seen in summer.

Beyond Abbotsbury the road follows the coast, 400-500ft (122-152m) below and 1 mile ($1^1/_2$km) away, with few access points until Burton Bradstock is reached. A few miles inland, **Bridport** is an old market town, aligned mainly along one long street, and was famous in the days of sail for its rope-making, which ended here in 1970, although nets are still made. The broad pavements are said to have been the ropewalks, where lengths of hemp were twisted to make rope. Continuous frontages, mainly dating from the days of prosperity in Georgian times, create a degree of unity which can be seen particularly clearly in South Street. In East Street, near the Town Hall, a Charity shop shows a fine, genuine late eighteenth-century façade, with two bowed shop windows and a nameboard along the parapet. It was formerly the George Inn, and Charles II stayed there during his flight to the Channel Coast after being defeated at the Battle of Worcester in 1651.

The A35 continues westwards to Lyme Regis, through undulating country, with hills between it and the coast, and **Charmouth** is one of the few places with access to the sea. **Golden Cap**, 626ft (191m) high, and the highest point on the coast of southern England, is the scenic centrepiece of a 2,000 acre National Trust estate. A steep, minor road from Charmouth gives access to part of it, where large areas of golden gorse brighten the landscape in early summer, and many miles of waymarked footpaths provide the most satisfying way to enjoy wide views and fresh sea breezes.

Lyme Regis is a delightful small town, predominantly late Georgian in character, though completely different from Weymouth. The 'Regis' dates from 1284 when Edward I granted the town its charter and used it as a port in his wars against France. Jane Austen wrote about Lyme in the early years of the nineteenth century, when it was enjoying its heyday; the town features prominently in her novel *Persuasion*. It also provides the setting for a modern novel, *The French Lieutenant's Woman* by John Fowles. The most important event in Lyme's history was the Duke of Monmouth's landing in 1685, as claimant to the English throne. He was Charles II's illegitimate son by his mistress, Lucy Walters, born in Rotterdam in 1649 during the King's previous exile. Charles had no legitimate sons and after his death in 1685 he was succeeded by his brother, who was crowned James II. The Duke of

Monmouth was persuaded to attempt to usurp the throne and, after land-ing (from Holland) at Lyme, built up a small army and moved north to Taunton, in Somerset, where he was locally proclaimed king. However, within 3 weeks of his landing, King James' troops had been mustered and, after a few skirmishes in North Somerset, joined battle with Monmouth's men at Sedgemoor and defeated the rebels. Monmouth escaped, and tried to head for the coast, as his father had done 34 years earlier, only to be captured a few miles north of Wimborne. A few days later he was executed at the Tower of London.

Lyme Regis is no longer a commercial port, but its small harbour, protected by the Cobb, a fourteenth-century breakwater, is used by a few fishing boats and many pleasure craft. Boats can be hired, fishing trips arranged, and sailing and windsurfing can be enjoyed, but Lyme's appeal is in the modest, colourful charms of its houses, cottages, shops and inns. A good local history museum displays many fine examples of fossils found in the limestones of nearby cliffs.

As a seaside resort, Lyme Regis is off the beaten track, and popular with those who prefer peace and quiet to brash commercialism. Nearby, but accessible only to walkers prepared for a 5 mile (8km) adventure through a unique stretch of English landscape, is the Landslip. Between Lyme Regis and Axmouth a huge mass of waterlogged chalk cliff fell away in an enormous landslide on Christmas Day 1839. The fallen rocks and land became colonised with plants, shrubs and trees. It is now a National Nature Reserve, with only one path through it; from Ware, west of Lyme, to a lane south of Axmouth. Be warned — walking is not easy, it is all very sheltered and sometimes feels claustrophobic, but the wildlife is remarkable.

From Lyme you should now head inland, by either the A3070 or the A3052. The latter soon picks up the A35, and is joined by the A3070, 3 miles (5km) from Lyme. Take the B3165 for Broadwindsor and Beaminster, enjoying wide views from this high road which sweeps round the northern rim of Marshwood Vale, at a steady 600-650ft (210-230m). Turn sharply to the east on the B3164 at Birdsmoorgate. Beyond here, it is worth pausing at **Pilsdon Pen** (National Trust), one of many Iron Age hill-forts, whose 900ft (274m) summit is easily reached by a short walk, rewarded by a superb panorama of a large area of West Dorset.

At **Broadwindsor** a small house, once an inn, has a plaque pointing out that Charles II slept there in September 1651 during his flight from Worcester. Three miles (5km) further east, on the B3163, **Beaminster** (pronounced 'Bemster') is the next focal point. This is a small market town, with small shops surrounding a market place which has a market cross at its centre. The church tower dates from about 1500 and is one of Dorset's finest. Nearby, Parnham House, an Elizabethan manor, now contains the workshop and modern furniture displays produced by the craftsman John Makepeace.

A cross-country journey, taking you into the quiet heart of the county, well off the beaten track, reveals perfectly its chalk downland intersected by southward-flowing rivers and streams. Take the B3163 eastwards from

Cerne Abbas, the junction of Abbey Street and Long Street, where the main medieval market was held

Beaminster, and in 3 miles (5km), cross the A356 on Toller Down, continuing to **Evershot**, Evershead in Hardy's novels. There is still a raised pavement down one side of the village street as there was a century ago. Beyond, cross the A37 at Holywell at the head of the Frome Valley and climb to **Batcombe Hill** for a glorious view of Blackmore Vale to the north (the Vale of Little Dairies), past the small, solitary stump of the 'Cross-in-Hand', and the descent to Minterne Magna.

Turn south on the A352 for **Cerne Abbas**, and soon the enormous, primitive chalk outline of the **Cerne Giant** can be seen to the east of the road. Cut in the green downland turf, 180ft (55m) tall and 167ft (51m) wide, holding a knobbed club 120ft (36m) long in his hand, the Giant is associated with fertility rites. Believed to date from the second century AD, the figure is thought to represent the Roman god Helith or Hercules. Significantly, when a monastery was founded at Cerne, the monks did not try to destroy the figure. The Cerne Giant and the downland immediately adjoining, is now safeguarded by the National Trust, and its outline is maintained by scouring every 7 years.

Cerne Abbas village has half-timbered Tudor cottages in Abbey Street, thatched stone cottages, some colour-washed, a few select shops, a general air of clean prosperity. However, very little remains of the great Benedictine abbey, apart from the three-storey porch of the abbot's guest-house, now in the courtyard of Abbey Farm which was built on the monastic site.

By taking the minor road climbing eastwards from Cerne, with the Giant on the left, you join the old Dorchester-Sherborne road at the top of the hill, to enjoy wide-ranging views. Head north, gradually descending from Downland into vale country, to join the A352 leading northwards to **Sherborne**, which, although it appears in many Hardy stories, especially *The Woodlanders*, is firmly rooted in historical Wessex. In AD705 Sherborne was the see of the Bishop of Wessex, its Saxon church remaining a cathedral until 1075 when the see moved to Old Sarum. In AD998 the cathedral became monastic, ceasing to be so at the Dissolution in 1539. After this the abbey church was sold to the town, whose people sensibly kept the whole of it for parochial use.

Historically and architecturally, Sherborne is the gem town of Dorset. The abbey church is largely fifteenth-century, with a superb fan-vaulted roof. To its north and west, former monastic buildings form the core of Sherborne School, most of whose buildings, Perpendicular and Victorian in style, date from the nineteenth and early twentieth centuries. Almshouses south of the abbey church maintain their medieval flavour and, nearby, a row of Tudor tenements with shops below is a rare survivor. Cheap Street ('cheap' means market) is Sherborne's spine; it is an attractive shopping street, mainly seventeenth- and eighteenth-century, with a tiny market area which has the sixteenth-century conduit, from the abbey cloister, at its focal point.

Sherborne's two castles lie to the east. The older (English Heritage), built by Bishop Roger of Salisbury 1107-1135, was sufficiently intact for Sir Walter Raleigh to start converting it into his mansion in 1592, although he soon gave up on the idea. The castle itself was abandoned after the Civil War. Across the lake to the south, Sherborne New Castle was started by Raleigh in 1594 but, after his downfall, it eventually passed to the Digby family, who added to it and have owned it ever since. The house contains fine furniture, porcelain and paintings, and 'Capability' Brown designed the surrounding park in the 1770s.

If you have not had your fill of fine country houses by now, there is a good group near Sherborne, conveniently reached by the A30 through Yeovil, beyond the Somerset border. **Brympton d'Evercy's** ensemble of house, gardens and associated buildings, chantry house and church, is memorably lovely. **Montacute House** (National Trust) evokes the splendour of Tudor building, displays Elizabethan and Jacobean paintings from the National Portrait Gallery, and has a beautiful formal garden with attractive gazebos. Colourful formality also characterises the gardens surrounding the more modest **Tintinhull House** (National Trust) a few miles north. A short distance up the A37, **Lytes Cary** (National Trust) is a perfect blend, mainly of the fourteenth- to eighteenth-centuries, in a gentle landscape. The gardens of Elizabethan **Barrington Court**, created in the 1920s, show the influence of Gertrude Jekyll, and there is a waymarked trail through the model estate (National Trust).

Take the main A303 eastwards towards Wincanton. If you have not made the detour to see the country houses, and are still at Sherborne, head north-westwards by the B3148 through Marston Magna and Queen Camel to pick up the A303 at Sparkford. A few miles west, the **Fleet Air Arm**

Museum at Yeovilton airfield attracts those with an interest in this aspect of modern naval history.

East of Sparkford, and south of the main road near South Cadbury village, far deeper historical roots are centred on the fort of **Cadbury Castle**. Imagination is needed to flesh out the bare factual bones relating to this now partly-wooded hilltop. It was used in Neolithic times, during part of the Bronze Age, and prominently in Iron Age times before the Roman invasion. It was an important post-Roman base of Celtic resistance during the so-called Dark Ages — the Camelot of Arthurian legend — and again as a Saxon stronghold resisting Danish invaders about AD1000. The site is known to have been occupied about the time of King John, after which it declined from being a small defended town to become part of the quiet agricultural landscape of South Somerset.

Continuing eastwards on the A303 past Wincanton, where there is one of England's many attractive country racecourses, you soon cross from Somerset into Wiltshire. It is worth continuing as far as **Mere**, whose name indicates that it has always been a boundary settlement, between the quiet meadows of the upper valley of the Stour, and the bare, vast chalk landscapes of Salisbury Plain to the east. The 100ft (30m) church tower dominates the small town, and The Ship and The Talbot, historic and admirable inns, face each other across the former main road. The Ship boasts a superbly-decorative wrought iron sign dating from the early eighteenth century while upstairs, in what is now the dining room, there is some wonderful oak timbering. The medieval castle on Castle Hill, above the town, has long vanished, but the climb of the grassy hill is well worth it for the widespread view from the top, embracing vale, fields, town, villages, downland, and, to the north, the woods of Stourhead.

From west of Mere, the B3092 leads northwards to Frome, and soon a side-road drops down to **Stourhead** (National Trust). The great Palladian mansion of Stourhead was designed by Colin Campbell for Henry Hoare, the banker, in 1721, with wings added about 1800. From 1741 extensive pleasure grounds were laid out with lakes, woodlands and temples. Today they form one of the finest English examples of eighteenth-century landscape design, with conifers, beeches, tulip trees, rhododendrons and azaleas. The grounds are lovely throughout the year, but late May to early June, and late October, are the most colourful times. Reasonably level drives and paths give access to most of the grounds, but allow plenty of time to walk around and appreciate the artfully-contrived vistas.

Return to the road, turn left for Kilmington and left again for **Alfred's Tower**, an enormous, three-sided brick folly built in 1772 to commemorate the victory by King Alfred in 879 over the Danes, on the edge of the town a few miles to the north.

Return to the B3092 again and soon join the A361, by-passing Frome and Beckington. Take the A36, then the B3110 for a small diversion to **Norton St Philip** which is justified if only to see, and possibly experience more closely, the famous fifteenth-century George Inn, with mullioned and bow windows, much half-timbering, a large stone porch and an interesting rear

The restored Saxon church dedicated to St Laurence, Bradford-on-Avon

courtyard. It was probably built by the monks from nearby Hinton Priory as a wool hall and inn. The Duke of Monmouth stayed there on 26 June 1685, 10 days before the Battle of Sedgemoor, and the diarist Samuel Pepys dined there, in less troubled times, 17 years earlier. The nearby church, mainly seventeenth-century, has a particularly unusual tower, very much the design of a local wealthy citizen called Jeffrey Flower, who died in 1644.

Now head eastwards on the A366, across the A36, through Farleigh Hungerford to the B3109 crossroads, turning north towards **Bradford-on-Avon**; this is something of a rarity in England — a hilltop town. Shaftesbury in Dorset is another, but not so spectacularly situated as Bradford, where the southern approach shows a series of terraces, stone houses and cottages with much modern in-filling, on the steep valley-side north of the river.

Again, the thing to do is walk. A large car park near the station is well-placed for a short walk to the great tithe barn, built in the early fourteenth century for the Abbess of Shaftesbury, who owned estates at Bradford. Huge porches, big buttresses, fine masonry outside and massive timber-framing within, leave a memorable impression. Walk across nearby Barton Bridge (dating from the same time as the barn), over the railway, to gain the closer view of Bradford. This is the most rewarding approach, which brings you to the parish church, and, more importantly, the Saxon church almost in its shadow. Founded as part of a monastery around AD705, the ground-plan of the building dates from then but most of the unusual building, which is very tall and narrow, is probably of the late tenth century, making it one of the most important late Anglo-Saxon churches in Britain.

Bradford-on-Avon prospered as a clothing town, especially from the sixteenth to late eighteenth centuries, and its buildings are largely of that period. Terraced cottages contrast with Georgian houses of rich merchants, all built of stone quarried locally. The town bridge, widened on its western side in the seventeenth century, has a lock-up on it, formerly a small chapel for prayers. At the western end of the highest of the terraces, St Mary's is a Victorian reconstruction of an early hospice's chapel.

Take the B3107 eastwards to Holt, and follow the signposts, along narrow lanes, to **Great Chalfield Manor House** (National Trust), one of the earliest non-fortified manors in the country, although it is moated on three sides. Built by a wealthy clothier about 1480, it has had remarkably few alterations, and retains three spy windows in its hall in the form of stone masks with open eyes and mouths, something which is very unusual in England. If the house is not open, you will be well-satisfied with the view of its north front, gently illuminated by evening sunlight, modest, balanced and mellowed, gloriously off the beaten track, and almost continously lived-in and cared for.

Continue northwards and eastwards to Melksham, a small town rather dominated by the Avon Rubber Company's works. Take the A350, following the broad vale of the River Avon, to **Lacock**. This is a beautiful village which, for photographers at least, must be a place of pilgrimage. It was here, in his home at Lacock Abbey, that the local squire, W.H. Fox Talbot, invented in 1835 the photographic process named after him, which subsequently formed the basis of modern photography. His first recognisable photograph, an interior shot of an abbey window, can be seen in the house.

Lacock Abbey originated in 1229 as a nunnery which, after the Dissolution of the Monasteries in 1539, was bought by Sir William Sharington. He adapted it for his house, while keeping most of its monastic features — chapter house, cloisters, kitchen and sacristy — all of which are still there today. In 1754-6 the architect Sanderrson Miller changed much of the interior into the new, Gothick style, for John Talbot. Lacock Abbey and the nearby sixteenth-century barn which now houses the Kodak Fox Talbot Museum displaying some of his equipment and work, together with most of the village, have all belonged to the National Trust since 1944. The village is a square of streets, with cottages and houses of various materials and dates; all compact, colourful, and on a friendly scale. High Street is very wide and handsome, and Church Street leads to the unusually-dedicated St Cyriac's Church, which is impressively Perpendicular, with very good monuments.

It is a short journey south-eastwards, climbing up from the Avon Vale along the minor road which used to be one of the main roads between London and Bath, to join the A342 at **Sandy Lane**. This not only has thatched cottages, but a thatched church too. Head south-west now for **Devizes**, whose name derives from the Latin, *ad Divasas*, meaning 'on the boundaries'. Probably on the edge of three manors, it was chosen by a twelfth-century bishop of Salisbury as the site for a castle, which is now occupied by a strange Victorian re-creation which does have a few bits of Norman masonry in its walls. The town of Devizes grew up to serve the castle, and was planned in the segment of a circle to its north-east, and the original town shape and street-pattern survives remarkably intact after 800 years.

St John's is the finest of three distinctive churches, with much Norman work in its central tower, and a magnificent Tudor chapel to the Beauchamp family. Some half-timbering is still evident in the town, but most of the buildings are of Georgian brick, even though a number are of the more aristocratic Bath stone. The Bear Hotel, in the market place, has been the town's leading hostelry for 200 years, and consists of two distinct adjoining buildings — an early seventeenth-century one on the right and one about 1760 on the left. Notice particularly its beautiful central windows, carved about the time when the father of the future great portrait painter, Sir Thomas Lawrence, was landlord.

In 1810 the Kennet and Avon Canal, linking Bristol to London, came to Devizes, bringing new trade and prosperity, and more easily available Bath stone, to the town. Today, after a long period of restoration, the canal operates for leisure cruising. To the west of Devizes one of the most impressive staircases of locks, at Caen Hill, lifts the waterway 300ft (91m) from the Avon Vale, to Devizes on its downland spur, and from there eastwards along the pastoral Vale of Pewsey.

For road travellers the A361 is the route, north-eastwards across the clean-contoured downs to Beckhampton and the A4. Halfway along this stretch the road crosses the Wansdyke, probably built in the early sixth century as a defence earthwork. **Beckhampton** has important racing training stables and horses are frequently exercised on the downland gallops between the A361 and the A4, usually early in the day. By continuing on the A361 beyond the roundabout, you will reach **Avebury**. Use the first car park on the left and walk the short distance into the village, which is pleasant enough in itself, but is unusual for having been partially built within the greatest prehistoric stone circle in Britain.

Probably because of its less dramatic situation, the Avebury circle is far less known than Stonehenge, and lacks the ordered, concentrated unity possessed by its more famous contemporary. However, Avebury is much grander in scale, with its huge banks and ditch, almost 1 mile ($1^1/_2$km) round , enclosing an area of 28 acres. At least a hundred stones formed a circle within this, but only twenty-seven remain. Sites of many others are identified by small concrete pillars; most of the missing ones were broken and used for buildings in the village and neighbourhood. Avebury circle seems to have been used from about 2600BC to 1600BC, but its purposes have never been proved. The best quadrant is the south-western one, but equally impressive is the stone avenue by the side of the minor road, the B4003, leading back to the A4 at West Kennett. This avenue had about a hundred pairs of large stones in a double row of $1^1/_2$ miles ($2^1/_2$km), but only about a third remain.

A short detour 1 mile ($1^1/_2$km) westwards along the A4 is worthwhile for the close view it provides of the enigmatic Silbury Hill, Europe's largest man-made prehistoric mound, believed to date from approximately

Avebury stone circle which dates back to the late Neolithic period

2500BC. Repeated excavations have yielded very little evidence to explain its significance; perhaps it is best that we can still look and wonder. Nearby, on the opposite side of the road, a footpath points the way to West Kennett long barrow, $^1/_2$mile (1km) away on the downs. Part of this huge chambered Neolithic tomb has been excavated and is open to view. Excavations have revealed that forty-six burials took place here, extending over the period 2000-1000BC, broadly contemporary with the Avebury circle, and emphasising the importance of this part of Wiltshire over 3,000 years ago.

The road to Marlborough, the A4, follows the upper reaches of the River Kennett. Now that the M4 takes much of the London to Bath and Bristol traffic, the A4 is a much pleasanter road to drive on, passing through gently-contoured landscapes generous with trees, between flowing downland skylines.

Marlborough today is probably most famous for its great public school, Marlborough College, which started in 1843 with 200 boys and now has many times that number. The Bath road enters the town between groups of college buildings. It then turns sharply by one of the town's two parish churches into the spectacularly long, broad High Street. The latter's width is historically explained by its having evolved as a great open sheep market in late Saxon times, and a planned town was developed around it in the early thirteenth century. A great fire in 1653 destroyed most of the timbered houses, so the present town shows a remarkably unified appearance, most of the houses, shops and inns are brick-built, with some tile-hanging, from Georgian times.

Excellent hotels, restaurants and shops make Marlborough a popular stopping-place, or a place at which to stay, maintaining a 300-year-old tradition, especially for travellers from London to Bath. The Castle and Ball Hotel, and many shops on the north side of High Street, have colonnades at ground floor level, and the handsome Ailesbury Arms has a large pillared porch. Many properties along the south side have archways to yards or lanes leading down to the River Kennett. From the eastern end of High Street, Kingsbury Street and Silverless Street there are gabled, late seventeenth-century houses, and The Green to the east achieves a village-like atmosphere.

From Marlborough the A4 provides a pleasant and direct route to London. Alternatively, to complete the Wessex circle, a return to Salisbury can be made by the A345, through Pewsey to Amesbury. There, take a minor road down the winding valley of the River Avon, passing a series of charming villages. At Great Woodford, visit the beautiful gardens at Heale House and reflect, in this quiet place, how King Charles II must have appreciated the week's safety at Heale House in early October 1651, during the last stages of his long escape journey from Worcester to the English Channel. A few miles down the valley will take you past Old Sarum, with the graceful spire of Salisbury Cathedral beckoning you ahead.

Further Information

— Wessex —

Places of Interest

Athelhampton House
Open: Easter to October Wednesday, Thursday, Sunday, Good Friday and Bank Holidays. Monday and Tuesday in August, Tuesday in July and September 2-6pm.

Avebury
Museum of Wiltshire Folklife
Open: Easter to October daily; November-Easter week-ends.

Alexander Keiller Museum
Open: April to September daily; October-March weekends.

Barrington Court Gardens
(National Trust)
Open: April to mid October daily except Thursday and Friday, but open Good Friday 11am-5.30pm.

Beaminster
Parnham House
Open: April to October, Wednesday, Sunday and Bank Holidays 10am-5pm.

Blandford
Royal Signals Museum
Open: Monday to Friday 10am-5pm. Weekends June to September 10am-4pm.

Clouds Hill (National Trust)
Open: April to early November, Wednesday, Thursday, Friday, Sunday and Bank Holidays 2-5pm; November to end March, Sundays 1-4pm.

Bovington Camp Tank Museum
Open: daily 10am-5pm, except Christmas and New Year.

Yeovil
Brympton d'Evercy House
Open: Easter weekend, then May to September, daily except Thursday and Friday 2-6pm.

Calne
Bowood House
Open: End March to end October daily 11am-6pm.

Corfe Castle (National Trust)
Open: mid-February to early November daily 10am-5.30pm; November to February, Saturday and Sunday 12noon-3.30pm.

Corfe Castle Museum
Open: April to October, daily 9am-5pm.

Devizes Museum
Open: daily, Tuesday to Saturday.

Dorchester
Dorset County Museum
Open: daily, except Sundays.

Hardy's Cottage (National Trust)
Higher Bockhampton
Open: Garden; April to early November daily, except Tuesday 11am-6pm. Interior; by prior appointment with custodian.

Heale House Gardens
Open: daily 10am-5pm.

Kingston Lacy (National Trust)
Open: House; April to early November daily except Thursday and Friday 12noon-5.30pm. Park; 11.30am-6pm.

Lacock Abbey (National Trust)
Open: House; April to early November daily except Tuesday 1-5.30pm. Cloisters and Grounds; daily 12noon-5.30pm except Good Friday.

Lacock Fox-Talbot Museum
(National Trust)
Open: March to October daily 11am-5.30pm except Good Friday.

Langton Matravers Museum
Open: April to October daily 10am-12noon, 2-4pm.

Lytes Cary Manor (National Trust)
Open: early April to early November, Monday, Wednesday, Saturday 2-6pm.

Lyme Regis Museum
Open: April to October, Monday-Saturday 10.30am-1pm, 2.30-5pm, Sunday 2.30-5pm.

Montacute House (National Trust)
Open: April to early November daily except Tuesday 12noon-5.30pm. Gardens and park daily, except Tuesday throughout year 11.30am-5.30pm.

Portland
Castle (English Heritage)
Open: Easter (or 1 April if earlier) daily 10am-6pm.

Museum
Open: summer, daily 10am-1pm, 2-5pm; winter Tuesday to Saturday 10am-1pm, 2-5pm, Sunday 11am-1pm, 2-5pm.

Salisbury
Mompesson House (National Trust)
Open: April to early November daily except Thursday and Friday 12noon-5.30pm.

Museum
Open: daily throughout year except Sundays. July and August Sundays as well.

Shaftesbury Museum
Open: Easter to September. Weekdays 11am-5pm, Sundays 2-5pm.

Sherborne
Sherborne Castle
Open: Easter Saturday to end September, Thursday, Saturday, Sunday and Bank Holidays. House; 2-6pm. Grounds; 12noon-6pm.

Sherborne Old Castle (English Heritage)
Open: April to September daily 10am-6pm; October to March, Tuesday to Sunday 10am-4pm.

Stourhead (National Trust)
Garden Open: all year 8am-7pm (or dusk if earlier)
House Open: April to early November, Saturday to Wednesday 12noon-5.30pm (or dusk).

Wareham Museum
Open: Easter to mid October, Monday to Saturday 10am-1pm, 2-5pm.

Wilton House and Grounds
Open: Easter to mid-October, Tuesday to Saturday and Bank Holidays 11am-6pm, Sunday 1-6pm.

Wimborne Museum
Open: Good Friday to September daily 10.30am-4.30pm.

Winchester
Great Hall of Castle
Open: daily.

City Museum
Open: all year, Monday to Friday.

Yeovilton
Fleet Air Arm Museum
Open: daily throughout year.

Tourist Information Centres

Blandford
West Street Car Park
☎ 0258 51989

Bradford-on-Avon
Silver Street
☎ 02216 5797

Bridport
South Street
☎ 0308 24901

Devizes
The Wharf
☎ 0380 71069

Dorchester
Aceland Road
☎ 0305 67992

Lyme Regis
Guildhall
☎ 02974 2138

Marlborough
High Street
☎ 0672 53989

Mere
The Square
☎ 0747 860341

Portland
St George's Centre
☎ 0305 823406

Salisbury
Fish Row
☎ 0722 334956

Shaftesbury
Bell Street
☎ 0747 3514

Sherborne
Hound Street
☎ 0935 815341

Wareham
Town Hall
☎ 09295 2740

Weymouth
The Esplanade
☎ 0305 785747

Wimborne Minster
Cook Row
☎ 0202 840125

Winchester
The Guildhall
☎ 0962 67871

4 • The Cotswolds

T he Cotswolds is the name given to an area of gentle upland country covering less than 700sq miles (1,814sq km), mainly in Gloucestershire but extending slightly into Oxfordshire, Worcestershire, Wiltshire, Avon and Warwickshire. Its nature is that of a plateau averaging 500ft (152m) above sea level, tilted slightly from west to east, with the highest points on its western escarpment just reaching the 1,100ft (335m) contour and providing the most rewarding and wide-ranging views. Nowhere is the scenery spectacular, but everywhere it is charming — the result of 4,000 years of man's labour.

It lies many miles inland from the nearest sea, although the silvery tidal waters of the Severn Estuary gleam in many views from the western edge. However, the limestone of its friendly hills was formed in the sea, as the accumulated deposits of tiny organisms which, compressed and subsequently raised above the surface, have provided the most gracious of building stones. This oolitic limestone exists as an almost continuous belt across England, stretching from the Dorset Coast to Yorkshire, but in the Cotswolds it reaches perfection in quality and colour. Occurring near the surface, it has been quarried or mined since prehistoric times. Medieval abbeys and castles, fine mansions, smaller though equally elegant houses in town and country, farms, barns and more modest houses are all built of it and this imparts a unique architectural unity to the area. However, subtle differences in the colour and texture of the stone ensures that there is no dull uniformity.

Each of its small towns has its individual character and appeal, while many of the region's hundred villages are regarded as the most beautiful in Britain, wholly in harmony with Cotswold landscapes. Most towns and villages are dominated by their churches, largely paid for from the profits of a prosperous medieval wool trade. In later centuries cloth-making produced the wealth which has given us scores of substantial stone houses, particularly from the late sixteenth century onwards.

History has dealt kindly with the Cotswolds. No great battles have been fought here, although Edge Hill to the east, and Lansdown above Bath did see fighting during the Civil War. King Charles I's headquarters were at Oxford, and there was strong Royalist support in Wales and the south-west of England, while opposing Parliamentary forces were garrisoned at Gloucester. The period between 1642 and 1646 was one of local unrest, with

*The gently
rolling landscape
of the Cotswolds*

many small bands of foot soldiers and cavalry engaged in minor skirmishes, while larger numbers of troops marched and counter-marched
across the open wolds, occasionally meeting in battle. Churches at Burford,
Cirencester, Painswick and Stow-on-the-Wold were used to house prisoners temporarily.

Peaceful conditions since then have contributed to the calm,
unspectacular landscapes of the Cotswolds. Enclosures of their former
open fields from about 1720 to 1830, by hawthorn hedges or stone walls,
have given them their ordered appearance. Sheep and cattle graze rich
pastures, while corn thrives on the shallower soils of the uplands, its
ripening in summer adding colourful contrasts to open views, as do the rich
browns of new-ploughed soils in autumn.

Majestic beechwoods crown the crest of the escarpment almost continuously from Dover's Hill above Chipping Campden to Wotton-under-Edge,
40 miles (64km) to the south-west. Their greening in late spring and bronz-
ing in late October are memorable seasonal glories. Ashes are the trees of
hedgerows, willows and alders of the gentle, secretive rivers, Evenlode,
Windrush, Leach, Coln and Churn draining southwards and eastwards
from the plateau to join the Thames, which has its source near Cirencester.
Near Stroud, the Frome has carved a gorge in its westwards course towards
the Severn.

Woodlands, hedgerows, and the few areas of limestone grassland now
preserved as commons are of particular interest to naturalists for their rich
variety of wild flowers. Many miles of footpaths throughout the Cotswolds
encourage walkers to explore these quiet places in this most rewarding

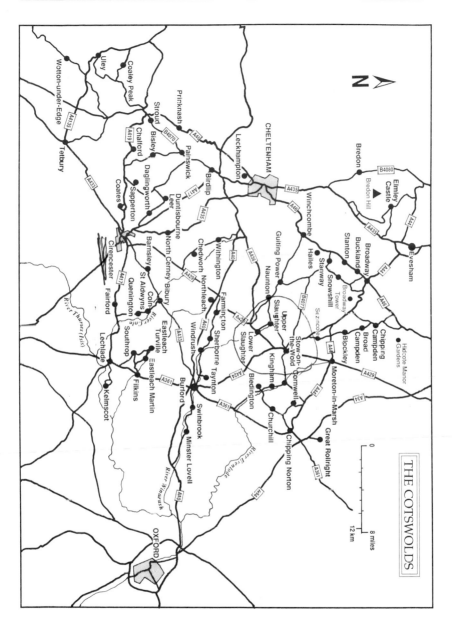

way. Horse-riding is very popular, and although good bridlepaths are plentiful, it is almost inevitable that riders have to use public roads, particularly those minor ones which wind intricately across the wolds and in the valleys.

Public transport in the Cotswolds is fragmented, with local bus services operating from various villages to market towns mainly on market days.

Only one main railway line now serves the area, with inter-city trains running from London (Paddington) to Worcester via Oxford and Moreton-in-Marsh. A more frequent service operated by 'Sprinter' units between Oxford and Worcester, stops at local stations in the Evenlode Valley. Inter-city trains between Paddington, Cheltenham and Gloucester, stopping at Stroud, are also supplemented by 'Sprinter' units.

No motorway touches the Cotswolds, although the M4 to the south, the M5 on the west, and the M40 on the east and north offer fast routes to the periphery, with Swindon, Bath, Cheltenham, Stratford and Oxford the main towns near the edges of the area. The trunk roads, A34, A420, A46 and A435 bring motorists closer. However, as the map shows, the A40 Oxford to Cheltenham, and A429 Cirencester to Moreton-on-Marsh roads, with the A429 and the A433/A46 continuing south-westwards from Cirencester, are the most useful main routes crossing the heart of the Cotswolds.

Cirencester, with a population of 16,000, is the Cotswolds' largest town, and shares with Stow-on-the-Wold (with a population of under 2,000) the claim to be the best centre for exploration. Hotels here, and in other towns, are modest and comfortable. More expensive accommodation is available at a number of the 'Country House' style of hotels, often in converted and enlarged manor houses. However, these do not always represent the best value for money. Many pubs in villages and country towns provide good midday lunches and bar meals, and some display imaginative menus for evening meals, based on good home cooking. Of the three large towns (Bath, Cheltenham and Oxford) convenient for exploring the Cotswolds, with a much greater variety of accommodation, Cheltenham is the closest to the heart of the area, with the A40 main road from Oxford neatly bisecting the Cotswolds.

Visitors driving from London should use the M40 as the quickest approach to the Cotswolds, branching off to join the A40 east of Oxford. This by-passes the University city and continues westwards, by-passing Witney and giving increasingly wide views, particularly across the Windrush Valley. If one continued to Cheltenham, the Cotswold plateau would be crossed within an hour's easy driving, and a first impression would reveal an apparently unpeopled landscape of patterned fields, woodlands and shelter-belts, hedges and stone walls, but few signs of habitation other than a distant church tower or a closer stone-built farm, and an occasional wayside inn. Such an impression would be wholly false, and needs correcting.

Burford, lying just to the north of the A40, is reached by the A361 which plunges down the long main street of this compact, charming, but busy small town. A free car park near the bottom of High Street is conveniently placed to allow a stroll around. This is the only way to see Burford and to appreciate its houses dating from the fifteenth to eighteenth centuries. Although most High Street properties now have shops or offices on their ground floors and are stone-built, some of the older ones reveal their late medieval origins by their exposed timber frames. A particularly good group of these lines the eastern side of High Street, almost opposite the

Minster Lovell; the church and ruined hall

Tolsey, a small gabled sixteenth-century building, formerly the Court House where market tolls were collected. Below it, Falkland Hall (1558) was probably the first Burford house constructed completely of stone. Below that, the courtyards of seventeenth- and eighteenth-century inns now reveal neat, modern cottage terraces, tastefully converted from half-timbered ranges of former inn buildings. Charles II is said to have stayed with one of his mistresses, Nell Gwynne, at the George Hotel, but Burford's history goes back at least five centuries before then. During the Middle Ages it was a prosperous wool town, administered by one of the earliest Merchants' Guilds. St John the Baptist's Church, near the car park behind the eastern side of High Street, reflects the growing medieval prosperity. Norman in origin, it was gradually enlarged with aisles and chapels. Monuments bear names of former wool merchants, and in the churchyard unusual decorative chest-tombs commemorate seventeenth-century clothiers.

The Industrial Revolution by-passed Burford, as did the railways of the nineteenth century, so it remained a roadside town, with scarcely any new buildings since the eighteenth century, although existing structures were refronted, modernised, enlarged or divided. Thus it preserves its medieval, Tudor, and seventeenth-century character.

A short detour down the Windrush Valley leads to **Minster Lovell**, with its single street of stone cottages, many of which are thatched, leading to the beautiful, if melancholy ruins of Minster Lovell Hall (English Heritage), memorably situated among stately trees on the north bank of the Windrush. Built by William, the seventh Lord Lovell (1431-42) the house was eventually dismantled in 1747, and its ruins evoke bitter-sweet memories of earlier greatness. Imagination may be needed to build up a picture of the surviving walls and gables, but a pastoral peace permeates a picturesque group. Nearby, the contemporary circular dovecote with a conical roof and lantern is worth seeing. So, too, is **Swinbrook**, a quiet, unassuming small village on the north side of the Windrush Valley. The Lords Redesdale were squires here from early last century until 1958, and two of the famous modern members of the family, Nancy and Unity Mitford, are buried in the churchyard. Earlier squires were the Fettiplaces, whose mansion was demolished in 1805. An unusual monument to seventeenth-century members of the family shows two groups of three, dating from 1613 and 1658, commemoratively stacked against the north wall of the chancel in the church.

Southwards from Burford, the A361 leads to **Lechlade**, an attractive small town at the south-eastern corner of the Cotswolds, its feet washed by the waters of the River Thames. A small diversion takes in **Filkins**, where modest houses and cottages line the village street, and many garden walls are made of upright slabs of local stone. A large, former barley-barn of 1720 has been converted into a centre for local crafts including wood-turning and other wood crafts, rush-weaving and wool-weaving. Tastefully displayed finished products are on sale and admission to the workshops and showrooms is free.

Three miles (5km) east of Lechlade, **Kelmscot Manor** is of particular interest as the home of William Morris for the last 25 years of his life. Poet, writer, craftsman, founder of the Socialist League and the Society for the Protection of Ancient Buildings, Morris was a profound influence on the Arts and Crafts Movement of the later decades of the nineteenth century. The sixteenth-century gabled house, occasionally open to the public, contains furniture and textiles designed by him and some of his friends.

Cotswold lanes are invariably more rewarding to follow than main roads, for they lead to secretive, unspoiled villages. Although the main A417 westwards from Lechlade reaches Fairford in only 5 miles (8km), a detour northwards along the Leach Valley allows one to incorporate a quintet of villages: **Southrop, Eastleach Martin, Eastleach Turville**, and, in the Coln Valley, **Coln St Aldwyns** and **Quenington**. Gentle river scenery, rich pastures and ordered parkland typify this corner of the Cotswolds, and Norman churches emphasise the depth of its historical roots; those at Southrop, Eastleach Martin and Quenington are the best.

Even these must bow in splendour to the parish church at **Fairford**, back on the main road. This small town is centred on a wide, elegant market place, with the glorious church nearby. It was built between 1490 and 1530 by wealthy wool merchants John Tame and his son, Sir Edmund, who could afford the best masons, sculptors, carvers and glaziers of the time. The church displays magnificent masonry, carved figures and armorial devices, and possesses the only complete set of medieval stained and coloured glass windows in any English parish church. These depict the Bible story from Adam and Eve to the Last Judgement. Among the many fine

The Dorset coast near Swanage, Wessex

The Georgian estate village of Milton Abbas, Dorset, Wessex

The seventeenth-century gatehouse of Stanway House, Cotswolds

A Cotswold landscape above Compton Abdale

churchyard memorials is a small modern one, opposite the south porch, to 'Tiddles, the Church Cat', a delightfully homely touch. A short walk along Mill Lane, north of the church, past the large free car park, leads to the mill adjoining the smoothly flowing River Coln. Here, with the church in the distance, is as perfect an English pastoral scene as you could hope to find.

The River Coln graces one of the Cotswold's most enchanting valleys. A narrow road leading north-west from Fairford, is known as the Welsh Way from its use for centuries as a route by which cattle-drovers from Wales brought their stock across country to the markets of London. In a few miles it joins the A433 Cirencester to Burford road near **Bibury,** where a small car park and some limited roadside parking are insufficient to cater for the hundreds of visitors who presumably agree with William Morris's assertion that this was the prettiest village in England. Across the clear river, **Arlington Row** is a group of cottages converted in the seventeenth century from a medieval wool barn to provide homes for weavers working at nearby Arlington Mill. Arlington Row is now owned by the National Trust, the cottages are tenanted and are not open to the public.

Seventeenth-century Arlington Mill still has its mill machinery operating, and its seventeen rooms display a variety of exhibits of rural life together with examples of craftsmanship, representative of the Arts and Crafts Movement, including work by Morris, with furniture by Gimson and Barnsley. Adjoining this is the long-established Bibury Trout Farm, where trout of all sizes may be observed and fed, while fresh and smoked trout, as well as smoked trout and salmon pâté are on sale. Excellent food and refreshments are available at nearby hotels and restaurants and, a few hundred yards away to the east, Bibury village and its historic church slumber quietly away, aloof from most visitors' exploration.

From Bibury the A433 offers an easy return to Burford in one direction, or, in the other, a few minutes' drive to Cirencester 7 miles (11km) south-west, passing through Barnsley village. There, Rosemary Verey's famous gardens at **Barnsley House** display, within the overall framework of a large garden, a creative array including knot and herb gardens, a formal kitchen garden, trees, shrubs, ground cover plants, herbaceous borders and a pond garden.

South Cotswolds' roads converge on **Cirencester**, many since Roman times, when *Corinium*, as they called it, was the largest town outside London. Today it could be fairly regarded as an almost perfect English market town. The Roman plan has been obscured by Saxon and medieval developments, whose winding and often narrow streets are visually much more satisfying. Scarcely anything survives of a great medieval abbey except a vast open space, the abbey grounds, north of the parish church. This is a complicated building of different dates, but predominantly a glory of Gothic grace and space. The south porch, overlooking the market place, built by the abbots at the close of the fifteenth century as an office, became the Town Hall after the Dissolution.

Walk the streets of Cirencester to appreciate domestic architecture dating from three centuries ago, with the Classical formality of Georgian times making the strongest impression. There is much to delight, little to displease. Care has been taken in recent years over the location of car parks which are tucked away behind street frontages. The Corinium Museum, in Park Street, shows aspects of the Roman town and its life, imaginatively displayed in full-scale reproductions. Beautiful mosaics discovered during local archaeological excavations are also shown.

If the Corinium Museum whets the appetite for things Roman, a visit to the Roman villa at **Chedworth**, a few miles north, well-signposted but still elusive and reached only along narrow lanes, is an obvious corollary. Sites of a dozen Roman villas have been found within a few miles of Cirencester, which is proof that this was a desirable area in which to live 1,600 years ago. Excavations at Chedworth have revealed the extensive layout of a large Roman farm and its outbuildings, although what remains above ground is meagre. With a little imagination it is possible to picture the opulent lifestyle of the occupants, and to recognise what an enormous peasant labour force would have been essential to service it. Many mosaic floors are visible and an on-site museum displays the more important relics from excavations.

Beyond Chedworth this northern excursion from Cirencester could continue to embrace the attractive, if little-known, village of Withington, then taking a straight road to join the A436 and swing westwards to the important cross roads at **Seven Springs**. This gains its name from the springs of clear water in a small copse nearby, easily reached from a convenient layby, which form the source of the River Churn, formerly thought to be the birthplace of the Thames, as a Latin inscription claims. Opinions still differ on this subject, and Thames Head, south-west of Cirencester, has gained credence, as an alternative site although Seven Springs is a greater distance from the main river at Lechlade.

Seven Springs is a good point from which to sample the Cotswold Way. A well-signposted and easy walk follows the route northwards up to and along the escarpment, around Charlton Kings Common and **Leckhampton**. There, a short detour leads to the famous landmark, the **Devil's Chimney**, an isolated rock pinnacle left by quarrymen, close to the famous Leckhampton quarries which yielded early last century most of the stone from which the elegant houses of Cheltenham were built. By returning the same way, the wide-ranging view can be enjoyed again in a 5 mile (8km) round trip for which 2 to 3 hours should be allowed.

The return to Cirencester is by the A435, down the winding, well-wooded and scenic, Churn Valley. Make a detour at North Cerney to see one of the best village churches. Dating from the twelfth century, it is full of exquisite details and delights, whose beauty and fine condition are preserved as the result of generous benefactions by William Croome since 1910.

The A417 is, and was in Roman times, the main road from Cirencester to Gloucester. Its uncompromising directness may speed travel, but it lacks scenic interest and does not pass through any villages. Immediately to its west is the secretive and charming Duntisbourne Valley which gives its name to a string of tiny villages, although before these is **Daglingworth**, whose manor house and circular dovecote grace the valley while the church with rare Saxon sculptures stands above the village. From the village crossroads follow the narrow road up the valley, visiting **Duntisbourne** on the way, for little over 2 winding miles (3km). **Duntisbourne Rouse** has a tiny Saxon church in a lovely churchyard above the valley; **Middle Duntisbourne** is little more than a farm group, **Duntisbourne Leer** has farms, barns, houses, cottages embracing a ford amid sloping valley fields, and at **Duntisbourne Abbots** the hill-perched church stands at the heart of its friendly village.

A lane leads westwards towards the next secret valley, that of the River Frome, down which there is no road. However, a good minor road heads southwards above the valley's eastern rim to **Sapperton**. Originally the 'place of soap-makers', early this century it was a village of wood-carvers, furniture makers and architects, all influenced by, and continuing the traditional crafts of the Arts and Crafts Movement. Ernest Gimson, Sidney and Ernest Barnsley, and later Norman Jewson, all lived in the village, established workshops, revived Cotswold masons' skills, built houses and cottages, and restored others in the district. Their simple memorials are in the churchyard, where the church was almost wholly rebuilt in Queen Anne's reign, and still retains its calm, early eighteenth-century atmosphere.

Below the village the towpath of the old Thames-Severn Canal leads to the northern portal of the tunnel constructed in 1789; at over 2 miles (3km), it was the longest tunnel that had ever been built in Britain. The canal has long been derelict, its bed dry and overgrown, but the tunnel's southern portal, near the village of Coates west of Cirencester, has been restored to its former Classical elegance.

Westwards from Sapperton, the Frome Valley is known as the Golden Valley, a soubriquet justified when October burnishes the beech woodlands that clothe the hillsides. At **Chalford**, where virtually nothing is on the level, most local streets are too steep and narrow for vehicles. Stepped paths and alleys link a bewildering jumble of clinging cottages, and a walkabout is challenging but rewarding in this unique corner of the Cotswolds. The cloth industry reached its heyday here early last century. Further west the valley becomes more industrialised with modern development around Stroud, so to escape from these intrusions it is as well to head northwards to **Bisley** to regain true Cotswold country and character. This upland village enjoys a well-dressing ceremony each Ascension Day and, in the large churchyard, a rare, thirteenth-century 'Poor Soul's Light' retains its carved niches for candles used in outdoor mass. Among the splendid, yet modest houses in outlying parts of this widespread parish, Nether Lypiatt Manor is an outstanding example — it dates from 1702-5.

By continuing northwards to Birdlip on the B4070, the A417 can be regained, offering a quick return to Cirencester. A short 'there-and-back' detour to **Barrow Wake**, 1 mile (2km) beyond Birdlip, gives the reward of a panoramic view illustrating perfectly what an escarpment is, with the Cotswold edge stretching away to the north-west, the Vale of Gloucester below, and the sprawling city reaching almost to the foot of the hill.

Turn off the A417 a few miles down the road to visit **Elkstone**, lonely on the uplands to the east. Here is the outstanding Norman village church of the Cotswolds. It is full of rich and fascinating details both outside and in, including an unusual dovecote above the chancel, reached by climbing a spiral stair behind the pulpit. Eight centuries of sanctity and worship have created an eloquent ambience at Elkstone. If you were limited to seeing one Cotswold village church, this should be it.

Although the area around Stroud is the most industrialised in the Cotswolds, within a few miles the 'real' Cotswold character asserts itself, particularly at **Painswick**, 3 miles (5km) north of Stroud along the A46. Compact and huddled, so different from Burford, it has short, narrow streets, few of which are level, all with houses and cottages fronting directly on to them, and all of silvery-grey stone. Wool merchants and later clothiers built and lived in them, and are remembered in the best display of memorials in any English country churchyard. Useful trail leaflets explain their history. Also in Painswick is the Rococo garden recently restored to resemble its 1748 origins.

Prinknash (pronounced 'Prin-age') Abbey, close to the A46 north of Painswick, is a modern Benedictine abbey, functional in appearance, with limited access. However, nearby are the workshops and showrooms of its famous pottery where today's monks, helped by lay craftsmen, throw, fire and decorate their distinctive wares.

Cirencester's situation is convenient for a short tour round the southern tip of the Cotswolds. **Tetbury** is only 10 miles (16km) away down the A433, another small town which prospered through the wool and cloth trade. Centred round a handsome, pillared Market House built in 1655 but altered in 1817, pleasant hotels, inns, and a range of shops occupy mainly seventeenth- and eighteenth-century buildings. Many are famous for their antiques, while one concentrates solely on cheese. Royalty live nearby — Prince Charles' home is Highgrove House, while his sister, the Princess Royal, has Gatcombe Park. Neither house is open to the public, and local people, as well as visitors to the area, respect the privacy to which they are entitled. The spire of St Mary's Church pierces the skyline, and the building itself is large and light, a latecomer of 1781, and, unusually for the Cotswolds, a graceful essay in Gothic Revival architecture.

Travel westwards along the A4135, across the A46, gradually swinging south-westwards on the B4058 into **Wotton-under-Edge**. This is much more a workaday place than most other Cotswold towns, and is none the worse for that. Very much off the beaten track, it is the sort of place that exists for its own 5,000 residents rather than for visitors. However, the Cotswold ethos prevails although the stone is greyer, and some roofs are pantiled. The Perry and Dawes Almshouses in Church Street, were built and endowed by former worthies in the seventeenth century. Now modernised internally, they house local elderly people. Heed the welcoming inscription above the doorway, go into the quiet courtyard and, if you wish, say a silent prayer in the tiny chapel. Wotton looks, feels and is friendly.

Head now for Dursley, which is industrial, and seek the B4066 which leads eastwards to **Uley**. This is a long village climbing the lower slopes of the Cotswolds. The road winds up to the crest, past the large grassy mound to the west which is Hetty Pegler's Tump, a prehistoric chambered long barrow. You can gain an impression of what it is like by continuing to the large car park and picnic site at Coaley Peak, where the small Nympsfield long barrow has been excavated and left uncovered. More wide views are the main rewards at Coaley, and the Cotswold Way footpath passes through, running along the crest before entering fine beech and ash woodland on its 100 miles (161km) from Chipping Campden to Bath.

Stow-on-the-Wold lies 19 miles (31km) north-east of Cirencester along the A429 which follows the direct, if gently undulating Foss Way. It is a hilltop town, bracing but often windswept. Eight roads, mainly of ancient origin, converge upon it, making it an obvious site for the market charter which Henry I granted to its manorial landowner the Abbot of Evesham in 1107. This was an entreprenurial move which brought success, and the town's layout today, based on a large market square, by-passed by main through-roads, preserves the original plan.

The continuous frontages facing the square are varied and attractive, with a small green at its north-eastern corner giving a village-like touch. Stow prospered as a wool town, although its church is unusually undistinguished. Seventeenth- and eighteenth-century inns dignify and impart a great deal of character to Stow's townscape. Stow Fair, where 20,000 sheep at a time would be sold, has largely been transmuted into Stow Horse Fair held each July and October.

Villages near Stow which should not be missed are Lower and Upper Slaughter, in the little valley of the River Eye, a feeder of the Windrush. **Lower Slaughter** is the prettier of the two; the clear stream flirts tantalisingly close to delightful cottages, and small, neat bridges link grassy banks. A narrow road climbs and winds its way to **Upper Slaughter** where cottage gardens with flowers and vegetables suggest the more homely, less self-conscious twin, and the stream is kept at arm's length behind the village. The nice central grouping round a triangular space was remodelled by Sir Edward Lutyens early this century. To savour both villages explore them on foot — better still, walk from one to the other, only 1 mile (2km) each way along an inviting path.

A few miles to the west, by the B4068, **Naunton** is equally well-worth visiting, elongated in the Windrush Valley where clear waters trickle along behind cottages and vegetable gardens. Here, as in most Cotswold villages, is unplanned evolution, where houses, cottages, barns, dovecote and church illustrate complete harmony and instinctive good taste. The few recent additions, though obviously raw in appearance, continue the traditional Cotswold style of building. The Cotswold Farm Park, with its rare breeds of livestock, is a few miles to the north.

Beyond Naunton a minor road cuts north-westwards across country, through **Guiting Power**, a village revitalised through a self-help housing trust, with good cottage groups around a small green. The road climbs gradually to the Cotswold crest on Round Hill (950ft, 290m) before the long descent into **Winchcombe** on the busy A46. Winchcombe's roots go deep into England's past. It was a seat of Mercian royalty, with a great Benedictine abbey refounded here in 969 which flourished almost continuously until the Dissolution of the Monasteries in 1539. It was one of four Domesday boroughs in Gloucestershire, when its population was 1,000, and the town was on an important trade route along the western foot of the hills. The comings and goings of its monks, together with pilgrims to the abbey, and Tudor visitors to nearby Sudeley Castle, must have ensured constant activity.

A main street with continuous frontages on both sides provides a fascinating stroll, passing the parish church on the way, with its fierce array of grinning or grotesque gargoyles looking down. Abbot William initiated the building of the church in 1460, the work was finished by the parishioners and helped financially by Sir Ralph Boteler of Sudeley. A few timber-framed late Tudor buildings survive, including the galleried courtyard of the George Inn, built for abbey pilgrims shortly before the Dissolution, but much altered since. However, seventeenth- and eighteenth-century stone houses predominate, and nothing survives above ground of the once-famous abbey. **Sudeley Castle** has fared better although, on the whole, its superb, parkland setting and apparent medieval appearance is rather better than its largely Victorianised interior. It is privately-owned but regularly open to visitors.

Two miles (3km) north-east from Winchcombe are more ruins, those of **Hailes Abbey**, the only Cistercian monastery in the Cotswolds, and very much off the beaten track. The ruins of their wooded setting are hauntingly beautiful, and an excellent museum displays many fine pieces of carved masonry, together with an interpretative exhibition depicting monastic life. The tiny church nearby, a century older than the abbey, fully merits a visit for its own sanctity, medieval wall-paintings, stained-glass and excellent seventeenth-century furnishings.

North of Winchcombe a number of Cotswold 'outliers' form isolated, island hills above the Vale of Evesham. **Bredon Hill** is the highest, its summit plateau accessible only by footpaths. It is girdled by villages, each worth visiting, with **Bredon** at the south-west and **Elmley Castle** diametrically opposite. They are especially appealing because their black-and-white half-timbered houses provide a happy contrast to the stone ethos of most Cotswold country. At Elmley, only a few mounds and bits of masonry in the thick woods of the deer park survive of the medieval castle of the Despensers and Beauchamps.

Although there are no villages on the A46 between Winchcombe and Broadway, the gems of Stanway, Stanton and Buckland, each less than 1 mile (2km) east from the road, should not be missed. **Stanway**'s pride is an elaborately decorated Jacobean gatehouse, built of one of the noblest of all Cotswold stones, the rich orange-yellow from Guiting quarry up the road. The great house beyond has too many windows and looks rather bleak, but the huge fourteenth-century tithe barn was built nearby when Tewkesbury

Sudeley Castle, the ruined banqueting hall

Abbey owned the manor.

A minor road leads northwards through parkland to **Stanton**, which exudes Cotswold perfection in the apparent authenticity of the great period 1570-1640. Much, however, dates from the early decades of this century when the architect-squire, Sir Philip Scott, skilfully and sympathetically restored many cottages and houses. The church is distinguished by good modern furnishings, and glass by Sir Ninian Comper. Further north, **Buckland**, podded in a sheltered combe beneath wooded hills, also has interesting church furnishings, while the old rectory at the western end of the village is a rare pre-Reformation survival, a fifteenth-century hall, with open timbered roof. The north-west front is largely unaltered.

Busy Broadway, Cotswold in appearance but in thrall to tourism, is as undeniably attractive as a practised courtesan. Take the minor road by the green and head for **Snowshill**, apparently snugly-situated in its woodlands, yet one of Cotswold's highest villages, at 800ft (280m), and scenically one of the best, with clutches of cottages at different levels, centred on a triangular green with open westward views. Near the Snowshill Arms — an excellent pub for a lunch break — Snowshill Manor (National Trust, mainly seventeenth- and eighteenth-century), has terraced gardens, flowers, shrubs and ponds. The house contains a breathtaking array of curios and bygones collected by the eccentric Charles Wade earlier this century. They fill every available space in every room, and are not necessarily attractive, but utterly whimsical and un-missable.

Swinging eastwards up the hill to the crest, a minor road leads back to the A44 at the top of Fish Hill, passing on the way **Broadway Tower Country Park**, one of the few places along the edge which reaches 1,000ft (305m), and an obvious site for one of Britain's best-known follies, **Broadway Tower**. Built by the Earl of Coventry in 1800, it dominates the skyline and commands a vast, panoramic view. It now houses a series of exhibitions including one devoted to William Morris, who used the tower for holidays late last century and entertained some of his friends there, while another is a Sheep and Wool Exhibition. The 35-acre Country Park has Nature Trails and Country Walks, and the Cotswold Way, coming from the north, touches the tower before descending the escarpment into Broadway.

By following the A44 eastwards for 1 mile (2km) and then turning left at historic Cross Hands on the B4081, you will enjoy a scenic approach to the most attractive of all the small towns in the Cotswolds, **Chipping Campden**. Not being on a main road or a sizeable river provides unusual advantages, and the zealous concern of the Campden Trust, initiated in 1929, created an early awareness of building conservation. High Street, laid out by a lord of the manor after obtaining a market charter about 1180, curves gently along the line of an important trading route, widening to accommodate a central market place. Continuous frontages along both sides represent six centuries of building and growth. Inns, houses and shops now occupy properties of wool merchants, clothiers, craftsmen, artisans and shop-keepers. Some early timber-framing survives but stone dominates, honey-gold and always lovely.

Walk southwards down the eastern side, returning along the higher western side to appreciate the curve, the narrow grass strip with small trees, the gabled Market Hall of 1627, and shops selling everyday things rather than antiques. Grevel's House dates from 1400 and the contemporary Woolstaplers' Hall stands opposite — it is now a museum. The tower of the church focuses the scene, beyond the roof tops to the north. This is another 'must', a noble, well-proportioned wool church, and nearby is a dignified row of almshouses exemplifying Sir Baptist Hicks' philanthropy in 1612. However, only the lodges of his great mansion survive.

For those who delight in gardens, a short detour northwards to **Hidcote Manor** (National Trust) will bring a special joy. Ten acres of unique and glorious gardens were created from a bare hillside earlier this century by Major Lawrence Johnstone. Trees, grassy walks, dells, terraces, spring slopes and rocky banks display — often in the form of outdoor rooms each created round a different theme — a planned cornucopia of colour, scent and shape.

The unspoilt village of Blockley

Back at Chipping Campden, take the minor road through **Broad Campden** and up the hill to **Blockley**. This village is missed by most travellers but is full of delights. Cottages, modest houses and short Regency terraces, which are close-grouped on a hillside site, may have their busy industrial days behind them, but Blockley still retains the character of a 'lived-in' village.

Continue southwards to regain the A44 at Bourton-on-the-Hill. Visitors with an interest in trees should turn off at the foot of the hill for **Batsford Park and Arboretum**, best seen in spring for the seasonal colours of a rich variety of trees and woodland plants. On the opposite side of the A44, another short detour can take in **Sezincote** (the first syllable pronounced 'seez') for the Cotswolds' most unusual and exotic house. Sezincote House was designed in 1805 by Samuel Pepys Cockerell for his brother Sir Charles and is essentially a late Georgian building in Greek Revival style, encased in an oriental exterior.

The beaten track is very much in evidence at Moreton-in-Marsh, for centuries an important stopping-place on the Foss Way (the A429). It lies at the northern point of a rectangular block of the north-eastern Cotswolds. The A44 leads south-eastwards to Chipping Norton — the 'Chipping' in so many English placenames merely means 'market' — with the A361 then running south-westwards to Burford, the A40 to Northleach, and the A429 returning northwards to Stow-on-the-Wold and Moreton-in-Marsh. Generally, the further east you go the less grand is the Cotswold ethos, although it is always apparent.

The most outstanding relic of prehistoric Cotswold is to be found a few miles east of Moreton. The **Rollright Stones** comprise three separate Bronze Age sites. Most impressive is a large circle of about seventy stones, most less than 4ft (1m) high, known as The King's Men. Opposite them is a solitary King's Stone — an 8ft (2m) monolith, pitted and weathered — while $1/_2$ mile (1km) away are The Whispering Knights, a group of five large stones once forming the core of a burial chamber. In the bright light of a summer's day, all these sites look quite ordinary. In the fading light of dusk, or on a winter afternoon, they can arouse atavistic sensations, and legends associated with them seem more believable.

Chastleton House, off the A44 to the west, was built in 1603 by Walter Jones, a Witney wool merchant, and has changed remarkably little, with original panelling, furniture and tapestries. Its gables and pinnacles make for an interesting skyline, and this modest, unusual house faces southwards to an elegant, gabled dovecote in the wooded park opposite.

More parklands nearby, at Adlestrop, Daylesford and Cornwell, emphasise man's controlled contribution to the Cotswold landscape, a contrast to the farmed countryside of the corn-growing wolds. **Adlestrop**'s name attracted the attention of the poet, Edward Thomas, during a train stop there in the early days of World War I. **Cornwell** is a tiny essay in Cotswold Picturesque, neo-Georgian of the 1930s by Clough Williams-Ellis, with stone cottages, village hall, walled gardens, cobbled paths, all neat and charming, but no access for visitors' cars. A brief stroll is rewarding.

Nearby, **Oddington** illustrates how a village can move, either due to a change of farming practice, a change of landlord, or a series of visitations of the plague during medieval times. The present village extends for nearly 1 mile (2km) just south of the A436 east of Stow-on-the-Wold. Half a mile away (1km), down an inviting lane, St Nicholas' Church, mainly twelfth- and thirteenth-century, is all that remains of the medieval settlement. It is a building for the connoisseur of churches, with wall-paintings, fine furnishings, monuments, hatchments, and an indefinable aura of continuing, loving care.

Although time seems to rest lightly on the villages in the broad valley of the Evenlode, **Bledington, Kingham** and, to the east, **Churchill**, they have the advantage of being served by the only main railway line through the Cotswolds. There are trains between London, Oxford and Worcester, stopping at Kingham station, as well as at Shipton-under-Wychwood to the south, and Moreton-in-Marsh. No main road accompanies the Evenlode, but a series of minor winding country roads threads the valley. They link more small villages with Stow-on-the Wold to the north, **Chipping Norton** in the east — another lively, friendly small town round a large, sloping market place — and Burford in the south.

Westwards from Burford, the A40 quickly gets you to the important crossroads with the A429 (Foss Way) near Northleach, 9 miles (14km) away, keeping at 500-600ft (152-183m) all the way, and not passing through any villages. This well-used road gives one impression of the Cotswolds. A parallel route, 1 mile (2km) to the north, up the Windrush Valley, 200ft (61m) lower and passing through six villages, shows a completely different picture, an off-the-beaten-track journey well worth half a day. There is a peaceful quality about both the scenery and the succession of villages whose names roll musically off the tongue; Taynton, Great Barrington, Little Barrington, Windrush, Sherborne and Farmington, each representing 1,000 years of settlement, each with its church, and each with a long history of quarrying the noble Cotswold stone.

The secret of enjoying and appreciating the Cotswolds is to take your time. **Taynton**, with the best of churches, and **Great Barrington**, an estate village slowly reviving after being rather moribund, are on the north of the valley. **Little Barrington** and **Windrush**, each grouped with instinctive good taste round small greens, are on the south side, while **Sherborne** and its great park grace the Sherborne Brook. Here, the park and most of the village are now National Trust property, and well-signposted footpaths encourage intimate exploration. A very narrow road winds on to **Farmington**, where the churchyard gate is made of horse-shoes welded decoratively together and, on the triangular green, a neat octagonal pumphouse of 1874 has been restored by the good folk of Farmington, Connecticut.

So to **Northleach**, lying just off the Foss Way and now by-passed by the A40. From three small settlements here, near the head of the Leach Valley at the Conquest, Northleach developed as a town with a market charter granted in 1220, about the time that the wool trade with Italy was being established. Cotswold wool was the best in Europe, and high prices were paid for it. Peasant flocks, and the huge numbers of sheep owned by Gloucester, Winchcombe, Evesham and Cirencester abbeys, yielded the fleeces that brought prosperity, particularly to the traders and merchants dealing with the sale and movement of wool, to London and the Continent. The wool merchants' wealth went into the rebuilding of Northleach Church in the second half of the century. Lofty, light, unified and beautifully-proportioned, its masonry and statuary, particularly in the tower and south porch, dating from about 1400, are of cathedral quality.

Inside, woolmen and their wives gaze piously from gleaming memorial brasses. Feet rest on sheep or woolsacks, and their own merchant's marks are included in the design. These memorials are the best group of medieval brasses in the Cotswolds, in what is, arguably, the best of Cotswold wool churches.

Although slightly aloof from the town, it still commands the small central market place. Some seventeenth-century houses survive, but Northleach shows largely an eighteenth-century face, representing rebuilding and new development when the London-Gloucester road was routed through the town in 1746. Today, Northleach is little more than a large village close to, but thankfully missed by, the two most important main roads crossing the Cotswolds. Close to their former crossing-place, the 1790 House of Correction — an early rural prison which later became a police station — has been very well adapted to house the Cotswold Countryside Collection. It displays spacious surroundings, a wide range of artefacts illustrating the agricultural and social history of the area, aspects of rural life, with indoor exhibits and, during the summer, a variety of outdoor events.

Further Information

— The Cotswolds —

Places of Interest

Barnsley House Gardens
Near Cirencester
Open: Monday, Wednesday, Thursday, Saturday 10am-6pm, or dusk if earlier.

Batsford Arboretum
Near Moreton-in-Marsh
Open: 1 April to 31 October, daily 10am-5pm.

Bibury
Arlington Mill
Open: mid-March to mid-November. 10.30am-7pm or dusk. Weekends only in winter.

Burford
Tolsey House Museum
Open: daily, Easter to September

Chavenage House
Near Tetbury
Open: Easter Sunday and Monday. May to September, Thursday, Sunday and Bank Holidays, 2-5pm.

Chedworth Roman Villa
(National Trust)
Open: March to October, Tuesday to Sunday and Bank Holiday Monday 10am-5.30pm. Closed Good Friday. November to early December, Wednesday to Sunday 11am-4pm.

Chipping Campden
Woolstaplers Hall Museum
Open: April to September daily 11am-6pm October weekends only.

Hidcote Manor Gardens
(National Trust)
Near Chipping Campden
Open: April to October, daily except Tuesday and Friday 11am-8pm (or dusk).

Kiftsgate Court Gardens
Near Chipping Campden
Open: April to September, Wednesday, Thursday, Sunday and Bank Holidays 2-6pm.

Cirencester
Corinium Museum
Open: April to September, daily 10am-5.30pm, Sunday 2-5.30pm. October to March, Tuesday to Saturday 10am-5pm, Sunday 2-5pm. All Bank Holidays except Christmas.

Guiting Power
Cotswold Farm Park
Open: Good Friday to September daily 10.30am-6pm.

Filkins
Near Lechlade Cotswold Woollen Weavers
Open: throughout year daily 10am-6pm, Sunday 2-6pm.

Hailes Abbey
(National Trust & English Heritage)
Near Winchcombe.
Site and museum open: Good-Friday to September daily 10am-6pm. October to Easter, Tuesday-Sunday 10am-4pm (except Christmas & New Year). Site open: daily, but museum may be closed occasionally between October and Easter.

About 130 miles (209km) of the Broadland waterways are navigable by boat, and every summer sees plenty of activity, with pleasure craft chugging up and down, occasionally making way for the infinitely more graceful sailing boats, including some of the old wherries, the trading versions of which plied the rivers with all manner of cargoes before the advent of the railways and road transport.

As with many other water systems, Broadland has been greatly affected by pollution — in this case, that of phosphate and nitrate enrichment which encourages the prodigious growth of algae, to the detriment of all other life forms in the water. The Broads Authority has had several successes in experimental projects to improve water quality, and these, including the introduction of millions of algae-hungry water fleas, will hopefully halt the decline, and indeed, allow plants and wildlife to flourish once more. Broadland is now the last refuge for the swallowtail butterfly, Britain's largest and rarest variety.

Wroxham and Horning, to the north-east of Norwich along the A1151 and A1062, are popular spots, and many boating holidays start here. Most of the Broads are clustered along the River Bure, and its tributaries the Ant and the Thurne, while the River Waveney, and the Yare, which carries sea-going vessels all the way to Norwich, link up with the northern Broads rivers by the tidal reaches of Breydon Water.

Across the river from **Horning**, reached by car from Woodbastwick, is a boardwalk nature trail leading along the river bank to **Cockshoot Broad**. Over the years, the broad had silted up with phosphate enriched mud, choking any aquatic life. The Broads Authority dammed it off from the river, and pumped out the equivalent of 44 Olympic-sized swimming pools full of mud. Within months, seeds which had lain dormant for 30 years started to germinate. Cockshoot Broad is now clear, and supports life once more.

The view from the tower of St Helen's Church in **Ranworth** is magnificent. The church also has one of the finest and best-preserved painted rood screens in the country. Nature lovers should visit the nearby Broadland Conservation Centre, reached by following a nature trail through the woods and marshes, to the unique thatched building floating on pontoons at the end of Ranworth Broad. There are displays about the Broads, and one may also sit in the upper gallery overlooking the broad, and observe many different species of waterfowl through the binoculars and telescopes provided.

One of the strangest sights is that of the unmistakable ruin of **St Benet's Abbey**, once a powerful monastery, but like so many, dismantled during the reign of Henry VIII. A windmill was built into the remaining walls of the gatehouse some 200 years ago, the remains of which form the rather confused structure seen today.

The Environmental Centre at **How Hill** is well worth a visit. Here you can take a trip on an Edwardian-style electric boat. It glides almost silently through the reeds, giving you the best opportunity to see a variety of birds without disturbing them.

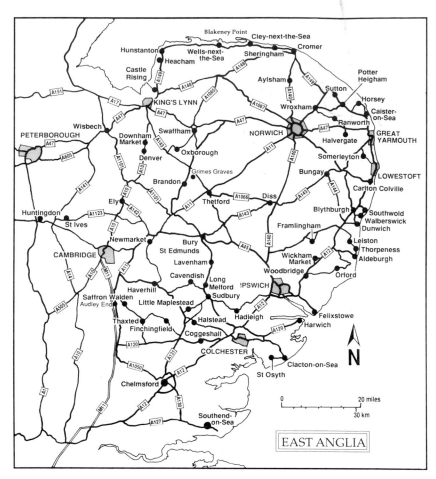

Anglia which thrust out into the North Sea may become decidedly chilly.

Perhaps the biggest delight of East Anglia is that there is so much for the visitor to discover, whether soaking up its interesting heritage, or taking it easy amidst areas of natural beauty.

The Broads

A unique system of lakes and waterways, recently recognised for their immense beauty and wildlife importance by being accorded National Park status, the Broads came about as a result of medieval peat digging. At the time, peat was the main fuel available in large quantities, and each of the diggings served the needs of a wide area. They flooded when the sea level rose in the Middle Ages to form the reed-fringed lakes of today, some now part of the system of five main rivers — the Yare, Bure, Waveney, Ant and Chet — and some on their own.

5 • East Anglia

East Anglia's location means that very few people visit the region on their way to somewhere else. Indeed, in the days before the Fens were drained, and much of what is now Cambridgeshire was under water, it would have been even more difficult for passing visitors. This is one of the reasons why much of East Anglia has retained its intrinsic character. Many people think of windmills as being the most characteristic feature of East Anglia, and these are certainly widespread, although many are actually wind-driven drainage pumps in low-lying wetland areas like the Broads and Fens. However, the area also has a major legacy from the wool and cloth weaving trade, which made East Anglia the richest part of the country from medieval times to the sixteenth century.

The most visible reminders are the churches, beautiful soaring monuments to the wealth of a past industry. Take a look in any of the wool churches, such as those at Lavenham or Long Melford, and you will discover a rich architectural heritage which has been passed on. There is a profusion of Norman and Saxon churches, and some fine cathedrals, castles and stately homes. Of more humble dwellings, the most characteristic in East Anglia are without doubt the timber-framed cottages with plaster infill. Villages like Kersey or Lavenham contain numerous examples of these.

A common misconception is that East Anglia is flat. Noel Coward's description 'Very flat, Norfolk', in *Private Lives*, seems to have rubbed off on its neighbouring counties. Cambridgeshire certainly is flat, but most of the countryside in Norfolk, Suffolk and Essex reaches for the horizon in gentle rolls and dips.

The area also includes England's latest National Park, the Norfolk and Suffolk Broads. Indeed, as a National Park, Broadland is unique in that it sets out to conserve a lowland water-scape, while the others are all upland areas with totally different pressures and needs. It is a popular area for boating holidays, but it is possible to see and appreciate Broadland without taking to the water.

While there is much talk at the moment of climatic change, and the possibility of the British Isles taking on a Mediterranean-style climate in the next 40 years, visitors to East Anglia already have less chance of experiencing rain than they would elsewhere in the country, as it is the driest area in Britain. At the same time, when winters are cold, the coastal parts of East

Check by telephoning property (0242 602398) or English Heritage Area Office (0272 734472)

Miserden Park Gardens
Near Stroud
Open: mid-April to September Wednesday and Thursday 10am-4.30pm

Northleach
Cotswold Countryside Collection
Open: April to October daily 10am-5.30pm, Sunday 2-5.30pm.

Keith Harding's World of Mechanical Music
Open: throughout year, daily 10am-6pm.

Painswick House Rococo Garden
Open: May to September, Wednesday-Sunday and Bank Holidays 11am-5pm.

Sezincote House and Gardens
Near Moreton-in-Marsh
House open: May, June, July and September, Thursday and Friday 2.30-6pm. Gardens throughout year, except December Thursday, Friday and Bank Holidays

Snowshill Manor (National Trust)
Open: May to September, Wednesday to Sunday and Bank Holiday Mondays 11am-1pm and 2-6pm. April and October, Saturday and Sunday 11am-1pm and 2-6pm, Easter Saturday, Sunday, Monday 11am-1pm and 2-6pm.

Stanway House
Open: June, July, August, Tuesday and Thursday 2-5pm.

Winchcombe
Sudeley Castle
Open: April to October daily 12noon-5pm. Grounds open: from 11am.

Winchcombe Railway Museum and Garden
Open: daily throughout year, except Christmas Day 1-6pm (or dusk during winter months).

Tourist Information Centres

Bath
Abbey Churchyard
☎ 0225 462831

Burford
Sheep Street
099382 3558

Cheltenham
Municipal Offices
☎ 0242 522878

Chipping Campden
Woolstaplers Hall
☎ 0386 840289

Chipping Norton
New Street Car Park
☎ 0608 44379

Cirencester
Market Place
☎ 0285 654180

Gloucester
The Cross
☎ 0452 421188

Northleach
Cotswold Countryside Collection
☎ 0451 60715

Oxford
St Aldates
☎ 0865 726873/726874

Painswick
Library
☎ 0452 812569

Stow-on-the-Wold
Talbot Court
☎ 0451 31082

Tetbury
Old Court House
☎ 0666 53552

Winchcombe
High Street
☎ 0242 602925

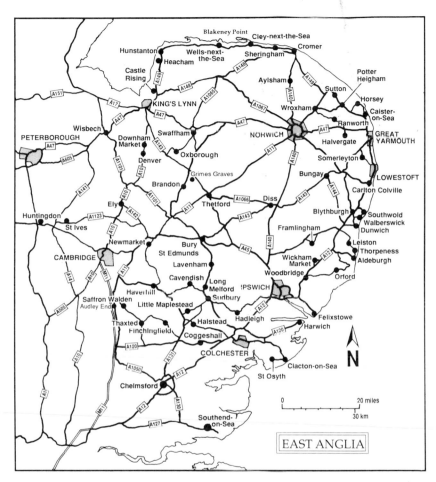

EAST ANGLIA

Anglia which thrust out into the North Sea may become decidedly chilly.

Perhaps the biggest delight of East Anglia is that there is so much for the visitor to discover, whether soaking up its interesting heritage, or taking it easy amidst areas of natural beauty.

The Broads

A unique system of lakes and waterways, recently recognised for their immense beauty and wildlife importance by being accorded National Park status, the Broads came about as a result of medieval peat digging. At the time, peat was the main fuel available in large quantities, and each of the diggings served the needs of a wide area. They flooded when the sea level rose in the Middle Ages to form the reed-fringed lakes of today, some now part of the system of five main rivers — the Yare, Bure, Waveney, Ant and Chet — and some on their own.

About 130 miles (209km) of the Broadland waterways are navigable by boat, and every summer sees plenty of activity, with pleasure craft chugging up and down, occasionally making way for the infinitely more graceful sailing boats, including some of the old wherries, the trading versions of which plied the rivers with all manner of cargoes before the advent of the railways and road transport.

As with many other water systems, Broadland has been greatly affected by pollution — in this case, that of phosphate and nitrate enrichment which encourages the prodigious growth of algae, to the detriment of all other life forms in the water. The Broads Authority has had several successes in experimental projects to improve water quality, and these, including the introduction of millions of algae-hungry water fleas, will hopefully halt the decline, and indeed, allow plants and wildlife to flourish once more. Broadland is now the last refuge for the swallowtail butterfly, Britain's largest and rarest variety.

Wroxham and Horning, to the north-east of Norwich along the A1151 and A1062, are popular spots, and many boating holidays start here. Most of the Broads are clustered along the River Bure, and its tributaries the Ant and the Thurne, while the River Waveney, and the Yare, which carries seagoing vessels all the way to Norwich, link up with the northern Broads rivers by the tidal reaches of Breydon Water.

Across the river from **Horning**, reached by car from Woodbastwick, is a boardwalk nature trail leading along the river bank to **Cockshoot Broad**. Over the years, the broad had silted up with phosphate enriched mud, choking any aquatic life. The Broads Authority dammed it off from the river, and pumped out the equivalent of 44 Olympic-sized swimming pools full of mud. Within months, seeds which had lain dormant for 30 years started to germinate. Cockshoot Broad is now clear, and supports life once more.

The view from the tower of St Helen's Church in **Ranworth** is magnificent. The church also has one of the finest and best-preserved painted rood screens in the country. Nature lovers should visit the nearby Broadland Conservation Centre, reached by following a nature trail through the woods and marshes, to the unique thatched building floating on pontoons at the end of Ranworth Broad. There are displays about the Broads, and one may also sit in the upper gallery overlooking the broad, and observe many different species of waterfowl through the binoculars and telescopes provided.

One of the strangest sights is that of the unmistakable ruin of **St Benet's Abbey**, once a powerful monastery, but like so many, dismantled during the reign of Henry VIII. A windmill was built into the remaining walls of the gatehouse some 200 years ago, the remains of which form the rather confused structure seen today.

The Environmental Centre at **How Hill** is well worth a visit. Here you can take a trip on an Edwardian-style electric boat. It glides almost silently through the reeds, giving you the best opportunity to see a variety of birds without disturbing them.

Thurne Dyke Windpump

The flat, marshy land west of Great Yarmouth represents the finest landscape of its type in the country. The windmills that can be seen around here are actually wind pumps, once used to keep the land drained so farmers could graze their cattle. Of the old windpumps, many have been restored, at least structurally, and are open to the public. The Stracey Arms Windpump, on the A47 opposite the turn-off for Halvergate, is a well-preserved example. Palmers Hollow Post Mill, the very last hollow-post plunger-pump can be found at Upton Dyke.

With a headroom of only 7ft (2m), the old bridge at **Potter Heigham** has been the downfall of many a holiday sailor. One mile (2km) north lies the village itself which, as the name suggests, was the site of a Roman pottery. The tallest tower windmill in the country can be found at **Sutton**. Last used in the 1940s, it is in the process of renovation.

Hickling Broad and much of the surrounding area forms a National Nature Reserve. The best way to see it is by taking the $1^1/_2$ hour guided Water Trail. Visitors are taken by boat to see a variety of Broadland features: reed and sedge beds, marshes and woodlands, and birds such as the marsh harrier and the bittern can be seen from the hides and observation hut.

Horsey Mere is about 1 mile (2km) up Meadow Dyke from Heigham Sound, and at the eastern end stands **Horsey Windpump**. Owned by the National Trust, this most impressive landmark affords some fine views.

Just upstream from the point where the Yare flows into Breydon Water, **Berney Arms** is the first safe place for pleasure boats to moor after running the tidal gauntlet of Breydon. The Berney Arms is probably one of the least accessible public houses by land, with no roads: only $^1/_2$ mile (1km) walk across the fields from the railway halt. Nearby Berney Arms Mill, the tallest of the Broadland drainage mills shares the same isolation, has been restored to complete working order, and houses an exhibition on windmills.

In Roman times, the waterways of Broadland were far more extensive than they are today; what is now flat marshland was then under the sea. The fort of *Gariannonum* was built on the banks of the vast estuary, with the town of Caister on the opposite bank. Now, all that remains of this huge river is Breydon Water, with the ruins of **Burgh Castle** standing at the southern end, where the rivers Waveney and Yare come together.

The most southerly of the Broads rivers, the Waveney passes close by the attractive Victorian estate village of **Somerleyton**. Somerleyton Hall dates back to Elizabethan times, although it was extensively rebuilt in 1846. The mansion has some lavishly furnished state rooms, and the gardens include a maze.

A popular place for mooring, **St Olaves** has the remains of a thirteenth-century priory, notable for its undercroft, a very early brick construction. Just down the road lies Fritton Lake, a country park, with lakeside gardens, woodland walks and a picnic area, together with opportunities for boating and fishing.

North Norfolk

The North Norfolk Coast between Cromer and Hunstanton runs for some 30 miles (48km) almost exactly east to west. While those towns, along with Cromer's neighbour Sheringham, bustle with holidaymakers in the summer, the commercial side of holidays tails off sharply in between. The countryside differs quite markedly along those 30 miles (48km). In the west, the coastline is a tortuous maze of creeks and inlets in a vast expanse of saltmarsh and mudflat. It is a birdwatcher's paradise, and whatever time of the year one visits, there will always be plenty to see. Further east, the countryside takes on more of a rolling aspect, with steep cliffs rising from the sea.

This strip of coast is rich in nature reserves; there are over a dozen, including Cley Marshes, the first of the County Naturalists Trust reserves which can now be found all over the country. The North Norfolk Coast is also an Area of Outstanding Natural Beauty, with its own long-distance footpath — the Norfolk Coast Path, which runs from just outside Hunstanton to Cromer.

One could spend an entire holiday nature watching on the North Norfolk Coast, but there are other attractions as well. The general character of the area is underlined by the houses, cottages and churches. They are built in the local flint, the prettiest ones with knapped flint walls, where the round flints have been split in two to expose a flat face of rich dark colour.

Castle Rising, north of King's Lynn, used to be a busy port before the sea receded. The Norman keep, largely intact, stands on earthworks of Roman origin. Caley Mill, at **Heacham**, is the home of Norfolk Lavender, the largest lavender producers in the country. The plants are a marvellous blaze of colour during the summer, and it is possible to tour the mill to see the various drying and distillation processes.

Hunstanton, the next place north on the A149, caters for those wanting a traditional family seaside holiday. It is the only East Coast resort where you can watch the sun set over the sea, and it has some magnificent cliffs with distinctive bands of colour formed from layers of red carr stone, and white chalk. Just around the coast, near Holme, there is some marvellous walking out in the dunes, and inland, on the chalk downs around Ringstead.

There are no less than six villages with the prefix Burnham, lying between Brancaster and Holkham. Most notable is **Burnham Thorpe**, birthplace of England's greatest sailor, Horatio Nelson. Although his father's parsonage no longer stands, a plaque beside the road marks the site. The cross and lectern in the church are made from timbers taken from Nelson's ship *HMS Victory*, as were the flags which hang in the nave.

The Norfolk home of the Earls of Leicester, **Holkham Hall**, is a magnificent Palladian mansion set in beautiful parkland. Using some of the ideas of 'Turnip' Townsend, Thomas William Coke turned the estate from what was almost wasteland into an agricultural success. Holkham Bay is a flat expanse of sand which gives you quite a walk to get to the sea when the tide is out. Fringed with pine trees, it makes a pleasant walk around to the small port of Wells-next-the-Sea.

Blakeney Point is a thin spit of land about 4 miles (6km) long, sprouting from the coast just north of Cley. The shingle bank makes walking heavy going, so most tend to take a short boat trip out to the nature reserve, a peaceful haven for birds and plants. There is also a good chance of spotting seals basking on the sandbanks.

Driving over the hill on the A149 into **Cromer**, with a first view of the sea, one can hardly fail to notice the magnificent church tower, the tallest in Norfolk. The climb up the steps to the top is well worth it for the view. Cromer is known far and wide for its crabs, and for the most famous lifeboatman of them all, Henry Blogg. Nearby seventeenth-century Felbrigg Hall is a National Trust property, and is worth visiting.

At **Sheringham**, there is the former Midland and Great Northern railway station. The North Norfolk Railway runs steam trains from here along the coast to Weybourne, and inland to Holt. There is another steam railway further along the coast, the Wells Walsingham Light Railway. **Walsingham** is famous for its shrine, a place of pilgrimage for hundreds of years.

Just outside the market town of Aylsham is **Blickling Hall**, a magnificent Jacobean building of red brick standing on the site of an earlier building which was the family home of Anne Boleyn. The house's long gallery has a superb plasterwork ceiling, and the grounds themselves are glorious. One of the outbuildings contains the Hawk Trust's National

Broad Water, in the Holme Dunes Nature Reserve

Centre for Owl Conservation, with a fascinating exhibition about barn owls.

The **Weavers Way** is so called because of the region's past importance in the weaving industry. A 56 mile (90km) long walking route from Cromer to Great Yarmouth, it passes through Blickling, North Walsham and Stalham. There are car parks at several places along the way, making it possible to walk short stretches. Taken with the Peddars Way/Norfolk Coast Path, Norfolk now has a major long-distance route offering probably more scenic variety than any other path in the country.

The Suffolk Coast

Rich in natural beauty and wildlife, and steeped in history, the Suffolk Coast stretches from Lowestoft to Felixstowe. It offers a variety of landscapes from eroding cliffs to steep shingle beaches, interspersed with the long, winding mudflat estuaries of the Rivers Blyth, Alde, Ore and Deben. In the hinterland there are vast stretches of heath and forest, all of them areas containing a number of important nature reserves and Sites of Special Scientific Interest.

Lowestoft is the most easterly town in Britain and is a fishing port. Only a stone's throw from the Broads, and at the northern tip of the Suffolk Heritage Coast, it is a good base for exploration. The beaches are sandy and safe for bathing, with the north beach at Corton designated a naturists' beach. The harbour is a bustling place, full of interest.

Just down the coast is the delightful uncommercialised seaside resort of **Southwold**, with its quaint old houses and sprawling open greens. In fact, part of the town's charming character is the result of a great fire in 1659.

Many of the houses destroyed were never replaced, resulting in the fire-breaks which are now seven pleasant greens. From any point in Southwold, the white lighthouse can be seen looming above the roof-tops. Not far away is the Mecca for all local beer drinkers: Adnams Brewery. Southwold Harbour stands on the River Blyth, about 1 mile (2km) south of the town, and just across the river lies the sleepy village of **Walberswick**. To reach it on foot is not too strenuous, just where the river joins Buss Creek there is a foot-bridge, or, one can take the row boat ferry across the river from the harbour. Motorists must take a longer route, about 9 miles (14km), via Blythburgh.

Once a great city whose fortunes depended on the all-powerful sea, and the centre of Christianity in East Anglia, **Dunwich** has existed for hundreds of years, but floods and drifting shingle banks spelt the end for it as a port. The ever-encroaching sea nibbled away at the town in successive floods, the last medieval church disappearing into the sea at the beginning of this century.

Bird lovers should not fail to visit the **Minsmere Reserve**. Awarded the Council of Europe Diploma in 1980, it is the flagship reserve of the Royal Society for the Protection of Birds, and internationally recognised as a model for nature conservation. Public hides are open along the beach, with free access. Entry onto the reserve itself is by permit only.

A small town north-west of Aldeburgh, **Leiston** became an industrial centre at the hands of the Garrett family in the nineteenth century. The town's engineering industry dates back to the Industrial Revolution, and the Long Shop, built in 1853, was a pioneer design for the manufacture and assembly of steam engines using production line techniques. The Long Shop is now a museum housing relics of the Richard Garratt Engineering Works, including steam engines, threshing machines, a trolley bus and two fire engines.

Thorpeness was originally conceived as an Edwardian fantasy holiday village in 1910 by the estate owner, Mr Glencairn Stuart Ogilvie. Its curious 'House in the Clouds', for example, is in fact a water tower. The upper part conceals the tank, while the creosoted portion below provides living accommodation. The nearby post mill is open to visitors; it houses exhibits about the mill itself and is also an information centre for the Suffolk Heritage Coast. Just down the coast from Thorpeness, **Aldeburgh** was another ancient large town to suffer at the hands of the sea. Inside the timber-framed Tudor Moot Hall (moot is the Old English for meeting) by the beach is a small museum with original 'before and after' maps. One shows the hall in roughly its current position, the earlier shows it standing in the middle of the town.

To the north of Orford, on the River Alde, is the nineteenth-century industrial complex, now a concert hall known as **Snape Maltings**. Opened in 1967, it is the home of Benjamin Britten's Aldeburgh Festival.

A visit to the castle can hardly be missed if you are visiting **Orford**. The great keep stands sentinel over the town, affording a superb view over what was once a thriving medieval port before the shingle bank of Orford Ness

Thorpeness Windmill

cut off direct access to the sea. Built by Henry II in the late 1160s, the castle was the first to be built with a keep which is cylindrical inside and polygonal outside, reinforced by three projecting rectangular turrets. It is the oldest castle for whose building there exists documentary evidence, in the form of the Pipe Rolls, the financial records of the King's Exchequer.

Inland Suffolk

About 6 miles (10km) north of Woodbridge, **Wickham Market** lies just off the A12, near the River Deben. Not far away is Easton Farm Park. The attractions of the Victorian farmstead include a dairy and vintage farm machinery. At Letheringham, an early eighteenth-century watermill survives on the River Deben, still in working order.

Framlingham, full of buildings with character, is best-known for its castle, built in 1190 by the famous Bigod family, and one of the first castles not to include a keep. Instead, it has thirteen separate towers, linked by a curtain wall, a Saracen idea brought back by returning Crusaders. It is possible to take a spiral staircase up one of the towers and walk right around the top of the walls, to enjoy magnificent views across the countryside.

While many stately homes have undergone a great deal of change since their original conception, **Heveningham Hall** has stayed almost the same as it was when it was built in the latter part of the eighteenth century. The interiors were designed by James Wyatt, its furniture designed to match the mood of each room. The park and gardens were laid out by 'Capability' Brown.

Stowmarket, to the west along the A1120, is a market town with a strong agricultural background, although it is now becoming slightly industrialised. The Museum of East Anglian Life provides a most interesting visit.

Exhibits relating to the rural life of the area are on display, including several ancient buildings rescued from demolition on their original sites, and re-erected here.

The only cathedral town in Suffolk, **Bury St Edmunds** lies in the western reaches of the county. A monastery was set up here in the seventh century, and the present name arose from the savage murder of the young East Anglian King Edmund at the hands of the Danes. Several years after his martyrdom, his body was brought to St Edmundsbury, where the shrine, and the abbey which rose around it, became a place of pilgrimage. Very little remains of the original abbey today, although the lines of the walls amongst the ruins in the abbey gardens may be seen. A plaque commemorates the meeting of the thirteenth-century English barons which led to King John's signing of the Magna Carta in 1215. Other places worth visiting include the Theatre Royal, one of only three surviving Regency theatres in the country, Moyse's Hall, probably the oldest Norman domestic building surviving in East Anglia, and Cupola House, a seventeenth-century inn where the author Daniel Defoe is reputed to have stayed.

Three miles (5km) south-west of Bury St Edmunds is **Ickworth Park**, some 1,700 acres of parkland and gardens surrounding an eccentric neo-Classical house. The house, basically a central rotunda with a domed roof, flanked by two sweeping wings with a total frontage of 625ft (190m), has been owned by the National Trust since 1956. The staterooms contain much late Regency and eighteenth-century French furniture, along with portraits by Gainsborough, Hogarth, Lawrence and Reynolds. There is also a collection of silver regarded as the finest in the country.

Every approach to **Newmarket** passes through the surrounding heaths, where racehorses can be seen exercising. Its main industry is racing, originally started here by Charles II. The fascinating story of horse-racing is told in the National Horse Racing Museum, whose exhibits include the skeleton of Eclipse, one of the three Arab stallions which founded the pedigree of English thoroughbreds. Today, the ancestry of around ninety per cent of all British racehorses can be traced back to Eclipse.

Constable Country

The valley of the River Stour, and the surrounding countryside, is closely associated with the artist John Constable. Many of the places immortalised in his paintings can still be seen, only superficially changed by the passage of time.

Constable was born in **East Bergholt** in 1776, and although his birthplace no longer survives, the small cottage which served as his studio still stands, as part of the Post Office. The west tower of the church was never completed, the top extremity capped with concrete to protect it against decay. A curious wooden building in the churchyard houses the bells intended for the tower, which was never finished. East Bergholt and nearby **Flatford** provided the young artist with the inspiration for many of his fine paintings. Flatford Mill featured in several of Constable's works. Here too can be found a quiet millpond, and Willy Lott's Cottage — a scene instantly recognisable as the setting for the famous *Hay Wain*.

Dedham, not far from East Bergholt, is where Constable went to school. Parts of the village are recognisable in several well-known paintings, including *Dedham Lock and Mill*, and the *Valley of the Stour*. Sir Alfred Munnings, another famous artist, made Dedham his home, and a collection of his work is on show at Castle House.

The church at **Stoke-by-Nayland** featured in more than one of Constable's landscapes, and it is easy to see why. The 120ft (36m) high Perpendicular tower rises majestically above the surrounding trees and Tudor houses. There are some impressive decorations inside, as well as memorials to the Tendring family, whose subsequent connection with the Howard family produced two of Henry VIII's wives: Lady Catherine Howard and Anne Boleyn.

The Church of St James at **Nayland** contains *Christ's Blessing of the Bread and Wine*. This was once criticised by someone who thought Constable's representation of Christ too closely resembled his own brother. The inn in the main street is reputed to be the last from which a Navy press-gang operated.

Hadleigh was one of the more important of the old wool towns. The church is surrounded by many old buildings oozing character, including the fifteenth-century half-timbered Guildhall, with its two overhanging upper storeys. The church, one of the largest in Suffolk, has an elegant lead spire. Inside, the 600-year-old Angelus Bell, one of the oldest in the country, bears an inscription which is best read with a mirror — the words appear backwards!

The colourful medieval village of **Kersey** has a strong weaving background, shown by the typical weavers' cottages — some half-timbered, some colour-washed plaster — lining the steep village street. A stream crosses the bottom of the street in a picturesque ford.

Virtually every street in **Lavenham** is lined with timber-framed houses, particularly fine being The Swan inn, and the Wool Hall behind it. The Guildhall is a magnificent early sixteenth-century building in the market place, which houses the local museum, while Little Hall dates from the fifteenth century and is now home to the Suffolk Preservation Society. The church, paid for by local wool merchants and the de Vere family, is a splendid example of late Perpendicular architecture, a mass of clear windows giving it a bright interior.

Like many other Suffolk towns, **Long Melford** enjoyed a long period of prosperity through the wool trade. Melford Hall, owned by the National Trust, stands at the edge of the Green. Nearby Kentwell Hall is a moated Elizabethan mansion almost lost through neglect before it was acquired privately in 1971. Since then, much renovation has taken place, including the creation of an award winning brick-paved Tudor Rose maze, in the central courtyard. Four miles (6km) west of Long Melford, on the A1092, **Cavendish** is a pretty village with a large green surrounded by thatched plaster cottages.

Sudbury, largest of the Suffolk wool towns, was home for many years to the painter Thomas Gainsborough. While Gainsborough loved to paint landscapes, it was the informality and grace of his portraits which won him far-reaching acclaim. A statue of him stands outside St Peter's Church, on Market Hill. Gainsborough's birthplace, formerly a sixteenth-century inn, is now preserved as a museum and exhibition gallery.

Seven miles (11km) south-west of Sudbury, **Hedingham Castle** is one of the best surviving examples of a Norman tower keep in Western Europe. Built in 1140, it was the home of the Earls of Oxford for over 500 years. Nearby, the Colne Valley Railway recreates the heyday of steam with its collection of locomotives, rolling stock and an old lever-operated signal box.

About 3 miles (5km) north of Halstead, **Little Maplestead** has a curious round church, once a common sight in medieval times, but now there are only five left in the country. Modelled on the Holy Sepulchre in Jerusalem, it was built by the Knights Hospitallers of St John as a stopping off point for pilgrims to the Holy Land.

Essex

Colchester's importance throughout history lies in its geographical situation. Situated 8 miles (13km) from the sea on the River Colne, the town was in an ideal trading position. It became the first major colony of the Romans in AD43, and its fortunes have risen and fallen over the centuries. Today it is a large garrison town, and the military tattoo, held in August, is well worth attending. The castle is now only the keep of what was once a huge fortress, built on the remains of the Emperor Claudius' Temple, still visible in places. The eleventh-century keep is the largest in Europe, despite a dismal attempt by a seventeenth-century ironmonger to become rich quickly by buying the castle with a view to demolishing it and selling the materials. The remains of St Botolph's Priory stand outside the old Roman walls. In about 1100, the priory became the first in the country of the Augustinian Order. The siege during the Civil War took its toll, and now only the west front and part of the nave survive.

Harwich, Britain's second biggest passenger port, has a distinguished history. Christopher Jones, the master of the *Mayflower*, lived here, a plaque marks his house in King's Head Street, and the renowned diarist Samuel Pepys was MP for Harwich. There was, for a time, a Royal Naval dockyard, and an interesting survivor can be found on Harwich Green. What looks like an enormous pigeon loft with gallows at one end is actually a double treadwheel crane, built in 1667, and in use right up to World War I. Nearby **Parkeston Quay** is the main terminal point for the port of Harwich, with regular sailings between here and Scandinavia, West Germany and the Netherlands. Over 2 million passengers pass through every year.

About 4 miles (7km) west of Clacton, **St Osyth** is a delightful and charming village with some attractive and fairly extensive historic ruins, including the thirteenth-century priory, and the flint-decorated fifteenth-

The attractive green at Cavendish, flanked by thatched cottages

century gatehouse. Osytha, an Anglo-Saxon princess, was forced to marry Sigehere of Essex, despite having taken vows of virginity. She escaped on her wedding night, and founded a nunnery here. The invading Danes, unable to incite her to give up her religion, beheaded her, and a fountain is said to have sprung up where it fell. The village was named in her honour.

The Paycocke family were rich merchants at the end of the fifteenth century. One of them built the splendid timber-framed house in **Coggeshall**, well worth a visit to see its intricate carvings and panelling. The close studding and the wooden uprights indicate it was built at a time when there was no shortage of good quality oak.

Situated in the calm upper reaches of the Blackwater Estuary, the ancient town of **Maldon** has a thriving yachting community, and a flourishing crystal sea salt industry which started in medieval times, when salt was important for preserving fish and meat. Today, the characteristic flaky crystals of salt are very popular for cooking.

Finchingfield, about 8 miles (13km) south of Haverhill, is in an idyllic setting. Its classic duck pond and village green, with tiled and thatched cottages gathered around, makes it a most attractive and picturesque village.

Thaxted's past wealth came from the manufacture of cutlery, and later, from the weaving trade. Like other East Anglian wool towns, its wealth is reflected for all to see in its fine church. The fifteenth-century timber-framed Guildhall is an unusual building with its arcaded ground floor, and overhanging upper floors topped by a twin gabled roof. It is possible that the legendary highwayman Dick Turpin lived in Thaxted. Gustav Holst certainly lived here when he was composing the famous *Planets Suite*.

Two miles (3km) west of Saffron Walden is **Audley End**, a magnificent Jacobean mansion in impressive parkland. Surprisingly, the present building is only a fraction of its former self. Three quarters of the original palace was demolished in the eighteenth century.

Breckland

The light sandy soils of Breckland once supported vast forests, but Neolithic man cleared them to grow his crops. In time, this combined with over-grazing and rendered the land unable to support further growth. The present afforestation, the second largest in the country, was planted in 1922 in what was virtually a desert.

Most of **Thetford Forest** can be explored along the various tracks and rides which intersect it, and the Forestry Commission has prepared a number of marked trails which can be followed from the information centre at Santon Downham. Elsewhere, there are picnic areas which are clearly signposted and also provide a good base for short walks. The forest is one of the last strongholds of the red squirrel in the south of England, and there are four species of deer, the most common being the roe.

Norfolk's own National Trail, the **Peddars Way**, runs through here, following the line of a pre-Roman route — indeed, much of the path is an ancient monument. Whether walked in sections, or perhaps over several days for a holiday, the Peddars Way from Knettishall to Holme-next-the Sea, the Norfolk Coast Path around to Cromer, offer the finest variety of landscapes of any of the major long-distance paths.

The water levels in the Breckland meres, such as Lang Mere and Ring Mere in **East Wretham Heath Nature Reserve** vary a great deal, rising and falling, even disappearing altogether, with no apparent connection to the weather. The determining factor is the water table in the underlying chalk.

Once the most important cathedral city in East Anglia, **Thetford** still has remains of its priory worth visiting. Local flint abounds, and the Ancient House Museum has displays about flint-knapping — shaping tiny flints for use in firearms. The statue of Thomas Paine commemorates Thetford's famous campaigner for human rights, who influenced both the American and French Revolutions.

Six miles (10km) east, off the A1066, is **Knettishall Heath**, 350 acres of Breckland heath and woodland, with walks and picnic areas. The western end of the heath also marks the beginning of the Peddars Way long distance footpath.

The village of **Euston** was moved to its present position in the seventeenth century — it originally obscured the view from Euston Hall. The hall itself is set in a great park, its gardens laid out by William Kent and 'Capability' Brown. It houses a fine collection of paintings, including works by Van Dyck, Lely and Stubbs. Only the church remains in its original position, interestingly built very much in the style of Sir Christopher Wren, and with a beautiful panelled interior.

At **West Stow**, 8 miles (13km) south of Thetford, is a magnificent Tudor brick gatehouse, part of what was once a large hall built by Sir John Crofts, Master of Horse to Mary Tudor. Half a mile (1km) north of the village is the King's Forest Information Centre, the start of a walk in the forest along the Forestry Commission's long-distance footpath. There is a large country park here, giving visitors the opportunity to stroll around heath and grassland, as well as to visit the reconstructed Anglo-Saxon village. Like Santon Downham, West Stow was buried in a sandstorm, and it was this which preserved the Anglo-Saxon site well enough for twentieth-century archaeologists to reconstruct it.

Not graves at all, but a vast collection of diggings where flint was mined, **Grimes Graves**, near Brandon, is the most important prehistoric site in East Anglia. Here, men dug down through the chalk, tunnelling in dreadful conditions. One of the shafts is open to the public.

The red brick manor of Oxburgh Hall, in **Oxborough**, has the largest fifteenth-century gatehouse in existence. Mary Queen of Scots was imprisoned here, and the needlework with which she whiled away her time is still here — the Oxburgh Hangings. Nearby is Cockley Cley, where an Iceni camp has been reconstructed on its original site.

According to local folklore, the lavishly appointed church in the market town of **Swaffham**, which lies to the north-east, was paid for by John Clapham, the Pedlar of Swaffham. He met a stranger in London who described having dreamt of finding a treasure in the Pedlar's garden. The Pedlar returned home to find everything just as he had been told, and celebrated his new found wealth by building the north aisle of the church.

Fenland

The result mainly of drainage and reclamation in the seventeenth century, Fenland, once a wasteland of marshes, is now the country's most productive agricultural region. Most of the important drainage was carried out by the Dutch engineer Cornelius Vermuyden, whose straight drainage channels short-cut the winding Fenland rivers.

Between Earith and Denver run the straight and parallel drainage cuts of the Old and New Bedford rivers. Apart from making the surrounding countryside fit for year-round agriculture, the drainage regime has turned the **Ouse Washes**, the thin island bounded by these rivers, into one of the few places in Fenland which can really be called Fens. It is managed in almost the same way as the land would have been in medieval times — grazed in the summer, and generally flooded in the winter. As such, the Ouse Washes are an important wildlife habitat. Winter flooding tends to vary in depth from several feet to a few inches, providing a wide range of habitats for a variety of waterfowl. The main places for observation can be found near Welney and Manea.

Almost inevitably, the first visit in **Ely** will be to the cathedral, which dominates the skyline from every viewpoint in and around the town. The striking building was begun in 1083, and not completed for 168 years. Had it not been for the untimely arrival of the Black Death, the nave and transepts would probably have been roofed in stone, but the building was actually roofed in wood. In the fourteenth century, an octagonal central tower was designed, replacing the former square one which had collapsed in 1322. This piece of architectural genius was accomplished in only 26 years, a considerable feat, and still a marvel to behold — 400 tons of masonry, suspended without any apparent means of support.

When Ramsey Abbey was the most important place of the area, **St Ives** was a satellite, being owned by the abbey. It was the monastery which built the quaint fifteenth-century bridge over the River Ouse, with its tiny chapel in the centre — one of only three in England.

Cromwell was born in **Huntingdon** in 1599, at Cromwell House, in the main street. The grammar school which he and diarist Samuel Pepys attended is now the Cromwell Museum, and gives an insight into the Cromwell family and his side of the Great Rebellion (1640 to 1660). Nearby Hinchinbrooke House, a thirteenth-century Benecdictine nunnery now used as a school also has associations with Cromwell and Pepys.

Peterborough is a curious mixture of old and new, the only cathedral city in the country also to be designated a new town. The cathedral is the focal point of the city. The present building is Norman, and is one of only three churches in Europe with an early painted wooden ceiling in its nave; Peterborough's is by far the biggest of the three. Catherine of Aragon is buried in the North Choir Aisle, and Mary, Queen of Scots lay in the South Aisle for 25 years after her execution, before being reinterred in Westminster Abbey.

Just to the east of the city is **Flag Fen**, the only place in the country where you can see the timbers of a Bronze Age village. The site, discovered in 1982, was a man-made defensive island, built in the marshes from over a million timbers. Whereas most archaeological remains decay in dry soil, everything found here has been perfectly preserved in the wet peat.

Although it is 10 miles (16km) from the sea on what is now the artificial River Nene, **Wisbech** maintains its long tradition as a sea port. The wealth created by years of shipping gave Wisbech two of the most perfect Georgian streets in England — the Brinks, sombre rows of mansions and warehouses on opposite sides of the river. On the North Brink is the National Trust-owned Peckover House, a handsome example of early eighteenth-century architecture and furnishings. The owner, banker Jonathan Peckover, merged his business with two others to become one of the founder members of Barclays Bank in 1896.

Further Information

— East Anglia —

Places of Interest

CAMBRIDGESHIRE

Peckover House
Wisbech
Open: Easter to mid-October, Saturday,
Sunday, Monday, Bank Holiday Mon-
days, 4-5.30pm.
Early eighteenth-century merchant's
house on North Brink of River Nene.

Bourn Windmill
Caxton Road
Bourn
☎ (0223) 243830
Open: April to September, last Sunday in
month, Bank Holidays, 4-5pm.
Open: trestle post mill, probably oldest
example in country.

Wicken Fen
Ely
Open: daily, dawn to dusk, permits
available from the warden on site.
Nearly the last remaining fen with
general access.

ESSEX

Colne Valley Railway
Castle Hedingham Station
Halstead
☎ (0787) 61174
Open: all year, daily, 11am-5pm. Steam
days most Sundays, Easter to October.

Hedingham Castle
Castle Hedingham
☎ (0787) 60261 or 60804
Open: Easter, May to October, daily,
10am-5pm.
Norman keep and Tudor bridge.

NORFOLK

Blickling Hall
Aylsham
Open: Easter to October, daily except
Monday and Thursday 1-5pm. Garden,
shop and restaurant open same days as

house and daily July to August. Garden
hours 12noon-5pm.
Jacobean red brick mansion with long
gallery containing fine plasterwork
ceiling.

Broadland Conservation Centre
Ranworth
Acle
Open: April to October, Sunday to
Thursday, 10.30am-5.30pm; Saturday,
2-5.30pm.
Displays on the history of the Broads,
and their conservation.

Fleggburgh Bygone Village
Burgh St Margaret
Acle
Open: all year, daily, 10am-5pm.
Reconstruction of a Norfolk village.

Grimes Graves
Weeting, Brandon
Open: Easter to September, daily, 10am-
6pm. October to Maundy Thursday,
daily except Mondays, 10am-4pm.
Huge network of 4,000-year-old flint
mines.

Horsey Windpump
Horsey Staithe, Winterton
Open: Easter to August, daily, 11am-
5pm.

National Centre for Owl Conservation
Lothian Barn, Blickling Hall
Aylsham
Open: April to October, daily except
Monday and Thursday, 12noon-5pm.

Norfolk Lavender
Caley Mill, Heacham
Hunstanton
☎ (0485) 70384
Open: all year, daily 10am-5.30pm.

North Norfolk Railway
The Station, Sheringham
☎ (0263) 822045
Open: Easter to October, daily.
Steam trains from Sheringham to
Weybourne and Holt every Sunday, and
daily in August.

Stracey Arms Windpump
Just off A47 near Stracey Arms Public
House
Open: April to October, daily, 9am-
10pm.
Fully restored drainage pump with
exhibition tracing history of Broadland
drainage.

Sutton Windmill
Sutton
Stalham
☎ (0692) 81195
Open: April to mid-May, Sunday to
Wednesday, 1.30-5.30pm; mid-May to
September, 10am-6pm.
The tallest mill in the country.

Wells & Walsingham Light Railway
Wells-next-the-Sea
Open: April to September, daily.
The longest $10^1/_4$in gauge railway in
Britain.

Wildlife Water Trail
How Hill
Ludham
☎ (069262) 763
Open: April to May, October, Saturday,
Sunday, Bank Holidays, 11am-3pm; June
to September, Monday to Sunday, 11am-
5pm.
Water trail by small electric launch along
rivers, dykes, marshes and fens of How
Hill Nature Reserve.

SUFFOLK

Dunwich Museum
Dunwich
Open: March to May, October, Saturday
and Sunday; June, July, September,
Tuesday, Thursday, Saturday, Sunday;
August, daily, 2-4.30pm.

Framlingham Castle
Framlingham
Open: Easter to September, daily, 10am-
6pm. October to Maundy Thursday,
daily except Mondays, 10am-4pm.
Twelfth-century castle with curtain
walls.

Gainsborough's House
Sudbury
Open: Easter to September, Tuesday to
Saturday, 10am-5pm, Sunday, Bank

Holiday Mondays, 2-5pm; October to
Easter, Tuesday to Saturday, 10am-4pm,
Sunday, 2-4pm.

Ickworth House & Park
Horringer
Bury St Edmunds
Open: April and October, Saturday,
Sunday, Bank Holiday Mondays. May to
September, daily, 1.30-5.30pm. Park
open: dawn to dusk.

Kentwell Hall
Long Melford
Sudbury
Open: Easter to September, days and
times vary.
☎ (0787) 310207

Lavenham Guildhall
Lavenham
☎ (0787) 247646
Open: Easter to October, daily, 11am-
1pm, 4-5.30pm.

Moot Hall
Aldeburgh
Open: Easter, Whitsun; June-September,
daily, 10.30am-1pm, 2.30-5pm.
Sixteenth-century building housing local
interest exhibits.

Museum of East Anglian Life
Stowmarket
☎ (0449) 612229
Open: Easter to October, Monday to
Saturday, 11am-5pm; Sunday, 12noon-
7pm. June to August, Sunday, 12noon-
6pm.
30 acre riverside site with watermill,
agricultural displays, traditional craft
demonstrations.

Museum of the Working Horse
The Wheatsheaf
Gainsford End
Toppesfield
Open: April to October, Saturday,
Sunday, Bank Holidays, 4-6pm.

National Horse Racing Museum
High Street
Newmarket
☎ (0638) 667333
Open: Easter to November, Tuesday to
Saturday, Bank Holiday Mondays, 10am-
5pm; Sunday, 4-5pm.

Orford Castle
Orford
Open: Easter to September, daily, 10am-
6pm. October to Maundy Thursday,
daily except Mondays, 10am-4pm.
The keep which revolutionised castle-
building.

The Priory
Water Street, Lavenham
Open: Easter to October, daily, 10.30am-
5.30pm.
☎ (0787) 247417

Thorpeness Windmill
Thorpeness
Aldeburgh
Open: Easter, May, June, September,
Saturday, Sunday, Bank Holiday Mon-
days; July, August, Tuesday to Sunday,
4-5pm.
Working windmill, Suffolk Heritage
Coast Centre.

Tourist Information Centres

Cambridgeshire
Ely
The Library, Palace Green
☎ (0353) 662062

Wisbech
District Library, Ely Place
☎ (0945) 64009/583263

Essex
Colchester
1 Queen Street, ☎ (0206) 46379

Harwich
Parkeston Quay, ☎ (0255) 506139

Maldon
Oakwood Arts Centre, White
Horse Lane, ☎ (0621) 56503

Saffron Walden
Corn Exchange, Market Square
☎ (0799) 24282

Norfolk
Cromer
Old Town Hall, Prince of Wales Road
☎ (0263) 512497

Fakenham
Red Lion House, Market Place
☎ (0328) 51981

Hoveton
Broads Information, Station Road
☎ (0603) 782281

Hunstanton
The Green, ☎ (04853) 2610

Mundesley
2a Station Road, ☎ (0263) 721070

Ranworth
The Staithe, NR13 6HY, ☎ (060 549) 453

Sheringham
Station Approach, ☎ (0263) 824329

Thetford
Ancient House Museum, White Hart
Street, ☎ (0842) 2599

Walsingham
Shirehall Museum, Common Place
☎ (0328) 820510

Wells-next-the-Sea
Wells Centre, Staithe Street
☎ (0328) 710855

Suffolk
Aldeburgh
The Cinema, High Street
☎ (072 885) 3637

Bury St Edmunds
6 Angel Hill, ☎ (0284) 763233

Lavenham
The Guildhall, Market Place
☎ (0787) 248207

Lowestoft
The Esplanade
☎ (0502) 565989

Santon Downham
Forestry Commission District Office
☎ (0842) 810271

Southwold
Town Hall
☎ (0502) 722366

Stowmarket
Wilkes Way
☎ (0449) 676800

Sudbury
Public Library, Market Hill
☎ (0787) 881320/72092

Blakeney Quay,
Norfolk, East Anglia

Denver Windmill,
Norfolk, East Anglia

Three Cliffs Bay, Gower Peninsula, South Wales

*Arthur's Stone, a prehistoric burial chamber in the Golden Valley,
Herefordshire, Welsh Borders*

6 • South Wales

T raditionally the name 'South Wales' has been applied to the heavily-populated former industrial region in the south-east, dominated by the large towns of Swansea, Cardiff and Newport. In future years this complex area will undoubtedly be of great interest to the visitor, but it has to be excluded by the terms of this guide, which covers some of the remarkably varied landscapes elsewhere in southern Wales.

A line drawn eastwards from Aberystwyth divides Wales roughly into two halves. Another line drawn from Aberystwyth to Swansea divides the southern half into two very distinctive regions. To the east the great upland mass of the Cambrian Mountains, the Radnor Forest, the Mynydd Eppynt and the Brecon Beacons stretches almost to the south coast, penetrated by the valleys of major rivers like the Usk, the Tywi and the Teifi. These rivers have always been vitally important — for centuries they were the only feasible routes through the mountains for soldiers and traders, and they still carry the main roads. They were also (and still are) valuable areas of fertile land for crop-growing and milk production to balance the sheep-rearing on the uplands.

To the west is Wales's southern peninsula, now forming the vast county of Dyfed but previously comprising the counties of Cardiganshire, Pembrokeshire and Carmarthenshire — names that are still used locally and which will be used in this chapter. The peninsula has one of the most spectacular and forbidding coastlines in Britain, but inland the country is green and fertile, supporting dairying and arable farming on a large scale.

There are curious political contrasts too. Cardiganshire and much of Carmarthenshire, lying behind the mountains, were never dominated by English influence, and remain today a preserve of Welsh language and culture. Southern Pembrokeshire, however, was colonised by the Normans and grew to be 'Little England beyond Wales', while the spread of English industrial enterprise along the south coast led to the virtual disappearance of the Welsh language there.

In recent years the small harbours of Cardigan Bay and the sandy beaches of Pembrokeshire, together with the opportunities for coastal walking and sailing, have become popular attractions for visitors. The Pembrokeshire coast is now a National Park, and a fine long-distance path runs along its entire length. However, the discerning visitor will find the inland areas largely unaffected by tourism, even at the height of summer. The Brecon

Beacons are also a National Park and a centre for activities like riding, climbing and walking, but again they have not been adversely affected.

Cardiganshire

Cardigan is an ideal starting point for exploring the contrast between the holiday coast and the Welsh heartland. It is a workaday market town of no great beauty but immense vitality, once a thriving port and strategically important for its bridge over the Teifi Estuary. The bridge area is still of great interest, with a castle of Norman origin and some handsome buildings, and it is worth seeking out the Guildhall and St Mary's Church, a spacious building with a fine east window and architectural features spanning several centuries.

This tour lies to the north, but before leaving the town there are two historic buildings in the vicinity that deserve a visit. Across the river to the west, the ruined abbey at **St Dogmaels** dates from 1115, although the remains represent several stages of building. **Cilgerran** Castle, 4 miles (6km) south-east of Cardigan, has a splendid site high above the wooded Teifi, and the huge thirteenth-century towers and curtain walls are well-preserved.

The tour starts on the A487, and after 6 miles (10km) a left turn leads to Aberporth, a pleasant settlement with good sandy beaches and cliff-top walks. However, those who enjoy a more dramatic coastline will prefer **Llangranog**, a little further up the coast. This unpretentious little place lies beneath the spectacular headland of Ynys Lochtyn, the property of the National Trust and an exceptionally fine destination for a walk. The charms of New Quay are rather more self-conscious. The picturesque harbour is believed to have been the inspiration for Dylan Thomas's village of Llareggub in his play *Under Milk Wood*. Its near neighbour **Aberaeron**, however, should not be missed. It was planned as a major harbour at the beginning of the nineteenth century and developed considerable prosperity from ship-building. Because of this early success the town centre was built within a short space of time, and the buildings in its grid layout are all early Victorian, colourfully painted nowadays to give the place a cheerful and uniquely attractive style. From here the route turns inland on the B4577, and the visitor driving into the hinterland quickly realises how superficial is the holiday atmosphere of the coast — Cardiganshire is fervently Welsh, and much of it is virtually untouched by tourism. Six miles (10km) along the road is Bethania, and shortly after it a minor road descends into the Aeron Valley to **Llangeitho**. This attractive village with its little square is a place of religious pilgrimage because the famous revivalist preacher Daniel Rowland (1713-1790) was curate here. His gravestone is in the church by the chancel steps (it may be covered by a carpet) and his statue stands beside the chapel above the church.

From Llangeitho take the B4342 for Tregaron, crossing a north-south Roman road on the way. **Tregaron** is a small grey town beside the River Teifi and beneath the looming hills of central Wales. As the only shopping

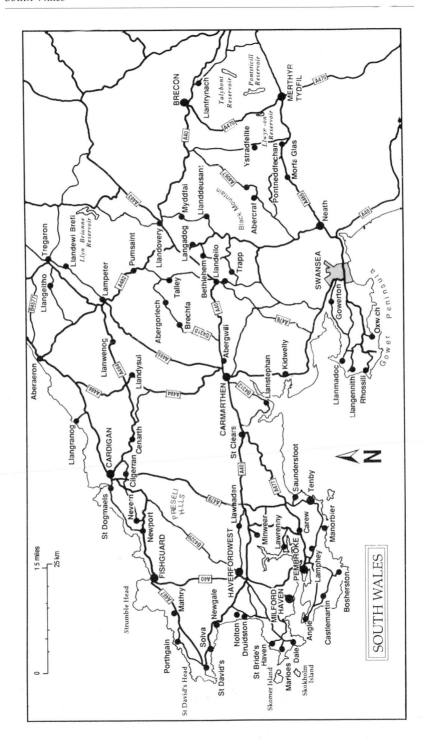

SOUTH WALES

centre for miles around, its miniature streets can be chaotic at times, but its varied architecture repays a stroll. The B4343 to the north passes alongside the nature reserve known as Tregaron Bog, the largest natural peat bog in Wales, where there are facilities for walkers and birdwatchers. Those wishing to sample the uninhabited mountains can take the old drovers' cattle road signposted Abergwesyn — not recommended in poor weather but superb on a fine day.

The tour continues south on the B4343 to **Llanddewi Brefi**. It is an unremarkable village, but its church is huge, with a great central tower and long nave and chancel. Some ancient inscribed stones are preserved. From here the road follows the Teifi closely along the valley bottom and eventually joins the main road into **Lampeter**. It is surprising to find a university town with elegant stuccoed houses in the middle of all this rural countryside, but it was here that a theological college was opened in 1827 in buildings modelled on the Oxford quadrangle style, and the town grew up around it. The college became part of the University of Wales in 1971. A pamphlet in the 'Dyfed Walks' series described an enjoyable walk along a wooded ridge above the town.

Continue now on the A475 (Newcastle Emlyn) road, and after about 7 miles (11km) turn off for **Llanwenog**. Few people seek out the remarkable church here. Of thirteenth-century origin, it is below the surrounding ground level and has a distinctly primitive air. The outstanding features are the irregular eighteenth-century barrel ceiling and the Norman font with twelve crudely-carved heads.

After another 6 miles (10km) it is worth the short diversion to **Llandysul**, where the riverside church, dating from the thirteenth century and unexpectedly sophisticated in style, contains some very ancient incised stones. Leave by the A486 to reach Newcastle Emlyn, another comfortable market town with no outstanding features but with a characteristic welcoming bustle. The modest castle ruins are part-medieval, part-Tudor and there is a good early Victorian church.

At nearby Cenarth the tourist industry begins to encroach again because the Falls here have been a famous attraction for many years, together with the sight of the small, round fishing-boats known as coracles. From here it is a straight run back to Cardigan.

Northern Pembrokeshire

South-west of Cardigan is Northern Pembrokeshire, with Fishguard as its only large town. **Fishguard** has three distinct personalities. To the east is the Lower Town at the mouth of the Gwaun River, forming a small, picturesque but quite unspoilt harbour. Quite separate at the top of a steep headland is the town centre, a place of narrow and intimate streets, a wealth of homely architecture and a tiny square that is cheerfully chaotic in the summer months. Few people discover the path that starts at the end of the road called Penslade and continues round the headland to reveal a panoramic view of Fishguard's third face — the ferry port at Goodwick. Originally intended for Atlantic liners, it was completed in 1906, but it could never compete with Liverpool and had to content itself with the Irish traffic.

A minor road from the Goodwick roundabout, signposted Strumble Head, leads to an attractive stretch of coastline. A National Park leaflet details walks that take in the main features, including Carreg Wasted point, where an ill-fated rabble of French troops tried to stage the last invasion of Britain in 1797. Cars can be driven to **Strumble Head** and its lighthouse.

From there a minor road leads due south to Garn Fawr, an Iron Age hill fort which overlooks the sea and can be easily climbed from a car park at its foot. Four miles (6km) south again the large village of **Mathry** is oddly draped over the top of a hill. There is a good pub and the church is worth a visit. The narrow road signposted Abercastle leads to a fromer slate port (limited parking on the quay) which still has some of its industrial buildings. Take the Trevine road out of Abercastle and after $^1/_2$ mile (1km) look for the lane to Longhouse Farm; beside it is Carreg Sampson, a fine Neolithic burial chamber.

From Trevine the road goes on to Llanrhian (with an interesting cruciform church) and from there to **Porthgain**, another former commercial harbour, with a well-restored row of quarrymen's cottages and the remains of huge brick hoppers that held quarried roadstone before shipment. A tramway from here (still traceable) passed round the headland to the south to link with slate quarries at Abereiddi, which is nowadays a tranquil beach with a few cottages. Visitors should walk the short distance along the coastal path to the north to see the 'Blue Lagoon', a craggy fishing harbour formed from a flooded quarry.

There is now a straight run to the tiny city of **St David's**. Its cathedral, described in detail in a pamphlet available inside, is famous and should certainly be visited, but just as remarkable in its way is the splendid ruin of the fourteenth-century Bishop's Palace close by. It is a most ambitious building, featuring a fanciful and near-unique arcaded parapet. Those wishing to escape the crowds should obtain the National Park walks leaflet for St David's Head and follow the 2 mile (3km) path that starts at the popular Whitesands Bay and takes in several ancient sites and fine viewpoints.

The National Trust owns most of the coastline around St David's Head, and this has helped to preserve the idyllic harbour village of **Solva**, about 3 miles (4km) west of the city. Like other natural inlets along this coast it was a busy commercial port in the nineteenth century, but it is unusual in having an integral settlement, which has turned it into something of a showpiece. The return to Fishguard can be made by way of a minor road that turns off the A487 at Penycwm, about 3 miles (4km) east of Solva, and joins the A487 near Mathry.

The second tour from Fishguard takes in the coast to the east and the Preseli Hills; start on the A487. Dinas appears unremarkable, but sideroads lead to Dinas Island, a headland traversed by a rewarding stretch of the coastal path linking the charming coves of Pwllgwaelod and Cwm-yr-Eglwys (the ruined church near the shore is St Brynach's, washed away

*The Pentre Ifan burial
chamber*

during storms in 1859). The extensive sands at Newport are a honeypot in
summer, but the cramped little town itself has considerable character. Just
beyond Newport a signpost indicates a minor road to the Pentre Ifan burial
chamber, and it is well worth visiting this spectacular example of a
Neolithic tomb, with its delicately-poised capstone.

The B4582 turns off almost opposite the Pentre Ifan signpost, but few
tourists seem to use it to reach **Nevern**, a tranquil riverside village set
against the backdrop of a wooded valley. The church is a sympathetic
restoration of a fifteenth-century building, but the main attraction here is
the tall, sculptured Celtic cross in the churchyard, probably dating from the
early eleventh century. It is one of three preserved in Pembrokeshire. Even
earlier (possibly fifth- to sixth-century) is the stone inside the church inscribed with the ancient Irish Ogham script.

Throughout the tour so far the **Preseli Hills** have loomed to the south. In
fact they are of modest height, and are high moorlands rather than
mountains, but they dominate the flat Pembrokeshire landscape and were
a notable centre of prehistoric settlement. Particularly rewarding is the
Bronze Age track that was once the main route from Salisbury Plain to
Ireland. Its east-west route is shown clearly on Ordnance Survey maps, and
it can be joined at Crymych on the A478 Cardigan-Narberth road.

It has to be said that because of the absence of roads only the walker will
make close contact with the hills, although some impression of their character can be gained by driving along the B4329 from Eglwyswrw (on the
A487 near Nevern). By negotiating narrow lanes it is possible to come
within striking distance of major features such as the hill fort of
Foeldrygarn (OS grid reference SN 157337) or the rare local example of a
Bronze Age stone circle at Gors Fawr (SN 135294).

The B4329 passes through the crossroads village of Greenway, and 4
miles (6km) later a minor road branches off for **Wolfscastle**. It is at the head

of the fascinating Treffgarne Gorge, carved out by melting ice. It is now heavily wooded and part of it is the route of a walk described in the leaflet *Wolfscastle-Treffgarne Walks*, available locally. Another walk traverses the craggy ground above the gorge, and both are highly recommended for a fine day. A signpost at Treffgarne points to Scolton Manor, 3 miles (5km) south-east, a nineteenth-century house and garden now open to the public as a museum and country park.

Before leaving Fishguard mention should be made of the **Gwaun Valley**, signposted at countless points in the area. Like Treffgarne it was scoured out by meltwater and now forms the long forested valley of the Gwaun River, stretching from Fishguard to Cilgwyn (SN 075361). It contains waymarked walks (a leaflet is available) and can be rather hazardously negotiated by car along a narrow lane — not recommended in the high season, but at other times an enjoyable, leisurely journey.

Southern Pembrokeshire

Southern Pembrokeshire is dominated by the former county town of **Haverfordwest**, from which roads radiate in all directions. The town traces its origins back to the Vikings, but it first gained importance after the Norman occupation, when its impressive castle was of great strategic importance. Later it developed into a thriving trading centre with its own port on the Cleddau River. The castle (adapted for many purposes and now housing the county museum) and the churches of St Mary and St Martin are worth visiting, but connoisseurs of architecture will find a rich variety in the older streets.

The first tour from here takes in the coast to the west and south of the town. The A487 leads to a string of beaches on the shores of St Bride's Bay, including the inviting length of sand at Newgale, the secluded inlet of Nolton Haven, Druidston (a long stretch of sand but with limited parking) and Broad Haven. Nothing remains of the industrial past at Little Haven, now a very pretty place where the tiny port is a much-favoured sailing centre and best visited out of season.

To the south of all these, **Marloes** is a sizeable village with a pub, a useful shop and an interesting church. Nearby is **St Bride's Haven**, an early centre of Christianity, where the church has a very early cemetery and the cove is very appealing. It is a good place to start a short walk along the coastal path to Nab Head with its promontory fort. The narrow lane from Marloes to Martin's Haven is something of a gamble in the summer because of the limited (and expensive) parking at the other end, but it is the only way to reach the boat for the fascinating Skomer group of islands.

Skomer, **Skokholm** and **Grassholm** are all official bird sanctuaries and access is restricted, but nevertheless possible and worthwhile for anyone interested in wildlife. Skomer itself is the most accessible, with daily summer trips, and information about these and other boat excursions is readily available locally; binoculars are a great asset here.

A minor road outside Marloes leads to **Dale**, a lively centre for sailing and water sports with a pub on the quay, and continues to St Anne's Head, which overlooks the entrance to the huge natural harbour of Milford Haven. Dale Fort, now a field centre, was constructed in the mid-nineteenth century as one of a series of installations designed to guard the port. Another can be seen across the water on Thorn Island.

Take the B4327 out of Dale, but after 2 miles (3km) turn on to the minor road for St Ishmael's and dive into the wooded dingle to reach the isolated church — restored but retaining a powerful, primitive atmosphere that justifies the diversion. The road to **Milford Haven** begins to reveal signs of the big oil installations that accompanied its development as a tanker port, but the old town is surprisingly unaffected, having the air of a modest seaside resort. From the pleasant waterfront it is possible to see both the old harbour and the new tanker jetties.

Milford's neighbour **Neyland** was created in the 1850s as a railway terminus and Irish ferry port, and in recent years has taken on new life as a waterfront town. Its latest venture is a large marina in a most attractive wooded gorge called Westfield Pill. There is an excellent walking opportunity here because the disused railway track between Neyland and Rosemarket to the north has been turned into a public footpath (information available locally). The return to Haverfordwest is by way of Johnston on the A4076.

The second tour from Haverfordwest explores some of the small villages and places of interest around the estuaries of the Eastern and Western Cleddau, the Cresswell and the Carew — four rivers which emerge to form a remarkable series of inlets and creeks to the east of Milford Haven.

Take the A40 (St Clears) road from Haverfordwest and after 4 miles (6km) turn right to The Rhos. Here is **Picton Castle**, a late thirteenth-century building modernised successively in the eighteenth and nineteenth centuries to produce a pleasant hybrid (restricted public opening). Its fine gardens are open from spring to autumn.

Continue on the A40 for just over 3 miles (5km) and turn left for **Llawhaden**, where, on a site high above the river is a notable castle, originally Norman but transformed in the fourteenth century into a palace for the Bishops of St David's. It is best to park in the village; at the time of writing the key is obtained from the post office. Llawhaden church should be sought out in its peaceful riverside dell below the castle.

On returning to the A40 take the right turn on to the A4075 almost immediately and then turn right again on to a minor road to Blackpool Mill, a superb four-storey structure now restored and with its water-powered turbine operating again. The minor road continues to **Minwear**, where the tiny church retains its medieval atmosphere and houses a font salvaged from use as a pig trough. Follow the road south to **Lawrenny**, a village with an unpretentious charm, dominated by the very tall tower of its church, beside which is a lane leading to a notable viewpoint over the estuary.

Continue on minor roads through Cresswell (another former coal port) to **Carew**, a place which has many attractions for the discerning visitor. The view on entering the village from this direction is striking — a ruined castle beside the river and a large mill beyond. The thirteenth-century castle was

Carew Tide Mill

rcmodelled in Tudor times and the mill is a rare surviving example of an early nineteenth-century tidal mill. A few yards from the castle entrance is the Carew Cross, a sculptured monument of the eleventh century like the cross at Nevern. The church (at Carew Cheriton to the south) is of fifteenth-century origin and has some notable memorials and a detached chantry chapel converted into a schoolroom. All these features can be visited in the course of a walk described in an informative National Park leaflet.

From Carew join the A477 for Pembroke Dock, but turn off after 4 miles (6km) for **Cosheston**, which provides access to Upton Castle. The castle is not open, but the grounds can be visited and contain a fine collection of specimen trees and shrubs. A National Park leaflet called *Upton Castle Grounds* gives a full description for the visitor. From here the return to Haverfordwest is via the Cleddau Bridge at Neyland.

The final tour in Southern Pembrokeshire starts in the very distinctive town of **Pembroke** itself. It is a long, thin settlement, spread along a limestone ridge headed by a magnificent castle on a promontory site and with a single main street as its spine — one of the most harmonious Georgian and Victorian thoroughfares in Wales. The town centre retains most of its fourteenth-century walls. The present castle, noted as one of the finest to survive in Britain, was begun in the mid-twelfth century. Neighbouring Pembroke Dock repays exploration. It was established in 1814, when a new planned town with a gridiron layout was begun, and closed in 1926, by which time over 250 ships had been built.

The tour, which is mainly coastal, begins on the B4320 at **Angle**, one of the most interesting villages in Pembrokeshire. An embattled place over the years, it has a ruined castle keep opposite the church; a walk round to the back of the churchyard will reveal a 'refuge tower' and a domed building beyond that appears to be a medieval dovecot. Also behind the church is a minute fisherman's chapel accommodating about a dozen people. The village itself contains some strange architecture — see the bizarre Globe Hotel. West Angle Bay has a pleasant beach with a large free car park, and a short walk along the coastal path to the north brings into view Thorn Island with its grim Victorian fortress, yet another of the elaborate defence works built to guard Milford Haven.

The road to Castlemartin threads its way through spectacular sand dunes and passes the rolling breakers of Freshwater West before turning inland. There are now constant reminders that this area is a tank firing range, and side roads may be barred at certain times. (Firing times are notified in all local information centres, and it is essential that this part of the tour takes place on a non-firing day.) **Castlemartin** church, in a beautiful setting well to the north of its village, should not be missed. Just beyond Castlemartin is a minor road to the right leading to a particularly dramatic stretch of coastline and providing a close-up view of the Elegug Stacks — tall, isolated rocks covered in sea birds. From the car park here an exhilarating cliff-top walk extends several miles to the east.

Three miles (5km) further on take the road to **Bosherston**. The car park just beyond the church is the starting point for a walk around the Bosherston Pools, once part of the Cawdor estate. These interlinked lagoons, barely separated from the sea at their southern end, are famous for their water-lilies and now shelter a variety of wildlife. Opposite the church, which is worth a visit, a military road leads to a car park above a long flight of steps down to St Govan's Chapel, an austere hermit's cell built within the rocks just above the waterline. It was once a noted place of pilgrimage with a holy well nearby.

From Bosherston it is a good idea to return to Pembroke and leave again on the A4139 (Tenby) road. This provides a chance to visit the Bishop's Palace at **Lamphey**, where the ruins include a thirteenth-century hall, a later great hall, a chapel and gatehouse. A little further on, the church at **Hodgeston** has a fine under-restored chancel with an ornate sedilia and double piscina. **Manorbier**, off the main road to the south, was the birthplace of Giraldus Cambrensis, the twelfth-century writer and historian. The castle where he was born is privately owned but open to the public. Curtain-walled and turreted, it spreads along a hill inland from the beach, and is best viewed from the church, which stands alone to the east and is reached by a lane leading off the beach road. The Norman nave, below ground level, has a simple primitive strength that is very impressive.

After the savage coastline characteristic of Southern Pembrokeshire **Tenby** comes as a surprise with sandy beaches, a picturesque harbour with a ruined castle and a wealth of charming early-Victorian domestic architecture that can be fully appreciated with the help of an excellent town trail. Boats leave from here for Caldey Island, which has a long history of monastic life. From Tenby the quick return route to Pembroke is via the B4318.

Manorbier Castle

Carmarthenshire

Carmarthen occupies a strategic bridging point at the head of the Tywi Estuary and has been an important centre since the Romans established a fortress here. A Christian settlement developed in the area abandoned by the Romans, but the present town centre grew up around Henry I's castle of 1109 and through the centuries became the business and administrative centre of western Wales. Nowadays its streets reveal a rich variety of domestic architecture with the occasional distinguished building (for example the Guildhall of 1770), and in Priory Street the remains of a Roman amphitheatre have been excavated. The town museum is on the eastern outskirts at Abergwili.

From Carmarthen it is possible to explore two very different areas — the hill and forest country to the north-east and, first, the coast to the south. The Tywi and the Taf meet at the sea to the south-west of Carmarthen, and a general lack of bridges makes a circular tour of the coastal area impossible, but a special trip on the B4312 to **Llansteffan** (or Llanstephan) is worthwhile. Apart from the charm of the village itself the remains of the promontory castle provide panoramic views. **Laugharne** (pronounced Larn) is only a short distance to the west, but reaching it involves returning to the A40 and turning off at St Clears. The poet Dylan Thomas spent his later years here before his death in New York in 1953, and it is an evocative experience to visit The Boathouse (his home on the shore) and to see the little hut (affectionately known as 'The Shack') in which he wrote. His grave is in the southern extension of St Martin's churchyard. The town itself, with a seaside castle and a fine town hall, repays exploration.

On the eastern side of the Tywi Estuary the A484 leads to **Kidwelly**, once a flourishing port until it silted up. It was also a centre of coal mining and tinplate manufacture, and both industries are featured at the Kidwelly Industrial Museum. Other attractions here include the substantial castle ruins by the riverside. Further south the Pembrey Country Park includes a dry ski slope among its attractions.

The main road passes through Llanelli and crosses on to the Gower Peninsula at Loughor. The **Gower Peninsula** is designated an Area of Outstanding Natural Beauty and manages to keep itself aloof from nearby Swansea, but it can be crowded in the summer holiday months, especially in the vicinity of its famous beaches. Nevertheless, even in high summer it is possible to find tranquillity inland and along the cliffs of its south-western coast.

Full details of the many attractions here are available locally, but a quick tour could begin on the B4295 west of Gowerton, which passes along an indeterminate coastline with immense stretches of sand and marsh. Two miles (3km) west of Llanrhidian, Weobley Castle stands on the cliff top. As a fortified manor rather than a castle proper it is of considerable interest, and substantial remains survive.

At Llanmadoc the road peters out, but there is plenty of good walking here. To the north a path leads to the dunes of the **Whiteford Burrows**, a national nature reserve, and there is a contrasting hill ramble to the south on to Llanmadoc Hill and the neighbouring hill fort called The Bulwark. **Llangennith** can be reached by way of a lane from Llanmadoc. It is a starting point for coastal walks above Rhossili Bay and perhaps to the near-island of Burry Holms, and there are also paths on to the exhilarating expanse of Rhossili Down.

Rhossili itself is reached by a long road detour from Llangennith which takes in the interesting church at Llanddewi. However, to enjoy the cliffs it is unnecessary to go as far as Rhossili since there are so many opportunities to walk to the coast from the approach road — for example from Pilton or Pilton Green to Paviland Cave, where the skeleton of a very early Stone Age man was discovered in 1823. There is a fine cliff path between Rhossili and Port Eynon to the east.

From Port Eynon the A4118 goes north and then sharply east. The right turn to Penrice leads to a small but attractive forest area and then goes on to the resort of **Oxwich**, which can be safely missed at the peak of the season, though at quieter times its isolated cliff-top church is worth a visit. For the enterprising visitor this is really an area for short and varied walking — from Penmaen to Three Cliffs Bay, or on the various tracks and lanes to the north of Parkmill. The Gower now begins to meet the outskirts of Swansea, and it is best to stay on the main roads for the return to the 'mainland' via Loughor.

The second tour from Carmarthen begins on the A40 to the east. After 5 miles (8km), at Nantgaredig, the B4310 turns off to the north. It winds steadily up into the hills and at Brechfa reaches the outskirts of Brechfa Forest.

This is fine and unspoilt countryside, penetrated by very few roads, although shortly after Brechfa it is possible to turn off for Gwernogle, an isolated forest hamlet with a primitive church. Perhaps the most attractive settlement is **Abergorlech**, 6 miles (10km) beyond Brechfa, a village with an ancient bridge and an interesting church. It is also the starting point for a number of forest walks.

At Llansawel, 4 miles (6km) further on, there is an attractive diversion on the B4337 south to **Talley**, a village notable for its lakes and the beautifully-situated ruins of its twelfth-century abbey (do not miss the adjacent church of 1722). To visit the Roman gold mines at Dolaucothi take the minor road off the B4337 in Llansawel to the A482 and make for **Pumsaint**, where the mines are signposted. There are underground tours through the workings (requiring suitable footwear and some agility) but also good walks above ground and an interesting exhibition.

From here the A482 takes a highly scenic route down to Llanwrda and on to **Llandovery**, an unpretentious market town that was once a starting point for drovers herding cattle to markets in England. The slight remains of a Norman castle indicate the town's strategic importance at the confluence of three rivers, and the Romans established a fort earlier still. The town's two churches are both worth visiting. Llanfair-ar-y-Bryn, on the north-eastern outskirts, is the burial-place of William Williams, the famous hymn writer, and like St Dingad's on the other side of the town, it has some good stained glass. Riverside walks at Llandovery are described in a pamphlet available locally.

To the north of Llandovery is the Llyn Brianne Reservoir, a fine objective for an excursion into the remote hills by way of a minor road running north from the town centre along the Tywi Valley.

The main tour resumes by tackling the hills to the south. Start on the minor road from Llandovery to **Myddfai**, a village on the edge of the Brecon Beacons celebrated for having produced many generations of skilled physicians around whom a considerable folklore has accumulated. The road continues, sometimes very steeply, into the hills to reach **Llanddeusant**, the starting point for several walks on to the Black Mountain. These include a 4 mile (6km) expedition (not to be undertaken lightly) to the beautiful and very remote lake Llyn-y-Fan Fach in its fine setting under a steep rock face.

After Llanddeusant the road begins its descent and joins the A4069. Make for **Llangadog**, situated in an area where several tributaries join the River Tywi. There is an opportunity here for a rewarding visit to Garn Goch, one of the largest Iron Age hill forts in Wales. Just over 2 miles (3km) after joining the A4069 look out for a turning on the left for Bethlehem, and on the outskirts of the village (named after its chapel) Garn Goch is signposted on the left. The sprawling fort, probably the home of an extensive community in the fifth century, provides panoramic views of the Tywi Valley.

On returning to the A4069 pass through Llangadog and make for **Llandeilo**. The pleasant small town is set in a commanding position above the Tywi, and it is no surprise to find Dinefwr (or Dynevor) castle here, standing in attractive parkland that makes for relaxed walking.

Carreg Cennen Castle is a different proposition altogether. Strikingly situated on a steep and craggy limestone ridge, it lies near the village of **Trapp**, reached by driving south a short distance on the A483 from Llandeilo and turning on to a minor road at Ffairfach. The ruins comprise a barbican and gatehouse, with an inner ward housing a chapel and hall. The work dates from the thirteenth and fourteenth centuries, during which the castle saw much conflict, but the 200ft (61m) tunnel through the rock is believed to have been used in prehistoric times. There is a rare-breeds farm close to the castle.

Return to Ffairfach and take the A476, branching right very soon on to the B4300, which runs above the remarkable meanders of the Tywi. The very attractive Gelliaur Country Park, a former private estate, lies on the left, while at Llanarthney there is a lane leading to Paxton's Tower, a folly of 1811 visible for miles around and built as a tribute to Lord Nelson. It is now National Trust property and a popular viewpoint.

Return for 2 miles (3km) on the B4300 and turn left. The road soon passes Dryslwyn Castle. Access is free, although something of a scramble. Continue up to the A40 for the return to Carmarthen.

The Brecon Beacons

The previous tour skirted the western edge of the Brecon Beacons National Park, and it is now time to look at this famous area in more detail. The Beacons are certainly mountains, but not of the familiar kind — they are more like a succession of long, flat-topped ridges, and this has misled people into thinking them less dangerous than such peaks as those of Snowdonia. In fact they are very high and very bleak, and any walking expedition on to their tops demands appropriate clothing and equipment. Luckily it is possible to appreciate their beauty from the security of the roads, and there is plenty of low-level walking.

Brecon is situated where the River Honndu joins the Usk, and has been an important settlement from the twelfth century. It is a small market town, but nevertheless has a cathedral, established in 1923 and formerly the medieval priory. In the eighteenth century it was a considerable social centre, which accounts for some handsome architecture, best appreciated by walking the narrow streets with the town trail available at the information centre.

The town is the starting point for a circular tour taking in the characteristic Beacons landscape to the south and west. The 'waterfall country' around Ystradfellte is included in the tour, and visitors wishing to walk around the waterfalls should pack suitable footwear and clothing and equip themselves with the leaflet *Walks in the Ystradfellte Area*, available from information centres.

Take the A470 on the western outskirts of Brecon, and after 4 miles (6km) turn right on to the signposted road for the Brecon Beacons Mountain Centre. It is open every day except Christmas Day, and its position, at 1,100ft (335m) on Mynydd Illtud, would in itself justify a visit, but the main reason for calling here is the wealth of information available about all aspects of the Beacons. After the visit continue the enjoyable mountain drive on the A470 (one of the highest trunk roads in Britain) and then branch right on to the A4059. After 7 miles (11km) a minor road on the right leads to Ystradfellte. The Old Red Sandstone that makes up most of the Beacons gives way to limestone here, and the River Mellte disappears underground at Porth yr Ogof and re-emerges to the south to form a series of fine waterfalls. The leaflet mentioned earlier shows parking places and the network of 'advised paths' that take in the best of the falls. An approach is also possible from the village of Penderyn nearby on the A4059.

From Pontneddfechan, 5 miles (8km) to the south, there are excellent alternative walks along the River Nedd to the falls of Sgwyd Gwladys and Sgwd Ddwli, and in the other direction to Sgwd yr Eira by way of some abandoned mines and the great rock of Craig-y-Ddinas. The tour resumes at Pontneddfechan, with a choice of two contrasting routes back to Brecon. One follows the main road to the west and provides a chance to visit the Craig-y-Nos Country Park and Dan-yr-Ogof Show Caves, while the other involves a drive through remoter country to the east.

For the first take the B4242 out of Pontneddfechan and turn right when it joins the A4109. At the point where the A4221 branches to the right a short lane (also on the right) leads to the Henrhyd Falls, owned by the National Trust. Continue on the A4221, and after another 3 miles (5km) turn right on to the A4067 to reach Craig-y-Nos. **Craig-y-Nos Castle** (not open to the public) is a Gothic mansion that became famous when bought by the renowned opera singer Adelina Patti in 1878. She entertained in brilliant style here, and the unique feature of the house was a small theatre which still survives. After Patti's death in 1919 the house became a sanatorium, but in 1976 the park was acquired for public access, and its 40 acres of water and woodland can be strolled through at will. It is only a short distance up the main road to **Dan-yr-Ogof**, where the main attraction is the series of spectacular caverns in which the limestone walls and roofs have formed fantastic and sometimes grotesque shapes that are cleverly floodlit for maximum effect. From here the road to Sennybridge passes over lonely hills with fine views, and the return to Brecon is along the valley of the Usk.

For the alternative route back to Brecon take the B4242 out of Pontneddfechan and turn right when it joins the A4109. This road joins the A465, which should be followed through Hirwaun to its junction with the A470 at Merthyr Tydfil. A left turn here leads after 3 miles (5km) to the **Llwyn-on Reservoir**, where the Garwnant Forest Visitor Centre has been established within old farm buildings, providing much information about the surrounding area and giving access to some pleasant short walks. Return down the A470, and just before the junction with the A465 look out for a minor road on the left signposted Vaynor. Continue through this old quarrying area and branch left just before the dam of the Pontsticill (or Taf Fechan) Reservoir. There is a parking place almost immediately for those wishing to walk to the dam. The Brecon Mountain Railway, with its vintage steam locomotives, passes on the other side.

The road now runs beside the Pontsticill and Pentwyn reservoirs, the last of a series designed to supply the industrial valleys to the south. At the northern end of Pentwyn branch right on to the mountain road, where there are several parking places with short walks, and drive beside the long Talybont Reservoir to the village of **Talybont** itself. The Brecon and Monmouth Canal passes through here, providing easy towpath strolling. From Talybont take the B4558 (Brecon) road, passing through Pencelli, another canalside settlement. A short distance further on it is worth the short diversion to the attractive village of Llanfrynach before returning to Brecon.

Further Information

— South Wales —

Places of Interest

THE BRECON BEACONS
Abercraf
Craig-y-Nos Country Park
At Penycae on A4067
☎ 0639 730395
40 acres of woodland and streams in former grounds of Adelina Patti's Craig-y-Nos Castle. Also tourist information centre.

Dan-yr-Ogof Show Caves
On A4067 north of Abercraf
☎ 0639 730284
Open: 1 April (or Easter) to end of October daily from 10am.

Merthyr Tydfil
Brecon Mountain Railway
Off A465 3 miles (5km) north
of Merthyr Tydfil
☎ 0685 4854
Narrow-gauge line running to Taf Fechan Reservoir. Timetables available in information centres.

Brecon
Brecknock Museum
Captain's Walk
☎ 0874 4121
Comprehensive collections illustrating local social and domestic history.
Open: Monday to Saturday 10am-5pm.

CARDIGANSHIRE
Cilgerran
Cilgerran Castle
☎ 0239 615136
Open: April to end of October, weekdays 9.30am-6.30pm, Sundays 2-6.30pm. November to March, weekdays 9.30am-4pm, Sundays 2-4pm.

Llandysul
Museum of the Welsh Woollen Industry
Cambrian Mill
☎ 0559 370329
Open: April to end of September, Monday to Saturday 10am-5pm. October to March, Monday to Friday 10am-5pm.

CARMARTHENSHIRE
Llandeilo
Gelliaur Country Park
☎ 05584 885
Open: all year except Christmas Day and Boxing Day.

Trapp
Near Llandeilo
Carreg Cennen Castle
☎ 0558 822291
Open: April to end of October, daily 9.30am-6.30pm. November to March, weekdays 9.30am-4pm, Sundays 2-4pm.

Carmarthen
Gwili Steam Railway
Bronwydd Arms
☎ 0267 230666

Restored standard-gauge railway, exhibitions.
Opening times vary so check by telephone.

Museum
☎ 0267 261391
Open: Monday to Saturday 10am-4.30pm.

Kidwelly
Industrial Museum
☎ 0554 891078
In former Kidwelly Tinplate Works.
Open: Easter to end of September, weekdays 10am-5pm, Sundays 2-5pm.

Castle
☎ 0554 890104
Open: April to end of October, daily 9.30am-6.30pm, Sundays 2-6.30pm.
November to March, weekdays 9.30am-4pm, Sundays 2-4pm.

Laugharne
Dylan Thomas Museum
The Boathouse
☎ 0994 427420
Open: Good Friday to end of October daily 10am-5.30pm.

Pumsaint
Dolaucothi Roman Gold Mines
☎ 05585 359
Open: April to end of October, daily 10am-6pm.

Gower Peninsula
Gower Farm Museum
Knelston
☎ 0792 391195
Open: June to end of September, daily 10am-5pm, weekends in April, May, October (plus Bank Holidays) 10am-5pm.

Weobley Castle
Llanrhidian
☎ 0792 390012
Open: mid-March to mid-October weekdays 10am-6.30pm, Sundays 2-6.30pm. Mid-October to mid-March weekdays 10am-4pm, Sundays 2-4pm.

NORTHERN PEMBROKESHIRE
St David's
Bishop's Palace
☎ 0437 720517
Open: mid-March to mid-October weekdays 9.30am-6.30pm, mid-October to mid-March weekdays 9.30am-4pm, Sundays 2-4pm.

Oceanarium
New Street
☎ 0437 720453
Open: daily 10am-sunset.

Farm Park
☎ 0437 721601
Open: daily all year 10am-5pm.

SOUTHERN PEMBROKESHIRE
Haverfordwest
Museum and Art Gallery
The Castle
☎ 0437 763708
Open: Tuesday to Saturday 10am-5pm.

Picton Castle
Off A40 east of Haverfordwest
☎ 043786 379
Grounds open: April to end of September, daily except Mondays 10.30am-5pm. Conducted tours of house on Sunday and Thursday afternoons from mid-July to mid-September 2-5pm. Gallery open daily except Mondays 10.30am-5pm.

Scolton Manor Heritage Park
Off A40 north of town
☎ 043782 457
Museum open: May to September, Tuesday to Sunday 10.30am-6pm. Park open all year.

Canaston Bridge
Black Pool Mill
☎ 09914 233
Open: Easter to end of October 11am-6pm.

Llawhaden
Llawhaden Castle
Open: April to end of October, weekdays 9.30am-6.30pm, Sundays 2-6.30pm.
November to March, weekdays 9.30am-4pm, Sundays 2-4pm.

Off the Beaten Track: Britain

Carew
Castle
☎ 0646 651782
Open: Easter to end of October, daily
10am-5pm.

Mill
Open: Easter to end of October, daily
10am-5pm.

Manorbier
Castle
Open: mid-April to end of September,
daily 10.30am-5.30pm.

Milford Haven
Museum
Mansfield Street
Open: weekdays May to October 10am-
12noon and 2-4pm.

Pembroke
Castle
☎ Pembroke 681510
Open: April to end of September, daily
9.30am-6pm, March and October daily
10am-5pm, rest of year weekdays 10am-
4pm.

Saundersfoot
Colby Woodland Garden
Amroth, near Saundersfoot
☎ 0834 811725
Open: April to end of October, daily
10am-5pm.

Tenby
Museum and Art Gallery
Castle Hill
☎ 0834 2809
Open: Easter to October, daily 10am-
6pm. Phone for winter opening times.

Tudor Merchant's House
Quay Hill
☎ 0834 2279
Open: April to end of October, Monday
to Friday 11am-6pm, Sundays 2-6pm.

Manor House Wildlife Park
St Florence
☎ 0646 651201
Open: Easter to end of September, daily
10am-6pm.

Caldey Island
Frequent boat services from harbour

mid-May to mid-September. Restricted
sailings at other times.

Tourist Information Centres

Aberaeron
The Harbour, ☎ 0545 570602

Brecon
Mountain Centre, Libanus, ☎ 0874 3366
also
Cattle Market Car Park, ☎ 0874 2485

Broad Haven
Car Park, ☎ 043783 412

Cardigan
Theatr Mwldan, Bath House Road
☎ 0239 613230

Carmarthen
Lammas Street, ☎ 0267 231557

Fishguard
4 Hamilton Street, ☎ 0348 873484

Gower Peninsula
Singleton Street, Swansea, ☎ 0792 468321
also
Visitor Centre, Rhossili, ☎ 0792 390707

Haverfordwest
40 High Street, ☎ 0437 763110

Llandovery
Broad Street, ☎ 0550 20693

Merthyr Tydfil
Glebeland Street, ☎ 0685 79884

Newcastle Emlyn
Market Hall, ☎ 0239 711333

New Quay
Church Street, ☎ 0545 580865

Newport
Long Street, ☎ 0239 820912

Pembroke
Drill Hall, ☎ 0646 682148

Pontneddfechan
☎ 0639 721795

St David's
City Hall, ☎ 0437 720392

Saundersfoot
The Harbour, ☎ 0834 811411

Tenby
The Croft, ☎ 0834 2402

7 • The Welsh Borders

Technically the Welsh border is simply a line drawn on a map in 1536 to settle the boundary between England and Wales once and for all. For 1,000 years before that the border had been disputed or ignored, despite the construction of Offa's Dyke, the remarkable ditch and bank running from the north coast to the south and constructed on the orders of King Offa of Mercia in the eighth century. That long period of uncertainty led to a strip of 'no-man's-land' many miles wide. On the map it can be detected through place names — English names in Wales, Welsh names in England — and through the myriad castle sites that recall centuries of border warfare. But more important has been the sense among those living along the border of being neither Welsh nor English — a feeling that survives today.

Geographically the border developed where the fertile English lowlands run up against the barrier of hills that has always protected Wales. This produces great contrasts. In the north the pastoral landscape of the Shropshire plain comes up abruptly against the massive Berwyn Mountains, accessible only through a series of narrow valleys. A little further south the Clun Forest of South Shropshire, an area of undulating wooded hills, gives way across the border to the barren moorlands of Radnor. South again, the rich pasture and arable land of Western Herefordshire is overlooked by the Black Mountains that form the eastern extension of the Brecon Beacons. Only at the most southerly end of the border is there a resemblance between the English and Welsh countryside, though even here the Forest of Dean in Gloucestershire jealously guards its distinctive personality.

Obviously the English side has always been much richer than the Welsh, and this is reflected in the character of the towns and villages. To the east a string of large and ancient towns — Shrewsbury, Ludlow, Leominster, Hereford, Monmouth, Chepstow — testify to military strength and economic prosperity. Welsh border towns such as Welshpool, Knighton, Presteigne, Hay-on-Wye and Abergavenny have never developed into more than modest market centres. Similarly there is a dramatic transition between the large villages of lush Herefordshire and the small grey settlements over the border.

It is these contrasts that make the Welsh border so fascinating, and this chapter will explore some of the most characteristic border regions, moving between the intricate English landscape and the lonely expanses of upland on the Welsh side. It should be pointed out at once that the long-distance path that runs the length of Offa's Dyke from Prestatyn on the north coast to Chepstow in the south provides the ideal way of discovering the border. Many fine lengths of the Dyke still survive, and from time to time during the chapter opportunities to walk short lengths of the Dyke path are mentioned. The effort is well worthwhile.

Tours From Monmouth

Monmouth is a good centre for exploring the southern border. Now in Gwent, it has never been strongly Welsh in character, in fact it has always been a key town in the English defensive system. It is an ancient settlement, squeezed onto a promontory between the rivers Monnow and Wye, and its centre retains the rectangular plan established in Norman times. Agincourt Square is the natural focus, dominated by the Shire Hall of 1724 and by the dignified Beaufort Arms. From here Church Street leads to St Mary's, rebuilt in 1736 and notable for its slender spire, while Priory Street runs above the Monnow, giving access to the Classical Market Hall, the home of the Monmouth Museum and the local history collection, which includes some remarkable memorabilia of Lord Nelson. The streets to the north of the square are full of good buildings, including the Gothic Monmouth School of the 1860s. The long, straight Monnow Street to the south arrives at the Monnow Bridge, straddled by its unique medieval defensive gate.

The A466 to the south runs through the Lower Wye Valley, which has attracted visitors since the eighteenth century. At first the road is undramatic, running beside the placid river and enclosed by a high bank, but after Bigsweir Bridge the views begin to open out, and the first major riverside settlement appears. This is **Llandogo**, where the houses are built largely on the steep hillside and screened by trees. Just over 2 miles (3km) further a narrow bridge allows a crossing to **Brockweir**, a pleasant place with a pub and a notable Moravian chapel. From here there is an attractive and easy walk along the riverside path to the former Tintern railway station, which has been thoroughly restored as a picnic site and tea room.

The road continues round a wide bend to reach the valley's most famous attraction. The ruins of **Tintern Abbey** are remarkable not only for their own beauty but also for their position on a riverside plateau with a dramatic backdrop of thickly-wooded cliffs. They are seen at their best in the early morning or late evening, although admission is only possible during the day.

At this point the Wye begins to meander through a spectacular limestone gorge, a view best appreciated further along the road by stopping at one of the parking places that give the walker access to the Wynd Cliff and Piercefield Cliff overlooking the river. After passing the racecourse the road drops into **Chepstow**, which was a major port in the Middle Ages and a centre of shipbuilding in the eighteenth and nineteenth centuries. The riverside still has a maritime air, but the upper part of the town is now a place of handsome Georgian and Victorian architecture. The medieval past

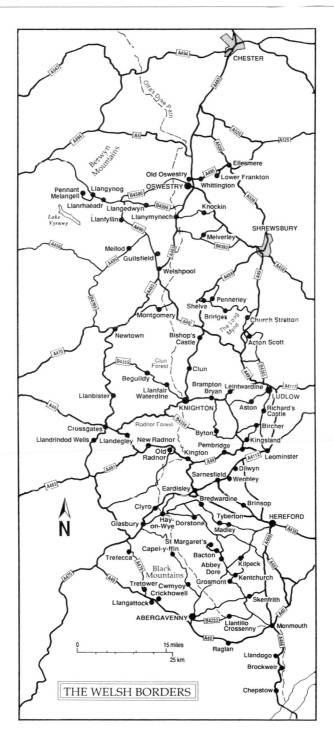

THE WELSH BORDERS

The magnificent ruins of Tintern Abbey

is recalled by the Town Gate set in the defensive Port Wall which runs through the town. From the fine iron road bridge over the Wye it is possible to see the former shipbuilding area on one side and the sprawling castle on the other. The castle is a major monument with a complex building history that started in the eleventh century and continued through the Tudor period. A leisurely inspection with the guide book is recommended. The town museum is opposite the castle entrance.

Castles are the theme of the second tour from Monmouth, and the first and finest of them is reached by taking the A40 west to **Raglan**. Raglan Castle is a very large and sophisticated example of its kind, dating from the later fifteenth century and designed for comfortable living as well as for defence. The remains of the hall, chapel and domestic apartments are of great interest, but the most eye-catching features are the massive gate and the hexagonal Great Tower, a formidable last refuge surrounded by a moat.

From Raglan take the old main road, which runs roughly parallel to the new A40, to Llanfihangel Gobion and then turn right on to the minor road which leads to Llanvapley. On joining the B4233 turn right for **Llantilio Crossenny**, where the church, well off the road, is unexpectedly splendid. The preserved moat by the village crossroads is Hen Gwrt, the site of a medieval palace of the Bishops of Llandaff. A short distance along the minor road to the north of the village is **White Castle**, well preserved and standing in rural isolation. It is one of three in the area (all visited on this tour) that were under common ownership and formed a triangular defensive system. The inner enclosure is twelfth-century but the gatehouse, towers and curtain wall were built a century later. It is freely accessible.

Continue along the minor road that passes the castle and join the B4521.

It leads to **Skenfrith**, the pleasant village where the second of the three castles stands — rather less substantial, consisting of a round keep within a curtain wall. A visit to Skenfrith church, with its fine, heavily-buttressed tower and notable monuments, is very worthwhile.

The third castle of the triangle is at **Grosmont**, reached by returning along the B4521 and turning north at Norton. With its late-Victorian town hall, Grosmont appears larger than it actually is, an impression reinforced by a church of impressive scale. On entering, however, visitors will find that the big nave is disused and that the present church is contained behind a screen within what was once the chancel and transept area. The ruined towers and walls of the castle stand in compact fashion on a motte, the unusual feature being a fine fourteenth-century chimney.

Stay on the road through the village and cross the Welsh border into **Kentchurch**, where the Court (signposted off the road) is open to the public in the spring and summer months. The minor road past the Court threads its way through empty countryside to **Kilpeck**, which has one of the country's finest Norman churches. A leaflet gives details of the riches here, but the outstanding work is the amazingly crisp and elaborate carving, particularly that on the south doorway and chancel arch. The route now is along the lane to the B4348 at Much Dewchurch and from there on to the A466 for the return to Monmouth.

Western Herefordshire

To the north of Monmouth and the Forest of Dean the landscape changes as the road begins to pass through the rich agricultural land of Herefordshire, famous for beef cattle, hops and cider. All roads lead to **Hereford**, the natural starting-point for an exploration of the deeply rural and largely unspoilt countryside that lies beside the Welsh border. The name 'Hereford' means 'the army river-crossing'. It sums up the importance of the town as a military centre from Roman times to the end of the Middle Ages, but Hereford was also an early cathedral city and later developed as a thriving market town. The dominant building, of course, is the cathedral, a Saxon foundation. The present structure dates from the late eleventh century and work continued well into the sixteenth century, so a wide range of architectural styles are represented, including the results of a major Victorian restoration. It is particularly famous for the riches of its chained library, which houses a volume of Anglo-Saxon gospels of the eighth century, and for the *Mappa Mundi*, an imaginative map of the world drawn in about 1300. The town centre was regrettably 'modernised' in the 1960s, but some fine streets and individual buildings survive, and should be walked with the town trail available from the information centre.

The first tour begins on the A438 to the west. Four miles (6km) after leaving the city the National Trust gardens at The Weir provide pleasant walks with fine views over the Wye towards the western hills. Shortly after turn left at Bridge Sollers and cross the river to reach **Madley**, where the large and splendid church has outstanding work dating from the twelfth and thirteenth centuries. The church at **Tyberton**, 3 miles (5km) away on the B4352, is very different, having been built in 1720 with the elegant furnishing of the period.

Continue through Blakemere to **Moccas**. Moccas Court (limited public opening) is one of the county's most distinguished eighteenth-century houses, designed by Robert Adam and standing in grounds laid out by 'Capability' Brown. The nearby church is authentically Norman. The Victorian diarist Francis Kilvert, for long the curate of Clyro (see the tour from Abergavenny) was Vicar of **Bredwardine**, 3 miles (5km) further on, from 1877 until his death in 1879; his grave is here. It is well worth strolling past Bredwardine Court to the bridge below the church for the excellent views. For even better views, drive up the lane beside the Red Lion, and at the sharp left turn park and walk along the track to the top of Merbach Hill, where the panorama includes vast stretches of Herefordshire and the Welsh border.

From Bredwardine a minor road leads to **Dorstone**, which stands at the head of the 'Golden Valley', thus named because the River Dore runs through it (rather unromantically the name turns out to be a mistranslation — Dore comes from the Welsh for 'water'). The village itself justifies a stop, although it is most famous for Arthur's Stone on the hill above it (signposted off the Bredwardine road). It is a Neolithic chamber tomb, about 5,000 years old, with vertical stones supporting a heavy capstone.

There now follows a 10 mile (16km) drive down the pleasant valley, passing first through its 'capital' **Peterchurch**, where the big Norman church has an unusual internal arrangement of four sections marked by a series of arches. At Vowchurch continue on the B4347, and after 4 miles (6km) look for a lane on the right leading to **Bacton**. This secluded church has a fine monument to Blanche Parry, a lady-in-waiting to Elizabeth I. Stay on this lane for the even remoter church at **St Margaret's**, primitive in character and atmosphere and containing a rare and beautiful rood screen and loft. Return to the valley road, which soon passes **Dore Abbey**, which has a curious history. The road now joins the A465 for the return to Hereford, but 2 miles (3km) before the city there is a worthwhile diversion to see the medieval monuments in the church at Clenhonger.

For the second tour leave Hereford once again by the A438, but 3 miles (5km) after Bridge Sollers turn left for the cider-orchard hamlet of **Monnington-on-Wye**, where the distinctive church of 1679 stands at the end of a lane overlooking the river. After this the A438 follows the route of a Roman road above the looping Wye and passes the hamlet of Letton (another interesting church) before reaching **Eardisley**, a well developed village with some picturesque houses and a church with a font that is an outstanding example of Norman carving.

From here there is an uneventful drive to **Kington**, an unpretentious old border market town. There are some interesting buildings here, including the seventeenth-century school built in stone by John Abel. Attractions nearby include the gardens of Hergest Croft (signposted from the town).

The route is now along the A44 (Leominster) to **Pembridge**. This was

The ruins of Grosmont Castle

once a medieval borough and is now a large village with a splendid array of timber-framed houses and a sixteenth-century market house. The unique feature here is the church's free-standing octagonal belfry, probably dating from the fourteenth century. There is more fine timber-framing at **Eardisland**, 4 miles (6km) further on — a smaller place, and made more attractive by the River Arrow running through it. Down a lane to the south, Burton Court (open to the public) has a fourteenth-century Great Hall and some interesting displays.

Two miles (3km) after Eardisland turn right on to the A4110 and then right again on to the A4112. The first village on this road is **Dilwyn**, another small settlement with an unexpectedly large church, containing an elaborate chancel screen and some good stained glass, but 3 miles (5km) further on and down a side turning is one of Hereford's showpieces. **Weobley** was an important medieval borough and is still a sizeable village today, with venerable houses flanking the main streets and a church made impressive by a tall tower capped by an elegant spire. There are some interesting monuments inside.

The church at **Sarnesfield**, 2 miles (3km) away is more modest, but it does have in its churchyard the tomb of John Abel, builder and carpenter, whose work enriched several Herefordshire towns in the seventeenth century. Just after Sarnesfield turn right on to the A480 and continue past Mansell Lacy, turning left just beyond it for **Brinsop**. The unassuming church has a rich interior, with examples of Norman carving and fine work by the distinguished modern church artist Ninian Comper. The road now runs back to Hereford.

The Black Mountains

Confronting Herefordshire to the west is the expanse of hills known as the Black Mountains. Together with the hills to the south they present a formidable barrier, and **Abergavenny** is strikingly situated at a point where the Usk Valley provides the only easy route into Wales. There was a Roman fort here and later a castle, though the remains of the latter are now insignificant (a small local history museum stands on the site). Today Abergavenny is a cheerful market town, with irregular streets and a surprising variety of buildings that include two fine old inns, an astonishing Victorian market hall and St Mary's Church, famous both for its size and for its splendid array of monuments. A town trail is available locally.

The tour around and through the Black Mountains begins on the A40, which runs west from the town between the river and the hills. After nearly 4 miles (6km) a minor road on the right provides a good route to the summit of the 'Sugar Loaf' mountain, a prominent local landmark. The first settlement along the A40 is **Crickhowell**, a small town of considerable charm with the scant ruins of a castle in its park and the rather more impressive gateway of a former Tudor mansion. Perhaps the most notable structure here is the long 13-arch bridge dating from the turn of the seventeenth century. Not many people cross it to reach **Llangattock**, a most attractive village beneath cliff-like rocks, where the church houses the ancient stocks and whipping post. The path to the Craig y Cilau nature reserve can be reached by a short drive along the minor road west of the village.

Two miles (3km) after Crickhowell branch right on to the A479 for **Tretower**, where the original modest Norman castle was replaced in the thirteenth century by a circular great tower which still stands. In the less turbulent fifteenth century this was superseded by the adjacent fortified manor house with its elaborate gate. The buildings are open to the public. Follow the minor road beside the Court back to the A40 and continue to Bwlch. Just beyond the village a lane turns off for Trebinshwn House. Three miles (5km) later another minor road on the right runs through to Pennorth and **Llangasty-Talyllyn**, where the outstanding church has the elaborate fixtures and decoration favoured by the nineteenth-century Tractarian movement in the Church of England.

There are further religious associations at **Trefecca** (variously spelt), reached by taking the minor road through Llanfihangel Talyllyn and on to the B4560. Hywl Harris (1714-73) was born here and became a leading enthusiast in the 'Methodist Revival', establishing at Trefecca a religious community that supported itself by farming. The buildings of the community have been altered and now house a study centre, but the story of Harris and his times is told in an interesting museum open to the public.

The B4560 joins the main road at Talgarth, where the church has a monument to Harris and the village centre is dominated by an unusual medieval defensive tower — a final place of refuge. Those interested in primitive churches may like to make the journey from Talgarth into the eastern hills to remote Llanelieu, and another possible diversion is to the castle keep by the roadside at Bronllys, 1 mile (2km) further along the A479.

Take the A4078 and A38 for Glasbury and cross the Wye. A mile (2km) beyond the village take the minor road on the left which runs up to the isolated Maesyronnen Chapel, a very early Noncomformist chapel built in 1696 and miraculously preserved almost in its original state (including the furniture). The countryside around here will be familiar to the many devotees of Francis Kilvert's *Diary*. Kilvert was a young curate at nearby **Clyro** in the mid-nineteenth century, and a preliminary reading of his diary will add a good deal of interest to a visit here. The church which he served and the house where he lodged can be seen at Clyro, off the A38, 5 miles (8km) from Glasbury.

Kilvert was a frequent visitor to **Hay-on-Wye**, just across the valley from Clyro. It is a fascinating town of narrow streets and alleys, most notable nowadays for being the 'second-hand book centre of the world.' The formidable Hay Bluff forms a backdrop to the town, and driving over it can be a memorable experience, especially early or late in the year when the crowds have diminished. The drive takes in the magnificent viewpoint at the 'Gospel Pass' (signposted in Hay) and then plunges into the Vale of Ewyas (or Llanthony Valley).

This is the only road that penetrates the Black Mountains. Three miles (5km) after the Gospel Pass it reaches an enclave of interesting buildings at **Capel-y-ffin**. St Mary's, at the road's edge, is a tiny box of a church, complete with miniature gallery inside. A Baptist chapel lies to the east. Up a lane on the other side of the road are the surviving buildings of 'Llanthony Abbey', founded as a monastic community by Father Ignatius (the Reverend Joseph Leicester Lyne) in 1869. The venture failed, but the tomb of Father Ignatius can still be seen in the ruined choir of his church. The main buildings, later occupied by the artist Eric Gill, are privately owned. Father Ignatius' inspiration was the priory of Llanthony, further down the road. Beautifully situated and remarkably substantial, the ruins date from 1175 and are open to the public. The site had a chequered history, and a shooting lodge built in the ruins in the early eighteenth century is now a hotel. The former infirmary became a parish church and contains some interesting memorials.

About 4 miles (6km) after the priory look out for a turning on the left for **Cwmyoy**. The primitive and atmospheric little church here was involved in a landslip which distorted its structure in astonishing fashion, but it remains standing. Another church not to be missed is **Partrishow**, reached by a narrow lane on the right just after the Cwmyoy turn. It stands alone in the hills, a remarkable example of medieval survival with a famous rood screen and a vast early Norman font.

The minor road joins the A465 at Llanfihangel Crucorny for the short drive back to Abergavenny. Just over $^1/_2$ mile (1km) up the minor road to the north of Llanfihangel Crucorny it is possible to join the Offa's Dyke Path for a memorable walk above the Llanthony Valley.

Radnor

The landscape to the north of the Black Mountains is not so dramatic but is almost as empty. The old county of Radnorshire was always notorious for being the least populated in Wales and nothing much has changed since it became part of the huge new county of Powys. It stretches from the Cambrian Mountains in central Wales across to the border, forming a bare and sometimes bleak expanse of hill and moorland cut by the occasional pastoral valley. Much of it remains comparatively unknown.

Its former county town (and now the administrative centre of Powys) is **Llandrindod Wells**, a place that always astonishes visitors, who hardly expect to find, in this deeply rural countryside, the impressive buildings of a nineteenth-century spa town. Nowadays Llandrindod Wells deliberately preserves itself as a Victorian survival, and few people can resist its unique period charm. Its fascinating history and old-fashioned attractions are well-documented at the information centre, and there is also a small local museum.

Llandrindod is well placed for the exploration of Radnor. The Elan Valley, to the west, is certainly worth visiting, the attraction being the series of reservoirs constructed in the 1890s to supply water to Birmingham. The dams are fine examples of Victorian engineering and the reservoirs, set in high moorland, are old enough to have acquired great natural beauty. They are reached by way of the small town of Rhayader, to the north-west of Llandrindod. There is a visitor centre at the first dam, giving details of drives and walks.

The A483 to the north provides a very scenic route as it winds its way over the hills to Newtown. Two miles (3km) after the roundabout at Crossgates a minor road on the left is signposted Abbeycwmhir and runs down a narrow valley to the ruins of a Cistercian abbey founded in the mid-twelfth century. The walls of its huge church (longer than many cathedrals) can be clearly traced, and a memorial slab commemorates the fact that the Welsh prince Llewelyn the Last is thought to have been buried there. The peaceful village nearby is very attractive.

Further along the A483, and off the road to the right, **Llanbister** has a church of great interest, but the church that should not be missed lies below the road on the left about 1 mile (2km) further on. It is called Llananno and looks very ordinary from the outside, but it houses what is considered to be the most beautiful rood screen in Wales, probably dating from the late fifteenth century.

The road continues to climb gently, threading its way around the hills before dropping steeply and tortuously into **Newtown**. In recent years

Newtown, the old parish church and Robert Owen's tomb

Newtown has seen much new industrial and residential development, but its centre has remained unspoilt. From the early nineteenth century it was a major textile town, thriving on wool and flannel, and a terrace of weavers' houses is preserved as a museum. The world's first mail-order business was started here, sending flannel all over the world, and its warehouse still stands. It was also the birthplace of Robert Owen, who, as a mill-owner near Glasgow, was a noted factory reformer and a founder of workers' co-operatives, including one in the USA. His story is told at a small museum, and his tomb is on the site of the old church. The information centre provides information on all these topics, and also on the town's varied buildings.

The return from Newtown starts on the same road, but after 5 miles (8km) there is a turn on to the B4355, signposted Knighton. The road runs over deserted hills into the peaceful valley of the Teme, passing through **Beguildy**, which has a good example of a motte-and-bailey castle and a church with a fine rood screen. A short distance further on, at **Llanfair Waterdine**, there are paths leading up to a superbly-preserved stretch of

Offa's Dyke, and the walk southwards along the long-distance path to Knighton is highly recommended.

Knighton stands right on the Welsh border. It is a useful rather than pretty town, but there is a centre devoted almost entirely to the history of Offa's Dyke, with every sort of information about the long-distance path. From here continue southwards on the B4355 and follow the signs for Walton into a broad, idyllic valley ringed with forested hills. A lane from Walton runs up to the hilltop church of **Old Radnor**, notable not only for its interior but for the panoramic view from its churchyard. Across the valley are the outlying hills of the Radnor Forest, an extensive and deserted upland area with virtually no roads. **New Radnor** lies below them ('new' because it did not become a borough until 1562). It still has its medieval ground plan and traces of its old walls, and the mound of its castle looms prominently.

Continue west on the A44, and less than 2 miles (3km) after New Radnor, a lane on the right is the path to the waterfall picturesquely known as Water-break-its-neck. The path can be followed north into the hills, although this is really countryside for the serious walker only. At the next junction stay on the A44, which curves round the bottom of the hills to reach **Llandegley**, where the sulphur springs once made the village something of a spa. A minor road outside the village to the north leads to The Pales, a remote Quaker meeting house built in 1717. The return to Llandrindod is via the roundabout at Cross Gates.

Northern Herefordshire

Once again there is a marked contrast between Radnor and North-West Herefordshire across the border, and the visitor is bound to be struck by the transition from rugged hills and small stone hamlets to gentle pastures and prosperous villages with ancient timber-framed houses.

Leominster, standing between the better-known attractions of Ludlow and Hereford, is more often passed through than visited. Few people realise that the town preceded Hereford as the diocesan centre, having a religious community as early as the mid-seventh century, although the size of the parish church, still known as the Priory, is a clue to its former importance. For most of its history Leominster was a thriving wool and leather town, and its prosperity is indicated by some good timber-framed buildings and handsome Georgian houses. However, the outstanding symbol of civic pride is the Town Hall built in 1633 by the renowned John Abel, whose name occurs elsewhere in this chapter. It originally stood in the High Street, but in 1854 it was re-erected at the Grange, near the priory. Its open ground floor has been boxed in, but its fine carving survives.

The tour from Leominster passes through some peaceful, undulating countryside and includes several places of historical importance. Start on the B4361, once the main road to Ludlow. After Luston there is a right turn for **Berrington Hall** (National Trust), a superb late eighteenth-century house with splendid furniture, standing in grounds by 'Capability' Brown.

On returning to the main road it is worth turning off after 3 miles (5km) for the village of **Orleton**, a picturesque place with timber-framed cottages, a manor house and a church with a famous font. At **Richard's Castle** turn left through the modern village to reach the old church and castle, the centre of the original settlement. The castle, now little more than a mound, is notable for pre-dating the Norman invasion, and there is a Norman nave in the church, although much of the work is medieval.

Return to Orleton, and just beyond it turn on to the B4362. **Yarpole** is soon signposted on the left, and it is worth driving the short distance to see the attractive village and the fourteenth-century church with its unusual detached tower. The next village is **Bircher**, and on the right of the road a lane leads up to Bircher Common (National Trust), a fine place for short walks with outstanding views over Shropshire and the Welsh border. Immediately to the west of the Common is Croft, dominated by its big castle (also the property of the National Trust) which hides its medieval origins behind later modernisation, particularly that of the eighteenth century, when the interior was refurbished. The church is also of interest, and there is a good walk up to the hill fort of Croft Ambrey, with more splendid views.

At the point 3 miles (5km) further on where the road crosses the river English Heritage have restored an eighteenth-century water mill, which is occasionally open to the public. It stands close to the crossroads at Mortimers Cross, the site of a major battle between Yorkist and Lancastrian forces during the Wars of the Roses.

Continue over the crossroads to **Shobdon**, which has one of Herefordshire's more unusual churches, rebuilt in the 1750s in the extravagant 'Gothick' taste of the time and given a delightful interior. Arches from the original Norman church were set up on the hill above as a folly. The road goes on towards Presteigne, but 2 miles (3km) after Shobdon a lane turns right for **Byton**, where the hillside churchyard commands panoramic views across the valley of the Lugg. The lane passes through Byton and joins a minor road to Lingen, which is the starting point of a road heading away west into the deserted hills close to the Welsh border — a worthwhile diversion for those who appreciate solitude.

There is more sparsely-populated countryside along the Wigmore road east of Lingen, which threads its way through an area of hill and forest before joining the A4110 south of Wigmore. This is a quiet hillside place now with a picturesque centre, but throughout much of the Midddle Ages it was the headquarters of the Mortimers, one of the most powerful of the near-independent families of the Welsh Marches. Little remains as a reminder of this, apart from the unobtrusive castle remains up a lane west of the church and the negligible ruins of Wigmore Abbey 2 miles (3km) to the north. The route now is the A4110, a relief after country lanes, and then the B4360, which branches off at **Kingsland**. The church here is large and architecturally rich — a rewarding place to visit before the return to Leominster.

South Shropshire

Herefordshire merges into Shropshire west of **Ludlow**, a town that for many is the epitome of England. Within its Norman boundaries it has a wealth of timber-framed buildings, some elegant Georgian streets, the most splendid parish church in the border region and one of the country's finest castles. To discover the equally rewarding border country to the west leave Ludlow by the Teme Bridge to the south and turn right almost immediately for **Whitecliffe**. This attractive area of heath and woodland has roadside parking places with walks, and after 6 miles (10km) it is worth stopping at the tiny hamlet of **Aston** to visit the church, which has some fine Norman features. Follow the minor road through Burrington, and pass above the Clun River's extraordinary meanders to reach **Leintwardine**, a village at the confluence of the Teme and Clun that was once the Roman settlement of *Branogenium*. The church here has an unusually grand set of choir stalls with carved misericords that may have come from Wigmore Abbey, a short distance to the south.

Take the Knighton road out of Leintwardine. After 3 miles (5km) it reaches **Brampton Bryan**, a village of great charm with picturesque timber-framed houses and a green. The castle (not open) has architectural features ranging from the early fourteenth century to Elizabethan times, and the church is rare in having been rebuilt in 1656 during the Commonwealth period. One mile (2km) further on, a right turn across the Teme leads into Shropshire at **Bucknell**, a village lying on the south-eastern edge of the Clun Forest, a sparsely-populated area of low hills and moorland stretching to the Welsh border. At its centre is **Clun** itself, reached by a minor road through Chapel Lawn. The town is in two distinct parts, separated by the river bridge (there is a car park here). To the south is the church, the centre of the early settlement, dominating its surroundings with a massive Norman tower. The interior is surprisingly rich. To the north is the town that grew up around the Norman castle, a powerful structure with massive earthworks and a great ruined keep set into the side of them. Clun is built on an intimate scale and is of great architectural interest, but its finest buildings — the Trinity Hospital almshouses of 1618 — have to be sought out.

A rewarding diversion into the remoter Clun Forest can be made by taking the B4368 along the river valley towards Newcastle. Half a mile (1km) before the village the Offa's Dyke Path crosses the road, and a walk along it to the south will reveal a particularly well preserved length of the Dyke itself. Another possibility is to take the B4368 east to Clunton and turn left on to a minor road which, after 2 miles (3km), arrives at a Forestry Commission car park, the base for forest walks up to the Iron Age hill fort of Bury Ditches.

From Clun the A488 continues north to **Bishop's Castle**, a friendly small market town which has as its heart a main street running uphill between the church and the site of the castle (the remains are negligible). The road north from the town runs along the Welsh border for several miles, passing the

Half-timbered cottages at Pembridge, Herefordshire, Welsh Borders

Ludlow Castle, Shropshire, Welsh Borders

Restored estate buildings at Erddig Hall near Wrexham, North Wales

The Pontcysyllte Aqueduct carrying the Llangollen Canal 120ft above the River Dee, North Wales

Stokesay Castle

conical Corndon Hill to the west. At this point watch out for a sign to Mitchell's Fold on the left. This Bronze Age stone circle with spectacular views is reached by a lane, a track and a walk.

The A488 now climbs into an area of old mines and quarries, where lead was extracted from Roman times to the nineteenth century. The dominant hills here are the Stiperstones, a series of jagged quartzite outcrops that have given rise to much folklore. To walk them (a memorable experience on a clear day; $2^1/_2$ miles, 4km, there and back) take the road to Shelve and Pennerley 2 miles (3km) after the Mitchell's Fold turn. At Pennerley follow the signs for Bridges and look out on the left for a small car park where the walk begins.

Continue on this minor road through Bridges and Ratlinghope where it starts to climb on to the Long Mynd. This extensive area of high moorland cut by deep ravines is one of the wildest parts of Shropshire and exhilarating whether traversed on foot or by car. Follow the road that drops steeply into **Church Stretton**, a town that has much of the atmosphere of a mountain spa — which it was for a few years in the nineteenth century. An excursion from here is to the Cardingmill Valley, one of the Long Mynd's more dramatic ravines (signposted in the town).

The A49 runs straight back to Ludlow from here, but there are two notable attractions on the way. Four miles (6km) south of Church Stretton a sign indicates the way to **Acton Scott**, a farm museum that is actually a working farm where all the operations are carried out by Victorian methods. Further south, just beyond Craven Arms, is **Stokesay Castle**, a remarkably complete fortified manor house with a thirteenth-century Great Hall. Historically it is one of Britain's more important buildings, restored under private ownership and now in the care of English Heritage.

Montgomeryshire

Facing Shropshire across the border is the old county of Montgomeryshire, and for once there is no immediate contrast because the landscape changes very little at first. In particular, the tradition of timber-framed houses continues well into Wales.

Welshpool is a comfortable market town with a long Georgian and Victorian High Street dominated by a grandiose town hall. The Powysland Museum near the church covers local history. In recent years a canal centre has been developed, and at the western end of the town is the terminus of the Welshpool and Llanfair Light Railway, a restored steam line that runs westwards through deep countryside to Llanfair Caereinion. The outstanding attraction is Powis Castle (National Trust) on the Newtown road, built in the thirteenth century and continuously occupied. The castle and its fine gardens are open to the public.

Four miles (6km) south of Welshpool, and reached by driving over a hill and along a ruler-straight road, is **Montgomery**, the former county town. Little more than a large village, it is a quiet and charming place, with its old town hall looking across a Georgian market square to the church on the opposite hill. The climb to the ruined castle, dizzily set on a rocky ledge, is justified by the vast views across the Severn Valley.

The main tour from Welshpool, however, runs through some of the less well-known countryside to the north and west. Take the A490 out of town, passing the Light Railway terminus, and after 2 miles (3km) turn right for **Guilsfield**, to see the most imposing church in the area. Most of the interior dates from the fourteenth and fifteenth centuries, including the splendid panelled roof, though the church underwent a major restoration in 1879, when the present chancel screen was installed.

The road now follows an abandoned branch of the Montgomeryshire Canal and joins the A483, which passes through Llanymynech (see the tour from Shrewsbury) to Llynclys. Turn left here on to the A495 and follow the signs for Llanraeadr-yn-Mochnant. Three miles (5km) later **Llanyblodwel** is signposted to the left. It is a well-camouflaged village with an extraordinary church created by a nineteenth-century vicar, the Reverend John Parker. A bullet-shaped spire dominates the exterior, and inside it is adorned with the vicar's own decorations in colour. Parker was also responsible for the eccentric school and vicarage. The pub by the riverside is a good stop for refreshment.

The road pushes west into the Tanat Valley, and the Berwyn Mountains loom ahead. **Llanrhaeadr** is the valley's principal village, full of rugged character and the starting point for a 4 mile (6km) drive into the Berwyn Mountains to Pistyll Rhaeadr, the highest waterfall in Wales and spectacular after rain. The Berwyns form a massive barrier, best appreciated at **Llangynog**, the furthest village on the road. It was once a busy mining and quarrying centre, and is surrounded by scarred hills. A spectacular road leads over the mountains to Bala, and a minor road along the valley floor reaches **Pennant Melangell**, the remote church containing the shrine of the legendary St Monacella (ask about the key at Llangynog Post Office).

Return to Penybontfawr and turn on to the B4396, a pleasant road that passes through Cwm Hirnant to reach Lake Vyrnwy. This reservoir was completed over 100 years ago to supply water to Liverpool, and the nearby village of **Llandwddyn** was built to rehouse the inhabitants of the village submerged in the process. The conifers and the Gothic straining tower give the lake a Rhineland appearance. Vyrnwy's history is explained at the visitor centre over the dam, where walking guides can also be obtained.

The return journey can be made on the B4393 which passes through **Llanfyllin**, an attractive small town with interesting buildings along its High Street and an early eighteenth-century brick church which is rare in Wales. Take the A490 out of Llanfyllin and join the A495, which runs above the River Vyrnwy to **Meifod**, a village of great architectural variety that was once the ecclesiastical centre for a wide area. Two miles (3km) beyond it, a minor road to the right (signposted Pontrobert) passes a lane leading to the Quaker meeting house at Dolobran, erected in 1700 after the death of Charles Lloyd of Dolobran, who accompanied William Penn to America and became Deputy Governor of Pennsylvania. On returning to the main road take the B4389, which joins the A458 for the return to Welshpool and runs beside the track of the Light Railway for much of the way.

North-West Shropshire

The final border tour takes in much of North-West Shropshire and begins at the county town. **Shrewsbury** was an important Saxon settlement, standing in a natural defensive position within a loop of the River Severn, but its present tightly-packed town centre developed after the establishment of a Norman castle, the headquarters of one of William the Conqueror's most powerful provincial governors. The town prospered as a commercial centre during the Middle Ages and Tudor period and as a social centre during the eighteenth century. As a result it possesses, like Ludlow, a rich mixture of timber-framed buildings and elegant Georgian houses. There are several museums, and among some notable churches are the Norman abbey, St Mary's (a fine medieval church, now redundant) and St Chad's, a remarkable eighteenth-century structure. The town trail, available at the information centre, is a mine of information on the ancient streets and wealth of historic buildings.

North-West Shropshire is a mainly pastoral landscape with occasional sandstone outcrops and the outlying Welsh hills towards the west. Leave the town through the old suburb of Frankwell and take the A5 (North Wales) on the outskirts. This is the Holyhead Road created by the great Scottish engineer Thomas Telford at the beginning of the nineteenth century, and he was responsible for the Severn crossing at Montford Bridge, 3 miles (5km) out of Shrewsbury. At Nesscliffe, 4 miles (6km) on, it is possible to walk on to the wooded sandstone ridge and see the cave of Humphrey Kynaston, a local Robin Hood figure.

Two miles (3km) later take the left fork for **Knockin**. It is a pleasant village with an attractive variety of houses along its main street, and there is a worthwhile diversion along minor roads through Kinnerley to Melverley. The little riverside church here is timber-framed, with an unspoilt, barn-like interior.

From Melverley follow the signs for **Llanymynech**, which straddles the Welsh border and has a fascinating history as a canal centre and quarrying village. There are exhilarating walks with panoramic views on the dramatic limestone cliffs above the village. The towpath of the dried-up Mont-gomeryshire Canal also provides walking opportunities. The canal, dis-used since 1936, runs north to a junction with the popular Llangollen Canal at Welsh Frankton which is included later in the tour.

From Llanymynech take the A483 to **Oswestry**, a much-fought-over border settlement in the past and now an unpretentious market town with streets of harmonious Georgian and Victorian buildings. Less than 3 miles (5km) to the west along the B4580 is the Old Racecourse, a high stretch of common with magnificent views into Wales. The Offa's Dyke Path leads from its southern end and makes a pleasant woodland walk. Just outside the town, to the north, **'Old Oswestry'** should not be missed. It is one of the most impressive Iron Age hill forts in the country and is easily accessible.

Leave Oswestry on the A495. **Whittington** is a sprawling village, and its centrepiece is a moated castle, largely ruined but with a fine gatehouse still standing. The distinctive Victorian church stands nearby. Continue on the A495 (Ellesmere), and after about 3 miles (5km) look for a minor road on the right at Welsh Frankton (signposted Lower Frankton). It leads to the canal junction mentioned earlier. Three locks have been repaired here in prepa-ration for the proposed restoration of the Montgomeryshire Canal, and the Llangollen Canal, passing the top of them, is always busy with boats in the summer months.

Return to the main road and continue to **Ellesmere**, a friendly small town with a canal wharf and the extensive lake called The Mere to the east of the town. It is the largest of several lakes in the area created at the end of the Ice Age, and a noted wildfowl sanctuary. There are opportunities for walking and boating here, and by walking along the canal towpath it is possible to pass the secretive Blake Mere on the way to Colemere, now designated as a country park. The return to Shrewsbury is via the A528, which is a most enjoyable rural highway, passing through several old villages typical of this tranquil countryside.

Further Information

— The Welsh Borders —

Places of Interest

THE BLACK MOUNTAINS
Abergavenny
Museum
The Castle
☎ 0873 4282
Open: March to October, weekdays
11am-1pm and 2-5pm, Sundays 2-5pm.
November to February closes weekdays
at 4pm and on Sundays.

Tretower Court and Castle
10 miles (16km) north-west of
Abergavenny on A479
☎ 0874 730279
Open: April to October weekdays
9.30am-6.30pm, Sundays 2-6.30pm.
November to March weekdays 9.30am-
4pm, Sundays 2-4pm.

NORTHERN HEREFORDSHIRE
Leominster
Berrington Hall
3 miles (5km) north of Leominster off
A49, ☎ 0568 5721
Open: May to end of September,
Wednesday to Sunday (and Bank Holi-
day Mondays) 2-6pm. April and October,
Saturday and Sunday 2-5pm.
Also Easter.

Burton Court
5 miles (8km) west of Leominster off A44
☎ 05447 321
Open: Spring Bank Holiday to end of
September, Wednesday, Thursday,
Saturday, Sunday and Bank Holiday
Mondays, 2.30-6pm.

Croft Castle
5 miles (8km) north-west of Leominster
☎ 056885 246
Opening times as for Berrington Hall.

WESTERN HEREFORDSHIRE
Hereford
Cathedral Chained Library
Open: April to October weekdays
10.30am-12.30pm and 2-4pm.
Restricted winter opening.

Churchill Gardens Museum
Venns Lane
☎ 0432 267409
Open: Tuesday to Sunday (summer)
2-5pm.
Closed on Sundays in winter.

Cider Museum
Pomona Place
Whitecross Road
☎ 0432 354207
Open: April to October daily 10am-
5.30pm. November to March, Monday to
Saturday 1-5pm.

Museum and Art Gallery
Broad Street
☎ 0432 268121
Open: Tuesday to Friday 10am-6pm
(5pm Thursday). Saturdays 10am-5pm
(summer), 10am-4pm (winter).
Open Bank Holiday Mondays.

The Old House
☎ 0432 268121
Open: Monday 10am-1pm. Tuesday to
Friday 10am-1pm and 2-5pm. Saturdays
(summer) 10am-1pm and 2-5.30pm,
Saturdays (winter) 10am-1pm.
Open Bank Holiday Mondays.

St John Medieval Museum
Coningsby Street
☎ 0432 272837
Open: Easter to end of September daily
except Mondays and Fridays, 2-5pm.

Kington
Hergest Croft Gardens
☎ 0544 230160
Open: May to end of October 1.30-
6.30pm.

Moccas
Moccas Court
Off B4352
☎ 09817 381
Open: April to end of September, Thurs-
days 2-6pm.

TOURS FROM MONMOUTH
Chepstow
Castle
☎ 02912 4065
Open: April to October daily 9.30am-
6.30pm November to March weekdays
9.30am-4pm, Sundays 2-4pm.

Museum
Bridge Street
☎ 0291 625981
Social and economic history of Chepstow
and district.
Open: March to end of October, weekdays 10.30am-1pm and 2-5pm, Sunday
2-5.30pm.

Monmouth
**Local History Centre and Nelson
Museum**
Priory Street
☎ 0600 3519
Open: weekdays 10am-1pm, Sundays
2-5pm.

Raglan
Raglan Castle
Off A40 west of Monmouth
☎ 0291 690228
Open: April to October daily 9.30am-
6.30pm. November to March weekdays
9.30am-4pm, Sundays 2-4pm.

Tintern
Tintern Abbey
☎ 02918 251
Open: April to October daily 9.30am-
6.30pm. November to March weekdays
9.30am-4pm, Sundays 2-4pm.

MONTGOMERYSHIRE
Llanfyllin
Bird and Butterfly World
☎ 0691 84751
Open: Good Friday to end of September
10am-6pm.

Oswestry
Bicycle Museum
Arthur Street
Open: weekdays except Thursday
9.30am-4pm.

The Marches Military Museum
Queens Head
Off A5 east of Oswestry

☎ 069188 335
Open: daily 10am-6pm.

Old Oswestry Hill Fort
On western outskirts of town
Unrestricted admission.

Welshpool
Powis Castle
Off A483 south of Welshpool
☎ 0938 554336
Open: 1 April to 30 June and 1 September
to 4 November daily except Monday and
Tuesday. July and August daily except
Monday. Castle open: 12noon-5pm,
Museum and gardens open: 11am-6pm.
Gardens open all year.

Powysland Museum and Canal Centre
Canal Wharf
☎ 0938 554656
Open: Monday, Tuesday, Thursday,
Friday 11am-1pm and 2-5pm. From
Whitsun to end of September, Saturdays
10am-1pm, Sundays 2-5pm.
Also Saturdays 2-5pm in winter.

Welshpool and Llanfair Light Railway
☎ 0938 810441
Terminus on western outskirts of town.
Narrow gauge line running to Llanfair
Caereinion. Timetables available at
information centre.

RADNOR
Llandrindod Wells
Museum
Temple Street
☎ 0597 4513
Open: Monday to Saturday 10am-
12.30pm and 2-5pm. Closed Saturday
afternoons from October to April, also on
Bank Holidays.

NORTH-WEST SHROPSHIRE
Atcham
Attingham Park
4 miles (6km) east of Shrewsbury on A5
☎ 074377 203
Open: Easter (or 31 March) to end of
September, Saturday to Wednesday 1.30-
5pm (Bank Holiday Mondays 11am-
5pm.) In October Saturdays and Sundays
1.30-5pm. Park open daily.

Shrewsbury
Castle and Regimental Museum
☎ 0743 58516
Open: daily 10am-4pm, closed on Sundays from November to Easter.

Clive House Museum
College Hill
☎ 0743 54811
Open: Monday 2-5pm, Tuesday to Saturday 10am-1pm and 2-5pm.

Rowley's House Museum
Barker Street
☎ 0743 61196
Open: weekdays 10am-5pm, Sundays 12noon-5pm (closed on Sundays from November to Easter.)

Wroxeter
Roman City of *Viroconium*
5 miles (8km) south-east of Shrewsbury off B4380
☎ 074375 330
Open: Good Friday (or 1 April) to end of September daily 10am-6pm. October to March Tuesday to Sunday 10am-4pm.

SOUTH SHROPSHIRE
Clun
Castle
Free admission and unrestricted access.

Ludlow
Butter Cross Museum
Church Street
☎ 0584 873857
Open: April to September, Monday to Saturday 10.30am-1pm and 2 5pm. Also Sundays in June, July and August.

Castle
☎ 0584 873947
Open: May to September daily 10.30am-6pm. In October and November and from February to April 10.30am-4pm.

Stokesay Castle
Off A49 north-west of Ludlow at Craven Arms
☎ 0588 672544
Open: April to September daily except Tuesday, 10am-6pm. In March and October daily except Tuesday, 10am-5pm. In November weekends 10am-dusk.

Tourist Information Centres

Abergavenny
Swan Meadow, Cross Street
☎ 0873 77588

Builth Wells
Groe Car Park, ☎ 0982 553307

Chepstow
The Gatehouse, High Street
☎ 02912 3772

Church Stretton
Church Street, ☎ 0694 723133

Hay-on-Wye
Car Park, ☎ 0497 820144

Hereford
Town Hall Annexe, ☎ 0432 268430

Knighton
The Old School, ☎ 0547 528753
also
Offa's Dyke Centre, At the Old School

Leominster
6 School Lane, ☎ 0568 6460

Llandrindod Wells
Town Hall, ☎ 0597 2600

Llanfyllin
Council Offices, ☎ 069184 8868

Ludlow
Castle Street, ☎ 0584 875053

Monmouth
Shire Hall, ☎ 0600 3899

Newtown
Central Car Park, ☎ 0686 625580

Oswestry
Mile End Services, ☎ 0691 662488
also
The Library, Arthur Street
☎ 0691 662753

Shrewsbury
The Square
☎ 0743 50761

Tintern
The Abbey
☎ 0291 689431

Welshpool
Vicarage Gardens Car Park
☎ 0938 552043

8 • North Wales

North Wales has an infinite variety of landscapes, a fact hardly appreciated by those who equate 'North Wales' with the mountains of Snowdonia. In the extreme west the Lleyn Peninsula, behind a formidable mountain shield, has been historically one of the least accessible parts of Wales. The stone and slate industries have largely declined, leaving their mark on many of the hills, but the farmers have ensured that it remains a working landscape and a stronghold of traditional Welsh life in spite of some holiday development around its long coastline. Much the same can be said about the island of Anglesey, where the fertile land and mild climate encouraged much prehistoric settlement, and where the Celtic way of life was able to develop independently of Roman rule. Its traditional character is summed up in its affectionate nickname Mam Cymru — the Mother of Wales. The island was for centuries the granary and dairy of the bleak North Wales mainland, and its fringe of beaches can easily hide the fact that the interior is still given over to agriculture.

The area known as Snowdonia, on the other hand, has been a National Park since 1951, and at the peak of the holiday season it suffers from a huge influx of tourists, walkers and climbers. In fact 'beaten tracks' become a physical reality. However, at other times of the year it is astonishingly easy to recapture the solitary grandeur that broods over the concentrated and intermingled mountain ranges of northern Snowdonia. In the southern part of the National Park the mountains are less dramatic, and the landscape is one of rolling hills, deep valleys and forests lying behind an attractive coastline — the northern stretch of the great sweep of Cardigan Bay, where Aberystwyth marks the divide between northern and southern Wales.

East of Snowdonia the mountain peaks give way quite suddenly to the more intricate landscape of Clwyd — the old counties of Denbighshire and Flintshire. The former industrial areas close to the English border are still densely populated, but are cut off from the rest of Clwyd by the striking hills known as the Clwydian Range, running north to south. On their western side the River Clwyd runs through a wide pastoral plain before the land rises again to present a vista of rolling hills and narrow valleys. The Berwyn Mountains form an effective barrier to the south. Apart from concentrated holiday development along the north coast, this varied region, rich in historical associations, has been largely neglected by visitors.

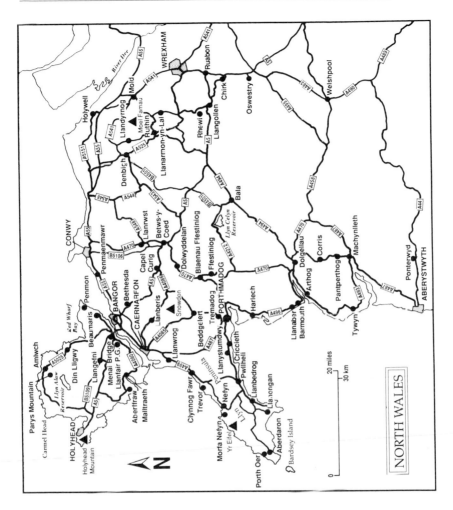

Apart from the Deeside conurbation, North Wales has few large towns. Even important cultural and administrative 'capitals' like Aberystwyth, Bangor and Caernarfon or industrial centres like Wrexham are modest in size and homely in character; nor do they have the picturesque quality that comes from centuries of steady development. What they have is the business-like solidity of the nineteenth century, whether that business was rural commerce, industry or tourism. If the suburban rash of modern housing is ignored they remain grey, unpretentious working towns.

A vast amount of tourist literature is now available from information centres, but its sheer quantity can be confusing as well as helpful. This chapter aims to provide a bird's eye view and to direct the visitor towards the authentic landscape and distinctive character of North Wales.

Anglesey

Until the 1820s Anglesey suffered severely from isolation, but that changed in 1826 with the arrival of the London-Holyhead road and Thomas Telford's magnificent suspension bridge. Although the main road now crosses by a later bridge to the south, it is worth travelling from Bangor on the old route and starting the visit to Anglesey in **Menai Bridge**, the small town that grew up afterwards. It has a Victorian character, but there is a reminder of much earlier life here in the fifteenth-century Church of St Tysilio on its small island to the west of the town.

A road along the shore leads to **Beaumaris**, where the squat castle confronts the mountain panorama on the other side of the Straits. It was built in the late thirteenth century by Edward I, and is one of the finest of a whole string of castles built across North Wales in order to subdue the country once and for all. Beaumaris was once Anglesey's main port, and it still has a cheerful maritime character. To the north of the main street the handsome parish church stands close to the grim gaol, which is open to the public. From here continue along the shore past the castle for **Penmon**. The very early priory was rebuilt in the thirteenth century and remains the parish church. The prior's house is still occupied. A path nearby leads to St Seiriol's Well, which may have been the cell of the founder, but perhaps the most striking building is the huge dovecot built in about 1600.

Return to Llangoed and pass through it, following the signs for Llanddona. The road passes the Iron Age hill fort of Bwrdd Arthur (or Dinsylwi), where there are fine coastal views, and descends to Llanddona on a road with panoramas of Snowdonia to the left and the sands of Red Wharf Bay to the right. Just before the village a lane on the left (fork right after turning) leads to Llaniestin church, a tiny L-shaped building with a dignified fourteenth-century monument to its founder.

To negotiate the concentration of holiday activity around Red Wharf Bay make for Pentraeth and take the A5025 for 5 miles (8km). At the roundabout go straight over and down the minor road to visit **Din Lligwy**, a well preserved hut settlement of the fourth century. More evocative perhaps is the nearby ruined Norman church, Hen Capel Lligwy, with its tiny crypt.

Return to the roundabout and continue on the A5025 (Amlwch). At Brynrefail the road to the right gives access to the sandy beaches of Dulas Bay, but an alternative is to take the left turn through Ty Mawr to a layby, where a track and path lead to the top of Mynydd Bodafon, a rocky outcrop from which just about the whole of the North Anglesey Coast can be seen.

On the approach to Amlwch the attention is caught by a brown and orange wasteland on the left. This is **Parys Mountain**, where the Romans mined for copper and where a rich vein was discovered in the eighteenth century, bringing the prosperity that created Amlwch as the exporting port. At the roundabout just outside Amlwch take the left turn, and after 2 miles (3km) a layby is the starting point for waymarked walks over this eerie and often spectacular landscape.

There is good cliff walking west of Amlwch, and the walk from the

Telford's suspension bridge over the Menai Straits

eastern side of the attractive little harbour of Cemaes to the promontory fort of Dinas Gynfor is particularly recommended. Another possibility is to drive a little way past Cemaes to the village of Tregele, where a right turn leads to **Cemlyn Bay**. This sweeping arc of shingle is a nature reserve, and from the car park on the western side there are paths to the headland of Trwyn Cemlyn and to the remote, tiny twelfth-century Llanrhwydrys church. It is possible to walk on from the church to the secluded cove of Hen Borth and further still to Carmel Head, an exhilarating place on a fine day.

The A5025 now moves inland, but roads on the right lead to a succession of small bays and beaches like Porth Swtan, Porth Trwyn, Porth Trefadog and Porth Twyn Mawr. Porth Swtan is particularly recommended for walking on its northern side.

Just north of Valley turn on to the B5109. There are signs indicating the way to **Llyn Alaw**, the island's largest reservoir, where a visitor centre gives information about walking and fishing. The nearby Church of Llanbabo is of interest. Further along the B5109, **Llangefni** was once Anglesey's county town and still provides a cattle market and shopping centre for the agricultural community. It has a good eighteenth-century church, and there is a pleasant riverside walk to the north of the town. From here it is a short distance back to Menai Bridge, but it is worth stopping at **Penmynnydd** to look at the church and attractive almshouses, and perhaps to visit the nearby Butterfly Palace.

The tour of southern Anglesey starts on the A4080 from Menai Bridge. Drive into **Llanfairpwllgwyngyll** (the much-publicised extended version of the name was a Victorian publicity stunt — it is usually known as Llanfair P.G.). Prominent here on its tall column is the statue of the Marquess of

Anglesey, who fought at Waterloo. The stairs inside can be climbed for the views.

Continue on the A4080 and very soon there are signs to Plas Newydd (National Trust), a late eighteenth-century house standing in fine grounds with views across to Snowdonia. The sumptuous interior includes a small museum devoted to the Battle of Waterloo, and the garden contains an early Bronze Age burial chamber. At the next turn to the right a road leads to Bryn Celli Ddu, another burial chamber, reckoned to be the finest of many in North Wales.

At the village of Newborough a road to the left runs through a forest to Newborough Warren, a vast area of sand dunes that is now a nature reserve. There are forest walks here, but the most interesting walk is undoubtedly along the shore to Llanddwyn Island, with its ruined church and old lighthouse.

Return to the A4080. The next village, **Malltraeth**, lies between the vast Malltraeth Sands and Malltraeth Marsh, a noted habitat for wildfowl which can be observed from the canalside footpath. Two miles (3km) further on at Llangadwaladr the church has an exceptional fifteenth-century east window and some fine memorials. There are further acres of dunes on the left before **Aberffraw**, an unspoilt place that was once the court of the Princes of Gwynedd in the post-Roman period. There is a good coastal walk out to the cliffs and round to Porth Cwyfan, with its ruined church on the shore. Two miles (3km) beyond Aberffraw a roadside car park is the start of a cliff path leading to the Neolithic chamber tomb of **Barcloddiad y Gawres**, restored to something like its original state, including the long passage to the tomb chamber.

The road now curves inland and joins the A5, crossing to Holy Island on Telford's massive Stanley Embankment of 1822 and entering **Holyhead**, a Victorian town that grew up in the nineteenth century as an Irish ferry terminal. The Church of St Cybi is of interest, being sited within the surviving walls of a Roman fort, and there is always plenty of summer activity around the old and new harbours. The town is dominated by Holyhead mountain to the west, reached by taking the South Stack road out of town. Opposite the first car park (provided by the RSPB) a short path leads to the remains of a group of Celtic huts of the Roman period, and from the final car park it is possible to climb to the top of the mountain and enjoy the spectacular views over a dramatic coastline. The west and south coasts of Holy Island offer good cliff walking, and while the area around Treaddur can be crowded in the summer with visitors to the very accessible beaches, at other times of the year it is a very rewarding destination.

The quickest route back is the A5, an uneventful journey which can be broken by a visit to the Henblas Country Park, reached by turning onto the B4422 (Llangefni) 4 miles (6km) after Gwalchmai.

The Lleyn Peninsula

The tour begins at Caernarfon. Take the A487 south, and after 3 miles (5km) turn on to the A499. Very soon the village of **Llanwrog** is signposted on the right. It is a nineteenth-century estate village built by the owner of nearby Parc Glynllifon, the grounds of which are open to visitors.

The road now begins to squeeze between the sea and the steep quarried hills of Bwlch Mawr and Gyrn Goch. At the foot of Bwlch Mawr lies **Clynnog Fawr**, with its unexpectedly magnificent church. Three miles (5km) later a right turn signposted Trefor leads to the quay where granite was loaded from the huge quarries above the village.

Meanwhile the main road turns to run south, and the tour continues on the B4417, which skirts the bottom of the hill with a triple peak known as The Rivals (a corruption of its real name **Yr Eifl**). The hill has one of the most important Iron Age hill forts in Wales, and a path to it begins on the right about $1/2$ mile (1km) out of Llanaelhaearn. There are further walking opportunities along the minor road that turns right in the centre of Llithfaen, 2 miles (3km) after. The road ends at a car park, and shortly before it a track starts across the hills, passing above the quarries and offering fine sea views.

Nefyn and its neighbour **Morfa Nefyn** have good sandy beaches, and since the Lleyn is so much bound up with the sea it is well worth visiting Lleyn Historical and Maritime Museum in the former St Mary's Church. It is possible to park near the shore at the western end of Morfa Nefyn to walk over to Porth Dinllaen, an idyllic hamlet a few yards from the sea, and from the neighbouring headland walks extend for many miles along the tranquil coast to the west.

After Morfa Nefyn the B4417 runs through Tudweiliog, and 3 miles (5km) after, where the road begins to run beneath Mynydd Cefnamlwch, a lane on the right leads to the lonely Penllech church with its unspoilt early nineteenth-century interior (key at the farmhouse). The next minor road on the right leads into a little wooded valley, where Llangwnnadl church is tucked away, extraordinarily wide and containing a sixth-century incised stone and a notable font.

After the village of Pen-y-groesion take the road that branches off to the right to reach **Porth Oer**. It is a good bathing beach, and the road past it goes on to approach the splendid coastline at the extreme end of the peninsula, much of which is National Trust property. From the road's end there are plenty of opportunities for walks to the headlands for views across the treacherous sound to Bardsey Island, an early monastic settlement and a popular place of pilgrimage. It is now a bird sanctuary.

It is possible to walk right round the headland to the seaside village of **Aberdaron**. It has an attractive small harbour with the old pilgrims' church, restored in the nineteenth century after being abandoned. At the village of Rhiw to the east Plas-yn-Rhiw (National Trust) is a seventeenth-century house modernised in Regency times and standing in large gardens with marvellous views. The house stands at one end of the long stretch of empty beach known as Hell's Mouth (bathing is dangerous here). The road moves well inland to reach the more sheltered shore at Abersoch, a lively sailing harbour of great charm. Nearby to the south-west is the outstanding church at the old lead mining village of **Llanengan**, noted for its fine medieval screens and font, while a walk above the beach to the south provides good views of the St Tudwal's Islands.

The coast immediately east of Abersoch is of no great interest, and it is pleasanter to go north and join the B4413 just outside Mynytho. Almost at once a lane leads left to Capel Newydd, dating from 1769 and probably the oldest Nonconformist chapel in North Wales (the key can be obtained from the house at the turning). Turn right now on to the B4415, which passes along the wooded Horon Valley towards Pwllheli, the peninsula's biggest town.

The village of **Llanystumdwy**, further along the A487, is famous for its associations with David Lloyd George, a controversial Prime Minister during and after World War I. A village walk directs visitors to various places connected with him, including his grave, and there is another enjoyable walk beside the River Dwyfor.

It is now only a short distance to the last town on the Lleyn Peninsula. **Criccieth** is a small and pleasantly old-fashioned holiday resort with an excellent bathing beach and a thirteenth-century castle on the shore. A coastal walk starts on the western side of the castle and runs along the shore to Llanystumdwy.

Snowdonia

The National Park is covered in four tours, and **Bangor** is the starting point for an exploration of northern Snowdonia. Modest in size, it is a cathedral city and university town at the northern end of the Menai Straits, with an important Museum of Welsh Antiquities, an art gallery and a theatre. There is an invigorating waterfront area, where the fine Victorian pier has recently been restored and opened to the public.

Leave the town on the A5 (Conwy). Almost immediately Penrhyn Castle (National Trust) is signposted — an extravagant early nineteenth-century creation in Norman style with a lavish interior that also includes some interesting special displays. The wealth that went into its building came from the next village, **Bethesda**, named after its impressive chapel and backed by the immense Penrhyn slate quarries. Usually dismissed as featureless, the village centre is worth a stroll to study the variety of building styles.

Beyond Bethesda the road begins to approach the Nant Ffrancon pass, and there are few more exciting vistas in Wales than the mountains that begin to loom intimidatingly closer. The top of the pass is reached at Ogwen Cottage, the starting point of the Cwm Idwal nature trail (a booklet is available). With the tranquil Llyn Ogwen and the Carneddau range on one side the road now passes beneath the menacing crags of Tryfan, a mountain where many great climbers gained their first experience. After an expanse of open moorland it descends gently into Capel Curig, a sprawling road-side village dominated by the peak of Moel Siabod and containing several Victorian hotels that catered for the early tourists.

The descent continues into a heavily-forested landscape until the valley bottom is reached at **Betws-y-Coed**. It is worth visiting the information centre to obtain leaflets about the wide variety of forest walks, and among the man-made attractions are a railway museum and Thomas Telford's splendid cast-iron bridge at the bottom of the village.

Take the B5106 (Llanrwst) from here. It runs up the Conwy Valley beneath the forested hills, and after 4 miles (6km) the Gwydir Uchaf Chapel is signposted on the left. Originally a private chapel for nearby Gwydir Castle, it was built in 1604 and has a notable painted ceiling and much fine woodwork. Just across the valley is **Llanrwst**, a cheerful little market town with a bridge that dates from 1636 and a church containing an exceptional rood screen and loft and the fine Wynn family chapel of 1634.

Back on the B5106 the next village is **Trefriw**, famous for its woollen mills and for its spa (both open to the public). A minor road west from here runs up the Crafnant Valley, and a left turn off it at the edge of the village leads to the remote and unspoilt Llanrhychwyn church.

Return to the B5106 and look for the signpost on the left to the attractive village of Roewen, the starting point for a good walk west along a Roman road to the Bwlch y Ddeufaen pass. The road now reaches **Conwy**, an ancient estuary town dominated by its magnificent late thirteenth-century castle. The information centre provides ample literature about the wealth of attractions in the town and its surroundings (including many fine walks), and a leisurely stroll of the town centre and quay will reveal a rich variety of architecture.

The busy A55 follows the coast to Bangor, but a preferable route from Conwy is the old coach road to Penmaenmawr that goes through the Sychnant pass, with the hill fort of Alltwen to the north. **Penmaenmawr** lies beneath a heavily-quarried headland that is notable for prehistoric associations, and a trail available in the town provides a useful guide to accessible sites. There is a similar trail for Llanfairfechan, another good starting place for mountain walks and an attractive little town in itself. The approach to Bangor is dominated by Penrhyn Castle, and it is worth stopping at Llandegai, the estate village, to see the Victorian cottages and the fine church with its many family monuments.

The second tour in the National Park includes Snowdon itself and begins in **Caernarfon**, like Conwy a town fortified by Edward I with a magnificent and well preserved castle. There is an information centre with details of this and several other attractions in the town, including a maritime museum and a Roman fortress.

The tour starts on the A4086 (Llanberis), which after 3 miles (5km) passes through Llanrug. The village is unremarkable, but signposted from it is Bryn Bras Castle, a mock-Norman creation of the 1830s, where panoramic views can be enjoyed from the gardens. A little further on the road meets the extreme end of Llyn Padarn and runs beside it to **Llanberis**, whose

The Miners' Track; a route to the summit of Snowdon for the more energetic

attractions include Dolbadarn Castle, a lakeside railway, The Power of Wales (a branch of the National Museum of Wales) and the Welsh Slate Museum, situated in the spectacular Dinorwic quarries on the other side of the lake. Llyn Padarn is a country park, and a leaflet describes various walks, including a complete circuit of the lake.

The quaint rack-railway to the summit of **Snowdon** (3,559ft, 1,085m) was established here in 1896 (there may be trouble in finding a seat in the peak season) but there are also half a dozen paths to the summit, all fully described in a set of National Park leaflets. The easiest, and longest, runs close to the railway and presents few problems. Two more start at the top of the Llanberis Pass, a beautiful and dramatic climb on the A4086, best appreciated from a Sherpa bus. The two paths — the Pyg Track and the Miners' Track — start from the Pen-y-Pass car park at the head of the pass. Like the other tracks they are suitable only for the reasonably agile and demand proper clothing and footwear.

The A4086 meets the A498 beyond Pen-y-Pass, close to the Pen-y-Gwrd, a legendary mountaineers' hotel. Turn on to the A498 and enter the beautiful valley of Nantgwynant. About 1 mile (2km) from Pen-y-Gwrd is a car park offering stunning views across to Snowdon and down the valley itself to Llyn Gwynant. Bethania, just below the lake, is the start of the Watkin path to Snowdon — recommended only for the fit — and the road then passes tranquil Llyn Dinas and runs into Beddgelert. Just before the village the Sygun Copper Mine has been re-opened, and there is a chance to be guided round the complex underground workings.

Beddgelert is a picturesque little place with a bridge near the confluence of two chattering rivers at its centre, and is an excellent stop for a meal. From here take the A4085 (Caernarfon), which runs through a deep valley with opportunities to park and walk in the Beddgelert Forest before arriving at Rhydd-Ddu. The car park at the entry to the village is the start of another route to Snowdon summit. The sixth path starts 2 miles (3km) further along the road. Both are fairly easy but unspectacular. An interesting diversion from Rhydd-Ddu is the B4418 over the hills to the dramatic Nantlle quarries. The A4085 now runs past Llyn Cwellyn and returns to Caernarfon.

The third Snowdonia tour takes in the central area of the National Park and starts in **Porthmadog**, which, like its neighbour Tremadog, takes its name from William Madocks (1773-1828) who did much to develop the area. The neat little planned town of **Tremadog**, with its interesting architecture, is well worth a visit, and much of Porthmadog's history is shown in the maritime museum. It is still very much a sailing centre.

Take the A497 across the embankment, and immediately there are signs to the right for **Portmeirion**, one of North Wales' most astonishing creations. Sir Clough Williams-Ellis, a gifted architect, bought this wooded headland in the late 1920s and proceeded to build on it an Italian fantasy village with several structures brought from elsewhere. It is a graceful and entertaining place and open to visitors for a fee.

The road passes through sprawling Penrhyndeudraeth and begins to run beneath heavily-forested land where there are several opportunities to park and walk close to the Ffestiniog railway track. Continue across the river to Maentwrog. The large house in the trees opposite is Plas Tan-y-Bwlch, the National Park Study Centre, once the home of quarry-owner William Oakley, who built Maentwrog as his estate village.

Continue on the A496 along the beautiful Vale of Ffestiniog. The valley gradually closes in until the road runs directly through the trees, with several parking places for exploration on foot. At Tanygrisiau much has been done to open up the pumped-storage hydro-electric scheme to the visitor, including a bus service to the upper storage dam from which there are spectacular views. The most remarkable views, however, are those on the approach to **Blaenau Ffestiniog**, where the straggling grey town seems in constant danger of being engulfed by the slate workings rising behind it. Two of the former quarries are open to the public.

Continue north on the A470 over spectacular hills and enter the Lledr Valley at Dolwyddelan. Signposted just before the village is the castle, which dates from the late twelfth century and was reputedly the birthplace of Prince Llewelyn the Great, but of equal interest is the sixteenth-century old church with its fine rood screen. The road now continues through the attractive valley and runs into Betws-y-Coed (described in the first Snowdonia tour).

Leave on the A5 which, over the next few miles, twists and turns as it follows a contour along the side of the Conwy Valley before emerging on to high moorland at Pentrefoelas and running through an expanse of scattered farms, sheep and dry stone walls. After Cerrigydrudion watch out on the right for the turn on to the B4501, which makes its way south across bare moorland totally unaffected by tourism before joining the A4212 at Frongoch and entering Bala.

Standing at the head of the largest natural lake in Wales is **Bala** with a long main street of varied and interesting buildings and useful shops. The information centre provides literature about the history of the town (very much tied up with the history of Welsh politics and culture) and about its attractions, which include a good deal of sailing activity and a lakeside narrow-gauge railway, easily the best way of viewing Llyn Tegid.

It is now necessary to return on the A4212, which winds its way around the Llyn Celyn reservoir. There are several parking places, including one by the little chapel that was built to replace one submerged beneath the lake. Beyond the reservoir the road runs between the peaks of Arenig Fach on the right and Arenig Fawr on the left. They are not readily accessible, although Arenig Fawr has a memorial on its summit to the crew of an American bomber which crashed on the mountain in 1943. Also visible on the left is the track bed of the dismantled railway that must have provided a memorable ride through this wild country.

At the village of Trawsfynydd the reservoir is dominated by the nuclear power station. Turn right on to the A470, and look out for a sign on the left indicating a parking place for a good walk along the north shore of the lake. After this the road goes on to rejoin the early section of the tour at Maentwrog.

The final Snowdonia tour covers the large area of the southern National Park, with Dolgellau as the starting point. **Dolgellau** lies near the confluence of the rivers Wnion and Mawddach, at the head of the broad Mawddach Estuary and beneath the heights of Cader Idris. Its older buildings (mainly nineteenth century) are distinctive in their granite and slate construction, and narrow, irregular streets lead away from the handsome central square. National Park leaflets describe various routes up Cader Idris, but there are good shorter expeditions here too, including the famous Precipice Walk and Torrent Walk and an enjoyable path along the Mawddach Estuary.

The tour begins on the A470, which heads north along the Mawddach Valley, running through Coed-y-Brenin (the King's Forest). With its rivers, streams and waterfalls this is fine walking country, and the Forestry Commission's visitor centre at Maesgwm, signposted off the road after about 5 miles (8km), provides a range of leaflets describing the features of the forest and waymarked trails within it.

The road runs out of the forest and passes Llyn Trawsfynydd (covered in the previous tour). Make for Maentwrog and take the A496 (Harlech), which soon begins to run beside the broad expanse of Traeth Bach Estuary with good views across to Portmeirion. **Harlech** is a small town best known for a superb castle built by Edward I as one of the series that included Caernarfon, Conwy and Beaumaris. Apart from its intrinsic splendour the castle offers panoramic views from its walls. The empty mountains to the east of Harlech, known as the Rhinogs, offer opportunities for walks of varying difficulty, and details can be obtained from the information centre. For the less active, one good way of experiencing the dramatic landscape is to drive up the lane from Llanbedr, 3 miles (5km) to the south, through the Artro Valley to the lake at Cwm Bychan and then walk along the ancient track known as the Roman Steps.

The A496 continues south past beaches that have been developed for holidaymakers, but just before Barmouth it is worth stopping at **Llanaber** to visit the unspoilt thirteenth-century church just above the sands and to look at the many graves in its churchyard. Barmouth itself is an attractive Victorian resort made accessible by the railway. Apart from its beach attractions there are several easy walks on to the hills above the town, and also the 'Panorama Walk' along the side of the Mawddach Estuary.

Pedestrians can cross the mouth of the estuary by ferry to the Fairbourne narrow-gauge railway or by way of the railway bridge. Motorists have to follow the estuary inland to the Penmaenpool toll bridge, on the far side of which is the start of a splendid estuary walk for bird-watchers along a disused railway track (an information centre is usually open by the bridge).

The road (now the A493) returns along the southern side of the estuary. At **Arthog** it is possible to walk up past the church to a series of waterfalls and a fine viewpoint or to drive along the narrow road to the Cregennen lakes. Soon afterwards the estuary disappears abruptly and the road and railway are forced close together between the sea and the hills, passing through the little seaside village of Llwyngwril. Just over 2 miles (3km) further on look out for the isolated church below the road on the left. It belongs to the tiny hamlet of Llangelynnin and has a rare unspoilt interior. A sharp turn inland now leads past Llanegryn and across the tortuous Dysynni River to Bryn Crug. A minor road here runs up the Dysinni Valley, passing beneath the remarkable crag called Bird Rock, a nesting place for cormorants, and further along the same road is Castell y Bere, the ruins of a thirteenth-century castle perched on a crag with magnificent mountain and valley views.

Back on the main road, **Tywyn** is the next town, situated well away from its popular sands and possessing a notable church as well as the terminus of the Tal-y-Llyn narrow-gauge railway, which runs for over 7 scenic miles (11km) to good walking country in the hills (there is also an associated museum). Continuing south, the road is forced inland once again by the Dyfi Estuary. Aberdyfi was once a commercial port and is now a very pleasant sailing centre and quiet seaside resort.

It is now time to leave the coast, as the road runs inland beside the estuary and through the village of Pennal. Shortly afterwards there is a worthwhile diversion to the old market town of **Machynlleth** before starting the climb north through the forested Dulas Valley. One of the more unusual attractions in the area is signposted at **Pantperthog**. In a former slate quarry opposite the village is the Centre for Alternative Technology, a fascinating place where research is conducted into conservation, energy-saving and wind, sun and water power. In addition to the exhibits there is a restaurant and an excellent bookshop.

Corris was once an important centre of slate production, but is now a quiet village with a small museum devoted to the railway which once carried slate from here down to the estuary. Not far beyond it is a turn to the left leading to a road that runs along the upper end of the Dysini Valley past Tal-y-Llyn lake to Abergynolwyn, another slate village that is now a centre for forest walking and the terminus of the Tal-y-Llyn Railway. The main road now crosses Bwlch Llyn Bach, a dramatic pass running between steep hills before dropping steadily back into Dolgellau.

Aberystwyth (region)

For powerful economic reasons Cardiff became the capital of Wales, but **Aberystwyth** has a good claim to be the spiritual capital. Lying on the dividing line between north and south, removed from strong English influence, the Principality's oldest university town and the home of the National Library of Wales, it has always been regarded as a stronghold of Welsh traditions and culture.

It has maintained this reputation in spite of the arrival of a railway across mid-Wales in the late nineteenth century, which gave the town its present character as a genteel seaside resort. It remains a pleasantly old-fashioned place with its shingle beach, small harbour and seafront of harmonious terraces closed off by Constitution Hill to the north (climbed by a cliff railway) and to the south by the extraordinary Gothic buildings originally intended as a hotel and later adopted for the University College. Much of the history of Aberystwyth and Cardiganshire is illustrated at the Ceredigion Museum, and there are regular exhibitions at the National Library of Wales on Penglais Hill.

To the east of the Aberystwyth is the **Rheidol Valley**, and for many years one of the pleasures of a visit here has been a ride on the narrow-gauge steam railway up to Devil's Bridge, a winding route with splendidly contrasting views of valley and forested hillside. Near the terminus there are waymarked walks around the spectacular gorge. It is possible to drive to Devil's Bridge on the A4120 and to visit on the way the Cwm Rheidol reservoir, 8 miles (13km) from Aberystwyth, where there is a circular walk and visitor centre.

After Devil's Bridge the road continues to **Ponterwyd**. From here a minor road leads north into the empty hills of Plynlimon to reach the big Nant-y-Moch reservoir, a magnificent landscape with signs of much prehistoric settlement. Just over 1 mile (2km) from Ponterwyd on the Aberystwyth road is the former Llywernog lead mine which has been turned into an interesting mining museum, and just beyond that a forest visitor centre with opportunities for walking. On returning to the outskirts of Aberystwyth it is worth looking at the church at Llanbadarn Fawr. Those interested in the religious history of Wales will find a visit to the Yr Hen Gapel museum rewarding. It is at Tre'r Ddol, 9 miles (14km) north of Aberystwyth on the A487.

Clwyd

The tours of Clwyd do not include the popular seaside towns on the northern coastal strip (despite the architectural attractions of Colwyn Bay and Llandudno for the connoisseur). The distinctive character of the county is to be found in the less-frequented interior.

The first starting-point is **Wrexham**, once the centre of an extensive area of coal-mining and heavy industry. The town itself has no great beauty, but the parish church of St Giles should not be missed. Its magnificent sixteenth-century tower proclaims its importance, and it has another claim to fame as the burial place of Elihu Yale, founder of Yale University.

Take the Rhostyllen road to the south-west of the town. After a few minutes **Erddig** (National Trust) is signposted to the left. It is a vast seventeenth-century house in formal grounds, of particular interest because the servants' quarters have been meticulously and vividly preserved. Continue on this road, cross the Wrexham by-pass and almost immediately turn right to reach the Bersham Industrial Heritage Centre, which has a permanent exhibition and much informative literature about the local industrial history and landscape.

The road now passes through Ruabon. On the other side take the A539 for Llangollen, and after 2 miles (3km) look for a left turn for Trevor and park at the canal basin. **Trevor** was once a strategic point on a projected canal to the River Mersey, and to take it across the deep valley of the River Dee the famous engineers Thomas Telford and William Jessop constructed the Pontcysyllte Aqueduct, a technological miracle at the turn of the eighteenth century and still immensely impressive today to any visitor who chooses to walk across it 120ft (37m) above the river.

Continue on the A539, which descends into the Dee Valley and reaches **Llangollen**, a town which is best known for its International Eisteddfod, a music and dancing festival held each year at the beginning of July. The information centre has details of the many attractions here, including Valle Crucis Abbey to the north, the romantic ruins of Dinas Bran Castle (an excellent walk to the top of a commanding hill) and Plas Newydd, the home of the eccentric Ladies of Llangollen.

Leave on the A5 (Oswestry) which runs back up the other side of the valley and into **Chirk**, where the castle is signposted in the centre of the village. It is unique as the only castle in Wales occupied continuously since the thirteenth century, and it combines medieval features with sumptuous accommodation modernised over the centuries. Finally a rewarding drive begins opposite the church in Chirk, where the B4500 begins its run along the Ceiriog Valley, starting in pastoral countryside and penetrating into spectacular mountain country after the old quarry village of Glyn Ceiriog.

The second and longer tour begins at **Mold**, now the county's administrative centre. The impressive office buildings outside the town include Theatr Clwyd, one of Wales's major theatres and concert halls; otherwise Mold is an unassuming but very pleasant place with a good parish church.

First a very worthwhile short excursion. Take the road up the main street

Plas Newydd, Llangollen

and join the A541. After about 2 miles (3km) the B5123 turns right (signposted Rhosesmor). It climbs gradually to emerge on Halkyn Mountain, a strange moorland area that has been exploited since Roman times for its lead and stone. There are superb views from here across the broad expanse of the Dee Estuary.

Follow the signs for Holywell, a fascinating place best explored by taking the Greenfield Valley road in the town centre. Right at the bottom, beside the river, are the ruins of Basingwerk Abbey, a twelfth-century foundation, and from here it is possible to walk up the valley through a succession of features that include a small farm museum and the remains of the valley's remarkable industrial history. At the top is the Holy Well itself, associated with the legend of St Winefride and a place of pilgrimage for centuries. In the fifteenth century an elaborate chapel was built over the pool. An information centre at the farm provides details of all these attractions.

The main tour begins on the A494 (Ruthin) and heads west towards the impressive Clwydian hills. After 3 miles (5km) the Loggerheads country park is signposted to the right, and the 70 acres provide relaxed walking along a river valley beneath the hills. To get on to the hills themselves continue on the A494 for another mile (2km) and branch on to a minor road on the right. This passes through a forested area with opportunities to park and walk, and emerges at the foot of **Moel Famau**, the highest peak in the range. From the car park here there are breathtaking views across the wide Vale of Clwyd to the mountains of Snowdonia. For even better views take the track (this is stony, so suitable footwear is required) that climbs quite gently to the top of Moel Famau.

It is a short drive to the town of Ruthin, visible below, but a longer and much more interesting route is possible by returning along the minor road and rejoining the A494, turning off after 2 miles (3km) for **Llanarmon-yn-Lal**. The church is of considerable interest. Follow the B5431 from the village centre through deeply rural, unspoilt countryside until it joins the main road. Turn left and very soon right on to the A542 to reach a roundabout. By taking the A5104 here visitors interested in the Yale family can reach Bryneglws, their parish church, where there are Yale monuments in the chapel.

Otherwise take the main road for Ruthin, which begins by twisting its way through the Nant-y-Garth pass and then emerges into the Vale of Clwyd, with the hills looming on the right. At **Ruthin** follow the signs for the craft centre, where there is also an information centre and large car park. It is a mellow old town with streets climbing to a hill carrying the castle and square (a new house was built on the castle site in 1826 and it is now a hotel). The church is worth visiting, and among other notable buildings is the rugged Town Hall and Corn Exchange.

From here the main road continues up the Vale to Denbigh, but a more rewarding road runs parallel to the east. Take the Mold road as far as Llanbedr Dyffryn Clwyd and after turning on to the B5429 beside the fanciful Victorian church follow the signs for **Llandyrnog**. Two good churches are tucked away off this road. About 3 miles (5km) from Llanbedr are the gates of Clwyd Hall; very soon afterwards a right turn leads to Llangynhafal, with its church lying on the slopes of Moel Famau, and a lane to the left threads its way to St Saeran's, Llanynys, where the main feature is a vast medieval wall-painting of St Christopher.

After Llandyrnog a minor road runs into **Denbigh**. In the summer it is best to use an outlying car park because the narrow streets of the ancient town are constricted. The thirteenth-century castle, with an impressive gatehouse and the substantial town walls, is reached by a path from the main street, which widens to form a companionable town centre lined with shops and pubs. Unfortunately the same cannot be said for St Asaph to the north. It is a tiny cathedral city, but distinctly lacking in charm, while the cathedral itself is largely a dull nineteenth-century creation.

To the north of St Asaph the fast A55 offers a quick return route to Mold. In the other direction it soon reaches Bodelwyddan, proclaimed by the gleaming 'Marble Church' by the roadside — in fact made of limestone in the mid-nineteenth century and worth visiting for its rich interior. On the other side of the road is the castle, an imposing building given battlements in the nineteenth century but deriving from a much older structure. It has now been restored as an authentic Victorian country house, with splendid furniture and pictures, and its gardens are most enjoyable.

Those who wish to explore the totally unspoilt hills and valleys of western Clwyd should make for Llanfair Talhaiarn (Llanfair TH on some road signs). It is on the A548 due south of Abergele, a road that can also be joined by taking the B5381 from St Asaph. Cross the river bridge on to the A544, which climbs into fine hill country before dropping into Llansannan. On the outskirts of this village take the B5384 which crosses the hills again to reach Gwytherin and makes the return journey north on the other side of the Cledwyn Valley. It joins the A548 near Pandy Tudor for the return to Llanfair Talhaiarn. This circular trip passes through a landscape of great beauty and variety, seldom sought out by visitors, and in the later stages there are unexpected panoramas of the mountains of Snowdonia.

Further Information

— North Wales —

Places of Interest

ABERYSTWYTH (region)
Aberystwyth (town)
Arts Centre
Theatr-y-Werin
☎ 0970 622887
Open: Monday to Saturday 9.30am-5pm.

Ceredigion Museum
Coliseum
Terrace Road
☎ 0970 617911
Open: Monday to Saturday 10am-5pm.

National Library of Wales
☎ 0970 623816
Open: Monday to Friday 9.30am-6pm, Saturday 9.30am-5pm. (Closed on Bank Holidays and first week in October).

Ponterwyd
Llwyernog Silver-Lead Mine Museum
☎ 097085 620
Opening times vary. Ring to check.

Tre'r Ddol
Yr Hen Gapel
☎ 0970 86407
Open: Easter week and May to mid-September, Monday to Saturday 10am-5pm.

ANGLESEY
Beaumaris
Beaumaris Castle
Open: May to September, Monday to Saturday 9.30am-6.30pm, Sunday 2-4pm. October to April, Monday to Saturday 9.30am-4pm, Sunday 2-4pm.

Beaumaris Gaol and Courthouse
Steeple Lane
Open: from end of May to end of September daily 11am-6pm. Courtroom 11.30am-5.30pm.

Museum of Childhood
Castle Street
☎ 0248 712498
Open: Easter to January, weekdays 10am-5.30pm, Sundays 12noon-5pm.

Bodorgan
Hen Blas Country Park
☎ 0407 840152
Open: daily 10.30am-5pm (summer). Winter times vary.

Brynsiencyn
Anglesey Sea Zoo
☎ 0248 430411

Holyhead
Holyhead Maritime Museum
Rhos-y-Gaer Avenue
☎ 0407 2816
Open: May to September, Tuesday to Sunday and Bank Holidays 1-5pm.

Seabird Centre
Ellin's Tower
South Stack
Open: Easter to September, daily 11am-5pm.

Llanfair P.G.
Plas Newydd
☎ 0248 714795
Open: April to end of September, daily except Saturday 12noon-5pm. October, Fridays and Sundays only.

Penmynydd
Butterfly Palace
Menai Bridge
☎ 0248 712474
Open: March to end of October daily
10am-5.30pm. 5pm in October.

SNOWDONIA
Bala
Lake Railway
Llanuwchllyn
☎ 06784 666
Narrow-gauge line running $4^1/_2$ miles
(7km) along Llyn Tegid. Timetable
available in information centres.

Bangor
Museum of Welsh Antiquities
The Old Canonry
Open: Tuesday to Saturday 12noon-
4.30pm.

Penrhyn Castle
☎ 0248 353084
Open: April to end of October daily
except Tuesday 12noon-5pm (11am-5pm
in July and August).

Pier
☎ 0248 362807
Open: daily 10am-10pm.

Beddgelert
Sygun Copper Mine
☎ 076686 595
Open: March to end of September 10am-
5pm (11am opening on Sundays, 4pm
closing on Saturdays). 11am-4.15pm in
October (4pm Saturdays).

Betws-y-Coed
Motor Museum Betws Farm
Village centre
☎ 06902 632
Open: Easter to end of October, daily
10am-6pm.

Blaenau Ffestiniog
Gloddfa Ganol Slate Mine
☎ 0766 830664
Open: Easter to end of September,
Monday to Friday 10am-5.30pm (also
Sundays mid-July until end of August.

Llechwedd Slate Caverns
☎ 0766 830306

Open: Easter or 1 April to end of October, daily 10am-5.15pm.

Caernarfon
Castle
Open: April to end of October daily
9.30am-6.30pm. November to March,
weekdays 9.30am-4pm, Sundays 2-4pm.

Maritime Museum
Victoria Dock
☎ 0286 830932
Open: May to end of September, daily
1-5pm. Extended opening during school
summer holidays.

Segontium Roman Fort
☎ 0286 5625
Open: Monday to Saturday from 9.30am,
Sundays from 2pm. Closes 4pm November to February, 5.30pm March and April
(5pm Sundays), 6pm May to September,
(5pm Sundays).

Conwy
Aberconwy House
☎ 049263 2246
Open: April to end of October, daily
except Tuesday, 11am-5.15pm.

Conwy Castle
☎ 0492 592358
Open: April to October daily 9.30am-
6.30pm, November to March weekdays
9.30am-4pm, Sundays 2-4pm.

Plas Mawr
High Street
Open: April to September daily 10am-
6pm, October daily 10am-4pm, Novem-
ber, February, March, Wednesday to
Sunday 10am-4pm.

Criccieth
Castle
☎ 0766 522227
Open: April to October daily 9.30am-
6.30pm, November to March weekdays
9.30am-4pm, Sundays 2-4pm.

Harlech
Castle
☎ 0766 780552
Open: April to October daily 9.30am-
6.30pm, November to March weekdays
9.30am-4pm, Sundays 2-4pm.

Llanberis
Bryn Bras Castle
Llanrug
☎ 0286 870210
Open: Sunday to Friday as follows:
Spring Bank Holiday to mid-July 1-5pm,
mid-July to end of August 10.30am-5pm,
September 1-5pm.

Lake Railway
Narrow gauge line running alongside
Llyn Padarn. Timetable available in
information centres.

The Power of Wales
☎ 0286 870636
Open: June to September, Monday to
Saturday 10am-5pm, Sunday 1.30-5pm.

Welsh Slate Museum
Dinorwic Quarry
☎ 0286 870630
Open: Easter Saturday to 30 April, daily
9.30am-5.30pm. 1 May to 30 September
daily 9.30am-6.30pm.

Machynlleth
Centre for Alternative Technology
☎ 0654 702400
Open: daily 10am-5pm.

Porthmadog
Ffestiniog Railway
Harbour Station
☎ 0766 512340
Narrow-gauge railway running to
Blaenau Ffestiniog. Timetable available
in information centres.

Maritime Museum
Greaves Wharf
☎ 0766 512864
Open: Easter week to end of September,
daily 10am-6pm.

Portmeirion
☎ 0766 771331
Italianate village created by architect Sir
Clough Williams-Ellis. Gardens, beaches,
hotel.

Welsh Highland Railway
Opposite Queen's Hotel
☎ 0766 513402
Short length of narrow-gauge line, but
developing. Timetable available in
information centres.

Tywyn
Tal-y-Llyn Railway
Wharf Station
☎ 0654 710472
Narrow gauge line running for 7 miles
(11km) to Abergynolwen. Timetable
available in information centres.

CLWYD
Chirk
Chirk Castle
☎ 0691 777701
Open: April to September, daily except
Saturday and Monday 12noon-5pm.
October Saturday and Sunday 12noon-
5pm. (Gardens close one hour later).

Llangollen
Valle Crucis Abbey
Open: April to October daily 9.30am-
6.30pm, November to March weekdays
9.30am-4pm, Sundays 2-4pm.

Ruthin
Craft Centre
Park Road
☎ 08242 4774
Open: daily 10am-5pm.

Wrexham
Bersham Industrial Heritage Centre
Bersham
☎ 0978 261529
Open: Easter to end of October, Tuesday
to Saturday 10am-12.30pm and 1.30-4pm.
Sunday 2-4pm. November to Easter,
Tuesday to Friday 10am-12.30pm and
1.30-4pm, Saturday 12.30-3.30pm. Closed
Sundays.

Erddig
☎ 0978 355314
Open: April to June daily except Thursday and Friday 11am-6pm (house
12noon-5pm), July and August daily
except Friday 11am-6pm (house 12noon-
5pm), September and October as for
April to June.

Wrexham Maelor Heritage Centre
King Street
☎ 0978 290048
Open: Monday to Saturday 10am-5pm.

LLEYN PENINSULA
Plas-yn-Rhiw
Near Aberdaron
Open: April to end of September, daily
except Saturday 12noon-5pm. October,
Sundays 12noon-4pm.

Clynnog Fawr
Museum of Welsh Country Life
Tai'n Lon
☎ 0286 86311
Open: April to end of September, daily
10am-5pm.

Llanbedrog
Plas Glyn-y-Weddw
☎ 0758 740763
Open: daily 10am-6pm.

Llanwrog
Parc Glynllifon
☎ 0286 830222
Open: all year, but precise admission
times vary.

Nefyn
Lleyn Historical and Maritime Museum
Church Street
☎ 0758 720308
Local seafaring history.
Open: July and August, Monday to Friday
10.30am-12.30pm and 2.30-4.30pm.

Tourist Information Centres

Aberystwyth (town)
Terrace Road SY23 2AR
☎ 0970 612125

Anglesey
Station site, Llanfair PG
LL61 5UJ, ☎ 0248 713177
also
Marine Square, Holyhead
LL65 1DR, ☎ 0407 2622

Bala
High Street, LL23 7AB
☎ 0678 520367

Bangor
Theatr Gwynedd, Deinol Road
LL57 2TL, ☎ 0248 352786

Barmouth
The Old Library, LL42 1LU
☎ 0341 280787

Beddgelert
Llewelyn Cottage, LL55 4YA
☎ 076686 293

Betws-y-Coed
Royal Oak Stables, LL24 0AH
☎ 06902 426

Blaenau Ffestiniog
High Street, LL41 3HD
☎ 0766 830360

Caernarfon
Oriel Pendeitsh, LL55 2PB
☎ 0286 672232

Conwy
Castle Visitor Centre, ☎ 0492 592248

Criccieth
47 High Street, LL52 0EY

Dolgellau
The Bridge, LL40 1LF, ☎ 0341 422888

Harlech
High Street, LL46 2YA, ☎ 0766 780658

Llanberis
Museum of the North, ☎ 0286 870765

Llangollen
Town Hall, LL20 5PD
☎ 0978 860828

Machynlleth
Canolfan Owain Glyndwr, SY20 8EE
☎ 0654 2401

Mold
Town Hall, Earl Street
CH7 1AB, ☎ 0352 59331

Porthmadog
High Street, LL49 9LP
☎ 0766 512981

Pwllheli
Y Maes, LL53 6HE
☎ 0758 3000

Ruthin
Craft Centre, LL15 1BB
☎ 08242 3992

Tywyn
High Street, LL36 9AD
☎ 0654 710070

Wrexham
Memorial Hall, LL12 7AG
☎ 0978 357845

9 • The Peak District

etween the cities of Manchester, Sheffield and Derby lies the bottom end
of the Pennine Hills which stretch up the backbone of England to
Scotland. Amongst these hills lies the Peak District, parts of which now lie
in Britain's oldest National Park. The Peak District National Park, established in 1951, is also the most visited National Park in Europe, welcoming
18.5 million visitors a year. Yet despite the popularity of some parts of the
region — the park alone extends to 550sq miles (1,426sq km) — it is still
quite easy to find areas which are comparatively off the beaten track.

The Peak District consists of two distinct geographical areas. Its core of
limestone is characterised by a rolling landscape of neat fields surrounded
by stone walls. The plateau is a chiefly treeless landscape except for isolated
clumps of trees or long lines of them planted on old and worked out veins
of lead ore. Cut into this plateau area are many valleys called 'dales', some
with rivers flowing down them and some devoid of water. On the whole
they are all particularly attractive and many are wooded. Some, such as
Dovedale and Lathkill Dale, have residual (or relict) ash woodlands, remnants of the original tree cover before it was cleared by early settlers.

Around the limestone regions are higher areas of moorland which lie on
top of gritstone, a coarse form of sandstone. In places it is a wild and rough
terrain interspersed with valleys, interestingly called 'cloughs' (pronounced klufs) and not 'dales'. Many of the cloughs are also areas of
significant beauty. The isolated little villages which characterise the limestone — or White Peak — area contrast with the moorlands, where individual hill farms stand four square against the wind and rain; rugged little
cottages that epitomise the very essence of the landscape, people and tough
way of life that is characteristic of the area. To explore the majority of the
Peak, visitors are recommended to use the Ordnance Survey 'Outdoor
Leisure' maps for The White Peak and The Dark Peak. They are to a scale
of 1:25,000 (approximately $2^1/_2$in to the mile) which means all footpaths
and fields are clearly identifiable.

The South-Western Moors

To the south-west of Buxton lies the moorland area known as **Axe Edge**. It
is a bleak area in the north; in fact the second highest inn in Britain stands
aside the A537 Buxton to Macclesfield road. It is the Cat and Fiddle Inn,
built in 1831 and standing at a height of 1,690ft (515m) in a treeless expanse

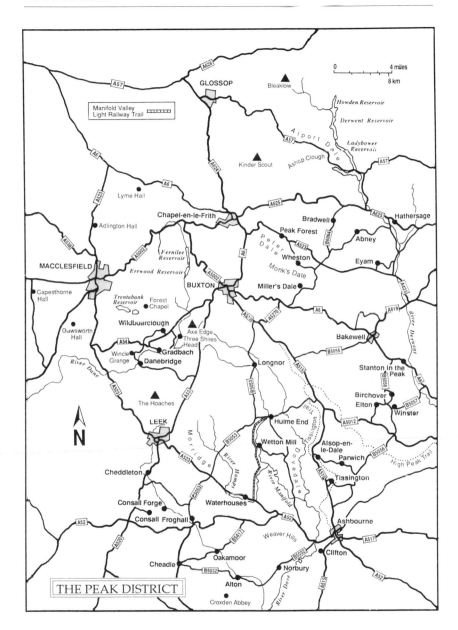

THE PEAK DISTRICT

of rough grass and heather.

Six miles (10km) due south of the Cat and Fiddle Inn are **The Roaches**, a large outcrop of gritstone escarpment. To the east of here lies **Morridge**, another treeless expanse that stretches southwards. Its ridge road affords tremendous views in all directions including the best view of The Roaches from near the Mermaid Inn. Much of Morridge (derived from Moor Ridge) is lower than Axe Edge and the land is cultivated, with farms situated in sheltered positions.

Six river systems find their head waters here — the Goyt, Wye, Dove, Manifold, Hamps and Dane. The rivers have created valley systems which are often unspoilt places — save the Goyt at its twin reservoirs of Errwood and Fernilee which not only inundated a beautiful valley but now draw nearly half a million visitors a year. There can be no greater contrast than the popularity of the limestone gorge of Dovedale and its neighbour, the Manifold with almost 2 million visitors and the upper reaches of the same rivers which receive only 5 per cent of this total.

Yet in their own way, the Dove Valley above Hartington and the Upper Manifold Valley can be equally interesting especially near the limestone reef hills around Glutton — the nearest one can find to 'peaks' in the Peak District which is named after a tribe and not its geography. Around the village of **Longnor** are a variety of narrow roads which enable us to explore the area more fully. Many of these lanes are old packhorse ways. Others were never surfaced with tar and remain as a delightful network of footpaths. Simply look for the green dotted lines on the White Peak map, figure out a circular route and take advantage of the network. One path (9 miles, 14km) runs down much of the Dove and it is possible to do a round trip from Longnor taking in both rivers. Take the path on the outskirts of the village near the Cheshire Cheese Inn that leads to Fold's End Farm. Leave the farmyard and walk through the river meadows reaching a road near Ridge End Farm. Continue downriver on the road until a crossroads is reached. Here, turn left and climb up the road up the north side of Sheen Hill and then drop down the green road (ie grassy track) to Pilsbury and the River Dove. Proceed up-river to Crowdecote and return to Longnor up the road. Alternatively continue upriver to Beggar's Bridge, cross it and then take the path to Longnor.

A little to the west of here, the River Dane rises and flows westwards towards the flat Cheshire plain. It rises near the Cat and Fiddle Inn, close to the Clough Brook, the source of its tributary. Both streams soon descend into pronounced and beautiful valleys where rough moorland heathland meets the cultivated fields, a patchwork of gritstone walls interspersed with areas of woodland.

The Dane Valley is well known for its packhorse bridge and four packhorse roads which lead down to it. This used to be an important highway with many salt-laden packhorse trains heading into the Peak from Cheshire. The bridge is at Three Shires Head (incorrectly called Three Shire Heads on the Ordnance Survey map) where the counties of Derbyshire, Staffordshire and Cheshire meet. The River Dane falls quickly through Gradbach which has no village but only a collection of isolated farms. It flows past an old silk mill which is now a youth hostel and skirts Back Forest with its huge cavernous landslip known as **Lud Church**. This was named after the Luddites, a group of fifteenth-century religious dissenters (as distinct from nineteenth-century activists with the same name). The cleft is situated high in the wood and is worth the trouble to visit it. It is situated

The market hall in Longnor, now a craft studio

off a footpath from Gradbach to Danebridge via the Hanging Stone and the northern boundary of Swythamley Hall park. There is a convenient path from Danebridge back to Gradbach through the river meadows which makes a marvellous circular route, with views up the tributary Clough Brook towards Shutlingsloe, its conical summit rising to 1,659ft (506m).

Above the hamlet of Danebridge is the village of **Wincle** where a road leads off towards the hamlet of **Wildboarclough** which sits adjacent to the Clough Brook in a pretty little valley also called Wildboarclough. Whether you wish to walk or ride, it pays to explore this area well. There is much to delight you although at weekends the area is busy with tourists but most visitors keep to the main villages and roads and it is easy to lose the crowds Just above Wildboarclough is the valley of **Cumberland Clough** which is worth exploring on foot, together with the eastern side of **Macclesfield Forest**. There is a visitor centre (and nearby heronry) adjacent to Trentabank Reservoir in the forest, together with a small Forest Chapel which still retains its annual rush-bearing ceremony. It is worth exploring the valley below Danebridge too, although this part of the valley tends to be more popular and can only be investigated properly on foot.

If one stands on the A53 Leek-Buxton road at the Ramshaw Rocks, north-west of Upper Hulme village and looks eastwards to Morridge, the isolated **Mermaid Inn** may be seen. This hostelry stands close to the top of a shallow valley which may be seen heading southwards beyond the adjacent gliding club. This is the Hamps Valley, a little known area frequented only by discerning ramblers and local farmers. A path (5 miles, 8km) runs down the side of the brook from Royledge Farm, through the village of Onecote to Ford. The latter now has a bridge and all the characteristics one expects of a hamlet off the beaten track. It is accessible by road but if you have come this far on foot you can return via **Butterton** and then an old road running north-westward from Butterton Moor, most of which is now metalled. Like most of the villages in this area, Butterton has a good village pub, full of atmosphere and selling good beer and food.

The National Park Authority owns two large estates in this part of the Park. It has 1,000 acres at The Roaches and 4,500 acres of the Western Moors purchased from the Harpur-Crewe estate and occupying the area north-west of Warslow village. Parts of The Roaches are open to visitors with well marked paths. The Western Moors estate is still being evaluated but contains many footpaths enabling it to be explored. It is a mixture of hill farm and moorland with some lower lying pasture land and is well recommended whether you prefer to explore on foot or by car.

The Churnet Valley

If one stands on Morridge and looks to the west, there is a clear view across the Cheshire plain often with Jodderel Bank Radio Telescope and the mountains of Wales visible. Much nearer is the town of **Leek** nestling in the valley of the River Churnet which has its source in a fan of small streams which drain the area between Morridge and The Roaches-Ramshaw Rocks escarpments. Below Leek, the valley changes direction and flows through a well wooded valley below Cheddleton.

This valley used to be referred to as the Hidden Valley but this is no longer appropriate at weekends. None the less in the week it recovers its seclusion. The valley contains not only the river but the Caldon Canal which must be one of the prettiest canals in the country between Cheddleton and Froghall where it now terminates. Although it has a railway line as far as Oakamoor, it lies unused. The aspirations of the railway museum at Cheddleton has still not extended in reality to regular tourist trains on this section of line.

The river maintains a south-easterly course to reach the River Dove at **Rocester**, a small village with a very good restaurant (Peck's) and the home of the JCB excavator plant. To the north of the valley rises the last bastion of the Pennine ridge. This smooth sided limestone feature is known as the Weaver Hills. Although it has a road over it and the views from the top can be tremendous, it is little known other than to local people.

From **Cheddleton**, about 3 miles (5km) to the south of Leek on the A520, the Caldon Canal runs to Wall Grange and just beyond it is the **Deep Hayes Country Park**. This used to be a reservoir, built to feed the canal but the dam became suspect and the water was drained off. Today it has woodlands, stretches of water and waymarked paths. It may be reached by taking the A53 from Leek towards Stoke-on-Trent. After rising up hill out of Leek you reach Longsdon where a left turn heads to Deep Hayes. Near the country park the canal splits into two, one canal passing over the other at Hazlehurst aqueduct. On the side of the lower canal is the Hollybush Inn where there are usually pleasure boats tied up. The whole of this area is well worth exploring from the canal towpath together with a trip into Cheddleton

The Upper Dove Valley near Hollinsclough, Peak District

The High Peak Trail, a former railway track, Peak District

*A barn above
Thwaite in
Swaledale,
Yorkshire Dales*

*Semer Water
near Bainbridge
in Wensleydale,
Yorkshire Dales*

village to see its ancient church. At Cheddleton alongside Caldon Canal is a preserved flint grinding mill complete with two waterwheels and a restored narrow boat moored on the adjacent wharf. A mile or so down river from here is the former Cheddleton railway station. This is now a steam railway centre dedicated to the North Staffordshire Railway Company. The valley becomes more picturesque below here. It may be viewed from the towpath of course, but no road runs down the valley until Oakamoor is reached. Two roads cross the valley, one at Oakamoor, the other at Froghall. A further road descends into the valley at Consall Forge where there is a canal-side pub. A new nature centre (an interpretation centre for the valley) has been established on the road from Consall to Consall Forge. To reach it from Cheddleton, take the A520 southwards to Wetley Rocks and bear left for Cheadle. After about $1/_2$ mile (1km) turn left for Consall.

Near Consall Forge, the River Churnet is canalised before separating in front of the Black Lion Inn. The valley is well wooded and very scenic. It retains this splendid characteristic all the way to Froghall. The Caldon Canal has terminated here since 1846 and used to be an important transhipment point for limestone from the Cauldon Low Quarry nearby. Today the canal is host to pleasure craft and a horse drawn passenger narrow boat which plies towards Consall Forge from Froghall Wharf. In the quiet of a sunny summer afternoon with the scent of flowers in the air, there can be no finer way of exploring the tranquillity of this valley than on the canal and at one horse power!

Froghall Wharf is now a country park, with picnic tables amongst the trees which have colonised the area amid the remaining railway and canal buildings plus a huge battery of stone lime kilns. The inclined railway which served the quarry from here dates from 1777 and is the second oldest in the country — it finally closed in 1920. Some of the rails survive at a gauge of 3ft (1m) which predates the standard British gauge. There is now a restaurant here in the old canal warehouse.

From Froghall the A52 proceeds towards Ashbourne and there is a turn off at Whiston for **Oakamoor** where there is also a country park, on the site of an old copper works of Messrs Thomas Bolton and Sons. The copper core was spun here for the first transatlantic cable which was unwound off the deck of Brunel's ship *The Great Eastern* in 1856. It is worth taking the valley road from here to **Alton** which is narrow but very pretty. After $1^1/_2$ miles (2km) a tributary valley on the right is also worth visiting. It is **Dimmingsdale**, a wooded valley with a series of large ponds; a walk along the path past the ponds is well rewarded.

Lying to the south of Alton is **Croxden Abbey**. This former Cistercian abbey is situated at Greatgate. Although a road now crosses over where the altar used to be, much of the huge west end of the building survives and gives a good impression of what the abbey must have looked like. The remains are now in the care of English Heritage. Croxden is close to Denstone where the B5032 leads to **Ellastone**. The Duncombe Arms in Ellastone is a reminder of Calwich Abbey near here which was owned by the Duncombe family who also still have a house near Helmsley in North Yorkshire and who built the Rievaulx Terrace above the Rievaulx Abbey remains. Across the River Dane at Ellastone is the hamlet of Norbury. A delightful church is hidden from view here and it dates from the early years of the fourteenth century, although there are the preserved fragments of two Saxon crosses. A large amount of fourteenth and fifteenth century glass may be seen together with several monuments (of a similar date) to the Fitzherbert family.

The latter built **Norbury Manor**, which is situated adjacent to the church. The rear portion dates from the mid-thirteenth century. It was enlarged in around 1305 and later extended with a Tudor addition to the south which was rebuilt in 1680. It is now in the ownership of the National Trust but is only open by prior arrangement. From Norbury a pleasant lane which is initially wooded on the left, runs up the valley to Clifton and then Ashbourne. Upon reaching open fields, the remains of **Calwich Abbey** may be seen across the valley. Just one gable end of the house survives, attached to the former stable block. In the valley bottom, the park lake and temple of 1797 survive. The scene is reputed to have inspired Handel to write his *Water Music*. He was a visitor here in the 1750s as a guest of Bernard Granville and he left Granville a folio of his manuscripts when he died.

Cycle Trails in the Peak

Cycle hire in the Peak enables the visitor to explore areas without intrusion of the motorcar. The withdrawal of railway services across the southern part of the Peak enabled the lines to be adopted for a new role. There are three lines used in this way plus a short length near Hayfield close to Glossop. In addition there are cycle hire facilities in the Upper Derwent Valley using roadways denied to vehicle traffic.

The Upper Derwent is a popular part of the Peak. Indeed it was like this years before the three reservoirs destroyed it together with Derwent and Ashopton villages. The visitor's centre at Fairholmes, below Derwent dam, is the proof of this. This part of the Peak received $1^1/_4$ million visitors each year. However, above Derwent dam, the road is closed in general to vehicle traffic. It is still popular with ramblers of course, but mid-week it is less so and is therefore worth including here.

There are plenty of routes to choose from at **Fairholmes**. There is a roadway up the side of Derwent dam and around the lake to Howden Reservoir. The road continues along to the King's Tree, an oak planted by King George VI on 25 September 1945 when he inaugurated the water-works scheme. A track continues here and the River Derwent is crossed by a re-erected packhorse bridge at Slippery Stones. It formerly stood in Derwent village, which is now beneath Ladybower Reservoir. One can return down the east side of the two reservoirs to Fairholmes. Additionally, you can continue down to the A57, cross Ashopton Viaduct over Ladybower Reservoir and cycle up the west side of the latter to Fairholmes.

A cycle trail in the Manifold Valley near Beeston Tor

Further to the south, between Buxton and Ashbourne, the **Cromford High Peak Trail** crosses the limestone plateau on one of the oldest railway lines in the country. Built like a canal, it has long flat sections and steep inclines. In fact it is the only railway in the country built to connect two canals — the Cromford and the Peak Forest. The rolling stock was originally hauled up the inclines and an old steam engine used for this survives at Middleton Top, just north of Wirksworth. Its location is easily identified by its tall slender chimney. There is a cycle hire centre here too. Much nearer to Buxton, at Parsley Hay on the A515, Buxton-Ashbourne road, the Cromford High Peak Railway met the railway from Buxton to Ashbourne. Here there is another cycle hire centre which serves the Cromford and High Peak Trail and the old line to Ashbourne — now the **Tissington Trail**.

From the lines you can view the limestone plateau particularly well and they are now important havens for wildlife. What is particularly interesting and quite rare to see is heather growing on limestone. Sometimes the soil is sufficiently acidic to permit this and a good example is the cutting under the A515 just south of Parsley Hay. To take a route to combine the Cromford and High Peak and Tissington Trails it is necessary to use minor roads to unite the two. Start off on the former trail from Parsley Hay and cycle pass Friden brickworks and across the A5012. At Gotham a track between two farms crosses the trail on a bend. This used to be the tightest curve on Britain's railways!

A little further on, one reaches the old Minninglow station where there are picnic benches and a car park. It is necessary to leave the line here and cycle southwards towards Parwich. From this little village, take the road through Alsop-en-le-Dale with its ancient church to the A515. Dismount and walk towards Ashbourne down this busy road for about a third of a mile where one can gain access to the Tissington Trail by an obvious railway bridge. From here simply cycle northwards back to Parsley Hay. It is even downhill once one reaches Biggin. At Hartington Station there is an interpretation and information centre in the old signal box together with some photographs showing the line in use.

Just to the west of Hartington is the **Manifold Valley** where a narrow gauge railway used the valley between 1904 and 1934. The Manifold is hardly off the beaten track, but the railway ran to Waterhouses down the Hamps Valley, leaving the Manifold roughly at its midway point — it was only 8 miles (13km) long. At the southerly end of the line is **Waterhouses**. There is a cycle hire centre in an old railway goods shed here. Simply take the Cauldon Low road at the Crown Inn and having passed under the old railway bridge, turn left. Far fewer people use the Hamps Valley than the Manifold and it is a beautiful place to walk or cycle — the track is metalled too. Although the River Hamps flows underground from Waterhouses for much of the year, it fails to distract from the overall beauty.

Continue up the Manifold from Beeston Tor where the River Hamps joins the River Manifold. **Beeston Tor** is the huge cleft just below the confluence. There is a tea room at **Wetton Mill** Farm which is 5 miles (8km) from Waterhouses, having passed the majestic looking Thors Cave en route. From just before Wetton Mill, $1^1/_2$ miles (2km) of the railway is also used by cars which is a nuisance. However, at Wetton Mill, one can cross the river and take the old valley road, which these days tends to be hardly used by vehicles. Upon reaching Swainsley, regain the old railway again. The line terminated at **Hulme End** where lunch can be taken at the pub and then cycle back again. Sixteen miles (26km) may seem a little daunting, but its very easy cycling and within the capacity of most people. Although this route enters into one of the most popular parts of the Peak, the majority is relatively peaceful especially if you use the old road between Swainsley and Wetton Mill or pick a week day.

Stanton Moor

In the south-eastern corner of the Peak District National Park lies an area of gritstone moorland known as Stanton Moor. It is also an area of great antiquity with numerous prehistoric burial sites and two stone circles. It is a tiny area of moorland and its paths are well trodden and easy to follow. However, it is not so well known to the occasional visitor and is missed by many. Two villages lie tucked into the western side of the moor — Stanton-in-the-Peak and Birchover. A little to the south lies Winster which was formerly an important centre for lead mining. Within minutes by car from Stanton Moor lies Lathkill Dale, Bradford Dale and Haddon Hall where tourists abound.

Stanton-in-the-Peak lies at the northern end of the moor adjacent to the private Stanton Hall with its deer park. The church is relatively recent, having been built between 1838-9. At the end of a terrace of stone built

Winster Hall, now a hotel

cottages is the Flying Childers Inn. It is named after a horse owned by the second Duke of Devonshire, which he purchased from Leo Childers in 1714. The village of **Birchover** lies just over $1^1/_2$ miles (2km) to the south and is connected by a road which skirts the moor and gives very good views towards the limestone plateau. Another good pub here, The Druid Inn, enjoys a good reputation for its inexpensive and wide ranging bar meals. A quarry for pinkish, fine-grained sandstone still exists here, with the stone in demand for fire surrounds etc. From the middle of the village a lane runs southwards to Upper Town where the village stocks may be seen. This road runs to Winster, which is the largest of the three villages.

Winster today gives no impression of its former importance as a lead mining centre. Its market hall survives in the main street and was the first acquisition in the Peak District by the National Trust. Its date of construction is unknown but Pevsner, in his *Buildings of England* series, considers it to be of the fifteenth or sixteenth century. The village has one or two pleasant properties including Winster Hall which is now a hotel. However, it is chiefly a village of leadminers' cottages built on the hillside to the south of the main street. In the 1970s a huge water pressure pumping engine — the only one in Britain and dated 1819 — was found in the fields to the south of the village. The engine was painstakingly removed and may now be seen in the lead mining museum at Matlock Bath. It is well worth going to see, especially when one considers that it was brought up a 400ft (122m) deep shaft by amateurs!

Stanton Moor is also worth exploring and one may park the car near Stanton-in-the-Peak or Birchover. The former access point is a footpath just past the last house on the left on taking the Birchover road. From Birchover, take the Stanton road to where the road turns sharp left. This is a T-junction and there is a footpath from either roadway just beyond the quarry which bounds both roadways. The paths are well defined and cross over the moor amid bilberry bushes and heather. The plateau was formerly forested but a big fire destroyed this during World War I. The tree cover is now creeping back at the northern end and has surrounded the stone circle known as Nine Ladies. This embanked circle of nine standing stones up to 3ft (1m) in height dates from the Bronze Age. Associated with it is the Kings Stone, some 130ft (40m) away. To the south-east of the Nine Ladies is a stone built tower above the Derwent Valley. It is known as Earl Grey's Tower and was built in 1832 to commemorate the passing of The Reform Act which widened the voting franchise and abolished electoral privilege.

A further stone circle confusingly known as Nine Stones Circle, exists about 1 mile (2km) to the north-west of Birchover. Only four of the original stones survive intact, with another now acting as a gatepost nearby. This circle really would have been impressive had it survived intact for these stones are 6ft (2m) in height. Although not on a footpath they may be seen from a path which runs in the direction of Cratcliff Rocks and Winster from Harthill Moor Farm. The rocks are easily identified by two protruding rocks, looking like chimneys on a roof, a feature known as Robin Hood's Stride.

For a circular route to cover the area by car, the following is recommended, starting for convenience in Winster. Leave the village for Elton, looking out for Elton Old Hall (now a youth hostel) which is dated 1668. Proceed straight through towards Dale End and upon leaving the village turn right for Alport. After a mile or so, look out for the Nine Stones Circle in the fields to your right opposite Harthill Moor Farm. Upon reaching Alport, the road crosses the River Lathkill, with the old mill on the downstream side. Bear to the left or right here to reach the Youlgreave road. Turn right and after nearly a mile turn right on the B5056. Take the first left and climb up the road to Stanton-in-the-Peak. The road climbs still further before levelling out and running southwards to Birchover. Return to Winster via the B5056.

Relics from the many archaeological digs on Stanton Moor may be seen in the Sheffield City Museum at Weston Park which also houses the collection of Thomas Bateman, a Victorian archaeologist who excavated many tumuli (or prehistoric burial sites) in the Peak. Another important collection is housed at Buxton Museum, including material from caves in the Manifold Valley.

Abney and Monk's Dale

At the north-eastern end of the limestone part of the Peak District lies **Eyam** village, well known as the Plague Village. Behind the village rises an elongated escarpment known as Eyam Edge. Beyond this lies a large area of upland. It is actually like an island extending to about 10sq miles (26sq km) with steeply sloping sides all around it. This high ground drains into a pronounced valley of the Bretton Brook which cuts through the moorland in a north-easterly direction. Although the road from Great Hucklow to Hathersage cuts over the moor, it is an area relatively unknown to the majority of visitors.

It is certainly worth taking the road from Great Hucklow, through Abney to Hathersage. It leaves the Great Hucklow to Bretton road and passes the gliding club before crossing Abney Moor to pass through the hamlet of **Abney**. From here, the road has good views over the Bretton Brook to Eyam Moor, and eastwards to the gritstone escarpment above the far side of the Derwent Valley. After a couple of miles it passes Highlow Hall, the sixteenth-century home of the Eyre family. The name is not the result of someone not knowing if they were coming or going, for 'low' is a common Derbyshire word for a prehistoric burial mound. There is much evidence of prehistoric settlement on Eyam Moor, but it is unfortunately not on a right of way.

It is also unfortunate that the large scale ordnance survey 'Outdoor Leisure' maps of the Peak — The White Peak and The Dark Peak — do not cover this area. The White Peak map covers the southern portion and the Dark Peak map covers the far western side only. However, if you are a rambler, this should not be allowed to temper enthusiasm! The paths are well defined and often signposted. There are two circular paths which afford good views and for the most part, allow you to wander in relative solitude. From Abney, a path leads off up a farm track in the direction of Bradwell. After $^1/_2$ mile (1km) or so, turn north to Shatton Moor. An unmade track is soon reached which passes a TV mast where there are good views to the north taking in Lose Hill, Win Hill and Ladybower Reservoir. At a sharp bend, where the tarmac is reached, the road drops downhill but a path contours along the hill to Offerton Hall where a road is reached. This is followed to Highlow Hall. Half a mile (1km) beyond here in the direction of Abney, a signposted path leads down to Stoke Ford where a path leads through a wood back to Abney. The route is about 6 miles (10km) in all.

The other route covers the area to the south-east, around Eyam Moor. Just to the east of the Barrel Inn at Bretton, the road turns sharp right and the road straight on is unmade. Park here and take the track along the ridge. The track crosses Sir William Hill, past a transmitter, before reaching the metalled road. Where the roads meet again, a path leads off to the left across Eyam Moor. There are good views across the Derwent Valley to the east. Upon reaching a road turn left and then left again on a track to Tor Farm. Beyond the farm, the path leads on to the Bretton Brook before climbing the side of Bolehill and then dropping to Stoke Ford. Here, a path up Bretton Clough is taken, past the ruined Bretton Clough Farm and up the valley bottom. It leaves the valley at Nether Bretton and an unmade track crosses the side of Bretton Moor back to your car. This route is also about 6 miles (10km) long.

If you wish to compare this upland gritstone area with a comparable limestone area, nothing could be easier. Four miles (6km) to the west of Great Hucklow is the village of **Peak Forest** on the A623 main road. Here the whole of the land surface has been given over to agriculture; there are no rough areas of heathland. The fields to the north and north-west gradually rise in height but the whole area is a network of small fields crisscrossed by footpaths. Just to the south of Peak Forest is a river valley, now chiefly devoid of water, which runs southwards to the River Wye at Millers Dale. The main section is known as Monk's Dale.

Monk's Dale

Some 6 miles (10km) east of Buxton on the A6 road to Bakewell, the B6049 leaves to the north side of the A6 for Tideswell. It quickly drops past Blackwell Hall and into Miller's Dale, crossing the River Wye and running alongside the river and under the twin bridges of the old Midland Railway. Just beyond the bridges, Miller's Dale's small village church sits adjacent to the road. Opposite here is the lane to Litton Mill. A few yards along the road is the Angler's Inn. Here there is a warm welcome, good beer and bar meals as required.

The path for Monk's Dale starts on the left side of the church, climbing over a small knoll and dropping into the floor of the dale. The latter is a National Nature Reserve. A footpath through such a sensitive area brings special responsibilities for the visitor. A permit to leave the footpath is required (and usually denied, except for scientific study). It is an offence to damage the environment in any way, and this includes picking flowers. The dale is fascinating in many ways both from its flora and fauna and the contrasts it valley floor affords.

It starts off like many Derbyshire dales, its valley floor a mixture of close cropped grass with some lush areas of herbs and shrubs. A trip in midsummer is particularly memorable, especially if the yellow rock rose and lilac flowers of thyme are in bloom among the limestone outcrops. The valley floor is unusual in that there are several calcareous 'flushes' which create wet habitats in places with several unusual plants. The flushes are the result of less permeable volcanic lava which flowed from a volcanic vent which existed in what is now Peter Dale, a part of the same valley system. Among the plants now found in these habitats are grass of parnassus and cotton grass.

The path leaves the valley floor to undulate along the valley side creating vantage points from which to view the dale. Eventually the woodland section is reached and the going becomes a little more difficult especially after rain when the many limestone cobbles become a little slippery. The wood consists chiefly of ash and sycamore; the latter being gradually reduced to encourage ash regeneration. The under storey is a rich habitat of herbs, many growing to waist height. All this along with a rich insect life and continual cocophany of bird song makes the dale a memorable visit without the many visitors associated with most other dales in the Peak.

Leave the woodland to cross a field and reach a minor road. Ahead is Peter Dale, a grassland dale compared to the woodland of Monk's Dale. One can return to Miller's Dale here or carry on up Peter Dale and then turn right to Wheston. From here an old lane — partly metalled and partly a green (or grassy) lane returns to Miller's Dale. It is this same lane which is picked up by climbing to the right up the road from the end of Monk's Dale. Upon reaching the flat plateau above the dale one turns to the right as soon as the lane is reached by a roadside cottage.

This circular route covering 5 miles (8km) has the advantage of combining a particularly good example of a dale with a return route through typical grassland of the Peak, with neat fields surrounded by drystone walls. These walls of limestone, built without mortar, prevail across the National Park and some date back to at least Roman times. Again, one is on a footpath little frequented by visitors, only dedicated ramblers. The views across the plateau are very good indeed, extending to several miles in some instances. The flower content of some of the fields is equally satisfying, with ox-eye daisy, meadow cranesbill, vetch and clover readily seen. Eventually the green lane begins to descend downhill, with views across to the two railway bridges and former quarry beyond — now part of a nature reserve controlled by the Derbyshire Wildlife Trust. Upon reaching Monksdale Farm, look out for yellow markers which direct you down to Miller's Dale where you emerge almost at your starting point.

The Woodlands Valley and Snake Pass

The A57 main road between Glossop and Sheffield takes advantage of the Woodlands Valley to provide an easy gradient to reach the top of what is now known as the Snake Pass. The road carries a great deal of traffic but it is surrounded by moorland of Kinder Scout (to the south) and Bleaklow to the north. Through agreements reached with landowners, much of this land is open access land, which means that having reached it along a footpath, one can wander at will in any direction.

There are two tributary valleys off the Woodlands Valley — Alport Dale and Ashop Clough. Both are well known to discerning walkers but are distinctly off the beaten track when compared with the neighbouring Derwent Valley which hums with tourists even on a bad day.

Alport Dale

From Ashopton Viaduct over the Ladybower Reservoir it is approximately 4 miles (6km) in the direction of Glossop to reach Alport Dale which lies to the north of the Woodlands Valley. Parking is difficult, but it is possible to pull off the road immediately adjacent to Alport Bridge which spans the stream draining Alport Dale. Here an access to farm land is wide enough to take a few vehicles. Park here and take the stile by the bridge. The path climbs upwards and away from the stream towards the farm track to Alport Castles Farm.

Although the mouth of the valley is quite broad, it soon begins to narrow up the valley. The sound of traffic soon dies away and one is drawn into a haven of peace and quiet. Behind, the north facing flank of Ashop Moor looks cold and uninviting and often under a mantle of snow in the deeper hollows which can lie until early summer. Alport Dale, however, catches the sun and the walk to the farm is a pleasant one.

Upon reaching the farm outbuildings, the path follows the roadway around a large barn. This is the site of the Alport Love Feast. This old custom is held annually on the first Sunday in July. A church service is held in the barn to commemorate three clergymen who were thrown out of their living in Derby for refusing to accept the Act of Uniformity in 1662. This remote barn enabled them to continue their religious persuasion far from the established church. The building is also a camping barn offering very basic accommodation for those people prepared to 'rough it'.

Above the farm, the west side of the valley has been planted with conifers by the Forestry Commission. The opposite side is completely different. Above the naturally regenerating Castle Wood, the moorland grasses lead the eye up to the steep gritstone cliff that marks the top of the valley. The path leaves the farm, crosses the flat valley floor before reaching a footbridge giving access to the far side of the valley. It then climbs up amid the sessile oak towards the exposed cliff, which is known as **Alport Castles**. Of particular interest is a huge detached mass of rock which has slipped away from the cliff face and is known as The Tower. Upon reaching the top of the valley side, the memorable vista of the whole of the valley unfolds below.

From here there are two options; either retrace your steps or if you are wearing appropriately stout footwear and have The Dark Peak 1:25,000 Ordnance Survey 'Outdoor Leisure' map with you return along the top of the valley. The route is across open access land for nearly 2 miles (3km), to reach the bridle path which drops down to the A57 close to Rowlee Farm. From here either walk back to the starting point of the walk up the main road, or cross the River Ashop and follow the path up river. It passes Upper Ashop Farm and then drops down to a footbridge directly in front of your car at Alport Bridge.

Ashop Clough

Some 6 miles (10km) to the west of Ashopton viaduct, as one climbs up towards the Snake Pass, the Snake Pass Inn is reached. It was built in 1821 by the Duke of Devonshire as a coaching inn. The road was built as a turnpike road by Thomas Telford and was one of the highest turnpikes in England. The name Snake Pass is derived from the snake in the crest of the Dukes of Devonshire. Some three-quarters of a mile beyond the inn is Birchin Clough. Here a tight bend in the road has been bypassed creating a useful car park for exploring Ashop Clough.

Opposite Birchin Clough is a Forestry Commission sign relating to its woodland walks. Follow the path from here down through the wood into Lady Clough. Upon reaching the stream, follow it downstream until a footbridge is reached which, when crossed, gives access to Ashop Clough. The conifer plantation hides the valley from the road, which is a blessing. The River Ashop is a broad, shallow stream flowing below the plantation, which is soon left behind. The river twists and turns creating interesting vistas as one walks through the moorland grasslands. Grouse and sheep seem to be everywhere against the backdrop of Seal Edge which rises dramatically some 200ft (61m) above the clough. This is the Snake Path, an old bridle path to Hayfield, and is well trodden and easy to follow. Another path runs much closer to the river and gives far better views of it. However, it is indistinct in places and peters out at the remains of an old shooting cabin. There is a footbridge at the cabin and a path climbs the hillside on the opposite side of the valley some way before contouring down the valley, eventually dropping down to a footbridge and reaching the A57 just below the Snake Pass Inn. An alternative route for hardy and adequately equipped ramblers is to continue up the Clough to Ashop Head, where the Snake Path reaches the Pennine Way, returning along Seal Edge before dropping down to the pub. This latter route should only be tackled by experienced ramblers with appropriate footwear.

There always seems to be cars parked at the head of the Snake Pass, at an altitude of 1,680ft (512m). Here Telford's new turnpike road took a new route towards Glossop and the old road, known as Doctor's Gate, was gradually abandoned. Although Doctor's Gate refers to Doctor John Talbot, vicar of Glossop between 1494-1550, this is in fact a Roman road. Standing where the Pennine Way crosses the A57 and looking northwards, one can see a tall signpost, about a quarter of a mile away. If one walks to the post Doctor's Gate is reached and by turning to the right, the original Roman causeway may be seen. It consists of pavestones with a kerbstone at each side. The track is 3 to 5ft (1 to $1^1/_2$m) wide and has been preserved as an amazing relic.

The Cheshire Fringe

The western moorlands of the Peak drop quickly to the flat expanse of the Cheshire plain with its emphasis on dormitory towns for Manchester and agriculture. Close to the boundary are a group of interesting country houses which are open to the public and worth visiting. Perhaps the most well known is Lyme Hall near Disley with its Palladian south front that lies on the foothills of the Peak itself and owned by the National Trust. The other three are grouped around Macclesfield and are privately owned. To the south is Gawsworth Hall, dating from 1480 and extended in 1701. It is a lovely black and white house with a large lawn linking it to a lake. There are three lakes at Capesthorne, to the west of the town. In contrast, the house is a marvellous example of High Victorian style. Further to the north is Adlington Hall, another house of great antiquity. Its Great Hall dates between 1480 to 1505. Like Lyme Hall and Gawsworth Hall, it has a much later addition. The south front and west wing dating from the mid-seventeenth century, with a large portico and four Ionic columns.

Gawsworth Hall

Two miles (3km) south of Macclesfield on the A52 to Leek is the delightfully named hamlet of Fools Nook, with a pub on the roadside with the same name. There is a sign to the right to Gawsworth. It crosses the Macclesfield Canal and winds through flat fields and into Gawsworth village. The hall is not signposted. However, look for the church tower across the fields to

Gawsworth Hall

the south of the village. The hall is next to the church and a couple of left turns soon brings you to the hall car park. The guide book to the house begins 'There are few prospects so appealing as the first sight of Gawsworth Hall. This long, low, half-timbered manor house reflected in its lake is a scene typically English in its serenity'. Unfortunately, most visitors head straight from the car park to the hall drive, completely missing this vantage point. Therefore turn right from the car park for a few yards to stand by the fence and look over the lake to the house. If your visit is in the afternoon, the sun is likely to be in a position for a good photograph of this tranquil scene.

Gawsworth is not a large house but a family home and the nearby steward could quite likely be the lord of the manor or one of the family. The first principal room is the library, a fine double cube with a nicely carved chimney piece of 1580. This leads on to the Long Hall and principal staircase where a door leads into the chapel. There is a lovely carved altar table and altar rail to be seen, with four stained glass windows by William Morris.

South of the Long Hall is the Dining Room, another part of the Tudor house as is the Drawing Room. Both are lovely, unpretentious and display a lot of original timber. The Green Room and the Solar above it are a reminder of the remodelling of the house in 1701 when these rooms — previously much larger — were truncated. The route then leads past several bedrooms to complete the tour.

There is a small formal garden to the west of the house — and perhaps the best vantage point to photograph the bulk of the house. Here, its half-timbered low and elongated form is perhaps seen to best advantage. A stroll around the garden and nearby church is recommended. To the south of the house is the Tilting Ground where jousting took place until the end of the sixteenth century.

Capesthorne Hall

Just to the west of Macclesfield, the A34 road cuts through pleasant fields and small villages connecting Stoke-on-Trent (The Potteries) with Manchester. To the south of Monks Heath on the A537, a sign indicates the turn off for the house. The lodge is small, the entrance to the drive lacking formality. It is a theme that is soon repeated. Rounding a bend in the drive by a clump of trees, the house suddenly appears ahead, with fields seemingly stretching almost to the front door. Nothing is allowed to distract from the impact of Salvin's reconstruction of the house after a fire destroyed the central block in 1861. Even the lake is off to the left, the eye staying on the brick and stone gables and turrets of the house.

One enters the house through its entrance hall and sculpture gallery to reach the Saloon, a charming room with many paintings and marvellous views into the garden. From here one moves on to the Drawing Room, occupying the centre of the rear of the house and dating from Salvin's rebuild. This is perhaps the most charming of the rooms open to the public. It contains some interesting Boulle furniture and an air of pleasing informality. From the Drawing Room, the main stairs lead up to several bedrooms; all different and all equally interesting. The State Bedroom contrasts with the eighteenth-century American Colonial furniture of the American Room. Returning down the stairs pass an intriguing nineteenth-century find — a huge Roman stone armchair — one reaches the State Dining Room, dominated by its fireplace; its table set with hand painted Coalport dating from around 1810. The house is the family home of the Bromley-Davenports and many features of the family connection appear around the building. For such a big house, the number of rooms open to view are few and far between. However, the garden does offer more to see. Situated between the house and the lake it is perhaps the most interesting feature of the estate with the early Rococo gates of the 1750s being a magnificent addition. The Milanese Gates, as they are known, came from a family house in Wootton, North Staffordshire. They were the gates to the main entrance until the house was sold in 1929.

There are four detailed short walks in a booklet produced by the house and other amenities include a café overlooking the garden. In addition it is permitted to picnic in the field by the upper lake where cars are parked.

Adlington Hall

The house is situated some 5 miles (8km) north of Macclesfield on the A523 to Stockport. Upon reaching the Legh Arms in Adlington, turn left. The hall is about 600yd (550m) down the road, on the left. There is nothing pretentious about this manor house. If anything, it lacks the stateliness of Capesthorne and Lyme Hall — the latter formerly belonging to another branch of the Legh family. Adlington's superb Great Hall dates from the fifteenth century. The house was extended in Elizabethan times — when the 'black and white' architecture — so typical of Cheshire — was added. More extensions came in the Stuart period, with major extensions on the south side in Georgian times. The latter is now the private quarters of the Legh Family and visitors are confined to the older north side of the house. It is obvious that this is a family house. As at Gawsworth, the lord of the manor — Charles Legh — can be found taking the admission fee, helping out in the shop or simply queueing with his visitors for a cup of tea in the tea room! An affable, relaxed man, he epitomises the continuity of succession that reflects in the ambience of a house like this; his family have been here for 650 years.

The house is much larger than Gawsworth, where a lack of repair resulted in demolition work as early as 1701. A succession of small rooms at first floor level brings one to the Drawing Room, with the Dining Room below it. The Drawing Room is wood panelled with fluted Corinthian columns. A rather pleasant pearwood carving over the fireplace is considered to be in the style of Grinling Gibbons who also did work for Lyme Hall. The Dining Room is plainer and makes an interesting comparison with Capesthorne's state Dining Room which was built a little over 110 years later. The latter is elegant, but much larger, perhaps reflecting Victorian affluence. The Great Hall is in complete contrast to the relative simplicity of the preceding rooms and was finished in 1505. Its east end is supported by two oak tree trunks, still in situ, complete with roots. The original Hunting Lodge on this site was built around these trees. Between the trees is the country's best preserved and largest seventeenth-century organ. Beneath the hall's richly carved hammer-beam roof are sixteenth- or early seventeenth-century murals, found behind the plaster. These dominate the room with their rich colouring. At the west end is the canopy, timber framed and divided into sixty panels showing armorial shields of Cheshire families and painted in 1581. It is an incredible survivor of a bygone age. This room whets one's appetite for an inspection of the Elizabethan East wing, but unfortunately it is not open to visitors. The formal garden is not extensive, but there is a woodland walk to the south of the house.

Lyme Hall

Nestled in the moorland south-east of Stockport is Lyme. The site of the house was given by King Edward III in 1346 to Sir Thomas Danyers for services rendered in the battle for Caen in northern France. His daughter married Sir Piers Legh in 1388 and the property remained in the Legh family until 1946, exactly 600 years after the king's initial grant. In that year, it passed to the National Trust and was leased to Stockport Metropolitan Borough. Major structural repairs since 1972 have secured the future of this lovely house.

It is approached by a long drive from the A6 at Disley. Red deer still roam the parkland and make a fascinating introduction to the estate. One approaches the north front which is Elizabethan, with Corinthian pilasters at each end. The house is set around a courtyard and it is the south front which is perhaps the most memorable feature of the exterior. In 1725 Giacomo

Leoni was appointed and made significant alterations to the house. His Palladian south front is reminicent of Chatsworth, completed 22 years earlier. However, Lyme is bolder in a way closer to Palladio's concept than Chatsworth. One is drawn back to it and the description (in the National Trust book on the house) that the front 'achieved a scale and weight which ensured that [it] held its own with the sweeping landscape of the Peak', sums it up well. Viewed across the lake it is particularly impressive.

Leoni was also responsible for the huge entrance hall modelled on the great hall of the original house. Here hang outstanding Mortlake tapestries woven in 1623. There are a substantial number of rooms to be seen here. The saloon includes Grinling Gibbon's carvings and eighteenth-century furnishings. A notice advises that the pea pods in the Gibbon's carving was his trademark. A pod is shown open which apparently meant that he had been paid for his commission. It is possible that Gibbon's commission also reflects the influence of Chatsworth and similarly the Chatsworth Cascade was repeated here in the garden. However, the pea pods at Chatsworth are closed!

Some of the rooms at Lyme are particularly attractive, such as the library, with its Compass Bay window and the long gallery, one of several Elizabethan rooms which have survived. Most of the house furniture was sold off in 1946 so several rooms are now noticeably lacking in furniture. However, there are some superb pieces such as the seventeenth-century settee in The Yellow Bedroom. Despite the noticeable lacking of ambience conveyed by the other houses described here, it would be wrong to allow this to influence one's enjoyment of this beautiful house.

It is recommended that you purchase the black and white National Trust booklet 'Lyme Park' — preferably before one's visit if possible. It describes the house, furnishings and paintings in far more detail than the full colour booklet of the same name.

The gardens include a sunken garden and a Dutch garden — laid out in sheltered beds below high retaining walls. To the east of the house are interesting herbaceous borders and the Orangery with three huge plants all at least 170 years old — a fig and two camellias.

Additional time should be allowed to visit the Countryside Centre which acts as an interpretation for the park plus the hall's Visitor Centre which covers life above and below stairs in 1910. This complements the staff in the hall who are dressed in Edwardian costume. There is a tea room here and a couple of shops. With the house, gardens and parkland walks, there is sufficient at Lyme to occupy you for the most of a day. It is a lovely house that should not be missed. Furthermore, one is spared the crowds of thousands who flock to the more popular parts of the Peak.

Although this feature covers four country houses on the fringes of the Peak, it should be mentioned that south of Gawsworth, and close to Kidsgrove, is Little Moreton Hall — perhaps the finest of all Cheshire's black and white timber-framed houses. It is owned by the National Trust.

Further Information

— The Peak District —

Places of Interest

Adlington Hall
Near Macclesfield, Cheshire
($^1/_2$ mile, 1km off A523)
Open: Good Friday, 13 April to 30
September, Sundays 2-5.30pm.

Capesthorne Hall
Near Macclesfield
☎ Chelford (0625) 861439 or 861221
Open: April, Sunday only; May, August
and September, Wednesday and Sunday;
June and July, Tuesday, Wednesday,
Thursday and Sunday. Good Friday and
all Bank Holidays. Park, gardens and
chapel 12noon-6pm; hall 2-4pm.

Croxden Abbey
Greatgate, near Rocester, Staffs.
In the care of English Heritage

Deep Hayes Country Park
Situated at Wallgrange, which is on the
road to Cheddleton from Longsdon,
south-west of Leek.
Visitor Centre open: May to September,
Saturday and Sunday 2-5pm.

Gawsworth Hall
Gawsworth, Macclesfield, $2^1/_2$ miles
(4km) south of Macclesfield on the A536
☎ North Rode (0260) 223456
Open: April to October, daily 2-5.30pm.

Cromford High Peak Trail
Former railway line from High Peak
Junction (Cromford Canal) south of
Cromford to Hurdlow.

Lyme Hall
Disley, near Stockport
☎ Disley (0663) 62023
Hall open: Good Friday, mid-April to
end of September, daily except Monday
and Friday but open Bank Holiday
Monday 2-5pm. Garden open: All year
daily except 25 and 26 December; summer 11am-6pm, winter 11am-4pm.

Middleton Top Engine House
Middleton Top, Wirksworth
Signposted off the B5036 Cromford to

Wirksworth road.
☎ Wirksworth (062982) 3204
Open: Easter to October, 10.30am-5pm,
Sundays (engine static); first Saturday in
month and Bank Holidays (engine
operating).

Nine Ladies Stone Circle
Stanton Moor
Situated north-west of Birchover.

Nine Stones Circle
Harthill Moor
North of Robin Hood's Stride, not on, but
visible from a public footpath.

Norbury Manor
Ashbourne, Derbyshire
Open: by prior written arrangement

North Staffordshire Railway Centre
Cheddleton Station, Cheddleton, Leek,
Staffs.
3 miles (5km) from Leek, off A520 Leek
to Stone road.
☎ (0538) 360522 (Sundays);
(0782) 503458 (other times)
Open: Easter to September, Sundays and
Bank Holiday Mondays 11am-5.30pm. At
other times by prior arrangement.

Peak District Mining Museum
The Pavilion, Matlock Bath
☎ Matlock (0629) 583834
Open: daily except Christmas Day 11am-
4pm (later closing in summer).

Sheffield City Museum
Weston Park
☎ (0742) 768588
Open: Tuesday to Saturday 10am-5pm,
Sunday 11am-5pm. Closed 24, 25, 26
December.

Tissington Trail
Former railway line from Parsley Hay to
Ashbourne.

Canal Cruises

Caldon Canal: Froghall Basin
Situated off the A52 on Foxt Road at
Froghall

☎ Ipstones (053871) 486
Regular $2^1/_2$hour horse drawn trips on
Thursday and Sunday at 2pm with
additional trips on Bank Holidays. On
the first and third Saturday in the summer months there is also a $3^1/_2$hour trip
including a four-course meal; Afternoon
teas on the canal are available. Telephone
in advance.

Caldon Canal: Cheddleton

A variety of different cruises are available during the summer months, taking
$2^1/_2$ to 6 hours.
Booking required to M.E. Braine, Norton
Cranes Docks, Lime Lane, Pelsall,
Walsall, Staffs.
☎ Brownhills (05433) 4888 or (0889)
881328
These cruises offer an opportunity of
seeing the beautiful Churnet Valley other
than on foot.

Cromford Canal: Cromford

Enquiries to Cromford Canal Society Ltd,
Old Wharf, Mill Lane, Cromford,
Matlock, Derbys.
☎ Wirksworth (062 982) 3727
40minute horse drawn trip from
Cromford Wharf. Currently Saturday,
Sunday and Bank Holidays 2 and 4pm
plus passenger and charter trips mid-
week. Details subject to change, so
telephone in advance.

Cycle Hire Centres

Tissington Trail, High Peak Trail.
Bikes may be hired from both Ashbourne
and Parsley Hay station sites. The latter
is situated just north of the old
Hartington Station. Also Middleton Top
Engine House. There is usually no need
to book except for parties. Similarly at
Waterhouses for the tarmac-covered
Manifold Valley Light Railway track.
Hire centre in old railway goods shed at
rear of the Crown Inn. Open: from March
to October.

Tourist Information Centres

* Information Centres run by the
National Park

Ashbourne

13 Market Place
☎ Ashbourne (0335) 43666

* Bakewell

Old Market Hall
☎ Bakewell (062 981) 3227

Buxton

The Crescent
☎ Buxton (0298) 5106

* Castleton

Castle Street
☎ Hope Valley (0433) 20679

* Hartington

Railway Station
No telephone
Open: Easter to September. Saturday,
Sunday and Bank Holiday Mondays.

Macclesfield

Town Hall, Market Place
☎ Macclesfield (0625) 21955

National Trust

East Midlands Regional Office
Clumber Stableyard
Worksop, Notts S80 3BE
☎ Worksop (0909) 486411

Peak District National Park

Head Office
Aldern House, Baslow Road
Bakewell, Derbys DE4 1AE
☎ Bakewell (062 981) 4321

Useful Addresses

Derbyshire Wildlife Trust

Elvaston Castle
Near Derby
☎ (0332) 756610

For details of conservation work involv-
ing volunteers, please contact either the
National Park or the National Trust,
Clumber Park, Worksop, Notts.

10 • The Yorkshire Dales and The North Pennines

The Pennines form a range of high country extending for about 140 miles (225km) from the Vale of Trent in the North Midlands to the Tyne Valley in Northumberland. Here we are concerned with the northern half, roughly from the Aire Gap to the Tyne Gap, transverse valleys carrying important trunk roads — the A65 and A59 in the south and the A69 in the north. Only two other main roads cross the North Pennines — the A684 through Wensleydale and the A66 between Scotch Corner and Penrith.

If the area is considered roughly rectangular, about 30 miles (48km) across, Skipton is at the centre of the southern edge and Alston is its northern counterpart. Motorways M1 (with A1) and M6 give convenient access on the east and west respectively without ever intruding into Pennine landscapes. Leeds is the nearest airport, and Manchester only slightly further away.

Within the Pennine rectangle there are no large towns, and only Skipton could be considered even partially industrial. The Pennines and their valleys are predominantly pastoral, with sheep on the fells, and cattle in the dales. These are words which, like those of other natural features of the landscape such as crag, scar, rigg, beck, gill, mere, moss and tarn, originated with Anglian and Norse settlers who colonised much of the Pennines between the seventh and tenth centuries. Scandinavian visitors may feel quite at home with these and other dialect words still regularly used by local folk.

Prehistoric occupation has left few sites and meagre remains. The Romans established a scattered pattern of small forts linked by a few roads, but the pastoral way of life was laid down in pre-Conquest centuries, with a baronial and monastic land-ownership imposed after the Norman Conquest, and continuing for five centuries.

Monastic landowners successfully managed huge estates, brought great farming and sheep-breeding skills and laid the foundations of much of today's farming pattern. By the end of the fifteenth century feudal power had declined, and soon afterwards the Dissolution of the Monasteries (1537-40) completed the break-up of large estates, which passed into large numbers of private hands. Within two generations a few new farmhouses were beginning to be built in the Yorkshire Dales, but many of the stone-

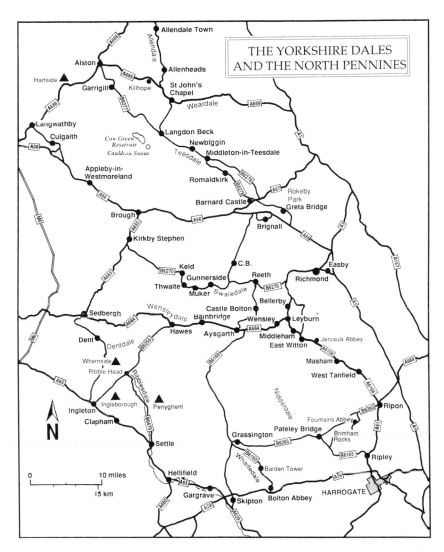

built farmhouses and larger houses in today's Pennine landscapes date from the seventeenth and eighteenth centuries. Generally, the area was not sufficiently prosperous to merit unnecessary ostentation, so function rather than fancy is the keynote. Traditional seventeenth- and early eighteenth-century houses are long — two or three bays wide — and narrow, only one room deep. They have a front entrance and an attached hay-barn under the same long roof, usually roofed with local 'slates', which are really thin sandstone flags. From about 1720 the Georgian influence slowly penetrated through the area, and can be recognised in the higher, squarer houses, with good masonry, sash windows and a more symmetrical appearance.

This style persisted, with modifications, until Victorian times, when large numbers of smaller cottages, often in short terraces, were built to house lead-miners, quarrymen and other artisans working in small local industries, usually mills. Lead-mining was an important industry, particularly in Nidderdale, Swaledale, Weardale and the Allendales, reaching a peak in the early decades of last century, but declining from the 1880s, to leave landscape scars.

Between about 1760 and 1850, hundreds of miles of stone walls were built to enclose valley-land into small fields, and to separate large common pastures on the hillsides. At the same time, especially in the upper valleys, stone field barns were rebuilt, to store the hay crop, harvested from late June to early August to provide winter feed for livestock. These barns and the walls which stitch the landscape, are unique features of Pennine valleys and hillsides.

Landscape and scenery give the Pennines their particular character. Buildings, though important, play the supporting role. Throughout the area there is visual harmony, in the intimate scene or the wide view from a hill. Colours are soft and muted, varying with the seasons, with brightest accents provided by wild flowers which greet the late-arriving spring and early summer, especially in the limestone uplands of the south, the Craven country of Wharfedale, Malham and Ribblesdale. Heather moors of the eastern ridges are washed with purple in August, while October sees the russets of hillside bracken and the golden tints of birch and beech.

In 1954 the Yorkshire Dales was designated a National Park, one of ten in England and Wales. Although almost all land within National Parks remains privately owned, National Park Authorities — essentially Planning Committees — have two principal duties. These are to protect and enhance the natural beauty of the Parks, and to ensure that the public has access to enjoy them. Generally, conservation of natural or man-made landscapes, and of wildlife, takes priority over recreation. Recently, a large area of the North Pennines, from the Yorkshire Dales almost to the Tyne Valley, has been declared an Area of Outstanding Natural Beauty (AONB), recognition of its particular landscape quality.

Since there is no single centre from which to explore this large area of Pennine country, the progression followed by this chapter will start in the south-east and travel mainly up the western side of the Pennines to the Tyne Valley, returning down the eastern margin, with frequent diversions to individual valleys and particular places of interest. Good, comfortable accommodation can be found in many modest hotels and guest houses in small market towns, but local farmhouses and villages are likely to provide the most homely hospitality, usually with a local flavour. Incidentally, this being pastoral country, livestock is often on the move, either on its own accord or being driven to or from market, or, with dairy cattle, for their twice-daily milking. From April to October, 8-9.30am and 4.30-6pm, are the likeliest times that you will be delayed by a herd of cows.

Harrogate is the start and finish point. Easily reached from the A1, 9 miles (14km) from Wetherby by the A661, or the M1, 16 miles (26km) from Leeds by the A61, it developed as a small spa in the late eighteenth century, blossomed in the early decades of last century, and became, architecturally at least, a handsome Victorian town. Now it has grown into a major conference and exhibition centre, with an extensive range of hotels, large and small. The Victorian stone buildings give dignity, while gardens, parks and The Stray — several hundred acres of grassy common land near the heart of the town — create a sense of spaciousness which sets the scene for subsequent journeys.

From the northern edge of the town take the A59 westwards to Blubberhouses, then across moorland country, before descending to Wharfedale. Turn right, along the B6160, reaching the village of **Bolton Abbey** in 1 mile (2km). Use the car park and walk the short distance to the ruins of Bolton Priory, founded in 1154 and completed 70 years later. The west tower was started in 1520 but the Dissolution prevented its completion, although the nave of the priory church was allowed then to continue in parochial use. The setting in riverside fields beside the sparkling Wharfe, with a background of woodlands, moors and hills, undoubtedly gives Bolton Priory its special appeal. Great English painters have found inspiration here — Turner, Girtin and Landseer among them.

Miles of public paths are an encouragement to explore the park and woods of Bolton Abbey estates, owned by the Dukes of Devonshire since 1748. Three miles (5km) upriver from the priory, along the B6160, Barden Tower's ruins evoke a long association with the great Clifford family, medieval lords of Skipton. Henry, the 'shepherd lord', Clifford built Barden in 1485, and his descendant, the redoubtable Lady Anne, restored it in 1658-9, adding a small chapel at the time. Recent restoration has adapted this into a guest house and restaurant.

Take the minor road south-west over the moors to Embsay and Skipton, enjoying superb views. Main roads now by-pass Skipton but the town is far too interesting to miss. Take advantage of large car parks and explore it on foot. If you are there on Saturday, Monday, Wednesday or Friday you will almost certainly find the High Street crammed with busy market stalls.

Skipton justifiably regards itself as the southern gateway to the Yorkshire Dales, with Grassington — a charming and busy small town a few miles to the north and always worth a detour up the B6265 — a good base for seeing Wharfedale. North and west of Skipton is the limestone country of the Craven uplands. Gritstone moors to the south, the pastoral Ribble Valley to the west and its own situation in the important Aire Gap all contribute to Skipton's frontier-like quality. The de Romilly family built Skipton Castle in the twelfth century, established a market, followed by a three-day annual fair. The castle passed into Clifford hands in 1309, was their family home for 350 years, and is still in their ownership. Lady Anne restored it 1655-58, although most of what we see today is early fourteenth-century work, and is well worth a visit, particularly for the high-level view it gives of the town that developed at its feet. The great round-towered gateway, surmounted by the Clifford motto, 'Desormais', meaning 'henceforth', nearly faces down High Street, and the parish church, which grew up alongside the castle, contains many Clifford memorials.

Skipton's townscape is largely of the eighteenth and nineteenth centuries, when wool-trading and livestock markets brought prosperity. The Leeds-Liverpool Canal brought more varied trade from about 1790, and new woollen and cotton mills were built near the canal banks, larger ones following between 1850-80. Rapid population growth saw terraces developed in the long plots behind High Street properties, reached by tunnel-like openings and alleyways which are still a feature of the present town.

Take the A65 westwards, following for a while the canal and River Aire to Gargrave, where the canal is crossed and then left. Beyond Hellifield the road enters Ribblesdale, where you soon leave the A65 to take the B6479 for **Settle**, a small, attractive market town beneath frowning limestone crags. Busiest on Tuesdays (market days), Settle is centred on its square, where the seventeenth-century Shambles — arcaded on the ground floor, Victorianised above — is an unusual focal point. Walk to its right, out of the Market Place, to see Settle's strangest building, The Folly, an extraordinary town house of 1679, with rich carvings and daringly original windows. Keep your eyes open elsewhere in the town, for decoratively-carved door-heads, often bearing date-panels.

Northwards now, into Upper Ribblesdale, the B6479 keeps close company with the railway, the famous Settle-Carlisle Line, part of the London-Leeds-Glasgow inland route completed in 1876. This particular stretch was the most expensive line ever built in Britain because of the number of tunnels and viaducts which were necessary. Threatened by closure, a prolonged campaign and much public outcry has saved it. Extensive repair work has been carried out, especially on the Ribblehead Viaduct, and regular train services now run, many stopping at village stations along the line for the benefit of locals and particularly of walkers who visit these western dales in their thousands, for the superb scenery of the famous 'Three Peaks' which dominate Ribblesdale. Penyghent, to the east of Horton-in-Ribblesdale, Ingleborough to the west, and Whernside beyond that, which comes into view at Ribble Head, are all over 2,200ft (671m) high.

Limestone marvels exist below the surface, too. Of the many caves and pot-holes in the area, most are accessible only to experienced adventurers, but a few 'show' caves are open to the public. Ingleborough Cave, near Clapham, and White Scar Cave near Ingleton, are the best of these. The A65, which we left near Settle, continues its north-westward course and passes these places, but access to Ingleborough Cave necessitates a 1 mile (2km) walk from Clapham village. From Ingleton, the B6255 links up at Ribble Head with the B6479 coming up Ribblesdale, at a point offering a splendid view of the great viaduct. Continuing northwards by the B6255, the road crosses a watershed at Newby Head, leaves the predominantly limestone country, makes a long, flowing descent into Wensleydale and the small, friendly town of Hawes. Just before Newby Head an unclassified road turns off left, into Dentdale, which is too charming to be missed. A few miles in a 'there-and-back' detour to **Dent** reveals its intimacy, its small, wooded river in a beautiful valley of scattered farms beneath sweeping fells. Dent is the most unusual of all Dales' villages, with close-clustered, whitewashed cottages fronting on to three cobbled streets meeting by the Adam Sedgwick memorial fountain near the broad, low-roofed church.

Return to the B6255 and the road to **Hawes**. Most market towns in the dales are at the lower ends of the valleys they serve, but Hawes is different, a relative newcomer whose charter is as recent as 1700. The A684 from Bedale and the A1 passes through the town, continuing westwards, across the Pennine watershed, down Garsdale to Sedbergh and Kendal, a convenient, popular and scenic 50 mile (80km) link between the A1 and the M6. Lesser roads north and south lead to Swaledale and Wharfedale, making Hawes a very useful touring centre for the main Yorkshire Dales. Tuesday sees its busy street market and, near the eastern edge of the town, a lively Auction Mart, with a huge throughput of sheep and cattle. The autumn lamb sales in late August and early September are an important annual event in Wensleydale's farming year. Wensleydale cheese, made locally, is a speciality in shops and restaurants, the Hawes Ropemakers continue an old traditional craft, and you can see ropes being made. Nearby, in Station Yard, there is a National Park Information Centre, and a former engine shed now houses the Dales Countryside Museum, displaying all aspects of local history.

A short journey down the A684 along the south side of the valley gives a good flavour of Wensleydale scenery. **Bainbridge** is one of the most attractive villages in the dale, where modest cottages face inwards around a large, well kept green. At Aysgarth, turn down a short, steep hill to cross the Ure at Aysgarth Falls, where the river flows over a series of low, broad limestone steps in a sylvan setting. Continue up the hill on the northern side to join the minor road coming along Wensleydale's northern side. Turn right, through Carperby, and in $2^1/_2$ miles (4km), left up the hill to **Castle Bolton**, a neat, grey village in the shadow of the massive ruins of Bolton Castle (not to be confused with Bolton Priory, seen earlier in Wharfedale). Built by Lord Scrope, Chancellor of England, about 1380, as a fortified, comfortable manor-house, three of its original corner-towers still stand to their five-storey height, with ranges of living quarters between them enclosing a square courtyard. From July 1568 until January 1569 Mary, Queen of Scots was imprisoned here, in some degree of comfort, with about twenty servants billetted in the village. The castle was partially dismantled at the end of the Civil War. Now owned by Lord Bolton, it is open to the public, houses a folk museum and a good restaurant, and from any viewpoint nearby, dominates Wensleydale.

Continue through the village, and at the first crossroads turn left, up a long hill, to cross the heathery Grinton Moor before dropping steeply into Swaledale. Pause at the brow of the hill for a superb view of Swaledale, with the little town of Reeth on a shoulder of wall-patterned Calva. Pass through Grinton village, cross the river, then Arkle Beck, and climb into Reeth, parking at the top of the green.

Like almost all the small towns in these northern dales, **Reeth** has no buildings of outstanding architectural or historic merit. However, the groupings of inns and houses at the top of the green, together with the

The dramatic ruins of Bolton Castle, Wensleydale

broad, breezy situation, with wide-ranging views, are memorable, an appropriate introduction to the journey up Swaledale by the B6270. This winds its way along the northern side of the valley, past small grey villages. Of these, **Gunnerside** is the largest and those with an interest in industrial archaeology will find much to fascinate them here in a 2 mile (3km) walk into the wild landscapes of Gunnerside Gill.

Further up the dale a different beauty distinguishes Swaledale around **Muker** and **Thwaite**, where the pattern of stone walls and field barns is more memorably concentrated than anywhere in England. If your visit coincides with the maturing hay-crop in valley meadows — usually in early July, bringing its own riches of flowers and ripening grass — the visual charm will be even greater. A walk through the fields, to the river and up the valley, provides a special dales' benediction. Richard and Cherry Kearton, born at Thwaite, schooled at Muker in the 1860s and 1870s, found inspiration here in the wildlife. They developed an interest in photography and, before the century's end, became pioneers of wildlife photography, wrote and illustrated many books and lectured extensively.

Continue along the B6270, climbing from Thwaite into the remote upper valley of the Swale, past Keld, the last village in the dale, and follow the river towards its source. The narrow winding road, still the B6270, climbs steadily into Pennine solitudes, crosses the watershed on the Yorkshire-Cumbria boundary at 1,700ft (518m), and descends the steep western escarpment to Nateby, joining the B6259 into another market town, **Kirkby Stephen** (the market day here is Monday). Follow the main road, the A685, north through the town to join the busy east-west trunk road, the A66, near Brough, heading westwards for Appleby, where a detour into the town soon convinces you that this is a place which is well-worth visiting.

In a loop of the River Eden, **Appleby** developed as a borough from Norman times, but today's castle, retaining its early keep, is largely a rebuilding, by Lady Anne Clifford, in the mid-seventeenth century, and is not open to the public. Boroughgate represents the spine of the medieval planned town, linking the castle to the parish church, inside which is Lady Anne's remarkable memorial which includes her proud family tree showing a relationship to twenty-four great families. In the upper part of the street is the neat little St Anne's Hospital, an almshouse founded by Lady Anne in 1651.

Trees, riverside greenery, and attractive buildings give Appleby an air of calm, solid prosperity. There is a lively Saturday market, good shops and inns and, in early June each year, a particularly colourful week when the town is host to the largest horse-fair in Britain, when gypsies from all over the country converge on the fairground just outside the town to buy and sell horses.

From Appleby continue north-westwards by the A66 for about 7 miles (11km), and just after Temple Sowerby turn right on the B6412 for Culgaith and Langwathby, where you turn right on the A686 to head for Alston. Beyond Melmerby the road climbs for 4 winding miles (7km) to **Hartside**, at 1,900ft (579m) the highest point on any 'A' road in Britain. If the weather is good, there is an enjoyable view from the top, westwards across the Vale of Eden to the Lake District and the Solway Firth, north and south for seemingly countless miles of wilderness north Pennine country. The A686 is the only trans-Pennine road for 30 miles (50km), and, a few miles to the south, Cross Fell, 2,930ft (893m) is the highest and most remote mountain in the whole Pennine range.

The road makes a long descent to the North Tyne Valley at **Alston**, which, at 1,000ft (305m), is one of the highest towns in England. Its market was created in the twelfth century, mainly for the benefit of its community of 'Kings' miners, who mined lead ore from rich veins deep beneath Alston Moor to the south and in upper Weardale to the east. Within a few miles of each other, three great northern rivers rise in the nearby fells, the Tyne taking initially a northwards course before swinging east, while the Wear and Tees carve valleys eastwards in their journeys to the North Sea. Roads follow these valleys, and another one links Alston with Allendale, so the town is at a focal point in the road system of these northern hills, and it is usually the first to be cut off by occasional heavy snows in winter. It is austere, dour, and fiercely proud of its bleak position, yet with relieving touches of sylvan and riverside charm, especially at the head of the South Tyne Valley around Garrigill, the first village encountered by the Pennine Way walkers after leaving Dufton, near Appleby, 16 miles (26km) away, with the Cross Fell range between.

Steep, cobbled streets meet at a pillared, covered Market Cross. Several eating places offer good food and a friendly welcome, and from the old

*The market place
in Alston*

railway station a few miles of the former South Tynedale Railway have been restored as a narrow-gauge line along the wooded valley northwards.

Our tour takes a different direction, however, by the A686 north-east-wards across another watershed before dropping down into the valley of West Allendale. Austere, upland scenery yield to mature woodlands above Cupola Bridge, where the waters of the East and West Allen Rivers meet to flow northwards to the main Tyne Valley. At **Allenbanks**, reached by a detour northwards along unclassified roads, the National Trust owns a stretch of the valley, where riverside and woodland walks are particularly colourful in early June when acres of rhododendrons are in bloom.

Two miles (3km) beyond Cupola Bridge, fork right along the B6305, and shortly turn right on the B6295, to head southwards for **Allendale Town**, in East Allendale. A sundial on St Cuthbert's Church records the latitude, 54°60", exactly midway between Cape Wrath and Beachy Head, and be-tween the East and West Coasts, so that, geographically, Allendale can claim to be the centre of Britain. In the eighteenth and nineteenth centuries it was certainly a busy centre of North Pennine lead-mining, and most of its stone-built houses, inns and hotels date from then.

Allendale is famous for its annual Baal Fire custom which occurs on New Year's Eve. This is a winter festival probably of pagan origins, in which a huge bonfire blazes in the market place, and men called 'Guisers' — strangely dressed and with blackened faces — carry barrels of burning tar in procession through the town.

The B6295 continues southwards along the East Allen Valley, woodlands and vegetation now clothe the old scars of earlier lead-mining, but terminal chimney-stacks of smelt-mill flues stand sentinel on skylines. Higher up the valley the pattern of small, walled fields is a relic of the days when Allendale operated a dual-economy system of farming, with miners encouraged to have small holdings, from which they could supplement wages earned by working relatively short hours in unhealthy conditions, with working outdoors on their own land where they kept a few livestock.

Allenheads marks the end of the valley, where more woods add a parkland quality to the landscape, embowering the little stone village, where the Allenheads Inn usually has a welcoming coal fire. Climb out from the village, over Burtree Fell, to Cowshill in Weardale, and make a short detour westward, up the A689, to visit the Killhope Wheel Leadmining Centre. As you have recently passed through so many places associated with the industry, it is a good idea to find out more about it, and Killhope is the best preserved site in the Northern Pennines. Centred on buildings associated with the former Park Level Mines — stables, smithy, sleeping quarters, and the great waterwheel — a Visitor Centre has been created to illustrate the history of local lead-mining and processing, and the life of the lead-workers and their families.

The wall-stitched landscapes of Weardale may be tempting but rewards of a different kind are to be found over in Teesdale. So, after a few more miles down the A689 to St John's Chapel, a long rather than a compact village, turn off southwards on a minor road to climb steeply to the watershed at 2,056ft (627m), and descend on an unfenced road into Upper Teesdale, at Langdon Beck.

Almost immediately you will see that, of all the Pennine dales seen so far, Upper Teesdale is the odd one out. It is more of an upland plateau than an obvious valley, although fells to the north and south rise to well over 2,000ft (610m). There are no apparent scars of old industries, and the settlement pattern is one of isolated farmsteads and small hamlets. Most of these are whitewashed, a long tradition on Lord Barnard's estate, to which they belong. Accidents of geology, and the effects of successive Ice Ages, the last one ending about 12,000 years ago, have created in Upper Teesdale a landscape and a plant life unique in Britain. This has been recognised by the designation of a huge area as a National Nature Reserve. Many of the plants are Arctic or Alpine species which were probably established after the last Ice Age, apparently suited to the altitude, 1,500-2,500ft (457-762m), a cold climate, high rainfall and a short growing season. These conditions are not suited to tree growth, so there are no trees in Upper Teesdale.

After joining the B6277, turn east to **Langdon Beck**, and take the minor road by Langdon Beck Hotel leading up to Cow Green, where there is a large car park at the end of the road. Information boards point out what is to be seen and what you can do. If you have time, walk the gravelled path across Widdybank Fell, providing fine views of Cow Green Reservoir and the bare fells in the distance. In half an hour you should reach the waterfall of Cauldron Snout, and the footbridge which carries the Pennine Way across the youthful River Tees. The period from late May through June and July probably sees Teesdale's flowers at their best but, being small and secretive, their impact may be insignificant in the broad scene.

Retrace your steps, and journey down Teesdale by the B6277 to **Middleton-in-Teesdale**, pausing on the way to visit High Force, England's most impressive waterfall. The Pennine Way footpath follows the south bank of the Tees closely between here and Middleton, with a useful access point near Newbiggin village.

Middleton was another important lead-mining centre last century, again showing the philanthropic influence of the London Lead Company. Keep on the B6277, cross the river, and follow the river's course, through a series of neat, stone villages (Romaldkirk being the best) to Barnard Castle, the chief market town in Teesdale (market day here is Wednesday). More information about this town is given in the Northumbria chapter.

Staying south of the River Tees, turn off the B6277 to **Egglestone Abbey**, where the riverside setting of the ruins of a thirteenth-century priory mark a return, in this tour, to the monastic influence in pastoral landscapes. Keep on the riverside road south-eastwards to join the A66 by the edge of **Rokeby Park** at the heart of the 'Scott Country' of Teesdale. Rokeby Hall was built in 1735 by Sir Thomas Robinson, son-in-law of the Earl of Carlisle, and himself a competent amateur architect, who favoured the Palladian style then in vogue.

The house and estate passed into the Morritt family, and in the early nineteenth century John Morritt was host to a distinguished group of artists and writers, including Turner, who painted scenes of the adjacent rivers Tees and Greta, and at nearby Brignall Banks. Girtin's painting of Greta Bridge, near the famous Morritt Arms, is regarded as one of his finest landscapes. Sir Walter Scott, the great novelist, frequently visited Rokeby between 1802 and 1831; Southey stayed there in 1812 and 1829, followed by Dickens in 1832.

From Rokeby head westwards along the busy A66 for a little over 2 miles (3km), turning left on an unclassified road which soon crosses the River Greta before making the long climb southwards, through Stang Forest and over high fells before descending into Arkengarthdale to join another minor road near the strangely-named hamlet of **C.B.** (after Charles Bathurst, local squire in the seventeenth century). Turn left and continue along the very scenic road a few miles down the valley to Reeth, where you pick up the B6270 to follow winding, beautiful Swaledale to **Richmond**.

High above a gorge of the River Swale, Richmond's situation gives it a visual excitement unusual in England, and nine centuries of history add to its unique character. It started as a Norman castle-town and even its name, 'Riche-mont' (strong hill) is French in origin. William the Conqueror granted Richmond to a distant relative, Alan the Red, who held the manor until 1089, when it passed to his son. The castle was started before 1100, yet, because it and its lands were so often connected with Brittany, it seems never to have played a part in England's political or military history.

The massive gatehouse-keep dominates the town, and was completed about 1180. Give yourself plenty of time to explore Richmond, first visiting the castle and most certainly climb to the top of the keep for the view.

Westwards is Swaledale and the distant hills, eastwards and southwards is vale country. Richmond is laid out at your feet, a maze of narrow streets, usually called 'wynds', radiating from a cobbled, semi-circular market place occupying the exact site of the castle's outer bailey, and filled with stalls on Saturdays. The medieval town walls, now largely hidden by buildings, ran parallel to the outer limits of the bailey, but about 50yd (45m) beyond them. One of the gates, Cornforth Bar, west of the castle, survives, and the old town covered a very small area within its walls. Holy Trinity, in the market place, is a bit of a mystery, and was never the parish church. It now houses the Green Howards Regimental Museum.

Castle Walk, which follows the foot of the curtain walls above the river gorge, is a complete contrast to the town's bustle around the market place. Richmond's only other medieval building is Grey Friars' Tower, north of the market place, all that remains of the Franciscan friary founded in 1258, although the tower dates from two centuries later.

Nearby is the Georgian Theatre, which looks like a warehouse but is a rare treasure. It was opened in 1788, closed in the 1840s and, after extensive restoration, re-opened in 1963, the best-preserved and most authentic Georgian theatre in Britain. Seating 237 people, not necessarily all in comfort, it has been redecorated in the original colours, and the narrow, deep, steeply-raked stage has original, painted woodland scenery dating from 1836, the oldest in the country. Regular performances and recitals are held at the theatre which, in its unique way, complements the theatrical nature of this predominantly Georgian town.

If you still have an appetite for abbeys, there are three more along these final journeys which should be seen. Easby Abbey, only 1 mile (2km) down-river from Richmond — a pleasant, easy walk — has a very large frater range, part of a guest-house, a large and impressive gatehouse, but very little of the church. Everything that survives dates from about 1300. Although it is a straightforward run southwards from Richmond to Ripon and Harrogate, it is more rewarding, if somewhat longer, to head for the dales again, following the A6108 along the winding, wooded valley of the Swale before swinging south to climb steadily over the eastern margins of the Pennines.

Keep on the A6108, cross the watershed to Bellerby and drop down to **Leyburn**, Wensleydale's main market town (market day here is Friday). Larger and less intimate than Hawes at the head of the dale, and with nothing of historic or architectural merit, it is nevertheless a good centre for exploring the mid and lower sections of Wensleydale and its tributary valleys, Bishopdale and Coverdale. Two miles (3km) to the west, on the A684, **Wensley** is a nineteenth-century 'estate' village at the entrance to Bolton Hall. Above it, Wensleydale's farming is pastoral, below are the first arable fields. Where one farming system meets another, markets were often established, and Wensley had one from 1200 to the early sixteenth century. Wensley Church is unusually rich in sixteenth- and seventeenth-century furnishings.

From Leyburn, the A6108 runs southwards, across the River Ure at

Middleham Bridge, and soon enters the village and former market town of **Middleham**. Historically far more important than Richmond, Middleham originated in early Norman times as a motte-and-bailey earthwork castle. However, the present massive building has a keep dating from 1170, a curtain-wall added later, with more comfortable living quarters round a courtyard added in the fourteenth and fifteenth centuries, together with a gatehouse.

The castle passed in the thirteenth century to the hands of the Nevilles of Raby, but saw its greatest days during the Wars of the Roses. In 1461 the young Duke of Gloucester joined the Middleham household to be tutored and trained by Richard Neville, Earl of Warwick, whose daughter Anne he courted and subsequently married in 1472. They lived at Middleham and their only son Edward was born there in 1473. After Richard's coronation as Richard III in 1483 he returned to Middleham only once, the next year, when his son died. Anne died soon afterwards, Richard was killed at Bosworth field in 1485, but the castle remained in crown hands until 1625. Below the castle, St Alkelda's Church was a collegiate foundation from 1478 until the middle of last century, when the novelist Charles Kingsley was its last canon.

Three-storey Georgian houses, inns and hotels round Middleham's market place add a touch of urbanity while, west of the castle, the open grassland of Middleham Low Moor provides superb gallops for the 200 or so racehorses currently trained at Middleham; expect to find many being exercised during mornings on local roads. As an important northern centre for horse-training, Middleham has a 200-year old tradition, and one set of stables actually adjoin the west walls of the castle.

The A6108 continues down the southern side of the widening valley, touching **East Witton**. Here, a long, sloping green is flanked by unassuming stone cottages, mostly rebuilt early last century by the landowner, the Earl of Ailesbury, on the precise sites of their predecessors shown on an estate map of 1627. The village was granted a market charter in 1307, largely as a result of its situation at the western edge of **Jervaulx Abbey** estate. The ruins of this Cistercian monastery, founded in 1156, a short distance down the main road, are in private ownership but are open to the public. Exquisitely situated in parkland they are famous, not so much for their architectural grandeur, but for the calm, informal beauty of the wild flowers that grow all around, unruled by either herbicides or the need for manicured lawns. Medieval monks are thought to have created the first Wensleydale cheese here, as well as breeding fine horses.

The road winds on through quiet countryside to **Masham** (pronounced Massam), another town of good stone houses and inns round a broad market place which was formerly cobbled but is now only partly so. From the eighteenth century until early this century the town's great annual sheep-fair in mid-September was one of the biggest in the north of England, with up to 70,000 sheep and lambs changing hands, and the market place crammed with temporary pens. Theakston's Brewery, a family affair since 1827, has brought new fame to the town; its most potent brew, served at many northern inns, is the 'Old Peculier'. The name marks an unusual aspect of Masham's history for, in medieval days, Archbishop of York freed Roger de Mowbray's manor, or Honour, 'from all customs and claims of his archdeacon and officials'. It was thus allowed to have its own 'Peculier Court', an ecclesiastical body with wide powers.

To the west of Masham a network of minor roads, narrow and winding, represents the routes by which stock was driven from the farms and small villages of the Pennine margins and Nidderdale to the great fair and markets at Masham. It is as much off-the-beaten-track country as you could wish for, with a number of surprises. Most unusual of these is near the tiny village of **Ilton** where, in a forestry plantation, you will find the so-called 'Druids' Temple'. This is a folly in the form of a miniature Stonehenge, with monoliths and trilithons composed in an elongated loop, the whimsical creation about 1820 of Squire Dalby of nearby Swinton Hall.

From there head eastwards for Grewelthorpe, and, to see a bit of earlier folly-building, walk to and through Hackfall Woods. In the late eighteenth century William Aislabie, of Studley Royal, landscaped this 350-years old, broad-leaved woodland on the south bank of the River Ure and added a number of folly ruins to create a place of secretive enchantment, with a rich diversity of habitats producing a wide range of woodland flowers.

Returning to the main road, the A6108, it is worth pausing at **West Tanfield**, midway between Masham and Ripon, if only for the view from the river bridge showing a fine grouping of church, village, and ruined gatehouse tower of the former Marmion stronghold, above the sparkling river. The castle has long-vanished, but medieval Marmions are commemorated by a large number of alabaster monuments in the church. The gatehouse-tower, which is open during normal hours, is tunnel-vaulted and dates from the fifteenth century.

So to Ripon, now a busy market town (market day here is Thursday) with cathedral status since 1836, although the first church there was that of a monastery founded by Scottish monks in AD660. Wilfrid became abbot shortly after and rebuilt the church on a different site, and his Saxon crypt of AD672 lies beneath the nave of today's cathedral. It serves as a strong-room in which ancient silver and treasures from many Yorkshire churches are displayed. The present cathedral, started in the twelfth century, shows features from most architectural periods, with the west front, 1220-30, one of the most noble Early English compositions in the country. Do not miss the gravestone outside the eastern end of the cathedral, commemorating an angler who died in the late eighteenth century. The epitaph is pleasantly humorous.

Architecturally, Ripon is undistinguished, although there are pleasant corners, with trees and gardens never far away. Many façades around the large market place are tastelessly modern, but on the west side the town hall of 1801 shows distinction, as well as a frieze with the town motto, 'Except Ye Lord Keep Ye Cittie, Ye Wakeman Waketh in Vain'. The Wakeman's House, fourteenth-century timber-framed, is a few doors away and now houses a small local history museum, but was formerly the home of the

*Fountains Abbey,
once one of the
richest Cistercian
monasteries*

Hornblower. The 1,000-year-old custom of Setting the Watch is marked
each evening at 9pm when the Wakeman, or Hornblower, blows his horn
in the market Square, which traditionally indicated that the town was then
in his care for the night. The tall obelisk commanding the square was
erected in 1781 to mark the sixtieth year for which William Aislabie, of
Studley Royal, served as Member of Parliament for Ripon.

A few miles west of Ripon, off the B6265, is the Fountains Abbey and
Studley Royal Estate (National Trust). Covering nearly 700 acres between
them, they form one of the supreme achievements of eighteenth-century
landscape gardening, recently recognised by their designation as one of the
few World Heritage Sites in Britain. They incorporate, in Fountains Abbey
itself (1132-1538), the greatest Cistercian monastic group in Europe;
Fountains Hall, 1598-1611, a characteristic Tudor house; the eighteenth-
century water gardens and deer park created by John Aislabie and his son
between 1720 and 1770. These were completely original in concept and
survive today as a gloriously green landscaped garden, virtually without
any introduced exotic species, with the abbey ruins forming the picturesque and romantic climax so necessary to a great Georgian garden and
park. Temples, gazeboes, grottoes and statues complement the man-made
landscape. Although you are free to wander at will throughout the vast
estate, separate guided tours of the abbey ruins and the water gardens are
available daily during the summer.

A final flourish to this tour of the hills and dales of the North Pennines
may be made by continuing westwards along the B6265 for another 4 miles

*Rievaulx Abbey,
near Helmsley,
North York Moors*

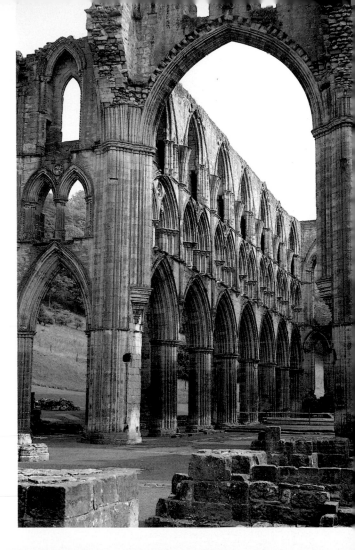

*Runswick Bay,
North York Moors*

Lower Eskdale, Lake District

A traditional farm building at Finsthwaite, Lake District

(6km), then turning off along a minor road to **Brimham Rocks** (National Trust, always open). Here, at about 1,000ft (305m), is an area of moorland, where heather and bilberry bloom among silver birches, and huge rocks of millstone grit have been worn by wind and weather into fascinating fantastic shapes, suggesting an almost alien world. Visited by tourists for two centuries, many of the rocks were given names by Victorians — Sphinx, Turtle, Anvil, Dancing Bear, Castle, Pulpit, and Druids' Altar. Paths twist among them; their gritty surfaces are easy to scramble on, and Brimham House now serves as an Information Centre with refreshments and toilets nearby. You need to walk a little way from the large car park to enjoy the rocks at close quarters, for vehicles are not allowed on the drive to Brimham House. The view from the rocks stretches westwards to moors and dales, and in the opposite direction to York Minster which is 20 miles (32km) away. A steep road descends southwards into Nidderdale to join the B6165 eastwards to Ripley, the A61, and Harrogate. **Ripley** is an estate village of great charm and unity, with houses built between 1780 and 1860 mainly in Gothic and Tudor styles. Ripley Castle, home of the Ingilby family since the early fourteenth century, is largely Tudor and Georgian, with elegant interiors and extensive gardens.

Further Information
— The Yorkshire Dales and The North Pennines —

Places of Interest

Allenheads
Heritage Centre
Open: March to October 10am-5pm, November to February weekends only.

Aysgarth
Yorkshire Museum of Carriages & Horse-drawn Vehicles
Open: most days Easter to October 11.30am-5.30pm.

Bolton Abbey
Open: daily throughout year.

Bolton Castle
Open: March to October, 10am-5pm. November to February by prior arrangement.

Brough Castle (English Heritage)
Open: throughout year (except 24 to 26 December) April to September 10am-6pm, October to March 10am-4pm.

Easby Abbey (English Heritage)
Open: throughout year (except 24 to 26 December) April to September 10am-6pm, October to March 10am-4pm.

Fountains Abbey & Studley Royal (National Trust)
Abbey and Garden open throughout year (except 25-26 December and Fridays in November, December and January). Winter 10am-5pm (or dusk if earlier). April to June and September 10am-7pm, July to August 10am-8pm, October 10am-6pm (or dusk if earlier).

Fountains Hall (National Trust)
Open: daily (except 25-26 December) April to September 11am-6pm, October to March 11am-4pm.

Grassington Museum
Open: April to October daily 2-4.30pm.

Hawes
Dales Countryside Museum
Open: Easter or 1 April to September, Monday to Saturday 11am-5pm, Sunday 2-5pm; October, Tuesday, Saturday, Sunday only.

Ireshopeburn
Weardale Museum
Open: May, June, September. Wednesday, Thursday, Saturday and Sunday, July, August daily 1-5pm, Sundays 1-4pm also Easter and Bank Holiday weekends.

Killhope Lead Mining Centre
Open: April to October daily 10.30am-5pm.

Middleham Castle
(English Heritage)
Open: throughout year (except 24-26 December) April (or Easter if earlier) to September 10am-6pm. October to March 10am-4pm.

Reeth
Swaledale Folk Museum
Open: April to September daily.

Richmond
Richmond Castle (English Heritage)
Open: throughout year (except 24-26 December) April (or Easter) to September daily 10am-6pm. October to March 10am-4pm.

Richmond Georgian Theatre
Open: daily 2.30-5pm. Also Saturday, Sunday and Bank Holiday Mondays 10.30am-1pm.

Green Howards Regimental Museum
Open: April to October daily.

Richmondshire Museum
Open: end of May to September, afternoons.

Ripley
Castle
Open: April, May and October, Saturday and Sunday 11.30am-4pm. June to September, daily except Monday and Friday 11.30am-4.30pm. Good Friday and Bank Holidays, 11am-4.30pm.

Settle
Museum of North Craven Life
Open: May, June, Saturday and Sunday afternoons. July to September daily (except Monday) afternoons.

Skipton
Castle
Open: throughout year except 25 December daily from 10am (Sunday 2pm) until 6pm (or dusk if earlier).

Skipton Museum
Open: April-September weekdays and Sunday afternoons.

Temple Sowerby
Acorn Bank Garden (National Trust)
Open: April to early November daily 10am-6pm (or dusk).

West Tanfield
Marmion Tower (English Heritage)
Open: throughout year.

Tourist Information Centres

Alston
Railway Station, ☎ 0498 81696

Appleby
Boroughgate, ☎ 07683 51177

Brough
Main Street, ☎09304 260

Harrogate
Royal Baths Assembly Rooms
☎ 423 525666/7/8

Kirkby Stephen
Market Street
☎ 07683 71199

Leyburn
Commercial Square
☎ 0969 23069/22773

Reeth
Folk Museum
☎ 0748 84373

Richmond
Friary Gardens, ☎ 0748 850252

Ripon
Minster Road, ☎ 0765 4625

Settle
Town Hall, ☎ 07292 3617

Skipton
Victoria Square
☎ 0756 2809/4357 (evening 2892)

Yorkshire Dales National Park
Grassington, ☎ 0756 752748

11 • The North York Moors

S t Aeldred, Abbot of Rievaulx Abbey in the twelfth century, was sufficiently moved by the tranquillity of Rye Dale to say; 'Everywhere peace,
everywhere serenity and a marvellous freedom from the tumult of the
world'. If he were alive today he would probably be horrified by the traffic
speeding along the B1257, Helmsley to Stokesley road above the abbey, but
it would be interesting to hear his thoughts on the rest of this valley. In his
time, Rye Dale would have been developing as an intensively farmed area
in support of the rapidly expanding abbey. Farming methods were certainly different to those of today; admittedly ploughed fields were smaller,
but the number of people needed to till them and look after domestic
animals were far in excess of those needed to maintain today's highly
productive undertakings. Another change he would notice would be that
the dale has fewer wildwoods than in his day; these have been partly
replaced by planted trees. As to whether St Aeldred would still think of Rye
Dale as a place where peace and serenity prevail, the answer is a qualified
yes. Despite the demands of a twentieth-century society with more time
and the means to enjoy the countryside, it is still possible to find out-of-the-
way places, where visitors can enjoy that 'marvellous freedom from the
tumult of the world'.

Even though the North York Moors National Park has 11 million visitors
a year, making it the third most popular park after the Lakes and Peak
District, quiet corners can still be found. Many visitors head for the open-
plan attractions of Hutton-le-Hole, and so many want to admire Farndale's
daffodils each spring that a one-way traffic scheme controls the number of
cars along the narrow, winding roads of this lovely dale. Pickering, just
outside the National Park, and Thornton Dale, inside an extension of the
park to the east along the A170, and considered by many to be the prettiest
village south of the Moors, can be so crowded that it is impossible to find
a car-parking space. However, villages like Normanby, in the flatlands of
the Vale of Pickering, are almost timeless. Normanby is where, according
to locals, nothing much has happened since 'Billy Norman [William the
Conqueror] went by t'end of road' during his harrying of the North.

The North York Moors are a roughly kidney-shaped block of uplands
rising steadily northwards from the Vale of Pickering, ending in an abrupt
escarpment above Teesside. A series of deep-cut valleys, with one exception, flow south into the lush farmland of the Vale of Pickering. Steep-sided

and remote, they were formed by a cataclysmic outpouring of melt-water at the end of the last Ice Age. A massive lake filling what is now Esk Dale, was unable to find its way into the still frozen North Sea. Held by ice on all sides but the south, it overflowed with awesome force, carving Newton Dale and changing the course of the Derwent. Gouged deeply into the landscape, the remote recesses of the deepest dales have never been heavily populated and, as a result, are places where nature rather than man is very much in control.

Long, broad airy ridges separating the valleys have for centuries been used as routes between centres of population north and south of the moors. Scottish drovers walked cattle and sheep from north of the Border, along the edge of the Cleveland Hills to English markets, and coach routes can still be traced across Rudland Rigg and Blakey Ridge. Some of these old roads have been metalled, are reasonably traffic-free and offer enjoyable motoring or cyling. Others, like the one on Rudland Rigg or across Fylingdales Moor, make excellent long-distance footpaths.

Several of the Central Dales and parts of the Northern Escarpment were once much busier places than now. Ironstone and coal found employment for over 3,000 miners and their families in Upper Rosedale. Iron-ore hewn from beneath the moors and calcined by heat produced from coal found near the Lion Inn on Blakey Ridge (which means black), was carried by a high-level moor-top railway which descended the steep Greenhow Incline on its way to the furnaces of Middlesbrough. It was once said that Rosedale Abbey beds were never cold, as they were shared by men whose shifts took over from each other. Today only 300 people live around the ruins of an abbey whose fortunes were made from iron-ore beneath its lands. Mining for alum, was an industry created by Henry VIII's attempt to break the Papal monopoly of its use as a mordant, or fixative, for the then popular Turkey Red dyes. Ironstone mining finished in the late 1920s, long after the clifftop alum mines were abandoned and nature reclaimed the land.

Heather is the dominant plant of the high moors, forming the largest expanse in England. Grouse feed on the young shoots of this upland plant but, after the 'Glorious Twelfth' of August (the start of the grouse-shooting season), many do not survive to enjoy the purple glory of the moors in the full bloom of summer. Ancient crosses, there are at least thirty of them dotted around the moors, and even older standing stones sit in isolation amidst the heather. One of the finest crosses, known as Young Ralph, is on Rosedale Head and has become the symbol of the North York Moors National Park Authority.

Forests created around the Upper Derwent Valley and in Newton Dale have been opened for public access and, although man-made, the plantations of 'foreign' conifers have become havens for wildlife. Miles of footpaths, trails and picnic sites offer a tranquillity that St Aeldred would have appreciated.

The Howardian Hills adjoining the south-western corner of the North York Moors National Park is an area of undulating wooded countryside dividing the Vale of Pickering from the Vale of York. Villages of attractive

red-roofed stone cottages and comfortable manor houses, or ruined abbeys fit into a green landscape amidst gentle, limestone hills. Grand houses, notably Vanbrugh's masterpiece Castle Howard, look out on to landscape parkland. In order to preserve this unique landscape, the Howardian Hills have been designated as an Area of Outstanding Natural Beauty. This does not carry quite the status of a National Park, but it means that this special area will be protected from undue development.

Some of the oldest passenger carrying railway lines follow the deep valleys of the North York Moors. The one linking coastal Whitby with Teesside follows Esk Dale and is run by British Rail; the other is along spectacular Newton Dale and is run by a preservation society, Moorsrail. Using steam locomotives wherever possible, it crosses Goathland Moor along an historically unique route to join British Rail's track at Grosmount. Both lines offer an ideal opportunity to enjoy a car-free day out on the moors.

In order to describe the off the beaten track places in and around the North York Moors, the text has been roughly divided into the following sections: the coast; Derwentdale and Fylingdales Moor; Newtondale and

Esk Dale; the central dales and moors; the Cleveland Hills and the Howardian Hills.

The Coast

Walkers following the coastal section of the Cleveland Way long-distance footpath have the best opportunity of finding out-of-the-way places along this exposed coastline. High cliffs alternate between exposed bays open to the direct wrath of the North Sea. With the exception of Staithes, Whitby and Scarborough, where river estuaries in the case of Staithes and Whitby, and a protective cliff at Scarborough have allowed the creation of harbours, fishing boats are normally beach-launched. Only Whitby and Scarborough have developed to any size and, due to the exposed nature of this north-east facing coast, tiny fishing villages snuggling beneath the haven of sheltering cliffs have kept much of their charm despite the demands of tourism and housing developments.

Most of the out-of-the-way places along this coast can only be reached on foot but, fortunately, it should not be necessary to walk very far from a safely parked car. Narrow side roads link the coast to the A174 and A171, the arterial links between Scarborough and Teesside. Never terribly busy roads, parking can usually be found in unofficial lay-bys set back from the sea, but it is important to park where it will not block access to someone's drive or farmers' fields.

Following the Cleveland Way south-east from its re-entry into the National Park, the path crosses **Boulby Head**, at 666ft (203m) the highest point on the North-East Coast. The path can be joined in Boulby village, just off the A174, and winds its way above a cliff which is now the haunt of sea birds, but was the scene of intense mining activity. Alum and ironstone were once mined nearby, as was jet, a form of fossilised wood. The latter was a fashionable ornamental stone in Victorian times and is now enjoying renewed popularity. Fossils of ammonites and other creatures can be found among the rocks, but take great care when exploring the unstable cliffs or if beachcombing beneath them. Steer clear of areas where rock falls are likely, keep an eye on the state of the tide, and make sure you can reach a safe beach access point in good time before high tide.

Moving on past Staithes with its fishermen's cottages grouped around a wave-washed harbour, where James Cook the navigator and explorer began his relationship with the sea, the coastal path climbs again past Brackenberry Wyke, a shallow unsheltered bay, to reach **Port Mulgrave**. Ships no longer carry ironstone from Port Mulgrave, but the abandoned harbour, once fed by a 2ft 6in wide underground railway, is an interesting place to explore. Substantial houses, once the homes of harbour officials, are the only links with what was a busy port only a few decades ago.

Runswick Bay is one of the prettiest harbourless fishing villages along this coast. Boats waiting above the high water mark are launched from the beach when conditions allow. Fishing is no longer a major industry, and many fishermen only work part-time.

The coast path climbs from the sandy beach and follows the curve of Runswick Bay, past a series of hollows where, according to local legends, a hob (a Yorkshire goblin) lives. He is apparently a friendly chap and is credited with curing children's ailments. The tiny clifftop hamlet of **Kettleness** marks the eastern arm of the bay; its cottages are the survivors of a village which disappeared when the sea cliff fell during a terrific storm in 1829. Kettleness is linked to the main road by a narrow winding lane past the site of a Roman signal station and, perhaps more important, a friendly pub. Remains of Roman signal stations feature all along this part of the coast, on high points between Saltburn and Filey, protecting a coast which was constantly under the threat of attack by land-hungry peoples from across the North Sea.

Continuing past almost inaccessible coves, the Cleveland Way joins the main road at sea level through aptly named Sandsend and the start of 3 miles (5km) of open sandy beaches leading to Whitby. Inland, **Mulgrave Castle** stands above a wooded ravine. It is the home of the Marquess of Normanby, whose ancestors made their fortunes from local ironstone mines. Deep inside the woodland are the romantic remains of an earlier castle built by Robert de Turnham in 1200, replacing an even older wooden Norman structure which stood on top of a circular mound above Mickleby Beck. Known as Foss Castle, it was supposed to have been the home of a giant called Wade and his wife Bel. Mulgrave Woods and the castle are privately owned, but public access is usually allowed on Saturdays, Sundays and Wednesdays.

Head on through **Whitby**, whose candy floss and penny arcades contrast sharply with the quaint intricacies of its harbourside streets and an ancient clifftop abbey. One hundred and ninety-nine steps known as Church Stairs climb from East Pier to St Mary's Church where Bram Stoker's Count Dracula sought refuge in the grave of a suicide.

Leave the tranquil ruins of St Hilda's Abbey where, in AD667, a compromise at the Synod of Whitby settled the difference between the Celtic and Roman methods of determining the date of Easter. Beyond a caravan site, the coast path follows 5 miles (8km) of clifftop without any road access until it reaches **Robin Hood's Bay**. Cars must be parked above the oldest part of the village and most visitors are content to walk down the steep and narrow street towards the open shore, or perhaps sun themselves in sheltered recesses along the protective sea wall. Pretty as the first view of Robin Hood's Bay is, the real attraction of the village lies in the narrow, almost hidden little side alleys and courtyards off the central, boat-cluttered lower main street.

Country lanes end at car parks above a rocky beach dotted with fascinating sea pools at the south-eastern end of Robin Hood's Bay. Leaving the sea, the coast path climbs to **Ravenscar**, the 'town that never was'. A grid pattern of clifftop streets lined with a scant handful of houses is all that remains of a grandiose scheme to build a resort rivalling Scarborough. The main reason it failed was due to the unstable geology of the area, a problem engineers had to cope with when building the Scarborough to Whitby

Railway. Part of the now undulating track is used by a Geological Nature Trail which begins in Ravenscar and also visits parts of the long-abandoned alum quarries nearby.

Heather-covered Howdale Moor — above Stoupe Brow, inland and to the west of Ravenscar — is littered with a complex of enigmatic tumuli left behind by a race of people who inhabited the area long before the Roman invasion. Several rights of way across the moor begin near the prominent radio mast at the top of the coastwards road descending Stoupe Brow.

A continuation of Bent Rigg Lane, one of Ravenscar's roads lies roughly parallel to the coast, but it has no official access link with the Cleveland Way footpath. The path follows the bramble and blackthorn-covered clifftop above wooded Beast Cliff and descends to **Hayburn Wyke**. This tiny bay is watered by Hayburn Beck where the Yorkshire Naturalists' Trust have created a 34 acre Nature Reserve based on a narrow densely wooded ravine carved through the exposed layers of Middle Jurassic rocks. Both the nature reserve and its waterfall backed rocky foreshore are accessible by a steep footpath below the Hayburn Wyke Hotel. An intriguing series of headlands, all with an everchanging seascape, lead onwards to the outskirts of Scarborough. Most of the headlands and intervening wykes can be reached alongside paths and tracks away from the narrow road between Cloughton and Ravenscar. **Cloughton Wyke** is at the end of a rough road eastwards from the junction of the Ravenscar road and the A171. Deep water in the wyke makes it popular with sea anglers, but it is also an ideal spot for picnicking. The coast path can be followed north from here along Roger Trod to Hayburn Wyke, returning to Cloughton by way of the old railway line.

Derwentdale and Fylingdales Moor

Before the last Ice Age, the River Derwent flowed due east and entered the North Sea at Scalby Mills to the north of Scarborough. A shallow stream, sluggish in all but flood conditions, still enters the sea at this point. However, the present, if unnatural, course of the Derwent is via the Vale of Pickering. This redirected course of the river was the result of a massive build-up of melt-water, which could not find a way into the still frozen North Sea when land-based ice melted about 10 to 12,000 years ago. Overspilling across a narrow gap, the Derwent gouged a new route for itself through Forge Valley and created a lake in what became the Vale of Pickering, before flowing on to join the Ouse below Selby, as it does to this day. When a natural dam at the western end of Pake Pickering below the A64 near Whitwell-on-the-Hill eventually collapsed, it left behind an area of silt rich agricultural land. Unfortunately, for centuries the vale was prone to flooding until Sir George Calley, an eighteenth-century landowner and an inventive man, had the brilliant idea of creating a flood channel — the Sea Cut along the prehistoric route of the Derwent. The road through **Forge Valley** is an attractive drive and short woodland and riverside footpaths retain much of the solitude that makes this sylvan ravine such a delight.

A quiet woodland path in Forge Valley

Dense plantations of conifers cover Upper Derwentdale and its se-cluded tributaries. Tributaries like the aptly named Whisperdales can only be reached on foot, and are waiting to be discovered. The latter are acces-sible from a forest track leading downhill from the Swarth Howe scenic car park on the ridgetop Scalby to Harwood Dale road, but parking is almost impossible around some of the remoter side dales. Reached only by the most determined, this apparent inaccessibility makes them even more delightful.

Long silent roads wind their way through forests where thoughtfully placed car parks and picnic sites, together with forest trails and waymarked walks, can be used to enjoy some of the remotest corners of this man-made amenity.

Tiny villages such as Hackness and Langdale End, where time seems to have stood still, have pleasant, unspoilt pubs and restaurants offering a remarkably high standard of cuisine. The quiet atmosphere of **Hackness** would be instantly recognised by St Hilda's nuns who settled there in AD680; but the scant remains of their abbey are in a field close by Lord Derwent's Georgian manor house. Scores of tumuli, those strange mounds erected by our prehistoric ancestors, are now hidden in the depths of the forests, but several Bridestones, a unique feature of the North York Moors, can be found surrounding the valley heads.

The Ordnance Survey Tourist Map of the North York Moors indicates that land to the east of the A169, near the hairpin bend of Eller Beck Bridge, is Ministry of Defence Property. What it does not show are the massive 'golf balls', soon to be replaced by a truncated pyramid covering the strategic radar antennae on **Fylingdales Moor**. As strange and obtrusive as the site may be, the surrounding heather moorland offers miles of little-used tracks and footpaths. Many were once commercial links between the coast and inland markets. Four of them converge on the highest point of the moor near the lonely cross marking the even older tumulus of Lilla Howe. The cross is said to mark the grave of Lillan, the faithful servant of a king of Northumbria who saved his master's life by intercepting an assassin's dagger. Forest walks and trails lead from car parks at May Beck in Sneaton Forest to the north of Fylingdales Moor.

Newton Dale and Esk Dale

If the melt-water flood which created Newton Dale had occurred in recent times, it would have been hailed as a natural disaster of unparalleled proportions. Tiny Pickering Beck trickles down a ravine gouged by billions of tons of water overflowing from 'Lake Esk' to the north. No roads, apart from short lengths of forest drive follow any part of the dale but, in the true spirit of entrepreneurial Victorian railway engineers, George Stephenson forced a track through the gorge. The valley bottom is barely wide enough to hold both railway and the river but, by following the stream, the line climbs steadily to its summit near **Fen Bog**. The bog is in a hole created by a huge overspilling back wash, and to cross it Stephenson's navvies had to literally float the track across on piles of brushwood and woollen fleeces. Fen Bog has become a haven for many unusual plants and insects and has been designated a nature reserve run by the Yorkshire Naturalists' Trust.

The best way to explore the hidden recesses of Newton Dale is from the railway. Steam locomotives, augmented by diesel during periods of drought, ply between the busy market town of Pickering and a link with British Rail at Grosmont. Halts such as Levisham or Newton Dale can be used as starting points for walks in Cropton Forest or on Levisham Moor. Minor roads from Pickering climb northwards through rich farmland towards the forest. One of them heads towards the tiny hamlet of Cawthorne and a lay-by nearby gives access to a curious group of earth mounds and banks (GR 785 900). These are the remains of an area where Roman military engineers were trained in the art of building camps. Not all are in the traditional 'playing card' shape and indicate a degree of innovation in Roman military thinking.

A Roman road linking Cawthorne Camps with the coast can be traced as a broad stony causeway above Wheeldale to the north of Cropton Forest. Known locally as Wade's Causeway, it was supposed to have been built by the Giant Wade and his wife Bel who, so the story goes, simultaneously built Mulgrave and Pickering castles. They supposedly shared a single hammer, throwing it the twenty miles or so to each other as needed! **Levisham**, a single street of farms and cottages topped by the Horseshoe Inn to the east of Newton Dale, is separated from the neighbouring village of Lockton by a dangerously steep road across the valley of Levisham Beck. Like the main valley, Levisham's dale was also carved by melt-water, possibly a secondary overflow from the main deluge. Footpaths across

Levisham Moor, or beside the beck, converge at Gallows Dyke above the mysterious Hole of Horcum, the reputed haunt of a giant. Both Levisham Moor and the Hole can be reached from the scenic car park, about 8 miles (13km) along the A169 to the north-east of Pickering.

As the railway descends through Goathland, it makes a broad sweep past Thomason Foss to reach Beck Hole. When the line was first built, Stephenson decided that it would be too difficult to continue alongside Eller Beck at this point and trains were rope-hauled up and down a 1 in 15 incline. Frequent accidents led to the creation, in 1865, of what was called the Deviation Line. Bridging Eller Beck four times and running through cuttings blasted out of solid rock, it cost £50,000 to create this section of line. The incline above Beck Hole is now part of a series of Historic Railway trails around Goathland.

Any motorist unprepared for narrow, twisting, steeply inclined roads should avoid **Esk Dale**. The railway follows the river with some difficulty but, apart from a few miles between Lealham and Castleton where the valley momentarily widens, roads tend to avoid the valley bottom and climb away from the river as soon as possible. It is this apparent inaccessibility which gives Esk Dale its charm. The villages have been slow to grow because of their difficult sites, and, as a result, are delightfully haphazard groups of architecturally interesting buildings. All of them are worth exploring and most have at least one welcoming pub. **Danby Lodge**, the North York Moors National Park centre in the upper dale is a most useful aid in helping visitors to understand this historic dale. Courses, exhibitions and guided walks from Danby Lodge not only cover Esk Dale, but the whole of the countryside in the park.

Working upstream from the railway junction at Grosmont, a complex of by-roads wind their way along the valley sides to **Egton Bridge** in one of the prettiest parts of the dale. They have held a gooseberry show here for over 200 years and, in keeping with this mild eccentricity, the main village of Egton, several hundred feet above the river, recently twinned itself with the mythical French village of *Clochemerle* created by the novelist Gabriel Chevallier. Like its counterpart, Egton fought bureaucracy over the provision of a public convenience, and won.

Beggar's Bridge, below Glaisdale station, is the first of two ancient single-arched bridges across the Esk. The other is Duck Bridge near Danby, and both are relics from a time when pack horses carried goods up and down the dale. Flagged ways, now relegated to footpaths, once echoed to the clip-clopping of ponies carrying salted or fresh fish from the coast, and returning with clothing and other essentials. **Glaisdale** was once an ironstone-mining village, but little evidence of the industry remains in this almost medieval backwater. Weaving was important locally in the sixteenth and seventeenth centuries; extra storeys in some of the older cottages indicate their use as weaving lofts.

Five narrow side dales enter the Esk between Glaisdale in the east and Westerdale. Dale bottom lanes and footpaths are an aid for their easy exploration and high level roads climb the intervening ridges. The name

Duck Bridge, an old packhorse bridge in Esk Dale

Fairy Cross Plain between Great and Little Fryup Dales often causes speculation. Old people living in the area not very long ago were convinced that little green men lived there and paid them due courtesies. The name Fryup has nothing to do with eating; the title is thought to come from the name of the original Norse settler, Friga, and 'up' is a corruption of 'hop', meaning a small valley.

Danby Castle, below Danby Rigg and to the south-east of opposite Danby village, is now a farmhouse, but was a fortified manor house in the fourteenth-century. Once owned by Catherine Parr, the sixth wife of Henry VIII, it still contains two towers and a dungeon. Elizabethan justices met there and Danby Court Leet and Baron still administers common land and rights of way. Its deliberations take place annually in the throne room which can be visited with the farm owner's permission.

The Camphill Village Trust have developed a self-supporting community at Botton Hall near the head of Danby Dale, where mentally and physically handicapped people make high quality goods for sale either locally or by mail order. **Westerdale** is in the heart of grouse moorland and the castellated hall, now a youth hostel, was once a shooting lodge.

Commondale is almost at the head of Esk Dale. Extensive earth dykes practically surround a side valley above the village and several moorland tracks, some of them paved, cross the nearby moors. One of them, Monk's Causeway, connected Whitby Abbey and Gisborough Priory. Long, roadless Baysdale marks the western limits of Esk Dale. The valley is carved deep into the Cleveland Escarpment where a remote farm below Battersby Moor was once an abbey.

The Central Dales

To the west of Newton Dale, four tributaries of roughly equal length, flow south to join Rye Dale, the main dale on the western side of the moors. Joined by minor streams, the River Rye enters the Derwent above the market town of Malton, regional headquarters for the Vale of Pickering and the western moors.

Starting in the east with **Rosedale** and its river, the Seven, this valley's population has shrunk to about a tenth of its former size in less than a hundred years. With the decline in ironstone-mining, nature is recovering from the ravages of man and the dale has returned to normality. However, as with many abandoned industrial areas, a number of relics have become interesting features in their own right. In the hey-day of ironstone-mining, **Rosedale Abbey** village was a much busier place than it is now. In order to move the ore from the south side of the moors to Middlesbrough's iron foundries, a railway was built around the upper dale's skyline. Footpaths and side roads out of the dale reach the cinder track bed of the long-abandoned line; it can be followed around the dale head with the minimum of effort. If you follow the line in a clockwise direction from Rosedale Abbey, a break may be made at the Lion Inn at Blakey Howe. On the way back make a diversion to examine the weird ruins of the old drying kilns above the east side of the dale. Take extra care when near abandoned trackside mine shafts.

Moorland roads across Blakey Ridge and Rosedale Moor converge on Rosedale Head near Ralph's Cross, the symbol of the North York Moors National Park. Known more correctly as Young Ralph's Cross, there is a smaller cross nearby in the heather known as Old Ralph. About $^1/_2$ mile (1km) east along the Rosedale Moor road, there is a stubby pillar topped by a white circular stone called Fat Betty.

The road leads down Rosedale where wild daffodils bloom in spring, and are less well known than their Farndale neighbours. Cutting through a corner of Cropton Forest, the road climbs up to the village which gives the forest its name. Just outside the National Park boundary, **Cropton** has grand views of the moors and forest. A village of stone cottages standing on either side of its main street, **Cropton** once had a castle, but only its earthworks remain. Lovers of real-ale should head for The New Inn to sample its home-brewed ale.

Lastingham is at the head of a short tributary of the River Seven and diagonally opposite Cropton. Considered by many to be the prettiest village on the moors, it is often missed by visitors to Hutton-le-Hole, barely $1^1/_2$ miles (2km) across the moor. Its church is a place of pilgrimage; one of the oldest in Northern England and admired by the Venerable Bede, it was founded in AD645 by Cedd, a Lindisfarne monk. A number of interesting well-heads can be found around the village, one of them dedicated to St Cedd. There is a pretty village post office-cum-general store, a cosy pub and a high class restaurant. Lidsty Cross, at the corner of the road to Appleton, commemorates Queen Victoria's Diamond Jubilee, and a seat erected at the time of Queen Elizabeth II's Coronation is a handy place to sit and admire the view. Once Farndale's daffodils are finished and left by the hundreds who walk beside the River Dove each spring, the dale resumes its tranquil rural charm. Known in Yorkshire as 'Lenten Lillies', they are the only true native daffodil. Tiny stone built hamlets and ancient water mills stand as reminders of a time when the valley was more intensively farmed. Roads run along each side of Farndale, but only link at Church Houses. Those leading to the dale head dwindle into tracks and footpaths climbing Greenhow Moor where the old Rosedale railway begins its descent towards Teesside at Bloworth Crossing.

Hodge Beck flows down Bransdale, probably the least-known of all the dales in the central moors. Hard by the dale head, **Bransdale Mill** can only be reached by footpath. Described as the 'Mill at the World's End' and now maintained by the National Trust, it was founded in the late thirteenth-century to grind flour for the Stuteville family estate. The present building dates from 1811 when William Strickland and his son Emmanuel developed a complex of cottages, sheds, forges and pigstys around the water-driven mill. Plaques in Hebrew, Greek and Latin around the mill indicate Emmanuel's classic upbringing. He was educated at King's College Cambridge and later became the incumbent at Ingleby Greenhow, to the north of the Cleveland Escarpment. Other inscriptions above the doors and on a sundial were left by William Strickland and his masons. The curious number AM 5822, beneath the initials W.S., are a reference to an archaic method of calculating the world's age. Invented by Archbishop Usher, Bishop of Dublin (1581-1656), who decided that the world was created in 4004BC. A.M. stands for Anno Mundi and 5882 was arrived at by adding 4004 + 1817 + 1 for year 0 between BC and AD.

Lonely moorland roads marked by venerable wayside stones climb out of the dale, linking it with Helmsley and Kirkbymoorside. No roads follow the Dove along Farndale, but side lanes and a handful of footpaths lead to isolated valley bottom woodlands and remote farms. About $^1/_2$ mile (1km) before the river flows beneath the A170 Pickering to Helmsley road, a side road following an earlier route of the main road fords the river and, almost hidden above it, is St Gregory's Minster. Almost untouched in later years, it is a fine example of a Saxon church. Notice the Viking sundial above the porch, erected by Orm, son of Gamal, in 1060.

A long, straight road climbs north from Helmsley, enters Carlton Plantation and descends the oddly named Cow House Bank into Riccal Dale. Scenic car parks, secluded picnic sites and wildlife are outstanding features of the forest, and the now undulating road leads across the moors into Bransdale. In late summer the narrow strip of surfaced tracks winds like a ribbon through a gloriously scented haze of purple heather.

The B1257 climbs out of Helmsley on its way to Stokesley, the scenic route from York to Middlesbrough. Following Rye Dale and its tributary, the Seph, the road skirts rural hamlets and often overlooked features set back from the road and away from the noise of speeding traffic.

A side lane behind Helmsley's Civil War-defiled castle, leads to

Duncombe Park. Built by Vanbrugh about the same time as Castle Howard, this ancestral home of the Earls of Feversham stands in 600 acres of beautiful wooded parkland above the meandering Rye.

Mock Grecian temples at either end of the Terrace Walk below Duncombe were originally intended to be linked by footpath with those above Rievaulx Abbey. Now owned by the National Trust, Rievaulx Temples and their Terrace are reached from a turning near the lane leading down to the abbey. Still maintaining their original purpose, the temples offer a romantic view of Rievaulx Abbey.

A scenic car park in a forest clearing marks the point at which the main road and Rye Dale part company. Narrow side lanes cross the dale and climb steeply towards the Cleveland Hills. Narrow plantations of mixed woodland fill the deeply indented side dales and, above the Hambleton Moors, the western limits of the North York Moors National Park are crossed by a lonely road climbing from Hawnby to Osmotherley.

When John Wesley preached at **Hawnby** in 1757, he called it 'one of the pleasantest parts of England', a sentiment he would probably echo were he alive today. Hawnby is in two parts, the upper a cluster of pantiled-roofed cottages, an inn and farmhouses on a sunny ledge sheltered by a glacial melt-water honed hill. The lower village is a scattering of farms lining the upper valley and a half-hidden church. All Saints has watched over the fortunes of the people of upper Rye Dale since the twelfth-century. The village lost more than its share of men during World War I, the unbelievably long memorial and poignant stained glass window bear witness to this. **Arden Hall**, almost hidden in dense forest, is about 1 mile (2km) upstream from the church. Home of Lord Mexborough, Arden Hall held Mary Queen of Scots for part of her long imprisonment and gradual journeying south towards execution. The hall is only open on specially advertised days.

Continuing upstream along the River Seph, the main road passes a thatch-roofed, sixteenth-century cruck-framed inn. Once known as the Sun Inn, but now called Spout House, the pub was the haunt of Bobbie Dowson, whipper-in for the Bilsdale Hunt. A painting of Dowson and other huntsmen drinking whisky in the inn was reproduced as an advertisement showing them drinking Bovril. Unfortunately for the Bovril company, this alteration infringed the artist's copyright, and after an acrimonious court battle, the artist was awarded considerable damages. Skirting the tiny villages of Fangdale Beck, Chop Yat and Seave Green, the road makes a steep descent of wooded Hasty Bank on its way northwards to Industrial Teesside.

The Cleveland Hills

A motorist driving north along the A168 has, on the right at its junction with the A19, a magnificent view of an abrupt, densely wooded escarpment. These are the Hambleton Hills, the south-western ramparts of the North York Moors. This escarpment continues northwards towards Osmotherley and, facing generally north-west with hardly a break, becomes the

Cleveland Hills. The hills enjoy a final fling above Guisborough before merging into the undulating ironstone landscape of Langbaurgh. Sharp-pointed isolated hills such as Roseberry Topping and Easby Moor feature prominently along the edge of the Cleveland Hills. Relics of a time when massive sheets of ice honed the landscape, their summits were never covered and are known as nunataks, an Eskimo word.

Snug villages, taking advantage of the protection offered by the escarpment to their north, line the lush rolling landscape between the Plain of York and the Hambleton Hills. **Coxwold**, in the far-left corner of the national park, was the home of the eighteenth-century novelist Laurence Sterne (1713-68). Vicar of Coxwold, he lived at Shandy Hall, a pleasant mixture of styles ranging from the fifteenth to seventeenth-centuries and now owned by the National Trust. Seventeenth-century almshouses and the Faucenberg Arms in the wide, main street help to create Coxwold's mellow atmosphere. Newburgh Priory is beyond the far end of the village. Now a private house, local tradition insists that Oliver Cromwell is buried there. The house, grounds and delightful water garden are open to the public at advertised times. Moving north towards the hills, the narrow road passes the noble ruins of Byland Abbey. It was founded by monks who came from Savigny in France by way of Furness Abbey in Westmorland. They built several small abbeys throughout the district before settling on Byland in 1177.

Ampleforth College can be glimpsed across the fields from Byland. Founded in 1802 by Father Bolton, a Benedictine priest and beginning with only two pupils, it is now one of the largest Roman Catholic schools in the country. Ampleforth Moors mark the southern limits of the Hambleton and Cleveland Hills. Partly wooded, the moors are crossed by footpaths; one of them, immediately north of the village, leads to Studford Ring, a prehistoric circular earth mound.

Timber stacked around **Kilburn** eventually becomes high quality furniture, made by the descendants of Robert Thompson, the woodcarver whose mouse symbol adorns ecclesiastical furniture in York Minster and Westminster Abbey. Kilburn's famous White Horse overlooks both village and the Vale of York. Built by local school children in 1857, it's surprisingly rough outline can be viewed at close quarters from the escarpment footpath. The path continues across the top of the little-visited Roulston Scar before reaching the popular viewpoint on Sutton Bank. Beyond Sutton Bank's often crowded car park, a short woodland footpath leads to secluded Gormire Lake. The ridge-top road was once used by cattle drovers and Dialstone Farm once echoed to the sounds of horse-racing. Fine bloodstock animals are still trained nearby.

The high-level road along the escarpment reached a 'T' junction at the top of steeply inclined Sneck Yate Bank, the end of the metalled version of the ancient drove. Beyond the junction a wide track continues for about another 8 miles (13km) to Osmotherley Moor. Followed by the route of the Cleveland Way long-distance footpath, the track can be visited on short walks from secluded villages such as Boltby and Kepwick, villages which

Byland Abbey, built by Cistercians in the twelfth century

are almost hidden in sheltering folds along the foot of the Hambleton Hills. It is easy to imagine that a witch spoken of in local legend still lives on Black Hambleton, the highest point along the western escarpment. The forest track above the woodland car park in Over Stilton Forest can be used to reach a breathtaking viewpoint on Black Hambleton.

The old drove road leaves the moors below Scarth Wood to the east of Osmotherley. To the north of this ancient stone-built village, a path in Arncliffe Woods leads steeply down to **Mount Grace Priory**. Owned by the National Trust, who have carried out an intensive restoration and preservation programme in recent years, this little-known Carthusian priory is the largest and best preserved in England. Living a life of austere silence, each monk had his own two-story cell complete with a small garden. They received their meals through an angled hole in the cell wall, which prevented them from seeing those who brought the food.

North-east of Osmotherley, the moorland escarpment changes. Still wooded, the Cleveland Hills are indented by narrow dales, unpopulated except for remote farms whose contact with the outside world is a series of narrow, winding lanes. Steep-sided, rounded hills — relics of the Ice Age — line the escarpment or sit in splendid isolation like Roseberry Topping, Cleveland's 'Matterhorn'. Crossed by the Cleveland Way and the Lyke Wake Walk, the Cleveland Escarpment is a popular walking area. Villages, once the home of ironstone workers, line the foot of the Cleveland Hills.

Elizabeth Harland, who lived to 105, and 8ft 6in tall Henry Cooper, both came from **Swainby**. Drovers rested here, but today the village is a gentle cluster of stone cottages, mainly commuter homes for Teesside executives. Of all the villages along this north facing foot of the moors, Ingleby

Mount Grace Priory; the ruins give a good impression of the austere but self sufficient lives of the monks

Greenhow can claim to be the most attractive. Its church is topped by a dovecote-like tower and was built in Norman times. The best view of it is from across the nearby ford. An incline once used by wagons loaded with Rosedale Ironstone, descends Greenhow Moor where massive Bronze Age cairns were left by the earliest settlers in Cleveland.

Across Kildale with its road and rail links to Esk Dale, the Cleveland Way path climbs Coate Moor to its memorial pinnacle to Captain Cook, then moves on over Great Ayton Moor above Guisborough. The Cleveland Hills can be said to end at the A171.

The Howardian Hills

This low undulating wooded ridge lies to the south-west of the North York Moors National Park. Sharing a mutual boundary between Coxwold and Ampleforth, the Howardian Hills run roughly south-east towards the gap created by the River Derwent. The B1257 Malton to Helmsley road follows the north-eastern foot of the ridge and where a line of charming villages sit above any danger of floods. Grand houses (Castle Howard is to the south-east) and secluded ancient villages, can be found at the end of winding lanes in this small but rewarding district.

Nunnington is to the north of the Howardians. Its seventeenth-century manor house, now owned by the National Trust, has a room supposedly haunted by the friendly ghost of a maid. She first came to Nunnington with her mistress and apparently liked it so much that she returned in death. The hall also houses the famous Carlisle collection of miniature rooms.

Sir Thomas Fairfax, Colonel of Oliver Cromwell's Model Army, lived at **Gilling Castle**. Altered many times since the fourteenth-century, but always with taste, the castle, near Gilling East, is now a preparatory school for Ampleforth College. The castle is open to the public at advertised times.

Brandsby is across the hills by the B1363 from Gilling. Like Kilburn, it also has its woodcarvers and their symbol is an acorn. To the east of Brandsby, along a hilltop road, the 'City of Troy' turf maze (SE 625 719) is one of the oldest in England; its design, linking it with the Minoan period, is found on every continent except Australasia.

If you have time to spare, look in on Terrington, further to the east. Typical of many of the delightful Howardian villages, its Georgian and Victorian houses sit back from wide grass verges. Roads appearing to go nowhere eventually reach Castle Howard, eastern Yorkshire's premier house, and bring to an end this short tour of little-known, off the beaten track places in and around the North York Moors.

Further Information

— The North York Moors —

Places of Interest

Opening times of buildings maintained by English Heritage:
Mid-March to mid-October, weekdays 9.30am-6.30pm. Sundays 2-6.30pm. October to March, weekdays 9.30am-4pm. Sundays 2-4pm. All English Heritage buildings are not open on Mondays.

Ayton Castle
Outskirts West Ayton

Beck Isle Museum
Pickering
Open: early Easter to mid-October 10.30am-1pm, 2-5pm (10.30am-7pm August).

Bransdale Mill (National Trust)
No interior access, but mill complex can be visited from public rights of way at the head of Bransdale north of Helmsley.

Byland Abbey (English Heritage)
6 miles (10km) south-west of Helmsley off A170 (Coxwold Road)
Open: All year.

Danby Castle
Near Whitby
Access only by prior arrangement.

Danby Lodge National Park Centre
Esk Dale
Open: April to October daily 10am-5pm (6pm July and August). February, March and November 10am-5pm weekends only.

Duncombe Park
Helmsley
Open: May to August 10am-4pm.

Ebberston Hall
Thornton Dale on A170
Open: Easter to mid September 2-6pm.

Gilling Castle
On B1363 near Helmsley
Open: Term time, daily (except Sundays) 10am-12noon and 2-4pm.

Gisborough Priory
(English Heritage)
Guisborough town centre

Helmsley Castle
(English Heritage)
West of town centre

Low Dalby Visitor Centre
Dalby Forest
3 miles (5km) north-east of Thornton Dale.
Open: daily April to end October.

Malton Museum
Market Place, Malton
Open: weekdays 11am-5pm, Sundays
2-5pm (4.30pm in winter).

Mount Grace Priory
(English Heritage and National Trust)
Off A19 1 mile (2km) north of
Osmotherley

Mulgrave Castle
(Private but near public footpath)
Woodland $1^1/_2$ miles (2km) south-west of
Sandsend (A174)

Newburgh Priory
Coxwold
Open: Wednesday from beginning July
to end August 2-5pm.

Nunnington Hall (National Trust)
$4^1/_2$ miles (7km) south-east of Helmsley
Open: Tuesday, Wednesday, Thursday,
Saturday, Sunday, April to October, plus
Bank Holiday Mondays, 1-6pm.

Pickering Castle (English Heritage)
North of town centre

Ravenscar National Trust Centre
Start of Geological Trail through nearby
alum quarries.

Rievaulx Abbey (English Heritage)
$2^1/_2$ miles (4km) north-west of Helmsley
off B1257 Stokesley road

Rievaulx Terrace and Temples
(National Trust)
$2^1/_2$ miles (4km) north-west of Helmsley
on B1257
Open: April to October 10.30am-6pm
every day except Good Friday.

Ryedale Folk Museum
Hutton-le-Hole, $2^1/_2$ miles (4km) north of
Kirkbymoorside
Open: daily Easter to end September
2-6pm (mid-July to end August 11am-
6pm).

Shandy Hall (National Trust)
Coxwold
Open: early June to end September,
Wednesdays 2-6pm.

St Gregory's Minster
Kirkdale, off A170, 1 mile (2km) south-
west of Kirkbymoorside

Tourist Information Centres

*Open summer only.

North York Moors National Park:
***Danby Lodge** ☎ Castleton (02876) 654
Helmsley Book Shop ☎ (0439) 70775
Pickering Station ☎ (0751) 73791
National Trust, Ravenscar ☎ (0723)
870138
Ryedale Folk Museum, Hutton-le-Hole
☎ (07515) 367
***Sutton Bank** ☎ (0845) 597426

Others:
Bridlington, Garrison Street ☎ (0262)
73474 (summer)
(0262) 78255 (winter)
***Filey**, John Street ☎ (0723) 512204
Scarborough St Nicholas Cliff ☎ (0723)
72261/73333
***Thirsk Museum**, 16 Kirkgate ☎ (0845)
22755
Whitby, New Quay Road ☎ (0947)
602674

12 • The Lake District

The time cannot be too far into the future when the Lake District National Park Authority is forced to adopt some form of traffic restriction in the more popular valleys. Places like the Langdales and Borrowdale can, on busier holiday weekends, generate a traffic flow way beyond the capabilities of their narrow road systems. Quite literally, some parts of the Lake District are in danger of being loved to death. Honeypot centres around Bowness-on-Windermere and Keswick can, within the limitations of their car and bus parking facilities, cope with the demands made by tourists, many of whom may also make their way to the National Park Visitor Centre at Brockholes. Several of the courses and day events on offer at this elegant Edwardian country house on the shores of Lake Windermere are aimed at helping the visitor to discover the lesser-known facets of the Lake District. A visit to Brockholes will help both first-time and regular visitors to find those quieter places which are off the beaten track.

A glance at the map of the Lake District shows that the most popular places are within easy access of the A591. Kendal, Windermere, Ambleside and Keswick can be reached (traffic permitting) within less than an hour after leaving the M6 motorway. However, once away from the busier arterial roads linking the Lake District to the rest of England, a network of minor roads leads into remote and often little-known dales. It is here that you will find sanctuary away from the bustle of the central part of this delectable region.

Most people come to the Lake District to enjoy its mountain scenery, either to simply admire the magnificent views from the lakesides, scenic car parks and picnic sites or if they are more energetic, to climb the high fells. At 3,000ft (915m), these are obvious attractions to the 'peak bagger' that is in many of us and, as a result, many of the well-used paths are badly worn. Despite the attractions of these busy routes, there are still quieter ways of reaching the high tops; many of these paths and also some of lesser-known fells are described in the following text.

Another glimpse at the Ordnance Survey Map of the Lake District shows that many side valleys and by-roads radiate from Ambleside. Using this busy central town as a starting point, and by moving eastwards to the boundary of the national park and beyond, you can then travel in a clockwise direction to explore the little-known valleys and villages away from the more central, crowded areas.

The Eastern Fells and Valleys

Of all the Lake District, this region of high, rolling hills and secluded valleys bordered by the A592 Kirkstone Pass road in the west and the A6 to the east, is probably the least-known. Further east still, beyond the National Park boundary and the M6's passage through the Lune Gorge, are that group of unenclosed fells known as the Howgills; strictly part of the Yorkshire Dales National Park, yet uniquely different to both the Dales and the Lakes.

Taking a line due east from Ambleside across sturdy Wansfell, where there is an easy climb to an excellent viewpoint, then crossing the Kirkstone Pass road (A592) you will come to the valley of **Trout Beck**. This deep-cut dale is fed by three tributaries draining the western outliers of High Street and where a footpath climbing the Hagg Gill tributary follows the line of a Roman road. There was once a racecourse on top of High Street, at 2,719ft (829m) the highest racecourse in Britain. Today, the only sporting activities are likely to be the occasional hound trail meet, the traditional method of fox hunting in the Lake District.

Eastwards again to follow the bridle-way over the Garbourn Pass from Troutbeck village to Kentmere. Once a drove road where cattle and sheep walked their long way to market, and also a route followed by packhorse trains, the 'road' is now only suitable for horse-riders and pedestrians or the sturdiest of four-wheel drive vehicles.

Although a branch continues up the steep eastern hillside to a group of farmsteads, the narrow winding public road along Kentdale effectively ends in **Kentmere** village. Kentmere is ancient, its church is dedicated to northern St Cuthbert and has sixteenth-century roof beams, but is built on older foundations. Kentmere Hall, to the west of the village, is built around a fourteenth-century pele tower.

The next dale to the east is **Longsleddale**, a valley which really is away from it all where the dead-end road serves a scattered farming community and continues as a rough bridleway across Gatescarth Pass into Mardale. This valley was flooded by one of the most attractive stretches of man-made water in the country. This is **Haweswater** which supplies drinking water to Greater Manchester. When the reservoir was built, the valley lost its links with the Holme family, self-styled 'kings' of Mardale, who lived as outlaws in this remote spot from 1209 to 1885.

Deer roam freely on the fells and in the forests surrounding Haweswater. This is a popular venue for sportsmen, especially fishermen who stay at the hospitable hotel about half way along its eastern shore. They pit their wits against the stock of brown trout and also char, that strange fish left behind by the last Ice Age which inhabits the cold depths of the deepest lakes.

Haweswater Beck flows north from the reservoir. About 2 miles (3km) below the dam, the river cuts through **Bampton** where it becomes the Lowther and joins the Eamont near Penrith. On the first Saturday in September they hold a Children's Sports Day in Bampton which used to take place on the summit of High Street. The Mardale Hunt use the village's St Patrick's Well Inn as their gathering point.

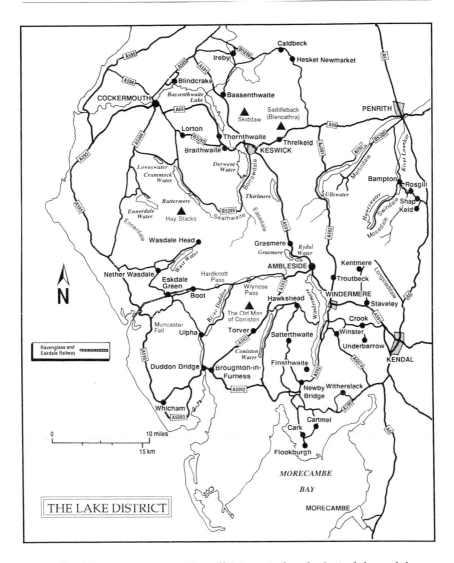

THE LAKE DISTRICT

South of Bampton, across Rosgill Moor, is lonely Swindale, a dale reserved for shepherds and walkers who must follow a long farm lane in order to reach footpaths leading to even remoter Mosedale. From Swindale Head you can still trace the Corpse Road along which, before 1736, Mardale's dead were carried for burial at Shap; strapped for their last journey to the backs of horses.

A minor road following the National Park boundary links Bampton with the A6 at **Shap**, a much quieter village since the M6 motorway was opened. An easily missed signpost off the Bampton road points the way to the tranquil ruins of Shap Abbey. The abbey stands beside the River Lowther and was built by the Pre-monstratensian canons in the twelfth-century.

Dissolved by the orders of Henry VIII, the remaining walls of the west tower and outlines of other buildings indicate its former size.

Linked by a footpath south-west from the abbey, the tiny village of **Keld** has a diminutive sixteenth-century chapel owned by the National Trust. Massive standing stones in nearby fields are the remains of an avenue leading to a stone circle 1 mile (2km) south of Shap.

Now make your way north-west across the fells towards Ullswater, where a narrow winding road from Pooley Bridge hugs its eastern shore to reach the almost hidden valley of Bannerdale. Lake steamers use Howtown pier as a stopping place on their journeys between Glenridding and Pooley Bridge. The road moves inland from here to climb steeply over into **Martindale**. Protected by its isolation, this is one of the most peaceful dales in the Lake District. Tiny clusters of houses, barely worth the title of hamlet, are grouped around the dale sides and the road, with another following nearby Boardale, serves only a handful of farms. Martindale has a history reaching back to before the sixteenth-century when the parish Church of St Martin was built on the site of one even older. The church may be ancient, but it is young in comparison with the stone circles and megaliths on the moors to the east of Martindale.

The Southern Fells

Most visitors who come to the Lake District by car will, if they are travelling from the south along the M6, leave it at Junction 36 to follow the A591 (T) past Kendal and into Windermere. Rather than join slow moving traffic beyond the National Park boundary south-east of Staveley, a left turn along any of the unclassified roads between Sizergh and Staveley will lead to a region of low wooded, fells and long, craggy limestone escarpments; very few visitors have discovered their delights.

This zone is bordered roughly by the A591 in the east and Coniston in the west, with Windermere and the River Leven dividing it into two contrasting parts. Neither section can compete with the high fells of the central Lake District. Indeed, very few places even reach 1,000ft (305m) and the highest point, Top o'Selside above Coniston Water, is only 1,091ft (333m), but what the district lacks in height it more than makes up for with interesting byways. Another positive feature is that, being protected by the high central fells, this part of the Lake District, especially to the east of Lake Windermere, enjoys better weather than the more mountainous areas. Moving south from Staveley, the unclassified road crosses across the B5284 Kendal to Bowness road at the scattered farming community of **Crook**. The hall was once the home of Robert Philipson, a Royalist officer during the Civil War. Apparently a bit hot-headed — he was known locally as 'Robert the Devil' — he once rode into Kendal church in order to capture a Roundhead colonel in revenge for the latter besieging Philipson on Lake Windermere's Belle Isle. Driven out by an irate congregation, Robert left his sword and helmet behind, where they are now on display.

A side road 1 mile (2km) west of Crook leads, by a series of steep hills, to

Winster where several of the houses date from the seventeenth-century. From the village a maze of narrow lanes south of the A5074, many of them with steep gradients and tight corners, leads to Cartmel Fell. Ludderburn Moss (SD 405 909), $1^1/_2$ miles (2km) south of Winster, is a quiet haven with picnic spots with an easy footpath to the panoramic view from its highest point.

Due east of here back across the A5074, **Crosthwaite** lies near the head of the Lythe Valley. The church stands on the site of a preaching cross — hence the village's name. Crosthwaite is the centre of rich farmland where fruit trees grow abundantly, especially damsons which fill the orchards and hedgerows with their fragrant blossom each spring.

East again is **Underbarrow**, a winner of the 'Best Kept Small Village of South Lakeland' competition. The village sits at a cross-roads of old coach routes, roads superseded by the B5284 to the north and the A5074 to the south. The 'barrow' referred to in Underbarrow is a 700ft (213m) crag to the east, part of a series of limestone escarpments running roughly north-south with their steepest sides facing west, on either side of the Lyth Valley. Whitbarrow Scar is west of the river and the A5074. Like the escarpments on the opposite side of the valley, it is the home of many interesting and often rare plants; on no account should these be taken. The lower slopes are filled with broad-leaved woodlands, again havens of unusual plants and other wildlife. Public footpaths cross Whitbarrow Scar and a Nature Reserve has been established at Chapel Head. **Witherslack** is at the foot of the scar and high above the danger of flooding by the River Winster. Its church, dedicated to St Paul, was built under the terms of the will of John Barwick (1618-69), a fervent Royalist who was born nearby and who was imprisoned in the Tower of London for his beliefs. A sundial in the churchyard is marked with his initials.

The A590, the only road towards the south out of shipbuilding Barrow-in-Furness makes a wide detour between the Leven and Kent rivers to follow lower ground around Newton Fell, the last of the interesting outliers of south-eastern Lakeland. With one minor exception no official right of way footpaths cross this triangular shaped fell, but a high-level road between High Newton and the Winster Valley follows a gap in its southern ramparts.

South of the main road the B5277 leaves **Lindale** to enter the Cartmel Peninsula. A cast-iron obelisk by the crossroads in the centre of the village is a memorial to one of the early Lakeland iron masters, 'Iron Mad' John Wilkinson (1728-1808). He intended that the 20 ton, 40ft high column should be erected over his grave, and that he should be buried in a cast-iron coffin made to his own design in his garden at Castle Head, south-east of Lindale. His wishes were carried out, but later owners of the house took a dislike to the garden's macabre ornaments and had him reburied in the local churchyard. The obelisk was re-erected on its present site in 1863.

The Cartmel Peninsula enjoys more hours of sunshine than any other part of the Lake District and the pleasant little seaside resort of **Grange-over-Sands** justifiably styles itself as the 'Torquay of the North'. The sands

*The gatehouse is all that remains of the priory at Cartmel,
near Grange-over-Sands*

referred to in the resort's name are those of Morecambe Bay which are uncovered every low tide, and where local fishermen use specially adapted tractors rather than boats to reach their nets. This is known as 'fluke-fishing'; the tide goes out so far that it is possible to erect a framework of staked nets at low tide and collect the fish after the next high tide. The famous Morecambe Bay shrimps are also caught at low tide, again from tractors or lorries.

For a really off the beaten track walk you could try the Morecambe Bay Walk. From medieval times until the last century, a crossing of the sands was used even by horse-drawn coaches, to save the long haul through Kendal to reach coastal towns to the south of the Lake District. Regular guided crossings at suitable low tides are organised throughout the summer; details can be obtained from Morecambe Corporation Tourist Department. On no account should unaccompanied crossings be contemplated. The sands are dangerous, cut by deep channels and the tides come in very fast.

Flookburgh and Cark, twin villages at the junction of two 'B' roads, the B5277 and B5278 and separated only by the railway, have a sleepy atmosphere which belies their long and complex history. Edward I granted **Flookburgh** its market charter in 1278, an event celebrated by a fair held on the nearest Saturday to 24 June. A sword, staff and halberd given to the former town at the time of its charter are housed in the parish church. The weather vane is in the shape of a fluke, acknowledging the unique local method of catching flat-fish in nearby estuaries around the bay. **Cark** was a busy place during the Industrial Revolution, having a few cotton mills.

Holker Hall, to the north-west of Cark, is set in 200 acres of deer park and has gardens which take advantage of this sunny corner of Lakeland and where the famous Lakeland Rose Show takes place every July. House and gardens are open to the public at advertised times.

Crossing the River Leven and the short but scenic riverside steam railway link between Haverthwaite and Lake Windermere, you come to a roughly oval-shaped complex of low, rolling fells and forest. The best-known parts of this remote corner are to the north around that delectable piece of National Trust land known as Tarn Hows and where nearby Hawkshead and its links with William Wordsworth's schooldays leads to Grizedale Forest, one of the few places where the Forestry Commission can be proud of the natural look of its plantations.

Tiny, remote villages lie almost hidden amongst folds in the Furness Fells, or deep within the forest. Screened by woodland and on a winding road to the west of Lake Windermere above Newby Bridge, **Finsthwaite** is typical of these villages. Now the home of workers in the nearby forest and retired folk, the village once hummed to the sound of Stott Park Mill, a water-powered nineteenth-century bobbin mill which used local timber. Restored to its former glory, the mill is open to visitors at advertised times.

South-west across the Rusland, the main river draining the southern portion of this area, the Nature Reserve of Hay Bridge near Booth specialises in the study of deer, both red and roe living in quiet seclusion in the nearby forest. The Hay Bridge Deer Museum is well worth a visit, especially for young people.

A mile (2km) north-west across the wooded fell is **Colton** with its fifteenth-century church perched on a hilltop overlooking the village. Short, easy footpaths lead from the village to views of Morecambe Bay and the Coniston fells.

Three road systems run roughly northwards from the A590 towards Grizedale Forest. The one from Finsthwaite follows Lake Windermere and the one serving Colton eventually reaches Hawkshead by way of Satterthwaite and Grizedale villages. The third and central road follows the Rusland Pool river as far as the village of Rusland before diverging towards Esthwaite Water. Rusland nestles in the shelter of hundreds of acres of deciduous woodlands and is home village for Rusland Hall, a Georgian mansion with gardens where white peacocks strut.

Two villages lie at either end of a clearing deep in the heart of Grizedale Forest. The southernmost is **Satterthwaite**, a village founded by Vikings who built a farm (*saeter*) in a forest clearing, a scene which is little changed in the twentieth century. According to local schoolchildren, the same Vikings kept their pigs at **Grizedale** (*gris* is still the Scandinavian word for 'pig'). The Forestry Commission have made their local headquarters in this village, the centre of an 8,000 acre forest. Trails and quiet footpaths radiating from the village lead into the forest where, if you are lucky, you may see the shy roe deer and other wildlife which abound in the forest. A novel feature of Grizedale is the Theatre-in-the-Forest which has given an average of 120 high standard performances a year since 1970. Theatregoers can complete a night out with a meal at the nearby, internationally renowned Ormandy Hotel.

Esthwaite Water is across the fells from the forest and, despite its closeness to Hawkshead and the easy access from nearby roads, it is a lake for solitary contemplation. Likewise, Claife Heights between Esthwaite and Lake Windermere are rarely crowded. Jewel-like tarns reached by woodland footpaths from Hawkshead, and the viewpoint on Latterbarrow, the highest point, are just some of the attractions.

The Western Dales and Fells

Shadowed by the obvious attractions offered by the central giants of Lakeland, the lower-lying fells to the west tend to be mostly moorland of interest only to sheep farmers. However, as in all cases where the exception proves the rule, several interesting hills await the attentions of those seeking new places to explore. Harter Fell and Dunnerdale Crag are but two heights quietly awaiting 'discovery'. This part of the Lake District has a series of little-visited valleys, many of them accessible to motor traffic and yet much quieter than the better known dales to the north and east.

This section is devoted to those dales which drain south and west towards the Irish Sea and range in a broad arc from the Coniston Valley to Ennerdale. As some of the intervening fells do not have official rights of way to their summits, permission should be sought as a matter of courtesy before venturing on to their little-trodden slopes. Also due to the remote nature of these fells, it is more important than ever to make sure you leave an exact note of your route before setting out from your holiday accommodation, and to ensure that you do not deviate from the plan. If threatened by mist or bad weather while out, always ensure you can recognise at least one landmark before it is obliterated and plan your retreat route accordingly.

Three main roads, the A5092, A5084 and A593 to the south-east of Coniston Water, make a rough triangle with the village of Torver at its apex. Within this triangle lie two distinct groups of low but steep-sided fells, **Blawith Fell** (the main mass) and Burney in the south, the continuation of a line of high ground running south to Barrow-in-Furness. A beacon once stood on top of Blawith Fell to warn the locals of armed attack, or to celebrate important events. Footpaths from Blawith beside the A5084 Greenodd to Torver road lead past Beacon Tarn towards the summit. There is also a beautiful path from Blawith along the shores of Coniston Water. Burney does not have a right of way to its summit, but a public footpath crosses the col to its south-east about 150ft (46m) lower down. This triangle of rolling fells is not simply a hill-walker's preserve. Winding hilly lanes from all of the three main roads wandering almost aimlessly across the heights make them accessible to motorists.

Of the countless thousands who thread their way across the barren summits of Coniston Old Man and its neighbour Wetherlam, few pay much attention to the lower fells beyond the Walna Scar Road. **Torver High**

Whistling Green Bridge in the Duddon Valley

Common, a little over 1 mile (2km) from its village, is littered with prehistoric remains. Hut circles, cairns and long enclosure mounds speak of its once greater importance; small wonder then that strange lights and unidentified flying objects have been sighted on these moors. A steep road leaves the A593 at Hawthwaite near Broughton in Furness and climbs across the Dunnerdale Fells, worthy of exploration, and descends into one of the most beautiful and romantic of all the Lakeland valleys, the **Duddon**. Wordsworth loved this valley so much that he wrote thirty-five poems using it as his theme. Despite it having a through road, but no doubt because this is a very minor and winding one, the dale remains almost unknown. The dale, followed by its road, begins at the foot of the Wrynose Pass and turns south-west past the junction of the valley road with that climbing towards Hard Knott. As you drive down the dale, look to the right above the forestry plantations at Hinning House towards the graceful cone-like symmetry of Harter Fell, 2,129ft (649m), a steep, hard climb but one rewarded by a perfect view of the Sca Fell range and Bowfell to the north. **Ulpha**, the only village in the Duddon Valley, takes its name from Ulph, son of Evard, who was granted lands around the dale soon after the Norman Conquest. The parish church though much altered over the centuries, has stood on the same little hilltop since before the reign of Henry III. This valley has evocatively named places like Whistling Green, High Dunnerdale and Hinning House.

The A5092 crosses the river at Duddon Bridge at the head of the tidal reach above Duddon Sands and where Wordsworth described 'majestic Duddon' making 'radiant progress towards the deep'. **Broughton in Furness**, an eighteenth-century market town, is on the opposite side of the estuary. Linked by a short footpath from the main road is a tower complete with dungeons, all that remains of a Norman castle built to control this part of the Furness district.

Keeping to the coastal plain, the A595 makes a wide loop around the long ridge of Black Combe. The hill rises abruptly from sea level to 1,970ft (601m), and as a result is an ideal vantage point for views across Morecambe Bay towards the Isle of Man. A footpath climbs steeply above Whicham close by the junction of the A595 with the A5093.

Return briefly to the Duddon Valley where two high level roads link it with Eskdale. The more southerly one crosses Thwaites Fell, a remote place known only to huntsmen and shepherds. The second road is arguably the most attractive; it climbs from Ulpha by a series of tight bends, then out onto Birker Fell not far from Devoke Water, a rewarding venue for anglers which is also accessible by public footpaths. Leaving Birker Fell, the road swoops down to Eskdale Green, the central habitation of a valley served by a narrow gauge railway, the Ravenglass and Eskdale. The River Esk starts its life beneath high, remote and little-visited crags buttressing the massive cirque of Scafell Pike and Bowfell. Only the hardiest fell walkers use this long but rewarding route to England's rooftop. However, the rewards of the walk-in from the foot of Hard Knott Pass are well worth the effort.

The Romans built their fort of *Mediobogdum* to command the western approaches to Hard Knott, a route used by their road from the sea port of *Glannaventa* (present day Ravenglass) and *Galava* at the head of Lake Windermere. The site of *Mediobogdum* is well-excavated and it does not need much imagination to visualise the fort in its heyday, or stand on the commander's dais and imagine the troops arrayed on the nearby parade ground.

The tiny village of **Boot**, about half way down the valley, once echoed to the tread of ironstone miners' and quarrymen's clogs. Mining both for copper and iron, as well as granite quarrying, finished many years ago, but the narrow gauge railway built to move the products of their labour still exists. Now affectionately known as 'La'al Ratty', the Ravenglass and Eskdale Railway operates a mostly summer service of passenger trains hauled by authentic scale replicas of famous steam and diesel locomotives; the latter only being used whenever there is a danger of sparks setting fire to surrounding woodland.

A journey on 'Ratty' can be combined with a walk over **Muncaster Fell**. This delectable and little known fell (it is only 758ft, 231m high), points directly towards the central fells and has one of the finest viewpoints in the whole of the Lake District. As the best views from the fell are to the north-east, park at either Irton Road Station or Eskdale Green and take the train south along the foot of Muncaster Fell to Muncaster Mill Halt. From the restored mill the path climbs through woodland, then descends to the main road, the A595, at Muncaster Chase. A sharp left turn at the junction joins a narrow, rough-surfaced lane climbing past woodland and wild rhododendron coverts. At the lane head, a path continues to climb across the summit of the fell and, with the view of the Lakeland giants forever in view above the dale head, gradually descends towards the village of Eskdale Green.

Wasdale can claim to be the cradle of Lakeland rock climbing. Many of the famous names in the history of British mountaineering used the Wasdale Head as a base for their explorations of the south-facing crags of Great Gable and Sca Fell. Not all lived to enjoy old age and poignant memorials in the tiny Church of St Olaf record tragedies both here and on Alpine expeditions.

Despite its early popularity, Wasdale has never been a place to attract the crowds. Being about the furthest dale from the main entry points into the Lake District has preserved a great deal of Wasdale's original charm, and it remains very much as those original mountaineers found when they turned away from the coast and followed one of the winding roads converging on Nether Wasdale. Possibly due to this comparative inaccessibility, most fell walkers and climbers turn their attentions to the highest fells surrounding Wasdale Head; Pillar, Great Gable and the Sca Fell range. Fascinating challenge though these giants may be, there are still slightly lower fells to the north of Wast Water lake which are worth far more than the scant attention usually given to them. Nether Beck which enters the lake about half way along its north-western shore, drains a moorland area known as Copeland Forest. The dale head is surrounded by a trio of fells, Red Pike, Steeple and Haycock. None cut the magic 3,000ft (915m) contour, but all offer a challenge to the hill walker in search of less-crowded fells. Scoat Tarn fills a glacier-scoured combe beneath Red Pike and Low Tarn is on the opposite side of its ridge. Seatallan stands aloof lower down the dale and tiny, almost hidden Greendale Tarn is between this conical hill and its neighbour, Middle Fell.

Another high-level tarn can be reached by the footpath south from Wasdale Head Farm which climbs between Sca Fell and scree-covered Illgill Head. This is Burnmoor Tarn, an excellent fishing lake owned by the National Trust. Long footpaths, used mostly by shepherds, wind their way north out of Lower Wasdale. One of them finds its way into remote Blengdale where a scattering of cairns and tumuli on the National Trust's Stockdale Moor (NY 10 08) remain as an enigmatic memorial to their prehistoric builders.

Ennerdale, the most westerly of all the dales, can also claim to fulfill the requirements of being off the beaten track. Reached only by minor winding roads from the A5086 Cockermouth to Whitehaven road, Ennerdale has the distinction of being closed to all except the few vehicles serving the needs of forestry workers and the handful of people living in the upper dale. Cars belonging to anyone wishing to explore this remote valley and its surrounding fells must be parked beneath Bowness Knott. There are several waymarked trails and mountain paths leading from the car park and the valley road is suitable for wheelchairs. The track along Ennerdale leads through miles of coniferous forest where fire-breaks point towards the summits of Pillar and Steeple to the south, and the High Stile ridge to the north. Green Gable, Great Gable's northern outlier, marks the dale head, part of an undulating skyline of rocky peaks.

Black Sail youth hostel is the only habitation in the upper reaches of Ennerdale. A former shepherd's bothy, it can only be reached by footpaths climbing out of the dale, across Scarth Gap Pass from Buttermere to the north, or by way of Black Sail Pass from Wasdale Head in the south. Immediately north of Black Sail youth hostel, a series of crags and boulder fields mark the lower slopes of Hay Stacks, a little mountain where jewel-like tarns backed by abrupt little crags make it a microcosm of all the Lakeland fells.

Buttermere and Crummock Water attract devotees in their thousands, but **Loweswater**, separated by an arm of Little Dodd to the north-west, is often overlooked by motorists entering the Buttermere Valley from the west. Small by Lake District standards, it has a reasonably quiet road on one side and a woodland footpath linking two farms on the other.

The B5289 links Buttermere to the market town of **Cockermouth**, birthplace of William Wordsworth (1770-1850). Attractive though the valley road may be, it is surpassed by the two older roads running parallel to it along Lorton Vale to the north of Crummock Water. The main village in this short fertile dale is **Lorton**, which, with apparent delusions of grandeur, divides into High and Low. Lorton Hall is in the lower part and is built around a fifteenth-century pele tower. A complex building, it has its own chapel containing much fine oak panelling, priest holes and seventeenth-century furniture. The house may be visited, but only by appointment (☎ Lorton 252).

Forests on either side of the B529 Keswick road across the Whinlatter Pass have been opened for public enjoyment, with picnic sites, nature trails and forest walks. The Forestry Commission's Whinlatter Forest Centre tells the story of the surrounding forest, aided by working models. There is also a lecture room where films are shown covering a wide range range of countryside and forestry topics particularly connected with the Lake District.

Now that the A66, using the route of the old railway line, bypasses **Braithwaite** and **Thornthwaite** at the northern end of the Whinlatter Pass road, the two villages have resumed much of their pre-motor traffic tranquillity. Both have friendly, unpretentious pubs. The Swan at Thornthwaite maintains the curious custom of whitewashing two rocks, which are called the Bishop of Barf and his Clerk. The latter is in the field opposite the inn, but the bishop, complete with pulpit, is an isolated pinnacle at the top of a steep scree slope about half way up the craggy hillside leading to the summit of Barf. Painting the Clerk would be easy, but imagine the problems involved in carrying a bucket of whitewash up the unstable scree slope towards the Bishop. The Bishop of Barf rewards this effort by being a prominent landmark for miles along Derwentdale.

Marsden Rocks on the Northumbrian Coast

Bamburgh Castle, Northumbria

Preserved lead mining equipment at Wanlockhead, South-West Scotland

The ruins of MacLellan's Castle, Kirkcudbright, South-West Scotland

The Central Fells and Valleys

Even though this is one of the most popular districts and therefore an area where roads and footpaths can become overcrowded at times, many little corners still remain free from the pressures troubling some of the honeypots.

The road through Borrowdale can sometimes almost grind to a halt with traffic congestion, but most of that traffic will be heading for the Honister Pass, or Seathwaite at the head of the dale. Few cars will turn off the valley road into **Stonethwaite's** secluded dale. This is a walkers' dale with footpaths climbing beneath crags where golden eagles might be seen, returning into the Lakes after centuries of ignorant persecution. One path turns south along Langstrath Dale, dividing in its upper reaches. One branch leads to Angle Tarn beneath Bowfell, and the other, an ancient inter-valley route, climbs to Stake Pass and the Langdale Pikes. There is also a lower level path on the west side of Borrowdale, climbing past the bastions of Castle Crag to Seatoller, a village well-served with cafés and, more importantly, a bus connection into Keswick.

A minor road pre-dating the A66 by centuries, climbs to the east of Keswick and passes the slumbering stone circle of Castlerigg before dropping into St John's in the Vale. The valley road links the A591 with the A66 at **Threlkeld**, home to the Blencathra fox-hounds of Lakeland's premier hunt. Granite was quarried nearby until recently and lead mining once employed many of the locals.

An old coach road, now accessible only on foot connects **St John's in the Vale** with Dockray above Ullswater. The name of this dale is supposed to link it historically with the Hospitallers of the Order of St John of Jerusalem who are said to have built a church here in the thirteenth-century. However, even though the present church dates from 1554, there is no trace of this ancient order. Pleasant as the valley road is, the footpath along the opposite side of the valley is by far the best way to enjoy this often-overlooked dale. A line of low crags divides the dale from Naddle Beck and in the east the fells of Matterdale Common sweep northwards from the Helvellyn range.

Thirlmere is a credit to the engineers who flooded the valley on behalf of Manchester Corporation towards the end of the nineteenth century. Mature forest surrounds this 4 mile (6km) long reservoir which can compete for attractiveness with many of the natural lakes. A narrow road follows the west bank of Thirlmere and, about half way along it, a woodland nature trail winds beneath Fisher Crag. The valley and its one-time twin lakes predating the reservoir was a favourite venue of the 'Wordsworth set'. A rock carved with Wordsworth's and other poets' initials now lies on the bottom of the reservoir, but fragments of it have been incorporated within a cairn standing above the A591. Other writers used the setting in their novels, amongst them was Sir Walter Scott who immortalised Castle Rock of Triermain above Legburthwaite.

The A591 crosses Dunmail Raise on its way to Grasmere and lovely Rydal Water. Justifiably famous though they may be, there are times when they

Elterwater and the Langdale Pikes

can be a trifle overcrowded and alternative corners become more attractive. **Easedale** drains the northern outliers of the Langdale Pikes and flows beneath Helm Crag to join the Rothay above Grasmere village. Easedale divides about 1 mile (2km) above the village, one arm enters a remote crag-bound upper valley, and the other can be followed beside Sour Milk Gill to Easedale Tarn, a frequent subject of works by the Grasmere-based artist Heaton Cooper.

A side road climbs Red Bank past High Close to reach Langdale, or for the more energetic, a series of footpaths linking Loughrigg Terrace above Rydal Water drop down to Skelwith Bridge and Little Langdale. Despite the proximity of some of the busiest roads in the Lake District, footpaths created by long-dead miners wander around the wooded fells surrounding Elterwater and its tarn.

The Northern Fells

Skiddaw, the 3,000ft (915m) benign giant overtopping the busy and ancient market town of Keswick, marks what for many are the northern limits of the Lake District. The roughly oval mass of fells to the north of Keswick is subdivided by remote high valleys into Skiddaw Forest, the Uldale and Caldbeck fells, and Mungrisdale Common. Skiddaw is climbed by thousands every year, but Blencathra (known also as Saddleback), across Glenderaterra Beck, will have only a handful of climbers on its summit while its neighbour is probably crowded. Steep and narrow ridges buttress Blencathra high above the A66, a test for the sure-footed only.

With the exception of the two major summits, the rest of this wild area is likely to be free of human activity except for the occasional shepherd or intrepid fell walker in search of solitude. The complex geology of this area makes it more interesting. Rocks which are not found elsewhere in the Lake District have created a strange and remote region of rolling fells and lonely deep-cut valleys; the unique nature of this area has led to its classification as a Site of Special Scientific Interest. Miners exploited the bounty of over twenty-three different ores and other minerals from ten major mines south of Caldbeck. The last to operate concentrated on the production of barytes (barium sulphate) for use in glass and paint industries. As with all abandoned mines, all of those beneath Caldbeck Fells are in a dangerous condition and should not be entered.

Sleepy villages surround this highland mass. **Bassenthwaite**, at the foot of Dash Beck and its lovely waterfalls, is linked to the A591 Keswick to Carlisle road by a system of narrow lanes. Joined to its lake by a series of fieldpaths, the village clusters around an attractive green. Strangely, Bassenthwaite church is almost 3 miles (5km) away to the south of the village. Dedicated to Saints Bridget and Bega, the twelfth-century church stands in the middle of a lakeside field at the end of a signposted track away from the A591.

Another isolated church is that serving the scattered nearby parish of Isel. Dating from 1130 or even earlier if Viking relics in the church come from an older foundation, it stands by the River Derwent about 2 miles (3km) from **Blindcrake**, the main village. Ignored by the A595 Carlisle road, Blindcrake is a pleasant cluster of mostly fifteenth-century houses and farms grouped around a pocket handkerchief of a village green. Narrow lanes gradually climb the sides of the northern fells, skirting conical Binsey, only 1,467ft (447m) high, but a miniature Matterhorn. Tiny villages huddle into protective hollows beneath the higher fells, villages like **Ireby**, a once-important market for people living in the scattered communities below Skiddaw Forest. Its market charter was granted in 1237, but all that is left is a moot hall and a market cross to indicate the site of the former market place.

Uldale is on the opposite side of the Ellen Valley from High Ireby. Most of its houses date from the eighteenth and nineteenth centuries and was the birthplace of Mary White who married John Peel, the famous Lakeland huntsman, in 1797.

Caldbeck, a former mining village and the main village to the north of the Skiddaw fells, is also the most northerly point in the Lake District National Park. It was the home of John Peel (1776-1854) who was made famous by the hunting song *D'ye Ken John Peel*. Peel was buried in Caldbeck's St Kentigern's churchyard as is Mary Robinson, the 'Beauty of Buttermere', who was seduced by a 'gentleman' rogue calling himself the Honorable Alexander Hope MP. A forger and a bankrupt, he was hanged at Carlisle; Mary eventually married a farmer and lived happily at Caldbeck. Her story of tragedy and deception is graphically told in Melvyn Bragg's *The Maid of Buttermere*.

Caldbeck is a village which must be explored in order to appreciate its charm. A row of cottages marked by a tall chimney was once a brewery in the days when Caldbeck was a much busier place. Moloney's Hotel and Restaurant should not be missed; the unpretentious barn conversion in the centre of the village gives no hint of the high standard of the cuisine on offer inside. Follow the short riverside path across the bridge from the car park, to an ancient pack horse bridge behind the church and look out for the carefully tended well where St Kentigern (the locals refer to him as St Mungo) baptised early Christians. Beyond the bridge you will come to Priest's Mill, a cleverly restored water mill which now houses a small complex of craft shops, a mining museum and a restaurant.

A fell road runs due south along the abrupt eastern edge of this remote region of rolling moors and narrow ridges, through **Hesket Newmarket**. The village added 'new' to its name in 1751 when it was granted its market charter but, apart from the regular shape of its market square and surrounding streets, the village never developed into another Penrith, the major market town for North-East Cumbria. The road continues south past Carrock Fell, then winding through Mungrisdale, another 'dale of pigs', it joins the A66 near the head of the Derwent Valley to complete this tour of the lesser-known corners of the Lake District.

Further Information
— The Lake District —

Places of Interest

Abbot Hall Art Gallery
Kendal
Open: Spring Bank Holiday to end October. Monday to Saturday 10.30am-5pm. Sunday 2-5pm. Rest of year Monday to Friday 10.30am-5pm. Saturday and Sunday 2-5pm.

Beatrix Potter Gallery
Hawkshead
Open: 1 April to 4 November, Wednesday to Sunday 11am-5pm.

Belle Isle
Windermere, Home of John Ruskin
Open: mid-May to mid-September, Sunday, Monday, Tuesday and Thursday 10.30am-5pm.

Brantwood
Lake Road, Coniston
Open: Easter to October daily (except Saturday) 11am-5.30pm.

Brewery Arts Centre
Kendal
Open: Monday to Saturday 9am-11pm.

Brockhole
Windermere
Open: early April to early November, daily from 10am.

Broughton Tower
Broughton in Furness
(English Heritage)
Open: any reasonable time.

Cars of the Stars
Standish Street, Keswick
Open: early March to end December daily 10am-5pm.

Cartmel Priory Gatehouse
(English Heritage)
Open: Spring Bank Holiday to Christmas, daily except Monday 10.30am-8pm. April to Spring Bank Holiday. Key available from Priory Hotel, Cartmel.

Castlegate House Gallery
Cockermouth
Open: early March to end December, Monday, Tuesday and Friday/Saturday, 10.30am-5pm. Wednesday 10.30am-7pm.

Cumberland Pencil Museum
Keswick
Open: all year except 25-26 December
and 1 January daily 9.30am-2pm.

Dacre Castle
Dacre, 5 miles (8km) south-west of
Penrith
Open: by appointment only
☎ (08536) 375

Dalemain House
Pooley Bridge, Ullswater
Open: daily from Easter to mid-October
(except Friday and Saturday) 2-5.15pm.

Dove Cottage
Town End, Grasmere
Open: daily 9.30am-5.30pm.

Grizedale Forest Park Visitor Centre
Near Hawkshead
Open: end March to end October daily
10am-5pm. 10-24 December 10am-4pm.

Hawkshead Courthouse
(National Trust)
Open: Easter, then May to September,
daily (except Monday) 2-5pm.
Bank Holiday Monday.

Heaton Cooper Studio
Grasmere
Open: summer, Monday to Saturday
9am-6pm. Sunday 12noon-6pm. Winter,
Monday to Saturday 9am-1pm and
2-5pm.

Hill Top
Near Sawrey, Ambleside
(National Trust)
Open: April-October, daily (except
Friday) 10am-5.30pm, Sunday 2-5.30pm,
or dusk if earlier.
Numbers of visitors may be restricted at
peak times.

Holker Hall and Park
Cark in Cartmel, Grange-over-Sands
Open: Easter Sunday to end October,
daily excluding Saturdays 10.30am-6pm.

Kendal Museum
Station Road
Open: Spring Bank Holiday-end October,
Monday to Saturday 10.30am-5pm.
Sunday 2-5pm. Rest of year Monday to
Friday 10.30am-5pm, Saturday, Sunday
2-5pm.

Lake District Dalehead Base
Seatoller, Borrowdale
Open: 1 April-30 September, daily 10am-
1pm, 1.30-5pm.

Lingholme
Portinscale, Derwentwater
Open: April to October 10am-5pm.
No dogs.

Muncaster Castle
Ravenglass
Open: daily except Mondays (Bank
Holiday Mondays excepted) from Good
Friday to end September.
Grounds: 12noon-5pm.
Castle 1.30-4.30pm.

Museum of Lakeland Life and Industry
Abbot Hall, Kendal
Open: Spring Bank Holiday to end
October, Monday to Saturday 10.30am-
5pm. Rest of year Monday to Friday
10.30am-5pm. Saturday and Sunday
2-5pm.

Ravenglass Railway Museum
Ravenglass
Open: April to October depending on
railway time-table.

Rydal Mount
Ambleside
Open: March to October, daily 10am-
5.30pm. November to mid January
(except Wednesday) 10am-12.30pm and
2-4pm.

Sizergh Castle (National Trust)
Kendal
Open: April to October, Wednesday,
Thursday, Sunday and Monday, 2-
5.45pm. Gardens open from 12.30pm on
same days.

Stott Park Bobbin Mill
Finsthwaite, near Ulverston
Open: 1 April to 30 September 10am-6pm
(or dusk if earlier).

Thornthwaite Galleries
Thornthwaite, Keswick
Open: mid-March to mid-November,
Wednesday to Monday 10.30am-5pm.

Townend (National Trust)
Troutbeck
Open: April to October, daily (except
Saturday, Good Friday, Easter Monday,

but open Bank Holiday Mondays), 2-6pm or dusk if earlier.

Whinlatter Visitor Centre
Braithwaite, Keswick
Open: 1 February to 31 December daily 9am-5.30pm (or dusk if earlier).

Windermere Steamboat Museum
Bowness on Windermere
Open: Easter to end October daily 10am-5pm.

Wordsworth House
(National Trust)
Cockermouth
Open: Summer, daily (except Thursday afternoon and Sunday, but open Easter Sunday) 11am-5pm. Sunday 2-5pm. Winter: November to 23 December and January to March, house closed, but shop open.

Tourist Information Centres

Bowness Bay
☎ (09662) 2895

Coniston
Yeardale Road
☎ (0966) 41533

Glenridding
Ullswater
☎ (08532) 414

Grasmere
Red Bank Road
☎ (09665) 245

Hawkshead
☎ (09666) 525

Keswick Moot Hall
☎ (0596) 72803

Lake District National Park
National Park Centre, Brockhole
Windermere
☎ (09662) 2231

Pooley Bridge
☎ (08536) 530

Seatoller Dalehead Base
Seatoller , near Keswick
☎ (059684) 294

Waterhead
Ambleside
☎ (09663) 32729

Weather Service
☎ (09662) 5151
(updated at 8.15am and 4.15pm daily.)

13 • Northumbria

Historically, Northumbria was a Saxon Kingdom stretching from the Humber to the Forth, a much larger area than is covered in this chapter. Today it embraces the north-eastern counties of England — Durham and Northumberland, together with the metropolitan county of Tyne and Wear, and the new county of Cleveland around the Lower Tees. These last two were created in 1974 by politicians and bureaucrats with no sense of history, and are rightly ignored by true northerners. This chapter is based on the old counties of Northumberland and Durham, that is, north-eastern England from the River Tees to the Scottish border.

As a region, Northumbria has played a major role in shaping modern Britain, yet until recently it was neglected by the tourist, except those with specialised interests in history and architecture, who came to see the Roman Wall, Durham Cathedral or a dozen castles. The designation of the Northumberland National Park in 1956 recognised the special quality of nearly 400sq miles (1,037sq km) of upland countryside from the Roman Wall to the Cheviot Hills. To the east, almost 40 miles (64km) of Northumberland's coast is 'Heritage Coast'. Only about one-tenth of the county, in the south-east around Newcastle, is industrialised. The rest is unspoilt countryside of hills and rivers, farmlands and forests, with scattered villages and a few small towns. Some favoured spots, such as Alnwick, Hexham and Rothbury, attract summer visitors, but for most of the year you can drive along Northumberland's roads in comparative comfort, appreciating the spaciousness, wide views and clean air.

Durham is unique. Roadside signs at its county boundaries describe it as 'Land of the Prince Bishops', a reminder of its County Palatine status from Norman times until 1832, when the Bishops of Durham had the right to enact their own laws, levy taxes and have their own armies. Under their strong control, Durham enjoyed peaceful conditions much earlier than their northern neighbours, for Northumberland was a frontier zone for centuries. Even before the nations of England and Scotland were named, the Romans had created a boundary; Hadrian's Wall, the first effective man-made frontier in Britain.

For almost 800 years following the Romans' departure the land north of the Wall was fought over, first between the emergent Kingdom of Northumbria and the Picts and Scots, later between England and Scotland. Eventually, high among the Cheviot Hills, a sketchy boundary evolved,

231

continuing north-eastwards to the River Tweed. However, the feuding, fighting centuries from about 1300 to the Union of Crowns in 1603 meant that until then life was not settled, conditions which retarded agricultural development and brought about a domestic style of medieval architecture unique in England. Powerful families lived in castles, lesser gentry in large fortified houses called peles, while farming families took refuge in bastle-houses. Many examples of these survive, but Northumberland has few stately mansions, none earlier than the seventeenth century.

In the seventh century Northumbria cradled an early Christianity and culture. Saxon churches have come down to us through 1,000 years or more. Durham boasts one of the greatest Norman cathedrals in Christendom. Coal-mining, iron and steel, and shipbuilding brought Victorian prosperity; railways originated here. Cuthbert and Aidan are great northern saints, and Grace Darling is a famous heroine. Catherine Cookson is a favourite modern novelist whose stories evoke Tyneside two or three generations ago, and the warmth of the northerners' character which makes them so hospitable and friendly. The climate is less so, being markedly cooler and less sunny than that of southern England, although it is reasonably dry, especially away from the western and northern hills. Spring comes late, but autumn often compensates by prolonging the summer, so that September and October are often very pleasant months.

Durham is roughly circular, Northumberland almost a triangle narrowing to its northern apex at Berwick-on-Tweed. Durham's roads are many, its neighbour's relatively few, so that the facts of geography impose some limits on the best way in which to explore an area so diverse in scenery, so rich in sites to see. Newcastle has a busy airport, but most visitors probably approach from the south, via the A1, or the M1, the M18 and the A1. Scotch Corner, about 230 miles (370km) from London, marks a gateway to the area, with **Durham** city another 26 miles (42km) away, by A1(M) and A177, and Durham county is best explored from the small city at its heart.

Lying in a bowl of hills, Durham is scarcely visible from any of its approaches but, ironically, the finest view of its citadel-complex of Norman cathedral and castle high-perched on a rocky peninsula above the River Wear's horseshoe loop, is from the windows of an Inter-City 125 gliding across the railway viaduct west of the city centre, although you can gain a similar view from the little garden above the station. Closer views from South Street, Prebend's Bridge, or the woodland paths above the river illustrate the cathedral's remarkable situation.

Durham has largely come to terms with the motor-car by building two new bridges across the river, with a link road between them and car parks nearby. Through-traffic is thus excluded from the historic centre, so the best way to explore it is on foot, preferably first by walking right round the peninsula, by riverside and woodland paths on the outer bank, clockwise from Elvet to Framwellgate, enjoying the changing views. Then go up to the market place, and Saddler Street to Palace Green, where various University buildings surround a gracious lawn between the Norman castle and the cathedral.

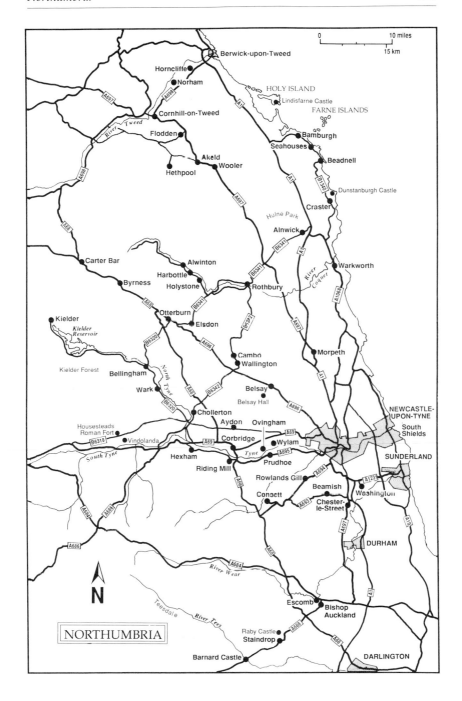

The city has other fine buildings, including many modest Georgian houses. Durham escaped industrialisation and has remained an episcopal and administrative centre through most of its history. Its University, founded in 1832, is the oldest provincial one in England after Oxford and Cambridge, and has expanded over the last 20 years. Many modern colleges have been added, particularly on the city's south-west, and some of these, together with other college buildings, provide accommodation for visitors out of term time. Durham's hotels tend to be pricey, but those in the surrounding villages offer more reasonably-priced, comfortable hospitality.

Durham county is relatively small, and good roads make it easy to explore from a central base in or near the city. It is not one vast, built-up industrial area, and the hilly roads, particularly to the west of the city, reveal unexpected landscapes from which all traces of coal-mining have vanished, although terraces of miners' houses climb the hills in old pit villages and drab Victorian churches and pubs do little to raise the spirit. A happier way to experience the north-east's social and industrial history of the past century is to visit the superb open-air museum at **Beamish**, a few miles north of the city, off the A167 at Chester-le-Street and along the A693.

Here, in 200 acres of parkland, you can visit recreated shops, pubs and houses of a small town street, go into miners' cottages, enter a 'drift' mine, ride on a tram and a steam train, and see a nineteenth-century farm. For northerners whose lives span two or three generations it is pure nostalgia; for visitors it is an ideal introduction to an important facet of Durham's story. Nearby, to the west, the Causey Arch is the world's oldest surviving railway bridge, built in 1726 to carry a wooden-railed wagonway across a steep-sided wooded valley — a 'dene' in Durham. Horse-drawn wagons would have transported coal along it from local pits the 8 miles (13km) to the banks of the River Tyne. A vast network of such wagonways once threaded the north-western parts of the county, many of these are now quiet tracks enjoyed by walkers, riders and cyclists.

By continuing north-westwards by minor roads towards Rowlands Gill in the Derwent Valley, you should see the signposts for **Gibside**. This is very much off the beaten track, a surviving fragment of a great eighteenth-century estate created by the Bowes family. Sir George Bowes was one of the so-called 'Grand Allies', three landowners who owned the best pits in the Durham coalfield between Tyne and Wear. Although the mansion has largely been demolished and other buildings are partially ruinous, the parkland can still be appreciated, with the great Column of British Liberty at one end of the Great Walk and Gibside Chapel (National Trust) at the other. James Paine's design dates from 1760 but was not completed until 1812 (the money ran out). It may have been inspired by Palladio's Villa Rotunda at Vicenza. The detail is magnificent throughout, the tooling of the masonry most delicate, and this elegant building is, architecturally, probably the most beautiful in Northumbria.

In contrast to the coal-mining villages and scenery of north-west Durham, countrysides to the south are much more rural, with good farmland

Gibside Chapel, a Palladian-style mausoleum in the Derwent Valley

and quiet villages. Because there is nothing spectacular or of special 'heritage' interest, the area is largely ignored by tourists. However, there are surprises. Travel southwards, from the city, by the A167 and the A688 to Bishop Auckland where, above the River Wear, Auckland Castle has been a spacious palace-home of the Bishops of Durham since the twelfth century, and their regular residence since 1832. The original medieval banqueting hall is now the chapel, but the whole building is faced in a mixture of Gothic and Restoration styles introduced by later eighteenth-century bishops. These are characterised by the rather playful gatehouse from the town and even more amusing deerhouse of 1760 in the 800-acre park, through which you are freely entitled to walk.

By taking the B6282 westwards from the town, and soon turning off to the north, another of Durham's unexpected secrets will be found, at **Escomb**, a former pit village. In its circular churchyard, ringed by modern houses, is a little-changed Anglo-Saxon church, a remarkable survivor of early Christianity, dating from the time of Cuthbert and Bede nearly thirteen centuries ago. Its darkened stones include Roman masonry and the ground-plan, without aisles, transepts or tower, shows the pattern from Roman Gaul fully developed here in northern England; austere, beautiful, and very moving. You can obtain the keys to church and churchyard from No 22 Saxon Green, behind the church.

Head southwards to West Auckland and join the A688 for Staindrop. The road passes **Raby Castle**, home of Lord Barnard's family since 1626. Before then, Raby's history was complex, starting in the fourteenth century as a fortified seat of the great northern family, the Nevilles. Its complex plan was a medieval compromise between the needs of comfort and defence, producing a castle of enclosure with a series of towers linked by curtain walls. After the Nevilles forfeited Raby in about 1570, successive owners made extensive internal changes, and today's castle contains many objets d'art in its eighteenth-century staterooms, contrasting with its medieval kitchens.

Staindrop is a particularly attractive example of a typical Durham 'two-row' village, with mellow stone houses strung out on opposite sides of an east-west village green, which narrows at its eastern end towards the church, where generations of Nevilles and Vanes are commemorated by a remarkable, if little-known series of effigies.

A few miles down the A688, **Barnard Castle** is the chief market town in Teesdale, taking its name from Bernard Baliol's early twelfth-century castle, whose gaunt ruins occupy a low, rocky cliff above the river. Richard III, as Duke of Gloucester, was a frequent visitor, and made a number of additions to the castle. Within the town, which has a busy market day each Wednesday, there are good seventeenth- and eighteenth-century buildings, particularly Blagroves House, and The King's Head Inn where Dickens stayed in 1838 while writing *Nicholas Nickleby*.

On the town's eastern edge is the extraordinary Bowes Museum, in size and style quite inappropriate for its setting; a French château in a northern dale. It was named after its founders, John Bowes and his French wife, Josephine, a Parisian actress and painter. Her ambition and taste, allied to his wealth, created this museum from about 1860, and within a few years it housed a huge and varied collection of ceramics, textiles, tapestries, clocks and fine paintings from the continent. Recent additions of English furniture, silver, costume, toys and antiquities have made Bowes one of the most important of English provincial museums.

From Barnard Castle it is an easy drive along the A67, through pleasant countryside, eastwards to **Darlington**. Although this is a large town and on the edge of the vast industrial spread of Teesside, it manages to retain something of a country-town atmosphere. Perhaps this is because its tall-spired, handsome parish church, surrounded by trees in a green graveyard, is at the town's heart. A huge open-air and covered market nearby, is surrounded by eighteenth- and nineteenth-century houses. Local industries then, and earlier, were created and managed by a prosperous and powerful community and it was a local Quaker banker, Edward Pease, who was one of the chief promoters of the Stockton and Darlington Railway. Opened in September 1825, this was the first public railway to use steam locomotives to haul trains carrying passengers or freight wagons.

North Road Station, built in 1842 and so elegant that it resembles a country house, is now the Darlington Railway Museum, and houses George Stephenson's famous *Locomotion*, which hauled that pioneer train. Other exhibits include the 1845 *Derwent*, together with examples of North Eastern Railway locomotives in their apple-green livery.

Hexham, to the north-west along the A68 and A695, is one of the most satisfying abbey towns of northern England, small enough to maintain a feeling of intimacy, and pleasantly situated on rising ground above the south bank of the Tyne. Although the Roman Wall is only a few miles away and the area is rich in Roman sites, Hexham's roots go back a mere thirteen centuries, to AD674 in fact, when Queen Etheldreda of Northumbria gave land there for her spiritual adviser, Wilfrid, to build a church.

Today's church, whose eastern end abuts the Market Place, is that of an Augustinian priory and dates from two periods, 1180-1250 and 1850-1910. However, it retains two wonderful survivals of Wilfrid's building — his throne, the Frith Stool, a stone chair with solid arms, and, reached by steps from the centre of the nave, the finest Anglo-Saxon crypt in England, constructed by Wilfrid using Roman masonry from the fort at *Corstopitum*. Wall-niches held oil lamps, and the wall-plaster is the original, as hard as concrete. In the body of the church are the unique Night Stairs, the processional way by which Augustinian canons came from their dormitory for the service of Compline. Now, at evensong, the white-surpliced, scarlet-robed abbey choir descend for their service.

For a good view of the abbey, walk into the parkland and gardens to the south and west, beyond the medieval precincts. The market place is the hub of town life, particularly on Tuesdays. Except for Beaumont Street leading to the south, the street pattern is a medieval one, but most of the buildings are Georgian or Victorian, with modern shop fronts. The Moot Hall frowns across the market place and was probably built in the late fourteenth century for representatives of the Archbishops of York, and served as a court house until 1838. Behind it is the equally dour Manor Office of 1330, England's first purpose-built prison. It now houses an excellent Tourist Information Centre as well as the Middle Marches Museum illustrating the history of the Border Country. A touch of more recent history can be seen at the southern end of Fore Street, where the Midland Bank premises, built in 1896, show on a carved sandstone frieze Britain's vanished coinage — sovereigns, shillings and pennies.

Hexham is well-placed as a base from which to explore the Roman Wall, the Tyne Valley eastwards, and that of the North Tyne towards the hills. In order to incorporate the best parts of the Roman Wall into a circular tour from Hexham it is most sensible to cross the river, turn left on the A69 for a short way, then take the A6079 northwards to **Chollerford** and join the B6318 heading west. Near Chollerford, on the river's south bank, is the extraordinary masonry of the original Roman bridge abutment.

The B6318 passes a series of Roman forts whose remains differ in size and content. **Chesters** (*Cilurnum*) (English Heritage) is in a parkland setting near the river and is best known for its baths complex and museum of finds. **Brocolita** has a temple of Mithras, and **Housesteads** — *Vercovicium* — (English Heritage and National Trust) a $^1/_2$ mile (1km) walk and climb from the road, is the most dramatically-situated, and displays a classic lay-out, with footings of many buildings including a flushing latrine. There is a superb museum and interpretative display, and the fort's north wall is incorporated into Hadrian's Wall. Indeed, the best sections of the Wall, with turrets and milecastles, run east and west from here, and the 3 mile (5km) walk along, or by, the Wall westwards to Steel Rigg, though quite demanding, is rewarding and memorable, following the crests of a series of crags. At **Crag Lough** there is the added attraction of a glacial lake far below the dark cliffs. This part of the Wall walk can be reached slightly more easily from the car park at Steel Rigg, signposted from the B6318 near the National Park Visitor Centre at Once Brewed.

Also near Once Brewed is the Roman fort, *Vindolanda*, where part of a civilian settlement has been excavated, and the Vindolanda Trust has built a replica of a section of Hadrian's Wall, together with a milecastle and turret. The fort formed part of an earlier Roman defence system guarding the route of the Stanegate along the Tyne corridor, and a minor road follows this today, offering a quick, convenient way back to Hexham, through the villages of Newbrough and Fourstones.

Those with an interest in racing may appreicate Hexham's National Hunt meetings in March, April, May, September, October and December. There is trout fishing in the Tyne, whose increasing cleanliness is already seeing salmon returning to the river.

A few minutes easy drive down the south side of the valley takes you to **Corbridge**, smaller and more compact than Hexham, and with roots going back to Roman times, when, in AD80, Agricola, marching his troops northwards from York, established the first fort at *Corstopitum* to guard the bridge across the Tyne, the main road west (Stanegate) and to serve as supply-base for his advance towards Scotland. Extensive remains of storehouses, granaries, military compounds, shops and houses testify to the importance of *Corstopitum* in Agricola's campaign.

The Roman fort lies 1 mile ($1^1/_2$km) west of Corbridge which was made a royal burgh by Northumbria's Anglian rulers, and by the thirteenth century was Northumberland's wealthiest town outside Newcastle — although this probably says more about the county's poverty rather than its prosperity. In the three centuries that followed, the Scots frequently raided the town. The Vicar's pele in the churchyard, dating from around 1300, attests to these Border troubles, as well as to the availability of Roman masonry from *Corstopitum*, earlier used by the Anglo-Saxon builders of the church tower. Most houses in Corbridge date from Georgian times; look out for the many 'pants' or conduits which provided the townsfolk with water from the early years of last century.

Return across the handsome bridge, the only one on the Tyne to survive the great floods of 1771, and continue eastwards along the A695, through Riding Mill and Stocksfield, towards Prudhoe. Two miles (3km) beyond Stocksfield, at Mickley Square, make a little diversion to **Cherryburn** (indicated by a brown signpost), recently opened for visitors. Thomas Bewick was born here in 1753, son of a farmer and a part-time miner. Bewick subsequently became a great artist, naturalist, and, above all, a woodengraver, particularly of birds, animals and familiar countryside scenes. Cherryburn now displays much of Bewick's work, and on most afternoons there are demonstrations of printing on an early press, using wooden

George Stephenson's birthplace, Wylam

blocks in the traditional manner. You will also, in surroundings that have changed little since his day, experience just a hint of the Tyne Valley in mid-Georgian times.

At Prudhoe the hints become more urban and industrial, with the centre of Newcastle only 10 miles (16km) away. However, by turning sharp left (signposted 'Ovingham') you will find at the bottom of a hill the very impressive **Prudhoe Castle**, with extensive remains of gatehouse, curtain wall and keep. There is an early nineteenth-century 'Gothick' house in the inner ward now containing an exhibition about Prudhoe, with a video about other castles in Northumberland.

Across the river is the charming village of **Ovingham**, in whose churchyard Bewick is buried, and a riverside road leads eastwards to **Wylam**, formerly a pit village but now a prosperous rural village on the edge of industrial Tyneside. George Stephenson, the 'Father of Railways', was born in 1781 in a small cottage nearby, reached only by a bridleway along the track of a former wagonway. The property is now owned by the National Trust but only one room is open, furnished largely as it must have been two centuries ago. For railway enthusiasts Wylam is probably more important than Darlington. It was from Wylam Colliery that the first of all locomotive engines, William Hedley's *Puffing Billy*, hauled coal wagons to Lemington, a few miles eastwards, in 1813. Wylam Railway Museum commemorates these local railway pioneers, Stephenson, Hedley and Timothy Hackworth.

Retracing your route to Ovingham and continuing along the minor road following the north bank of the Tyne, you will come to **Bywell**; secluded, quiet and the most picturesque of Tyne villages. Its two churches face each other in a parkland setting. St Andrew's was built by the White Canons of Blanchland and retains a fine Saxon tower; St Peter's, built by the Benedictine Durham Monks, is mainly Norman. Nearby are the ruins of a fifteenth-century tower-house, and the tree-embowered Bywell Hall, both in private hands and not normally open. A place that is open, and — if your enthusiasm for castles has not yet waned — really worth seeing, is **Aydon Castle** (English Heritage), a few miles to the north-west, and reached by minor roads north of Corbridge and the A69. This is a superb example of a medieval, fortified manor-house, modest in scale, yet vividly illustrating domestic living conditions of the early fourteenth century. Although Aydon Castle was used and occupied as a farmhouse from the seventeenth century until 1960, it remains little-changed and represents as much space and comfort which could be expected in a Border home around 1300.

Leaving Hexham as a base, almost any road northwards takes you into off-the-beaten track country. The A6079 to **Chollerton**, a typical Northumbrian 'farm-hamlet', has a church with Roman columns forming its south arcade, a re-used Roman altar as a font, a tiny seventeenth-century organ, and an unusual headstone in the churchyard, to John Saint, a fuller. Take the minor road up the North Tyne Valley to Wark, joining the B6320 for Bellingham (pronounced Bellinjam), with Britain's most remarkable man-made landscapes a few miles to the west.

Kielder Water, opened as a huge reservoir in 1982, is a unique recreational facility catering for most types of watersports, and Tower Knowe Visitor Centre is an obvious starting-point from which to appreciate its amenities. Nearby is the jetty from which ferry services run regular trips. The south shore provides for the more active pursuits; the north shore, not accessible by road, is for walkers and naturalists, and all around the vast plantations of Kielder Forest stretch to far horizons. Kielder Castle, beyond the head of Kielder Water, is the Forestry Commission's Visitor Centre, with car-parking, exhibitions and displays, and details of the guided walks programme which operates during the summer.

The most convenient way to gain a closer impression of Kielder Forest — apart from walking in it — is by taking the Forest Drive of 12 miles (19km), running north-eastwards through different types of forest landscapes, and providing an excellent short-cut into Redesdale. The road is not surfaced the whole way, but is not unduly rough, and has many small parking areas on the way, before joining the A68 at Byrness.

The A68 is the most scenic of the main roads between Newcastle and Edinburgh, and crosses the Border at Carter Bar, 7 miles (11km) west of Byrness. Below Byrness are the unforested uplands of Redesdale; bare landscapes inhabited only by sheep, except for the military camps and training areas above Otterburn. Head south-eastwards down the A68, the A696, to **Otterburn**. Just off the road, Otterburn Mill, owned by the Waddell family since 1817, is open to the public as a showroom for the display and sale of the famous Otterburn Tweeds, although these are no longer made on the premises.

One mile ($1^1/_2$km) east of Otterburn, turn off along B6341 to **Elsdon**, the historic capital of Redesdale, and today a village which seems to sum up the Border. Everything is here: a huge village green with church and graveyard dividing it into two parts. Above is the best of all Vicar's peles, dating from about 1400, its gardens occasionally open; nearby is the little nineteenth-century school, while at the lower end of the green is the old village pound, and there were inns for Scottish drovers. A tranquil atmosphere prevails, and at the northern end of the village are the huge earthworks of a Norman motte-and-bailey castle, while many casualties of the fierce Battle of Otterburn (1388) are thought to have been buried beneath the stones of St Cuthbert's Church.

The B6341 climbs northwards from Elsdon before descending into Coquetdale. However, before going to its centre (Rothbury), it is well worth sampling the quiet beauty of the upper valley first, by taking the unclass-ified road above the west side of the river to Holystone and Alwinton. Pause at **Holystone** to enjoy a short walk from the village to Lady's Well, a large pool in a wooded grove, used in early Christian baptisms, and still pro-viding the local water supply. Easy waymarked walks from a Forestry Commission car park lead into fine deciduous woodland.

Alwinton is the last village in Coquetdale, gateway to the Cheviots, an extensive range of rounded, grassy, brackeny hills whose slopes run sharply down to this loveliest and loneliest of Northumbrian valleys. Challenging walks lead into the hills, but the winding road that follows the river for 10 miles (16km) into the heart of the hills below the Chew Green Roman Camps has no outlet, so it means a there-and-back trip. Merely going as far as Shillmoor is sufficient to provide a good flavour of Coquet country, and sense the secret charms of what were, in medieval times, the troubled 'Middle Marches', whose control on the English side was based on Harbottle Castle of which very little survives.

The Rose and Thistle at Alwinton marks in its name the Union of Crowns (1603) and is one of the best pubs in Border country. On the second Saturday each October Alwinton is the venue for the annual Shepherds' Show. This is a gloriously homely event in an idyllic setting, confined to shepherds, sheep and local rural skills such as stick-carving, home cooking, wrestling, hound-trailing and fell-racing, to the background sounds of Northumbrian pipes.

The more direct road to Rothbury crosses the Coquet below Harbottle and cuts off a large loop in the river's course before joining the B6341, with opening views southwards to the escarpment of the heathery Simonside Hills. **Rothbury** is a pleasant, small town with a large triangular green, a number of small shops, but limited tourist accommodation. An unre-markable church has the treasure of an Anglo-Saxon cross-shaft supporting the font, but the surrounding scenery is the main attraction. On the moors to the south, barrows, earthworks, forts, standing stones and hut circles testify to the prehistoric popularity of the area. An admirable Tourist Information Centre provides a wealth of leaflets and booklets outlining local attractions, walks, events and places to visit.

High on the list for most people is the Victorian mansion, **Cragside**. Its extensive grounds, now a Country Park, with scenic drives, woodland walks and lakes, and miles of rhododendrons seen best in early June. Cragside represents the wealth and vision of the industrialist Sir William Armstrong who transformed 900 acres of wild moorland between 1863 and 1883 into a superb country estate centred on Norman Shaw's mansion. This and its contents are a shrine to high Victoriana and Armstrong's inventiveness, which included developing his own hydro-electricity system, thus making Cragside the first house to be lit by water-generated power. The system has recently been restored by the National Trust, who now own this unique property.

Following the Coquet Valley downstream, the B6334 soon reaches **Brinkburn Priory** (English Heritage), although there is no close approach by car. A short woodland walk from the car park soon reveals the tranquil riverside setting of a church of the Augustinian canons, rebuilt in the late twelfth century, and showing the architectural transition from Romanesque to Gothic. The building was sensitively restored and re-roofed in 1858, its organ restored and windows replaced, and was licensed for services. The cool, calm perfection of its interior makes it very suitable for the occasional concerts and recitals held there.

A mile ($1^1/_2$km) down the road, the A697 provides a splendid way to head northwards along 20 miles (32km) to **Wooler**, at the north-eastern foot of the Cheviot Hills. Small, grey and austere, this is an important livestock market town with a few family shops and modest hotels, well-placed for exploring the northern valleys of the Cheviots and the fertile plain extending northwards to the Tweed.

Continue along the A697 westwards to **Akeld**, where there is a good example of a sixteenth-century bastle just off the road. Fork left on the B6351, following the northern boundary of the National Park. Stop at **Kirknewton** to visit the remarkable church whose vaulted chancel and transept appear to have been part of a medieval pele-tower. A small sculpture of the Adoration of the Magi shows them apparently wearing kilts, and probably dates from the twelfth century. Josephine Butler, the social reformer and crusader against the white slave trade is buried in the churchyard (she died in 1906).

Beyond Kirknewton a minor road leads a short way to **Hethpool**, in the beautiful Coquet Valley which runs for a further 5 miles (8km) into the heart of the Cheviots, accessible to walkers and horse-riders but only to motorists if they have previously obtained a permit from John Sale and Partners, Estate Agents in Wooler. Near Hethpool are the famous Collingwood Oaks, planted early last century to provide 'navy timber'. They did not thrive, but are more successfully managed today by the National Park Authority. There are plenty of good walks around Hethpool and, on the grassy hills to the west, the Pennine Way National Trail slowly descends from the Cheviots to its northern end across the Scottish border at Kirk Yetholm.

Our journey stays in England, however, and by turning off at Kilham, minor roads can be followed northwards to Branxton, nearest village to **Flodden Field**, site of the worst Anglo-Scottish battle. A tall Celtic cross set amid rolling cornfields commemorates, in a lonely, hauntingly beautiful landscape, 5,000 English and 10,000 Scots — almost the whole of the chivalry of the northern kingdom — who died on two September days in 1513. This is certainly a place for quiet reflection.

With the A697 only 1 mile ($1^1/_2$km) away, Cornhill-on-Tweed is easily reached, and from here the A698 offers an almost straight run north-eastwards to Berwick-on-Tweed. Two short digressions are justified on the way, first to **Norham**, whose castle was originally an early northern stronghold of Durham's Norman prince-bishops. Much of what is seen today was built about 1160 by Hugh de Puiset, the greatest builder of all Durham's bishops. The village stretches for nearly $^1/_2$ mile (1km) between castle and St Cuthbert's Church, with its majestic Norman chancel and south arcade contemporary with work at the castle. Neat cottages face a triangular green, with the village cross at a focal point.

The second diversion takes you to **Horncliffe**, not so much for the village but for the Union Chain Bridge 1 mile ($1^1/_2$km) beyond. Linking England to Scotland across the Tweed, this has the distinction of being the world's first large suspension bridge. It is an early essay combining grace and strength, designed by Captain Samuel Brown in 1820, 6 years before Telford's famous Menai Bridge in North Wales. Happily, it still carries a roadway, and is an elegant addition to a beautiful part of the Tweed.

The whole of the Tweed is attractive, even its estuary at Berwick. Unusually, for the last 4 miles (7km) of its course it does not form the Border line, and England, in the apex of Northumberland, extends a little way north of the river, so **Berwick-on-Tweed** is in our county and not in the county of Berwickshire. During the centuries of strife between the two countries the town changed hands thirteen times, an English army finally taking it, without any resistance, in 1482. Outside Durham, it is Northumbria's most historic and exciting town, small enough (the population is 12,000) to be appreciated on foot, ideally starting at the northern end of the handsome, long Old Bridge built in the early seventeenth century.

By following Quay Walls eastwards and continuing anti-clockwise, you pass some of the best of Berwick's many eighteenth-century houses and soon come to the great Elizabethan fortifications that make the town unique. These pioneering structures of military engineering took the form of low-profiled, earth-topped, star-shaped citadels, with projecting bastions giving all-round fire-power covering a wide moat. Earlier walls were built in the early fourteenth century, and fragments of these survive between the Brass Mount and Mary Gate. However, medieval types of fortification had become useless against the power of sixteenth-century artillery, so that Berwick's key position at the mouth of the Tweed had made it a worthwhile prize in the Anglo-Scottish wars, and in the duel between England and Scotland's old partner France.

Walk the grassy promenade which links the bastions and visit the town's buildings of special interest, perhaps starting with the eighteenth-century Barracks opposite Windmill Bastion (English Heritage), the oldest British barracks still in use. Holy Trinity Church to the west of the Barracks is unusual in having neither tower nor spire, since Cromwell would not allow one when it was built between 1648 and 1652, a rare date for an English church. Most towns have a 'town mark' which readily identifies them in almost any view, and Berwick's is its Town Hall in Marygate, whose 150ft (50m) high belfry can be seen from almost anywhere in the town, and particularly from across the river or its famous bridges. The old prison cells have been preserved upstairs, while an excellent coffee-shop, tea-room and gift shop operate in the Butter Market below. The salmon-netting season, for which Berwick, the south of the Tweed, and parts of the coast to the south are famous, is from 15 February to 14 September.

For almost 40 miles (64km) southwards from Berwick, Northumberland's coast has been designated as of Heritage quality. Vast stretches of clean sands, washed by every tide, alternate with rocky headlands and offshore reefs. The A1 runs parallel to the coast, never more than 2 miles (3km) from it, until Belford is reached, after which the B1342 to Bamburgh, and the B1340 and B1339 continue southwards near the coast, eventually making a more inland turn towards Alnwick. The North Sea looks inviting and many swimmers are prepared to brave its cool waters. Few access places to the sands ensure that commercialism has not seriously afflicted this coast. Saintly associations and the turbulent past which resulted in coastal castles, give special appeal. **Bamburgh Castle**, Norman in origin, and covering 8 acres, was over-zealously restored late last century, but its setting is majestic and memorable, while the village beneath its walls is proud of its memories of the heroine Grace Darling.

Holy Island, accessible by road between tides, has a crag-perched Henrician castle, brilliantly converted into a unique house by Lutyens early this century (National Trust). The beautiful ruins of Lindisfarne Priory (English Heritage) evoke associations with Northumbrian saints Aidan and Cuthbert. Neither Lindisfarne Church nor the local Lindisfarne Mead should be missed.

Seahouses is the largest and liveliest of the fishing villages, and small boats ply from there mornings and afternoons for the short trip to the **Farne Islands**, a group of rocky islands now owned by the National Trust, and an outstanding breeding place for thousands of seabirds. It is advisable to book in advance for a visit to the Farnes which are accessible from April to mid-May, and mid-July to the end of September. Landings are not made in bad weather.

Beadnell and, farther down the coast, **Craster**, are smaller fishing villages, the latter being famous for its kippers, which are smoked in sheds above the small harbour. From here a superb coastal footpath runs northwards to the prominent ruins of **Dunstanburgh Castle** on its wild headland, and continues past Embleton Golf Course to Low Newton, a level walk which is not only off the beaten track but which captures the essence of a lovely coast.

Minor roads wind inland from Craster the few miles to **Alnwick** (pronounced Annick), which is a good touring base. Alnwick has a distinct medieval feel about it, which is scarcely surprising since its history is

The dramatic, isolated ruins of Dunstanburgh Castle

intertwined with the castle and the House of Percy, the north's greatest family. The present castle originated in 1309 when the Percys obtained it, and to a large extent the family have been there ever since, for it is still the home of the Duke of Northumberland. Its interior, completely remodelled in the mid-eighteenth century, and again a century later, is decorated in Italian Renaissance style, contains fine paintings, porcelain and furniture, and most of its staterooms are open to the public. An array of battlemented towers creates a fascinating skyline, beautifully seen from the River Aln to the north. Look for some of the realistically carved figures on them.

Successive dukes have been considerate friends to the town and the pattern of its streets, now fronted by dignified grey stone buildings, reflects that of the medieval village centred on a triangular green, now the cobbled Market Square, funnelling eastwards to Hotspur Gate, part of the town walls. Alnwick Fair, held annually at the end of June, continuing a long tradition, is a week-long medieval costumed mock-up that attracts large crowds. A quieter picture is offered by Hulne Park, explorable only on foot, with permits from the Castle Estate Office. Landscaped by 'Capability'

Brown, it has at its heart the ruins of a rare Carmelite monastery, with a Gothic influence introduced by the first Duke, in 1776.

Warkworth, nearer the coast, a few miles south-east of Alnwick, should not be missed. The northern approach by the A1068 shows how dramatically the ruins of a fourteenth-century Percy stronghold dominate the very attractive little town, its streets lined with modest Georgian and Victorian houses. The castle is full of surprises — rooms, staircases, galleries, with a climactic view from its keep. If time permits, it is worth making the little boat trip on the River Coquet (arranged in conjunction with the castle visit), to the Hermitage, a fourteenth-century chapel and sacristy hewn from the cliff by the river, last occupied in the sixteenth century.

A journey southwards to Morpeth, Northumberland's bustling little county town, can continue westwards by the B6343, up the Wansbeck Valley to **Cambo and Wallington Hall**, the most gracious and elegant of Northumberland's mansions. Mainly dating from the mid-eighteenth century, it passed into the Trevelyan family, who made extensive alterations in the 1850s. Among these was the decoration of the central hall by William Bell Scott, a young Newcastle pre-Raphaelite, who painted famous scenes from Northumbrian history, lively pictures full of accuracy, colour and incident. These and other pre-Raphaelite work by Ruskin and Pauline Trevelyan, together with exquisite furniture and porcelain, add to Wallington's attractions. Beautiful gardens were planned partly by 'Capability' Brown, who was born at nearby Kirkharle.

The Wallington estate is a characteristic slice of eighteenth-century Northumberland, when local landowners were improving their land, draining it, laying miles of hedges, planting thousands of trees, creating fine parklands, growing corn which added to their prosperity.

From Wallington, head southwards to join the A696 and follow the signs for Newcastle. You will soon reach **Belsay**, one of the best-kept secrets of Northumbria, a microcosm of northern history and landscape. Even the village has a Grecian air about it, an 1830 rebuilding by Sir Charles Monck who lived at nearby Belsay Hall. The estate, now owned by English Heritage, had been in the Middleton family (Monck was a descendant) since 1370 when the first massive tower house was built. With more peaceful conditions after 1603, a handsome Jacobean house was added to it, one of Northumberland's earliest unfortified houses. Belsay Hall, over $^1/_2$ mile (1km) away, built between 1807 and 1815, was a product of the inspiration found on his Grecian honeymoon. Although it is now unfurnished, it is a Greek-Doric masterpiece, rare for this country. Its honeyed stone came from the park, and the resultant quarry garden is rugged, enchanting and utterly unexpected. Belsay summarises six centuries of Northumbrian history. The A696 continues directly to Newcastle, passing the city's airport on the way. Newcastle is one of the best of England's provincial cities, still retaining a vibrant blend of ancient and modern, appropriate to the North-East's commercial, industrial, recreational and cultural capital.

A short circular tour south of the Tyne, though involving built-up areas of Tyneside's conurbation, can include a visit to **Washington Old Hall**

(National Trust), on the site of the medieval home of George Washington's ancestors. This early seventeenth-century manor house has many items relating to its American connections. From Washington, the A1231 heads eastwards to Sunderland, where the A183 turns northwards up the coast towards South Shields, passing a rare strip of beautiful coast from **Lizard Point** to **Marsden Rocks** and **The Leas**, completely undeveloped and with free public access.

Turning inland, the A185 leads towards the Tyne Tunnel and Newcastle. Near Jarrow, St Paul's Church recalls the golden era of Northumbria's early Christian culture and learning. A dedication stone of 23 April AD685, when a monastery was founded by Benedict Biscop, and the present chancel survive from the church which Bede knew, thirteen centuries ago.

Further Information

— Northumbria —

Places of Interest

Alnwick Castle
Open: end April to early October daily except Saturdays in May, June and September, 1-5pm.

Auckland Castle
Dates and times vary, check locally.

Deer Shelter
Open: throughout year.

Aydon Castle (English Heritage)
Open: Good Friday (or 1 April) to 30 September daily 10am-6pm.

Bamburgh
Castle
Open: Easter to end May daily 1-5pm; June to August daily 12noon-6pm; September daily 1-5pm; October daily 1-4.30pm.

Grace Darling Museum
Open: Easter to early October daily; April to September 11am-6pm; June to August 11am-7pm.

Barnard Castle (English Heritage)
Open: Good Friday (or 1 April) to 30 September daily 10am-6pm; October to 31 March daily 10am-4pm except Mondays, 24 -6 December and 1 January.

Bowes Museum
Open: May to September, weekdays 10am-5.30pm; October, March and April 10am-5pm; November to February, 10am-4pm; Sunday, summer 2-5pm, winter 2-4pm. Closed one week Christmas and 1 January. Charge for admission.

Beamish
North of England Open-air Museum
1 January to 31 March daily 10am-5pm except Mondays; April to October daily 10am-6pm.

Belsay Hall
(English Heritage)
Castle and Garden
Open: Good Friday or 1 April to 30 September daily 10am-6pm. October to Easter, Tuesday to Sunday 10am-4pm except 24-6 December and 1 January.

Berwick-on-Tweed
Barracks Museum & Art Gallery
(English Heritage)
Open: Easter or 1 April to 30 September daily 10am-6pm.

Kings Own Scottish Borderers Regimental Museum
Open: October to Easter 10am-4pm except 24-6 December and 1 January.

Brinkburn Priory
(English Heritage)
Open: Good Friday or 1 April to 30
September daily 10am-6pm.

Cherryburn
Open: daily 20 March to 31 October,
Tuesday to Saturday 10am-4.30pm,
Sunday 2-4.30pm also Bank Holiday
Mondays.

Cragside House
(National Trust)
Open: April to October daily except
Mondays 1-5.30pm. Also open Bank
Holiday Mondays.

Cragside Country Park,
Power Circuit & Energy Centre
Open: April to October daily 10.30am-
7pm; November to March, Saturday and
Sunday 10.30am-4pm.

Darlington
Darlington North Road Station Railway
Centre & Museum
Open: throughout year except Christmas
and New Year daily 9.30am-5pm.

Dunstanburgh Castle
(National Trust, English Heritage)
Open: Good Friday or 1 April to 30
September daily 10am-6pm; October to
Easter Tuesday to Sunday 10am-4pm
(except 24-6 December and 1 January).

Durham
Castle
Open: July to September daily 10.30am-
4.30pm; October to June, Monday,
Wednesday, Saturday 2-4.30pm.

Cathedral Treasury
Open: throughout year Monday to
Saturday 10am-4.30pm; Sunday
2-4.30pm.

Heritage Centre
Open: late May to mid-September,
Saturday to Thursday 2-4.30pm.

Oriental Museum
Open: daily Monday to Saturday 9.30am-
1pm, 2-5pm; Sunday 2-5pm except
weekends November to February.

Elsdon Tower Garden
Open: 31 March to 15 September daily
10am-6pm.

Gibside Chapel (National Trust)
Open: April to October daily except
Monday but open Good Friday and Bank
Holiday Mondays 11am-5pm.

Hadrian's Wall
Forts & Museums, Chesters, Corbridge,
Housesteads (English Heritage)
Open: throughout year Good Friday or 1
April to 30 September daily 10am-6pm;
October to Easter 10am-4pm (Corbridge
closed Mondays). All Closed 24-6 De-
cember and 1 January.

Vindolanda
Open: daily July to August 10am-6.30pm;
May and June 10am-6pm; April and
September 10am-5.30pm; March and
October 10am-5pm; February and
November 10am-4pm. Closed December
and January.

Hexham Centre for Border History
Open: April to October Monday to
Friday 10am-4.30pm; July, August early
September also Saturday 10am-4.30pm,
Sunday 11am-4.30pm.

Jarrow
Bede Monastery Museum
Open: April to October Tuesday to
Saturday 10am-5.30pm, Sunday 2.30-
5.30pm; November to March, Tuesday to
Saturday 11am-4.30pm, Sunday 1.20-
5.30pm.

Lindisfarne
Castle
(National Trust)
Open: April to September daily except
Friday but open Good Friday 1-5.30pm.
October, Wednesday, Saturday, Sunday
1-5.30pm as tides permit.

Priory
(English Heritage)
Open: Good Friday or 1 April to 30
September daily 10am-6pm; October to
Easter, Tuesday to Sunday 10am-4pm (as
tides permit). Closed 24-6 December and
1 January.

Newcastle
Castle Keep
Open: October to March daily 9.30am-4.30pm; April to September 9.30am-5.30pm. Closed Mondays except Bank Holidays, Christmas and Good Friday.

Museum of Antiquities
Open: daily throughout year, except Christmas and New Year. Monday to Saturday 10am-5pm.

University
Open: Monday to Saturday 10am-5pm.

Laing Art Gallery
Open: daily throughout year except Mondays, Tuesday to Friday 10am-5.30pm.

Norham Castle (English Heritage)
Open: Good Friday or 1 April to 30 September daily 10am-6pm; October to Easter, Tuesday to Sunday 10am-4pm, except 24-6 December and 1 January.

Prudhoe Castle (English Heritage)
Open: Good Friday or 1 April to 30 September daily 10am-6pm; October to Easter, Tuesday to Sunday 10am-4pm, except 24-6 December and 1 January.

Raby Castle
Open: all Bank Holidays except Christmas and New Year; May to June, Wednesday to Sunday; July to September daily except Saturdays.
Castle open: 1-5pm, grounds 11am-5.30pm.

Wallington House (National Trust)
Open: April to October daily except Tuesday 1-5.30pm.

Walled Garden
Open: April to September daily 10am-7pm; October 10am-6pm; November to March 10am-4pm.

Grounds
Open: throughout year during daylight hours.

Warkworth Castle (English Heritage)
Open: Good Friday or 1 April to 30 September daily 10am-6pm; October to Easter, Tuesday to Sunday 10am-4pm except 24-6 December and 1 January.

Warkworth Hermitage
(English Heritage)
Open: Good Friday to 30 September weekends only.

Wylam
George Stephenson's Cottage
(National Trust)
Open: April to October Thursday, Saturday, Sunday, Bank Holiday Mondays and Good Friday 1-5.30pm.

Tourist Information Centres

Alnwick
Shambles, ☎ 0665 510665

Barnard Castle
Galgate, ☎ 0833 690909

Berwick-upon-Tweed
Castlegate car park, ☎ 0289 330733

Corbridge
Vicar's Pele, ☎ 0434 632815

Darlington
Library, ☎ 0325 469858

Durham
Market Place, ☎ 091384 3720

Hexham
Manor Office, ☎ 0434 605225

Kielder Forestry Commission
Castle, ☎ 0660 20242

Kielder (Water)
Tower Knowe, ☎ 0660 40398

Newcastle-upon-Tyne
Central Library, ☎ 091261 0691

Newcastle
Airport, ☎ 091271 1929

Northumberland
National Park Office
(Hexham), ☎ 0434 605555

Rothbury
Church Street, ☎ 0669 20887

Seahouses
Car Park, ☎ 0665 720884

Wooler
High Street Car Park, ☎ 0668 81602

14 • South-West Scotland

Nithsdale

North of Dumfries, the rounded Lowther Hills form the boundary between the Dumfries and Galloway Region and the Strathclyde Region. The headwaters of the River Nith rise to the north of the Southern Upland fault, having captured some of the streams flowing north into the River Clyde. The Nith is joined by swift-flowing tributaries from the Lowther Hills and the Penpont Moors.

The river runs along a mature valley throughout its course, which has been largely determined by the presence of basins of younger rocks, especially the Permian sandstones. The rocks are dune-bedded sandstones and breccias, which indicate that they were formed under desert conditions. The Nith passes through an ever-changing countryside, a patchwork of gentle rolling uplands, wide wooded valleys, pastureland and rich coastal plains — an area of fascinating contrasts.

In northern Nithsdale, just north of Sanquhar, the B797 leaves the main A76 road, ascends by a twisting route following the Mennock Water, and climbs the Mennock Pass to **Wanlockhead**. At 1,383ft (422m), this is the highest village in Scotland. The thin shales of the Lowthers crumbling away have produced smooth curving slopes. These hills are mainly rounded and grassy, but heather flourishes on some flanks. The upland village of Wanlockhead, along with the neighbouring settlement of Leadhills, just over the border in Strathclyde Region, were important centres for lead mining until earlier this century. Mining for lead and zinc carried on until the 1930s, when the workings closed. In the 1950s, the New Glencrieff mine was reopened, but closed at the end of that decade.

Wanlockhead is a unique settlement, rich in social history, with the evidence of a tremendous industrial enterprise still clearly visible. Some of the former miners' cottages line the two main streets, but others are set here and there without any proper planning. It can be a bleak place in winter, but sunshine highlights the colour-washed buildings huddled in a valley fold against a grey-green backcloth of hill slopes.

Today visitors can spend a fascinating time at the Museum of Scottish Lead-mining and also look at many other features associated with the area's mining heritage. The visitor centre has a display of local minerals and features outlining the history of lead-mining. One example is the Wanlockhead Beam Engine. This large structure was used to drain the

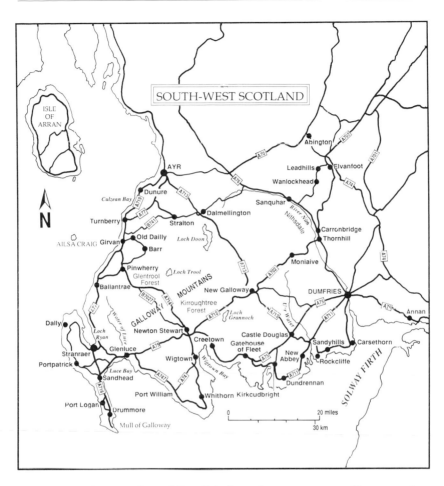

workings in the Strait Steps Mine. It is the only water-powered beam engine
of its type in Britain, and is now protected as an Ancient Monument. There
is also a horse powered engine nearby. Loch Nell Mine has guided tours
into the mine, where a surprise tableau is suddenly revealed when extra
lighting is switched on. Pates Knowes Smelt Mill consisted of four hearths
originally, now two of them have been partially reconstructed. The village
has a youth hostel, a general store/post office, miners' cottages with reconstructed interiors, the Miners' Library, founded in 1756, and the Walk Inn,
which has a tea-room.

The village of **Leadhills** lies $1^1/_2$ miles (2km) to the north-east along the
B797. The mines, now closed, were mainly concentrated round the head of
Glengonnar Water. Gold panned from the alluvial deposits was used in the
Scottish regalia, and individuals still try their luck panning for gold in
Shortcleugh Water. The Miners' Library, open on summer afternoons, was
set up by the local poet Allan Ramsey (1686-1758), the son of a local lead
mine manager, in 1741. The oldest circulating library in Britain, the building

houses a valuable collection of eighteenth and nineteenth century books. At the northern end of the village is a memorial erected in 1891 commemorating William Symington, a pioneer of steam navigation and the atmospheric pumping engine. He applied steam propulsion to a tug boat, the Charlotte Dundas, which was launched at Grangemouth in 1802.

The Leadhills and Wanlockhead Light Railway was opened by the Caledonian Railway Company in 1901. The line ran from the main line at Elvanfoot, and climbed to a height of 1,498ft (457m) at Wanlockhead. It closed in 1939. The line was the highest on British standard-gauge passenger railways. At the present time, the Lowthers Railway Preservation Society is planning and working on the construction of a 2ft narrow-gauge line on the existing track bed. It is hoped to operate a service with three stations on the 1^1/$_2$ mile (2km) stretch between Leadhills and Wanlockhead, first with diesel and later with steam traction.

Leadhills has a general store, a post office, the Hopetown Arms, and bed and breakfast accommodation. Look for the tall wooden structure with a large bell located in the centre of the village. The bell was tolled for shift changes, at funerals and to summon villagers to search the surrounding hills for missing persons. On the journey to Elvanfoot, spare a minute to view the fine old railway viaduct on the north side of the road. Although now in a sad and dilapidated condition, it stands looking across the heathery slopes of the valley of the Elvan Water.

There is a walk of 4 miles (6km) from Wanlockhead to Lowther Hill, 2,377ft (725m). Part of the Southern Upland Way, the route follows the private access road to the top of the hill. The road is marked with coloured poles which are of considerable assistance to the walker in winter, and the upper slopes can provide fair skiing conditions at times. The summit is a conspicuous landmark, dominated as it is by two huge golf-ball-like spheres in the area of the Civil Aviation Authority's radar station. There are extensive views from the summit towards the Draer Reservoir.

A 7 mile (11km) linear walk from Wanlockhead to Muiryhill follows a signposted path west of Stake Hill to meet the private road up Lowther Hill. After a short distance, leave the road and head for the col between Lowther Hill and East Mount Lowther. Descend, and follow the valley of the Enterkin Burn to Glenvalentine. Continue south, climb over the spur and walk along the ridge. The way proceeds down to a minor road junction to Inglestone and beyond to Muiryhill. This is an old, well known route through the hills, used in the past by Covenanters and the soldiers of Bonnie Prince Charlie came this way on their retreat from Derby. Motorists can make a very pleasant circuit of the area by taking in the Mennock Pass, through Wanlockhead and Leadhills to Elvanfoot, and returning to the Nith Valley by way of the Dalveen Pass, A702.

Returning to wooded, green Nithsdale down the Mennock Pass is particularly delightful when the heather and bracken on the hill slopes are changing colour. The A76 passes through **Sanquhar** on its way to Cumnock and Kilmarnock. The valley is open, the soil rich and red, and the pastureland supports many herds of dairy cattle. On entering Sanquhar from the south, a granite monument commemorates declarations read by two brave Covenanting leaders who challenged the king's authority.

Sanquhar was the original seat of the first Duke of Queensberry, and was given royal burgh status by James VI. The town holds an annual Riding of the Marches ceremony in summer, the climax of its gala week. The handsome Tolbooth, attributed to William Adam, was built in 1735. The building now houses a museum which covers the history of Upper Nithsdale. There is a tourist information centre downstairs.

Nithsdale has much to offer the discerning traveller, with many interesting locations tucked away behind lush woodland, or sited in one of the many quiet valleys leading into the hills. Where the Nith Valley narrows, and road, river and railway come close together, stately home enthusiasts should not miss the magnificent building of Drumlanrig Castle. Built of pink sandstone, it is a fine Renaissance example of Scottish domestic architecture. Visitors will find much to enjoy here; there are gardens, beautiful parkland, richly decorated apartments, period furnishings and galleries of paintings.

From Carronbridge, the A702 leads up the Dalveen Pass to Elvanfoot. Just north-east of Carronbridge, a minor road leads to the remote fourteenth-century Morton Castle. The ruins overlook Morton Loch against a backcloth of the Lowther Hills.

Further along the A702, leave the main road 3 miles (5km) north-northeast of Carronbridge, and bear right on a minor road to the remote settlement of **Durisdeer**, just over 1 mile (2km) ahead. The hamlet is dominated by the late seventeenth-century church, and contains the Queensberry Mausoleum. Just north of the church lies the well preserved remains of an Antonine fortlet, close to the line of the Roman road from Nithsdale to Clydesdale.

Thornhill is an attractive village south of Carronbridge, with a wide, tree-lined main thoroughfare overlooked by solid sandstone houses. A clear point of interest is the stately column headed by Pegasus, the winged horse, which is the emblem of the third Duke of Queensberry. A little to the south-west of the town is Keir Mill. Here, the world's first pedal cycle was built at Courthill Smithy, around 1840 by Kirkpatrick Macmillan. Daer Reservoir, reached via the Dalveen Pass, is a large stretch of water set amongst remote hills.

The Penpont Moors on the western side of Nithsdale, are cut by four glens; the Euchan Water, Scaur Water, Shinnel Water and Dalwhat Water. These lovely, lonely valleys are ideal for off the beaten track exploration along quiet, narrow roads. For example, the valley of the Scaur Water drives deeply into the surrounding hills, and provides many surprises for the traveller.

The road proceeds along the U-shaped glacial valley, following the stream on its wriggling course in the midst of the rolling hills and interlinking spurs. Soaring above the glen are the craggy precipices of Glenwhargen Craig, 1,581ft (482m), a totally unexpected sight. At the head of the valley the road ends just short of the Polskeoch Bothy, a simple, recently constructed building that offers good shelter for Southern Upland Way walkers.

Moniaive is an attractive village with colour-washed houses and narrow streets. It is a convenient centre for the exploration of the valley of the Cairn Water, the beautiful glen of Dalwhat Water, the hill roads over to the Glenkens, and beyond to the forests and mountains of the Galloway heartland. Moniaive used to be the terminus of the Cairn Valley Light Railway, opened in 1905 and closed down in 1945. Just east of Moniaive, off the B729, is Maxwelton House. This is the birthplace of Anna Laurie in 1682.

Below Thornhill the Nith Valley widens out again, and the river enters fine farming country, and an area associated with Robert Burns. At Ellisland Farm, despite the hard life on unproductive land, Burns had time to create some of his famous works, such as *Of A' The Airts, O, Were I On Parnassus Hill, Auld Lang Syne*, and *Tam O'Shanter*. The building houses a small museum and display area.

At Glenkiln Reservoir an extraordinary private collection of modern sculptures, including works by Rodin, Renoir, Epstein and Moore, is set out on the hill and watersides.

The Forest of Ae, north of Dumfries, is reached via the A701 and by turning left to Ae village. There are forest paths, parking facilities and a picnic site. There is a beautiful walk along the banks of Crawick Water from Sanquahr. Turn right before the clock tower on to a minor road and proceed for 2 miles (3km) to a small cottage called Plantainside. There is parking available here. Follow the route down through Moor Plantation to Crawick Water. There are bridges across the burn, and seats have been provided to view the surroundings.

A circular woodland walk from the car park at **Drumlanrig** follows the yellow arrows past Beech Loch, Coldstream Loch, Druid Loch, Mount Malloch viewpoint and the Roman Fort. The distance covered is 3 miles (5km).

A linear walk along the Southern Upland Way from Polskeoch Bothy to Benbrack, 1,903ft (580m). The journey there and back via Allan's Cairn and Black Hill is 10 miles (16km). The view from the summit of Benbrack is very expansive in all directions.

From the centre of Sanquhar, a 10 mile (16km) walk follows a section of the Southern Upland Way to Wanlockhead. Take the route uphill to Dinanrig, ascend the grassy slopes of Conrig Hill, and descend to Cogshead. In the grouse-nesting season and during the grouse-shooting season there is an alternative route from here. Proceed north above Cog Burn, and swing round the valley of the Glensalloch Burn. Walk through the afforestation above Glenbuie Burn, round the head of Back Burn, through another patch of forest and descend to Duntercleuch. The Way continues down the Wanlock Water to Wanlockhead.

The Solway Coast

The long, indented coastline of Dumfries and Galloway extends from the north shore of the inner Solway Firth, round the estuary of the River Nith, and continues in a series of ever-larger bays to the Mull of Galloway, the southernmost tip of Scotland. The Solway coastline may have been formed by the drowning of softer rocks, with the harder rocks of the Criffel and Bengairn hills rising steeply beyond the coastline. However, its character owes much to the different deposits from glacial origin, raised beaches, peat mosses and material brought down by rivers creating a picture of resistant rocky headlands separated by bays, where the sea has eroded away the softer rocks, resulting in a tattered coastline of sandy bays and rocky coves.

The Solway shores are also noted for their marshes, where sinuous channels are uncovered at every low tide. These networks of watercourses wind through the gleaming mudflats treasured by the ornithologist and marine biologist. The extensive coastal marshes of Lochar Moss lie east of the Nith Estuary. Another attraction for visitors who wish to explore this part of southern Scotland is the lovely, quiet countryside just inland. Here, a patchwork canvas of fields lie snugly between rocky hills, hollows, forests and salmon rivers.

The region contains a number of valleys in which the rivers drain into the Solway; the Rivers Esk, Annan, Nith, Urr, Dee, Fleet, Cree and the Water of Luce. These rivers rise amidst a rugged interior, a remote, unspoilt area of granite mountains, and hills and moorlands similar to the Border Country.

The wide sands of the Solway attract discerning visitors who enjoy a seaside holiday, although parts of this region are not good for swimming. The eastern end of the Solway is swept by very fast tides and has ever-changing channels. Powfoot and Sandyhills Bay, Colvend, are safe at high tides, but it is dangerous to walk out over long stretches of sand to meet incoming tides.

Administratively, Galloway consists of the old counties of Kirkcudbrightshire (the Stewartry) and Wigtownshire, bounded on the east by the River Nith and its catchment area around the upper tributaries of the Urr Water.

A new heritage trail has been designated along the Solway Coast westward from Annan to Stranraer. It is indicated by the blue-on-white symbol representing the Monreith Cross, one of the earliest Christian monuments in Scotland, which can be seen at Whithorn.

In the west, the gentle part of Galloway is a large triangle of land called the Machars (Gaelic for 'flat lands'). This area, bounded by Wigtown Bay and Luce Bay, has none of the rugged hills or numerous lochs associated with the Galloway mountain heartland to the north. The rolling, dairy farmland has been inhabited since the earliest communities were established around 6,000 years ago. Today, the story of these societies can be traced through conspicuous remains — grass-covered mounds, stone circles, inscribed stones, fortified settlements, abbeys, mottes and castles.

On the eastern side of the Nith Estuary, the minor road leads to the solid red sandstone splendour of **Caerlaverock Castle**. Built in the latter part of the thirteenth century, with later additions, it is the only triangular castle in Britain. It also has a double-towered gatehouse, fine living quarters and a water-filled moat.

Seawards, beyond the castle, lies the **Caerlaverock Nature Reserve** along the Solway Merse. The Wildfowl and Wetlands Trust has established a refuge covering many acres adjacent to the nature reserve. Every winter, barnacle geese fly down from Spitzbergen far beyond the Arctic Circle to the Solway Firth. The refuge is also the home of the rare natterjack toad. The Trust has provided excellent facilities to view and photograph the birds, with an observatory, three towers and twenty hides.

The small village of **New Abbey** lies on the A710, 7 miles (11km) south of Dumfries. Here are the impressive remains of Sweetheart Abbey, founded in 1273 by Devorguilla de Balliol in memory of her husband. The beautiful red stone building consists of an aisled nave with square-ended transepts. The tower, with its battlemented parapet contains traceried windows and there are rose windows in the south-west gables.

Just to the north of the village is Shambellie House, a Victorian mansion in the Scottish baronial style, it houses a Museum of Costume. West of Sandyhills, there is a path along the cliff edge which passes the Needle's Eye, a natural rock arch on the shore below.

Rockcliffe and **Kippford** are villages nestling close together on the Urr Water. The coastline here offers a variety of beaches, bays and inlets, some sandy, some rocky. Close by is the Mote of Mark, a Dark Age defensive citadel. Access to Rough Island can be gained at low tide from Rockcliffe or Kippford. It is the nesting site of terns and oyster catchers, but you are asked not to visit the island in the nesting season of May and June. **Orchardton Castle**, a short distance to the north, has a round tower house which probably dates from the fifteenth century. **Dundrennan Abbey** off the A71 to Kirkcudbright, is a fine example of twelfth-century medieval workmanship. It closely follows the style of architecture evident in Yorkshire Cistercian religious houses.

The ancient town of **Kirkcudbright** is situated at the head of the deep, sheltered estuary of the River Dee. As the capital of the Stewartry, it was once an important seaport, well-placed to trade with the transatlantic colonies. Close to the river are the substantial remains of MacLellan's Castle, a fine sixteenth-century tower house. The western part of High Street is the most ancient area of the town, with some very interesting houses. Broughton House is Georgian, with some fine panelled interiors; it is now the Hornel Museum containing many of the artists' paintings.

There are beautiful views from the rising ground above the town of Kirkcudbright, across the bay to the Solway, and also of the hills to the north. The countryside around is emerald green and dotted with farms. The coast between Kirkcudbright and Gatehouse of Fleet is carved with coves and rocky promontories. This picturesque stretch of the Solway Coast attracted the attention of famous novelists such as Robert Louis Stevenson, Sir Walter Scott and John Buchan. Near to Gatehouse of Fleet is the Fleet

Drumlanrig Castle in Nithsdale, South-West Scotland

Loch Einich, in the heart of the Cairngorms, seen from above the head of the loch

The harbour at Tobermory on the island of Mull, Scottish Highlands

A view across Loch Maree towards Slioch, Wester Ross, Scottish Highlands

Caerlaverock Castle

Oakwoods Interpretive Trail, which is a delightful way through attractive, broad-leaved woodland. There are other trails available, with a picnic area and information centre.

The road westwards from Gatehouse of Fleet is a particularly beautiful section, passing the commanding pile of Cardoness Castle. This strongly constructed fifteenth-century fortress guarded the approach to the Water of Fleet. The fascinating remains of Cairnholy Chambered Cairns and the well preserved, four-storeyed tower of Carsluith are also worth visiting. The Cairnholy Chambered Cairns lie on the southern slopes of Cairnholy Hill overlooking Wigtown Bay. The Neolithic culture spread north along the western coasts of Britain and these long cairns are good examples of gallery graves of the Clyde group. The southern cairn, Cairnholy I, consists of an inner burial chamber, an ante-chamber and a curved façade of eight tall stories.

Three miles (5km) east of Newton Stewart, off the A75, at Palnure, is the Kirroughtree Forest Visitors Centre. A number of well marked walks start here, varying in distance from $1^1/_2$ miles (2km) to 4 miles (6km), including a separate bird watchers' trail. North of Newton Stewart is a large area of ancient woodland, which is the location of the Wood of Cree RSPB Nature Reserve. It is open to the public at all times, and visitors are asked to keep to the trails which are clearly marked.

The A75 hugs the coastline of the Cree Estuary and reaches **Creetown**. Here there is the Gem Rock Museum which houses a fascinating collection of gems and minerals from around the world. **Wigtown Bay** is an important site for wintering wildfowl and waders. Ducks begin to arrive from the end of August and geese fly in from late November. They feed on the surrounding farm land during the day, and roost offshore during the night. Just south of Wigtown, on the A714, is the Bladnoch Distillery. A guided tour explains the distilling process.

Garlieston is a little further south of Wigtown. The gardens of Galloway House are open to the public. The village is also the home of the Wigtown Bay Trading Post. A converted grain mill contains a treasure trove of domestic delights.

The quiet village of **Whithorn** is renowned as an important historical settlement. In the sixteenth century, the splendour of the cathedral was renowned throughout Galloway. Today, all that remains is the shell of the nave at the western end of the cathedral, which was the church in the Middle Ages. The current archaeological 'dig' reveals the Whithorn story, a fascinating record of Early Christians, Anglo-Saxons and Vikings.

St Ninian (or Nynia) arrived here in the fifth century, and along the coast is a secluded cave where he came for peaceful meditation. A number of cross-incised slabs, now in the Whithorn Museum, came from this cave. The museum houses the fifth-century Latinus Stone, the earliest Christian memorial in Scotland. St Ninian's Cave is near to Kidsdale Farm. The walking distance from the farm is nearly 2 miles (3km). Near Whithorn is Rispain Fort — this was the site of a second-century fortified homestead, with a massive ditch and inner and outer ramparts.

From the Isle of Whithorn, the exposed nose of Burrow Head juts out into the sea, and the coastline, with its fine cliff scenery, streams away to the north-west, uncluttered by houses. The A747 hugs the shores of Luce Bay, but is checked for a few moments by the pleasantly situated seaside village of **Port William**, which is mostly set round the little harbour. The road quietly continues without interruption, keeping the sea alongside and affording lovely views across the bay to the raised outline of The Rhins and the Mull of Galloway. **Glenluce**, situated close by the Water of Luce and straddling the A75, is the gateway to the moors. Glenluce Motor Museum has a display of vintage cars and motorcycles. Glenluce Abbey dates from the thirteenth to fifteenth centuries.

Leaving behind the lowland area between Luce Sands and Loch Ryan, the A715 passes through the village of Sandhead with its magnificent stretch of sandy beach. Nearby Kirkmadrine is a nineteenth-century burial chapel with ancient Christian monuments. The B7041 takes over for the final part of the journey, rising towards the Mull of Galloway, the finger tip of the knobbly peninsular of The Rhins. Here, bold cliffs point towards England, Ireland and the Isle of Man, and the tall lighthouse keeps watch over the area where nine tides meet.

Moving northwards, the exciting windswept western coastline of the peninsular is an interesting sequence of cliff tops and small bays. **Port Logan** is a peaceful spot, with a pleasant picnic area by the harbour, which is overlooked by a stubby lighthouse tower. At the north end of the bay is the Logan Fish Pond, where the fish can be fed by hand. The mild climate of the area, due to the warming influence of the Gulf Stream, has enabled a fine collection of plants from other regions of the world to be grown outdoors. A lovely display of magnificent rhododendrons, cabbage palms, tree ferns, a peat garden and a woodland area may be viewed at the nearby Logan Botanic Garden.

At the north end of the peninsular country lanes lead down to Dally Bay, where the immediate surroundings are rich in birdlife. A walk of approximately 1¹/₂ miles (2km) extends north from Dally Bay over fine coastal scenery.

A good walk can be started from **Ardwell Farm, Criffel**. Take the A710 south from New Abbey for 2¹/₂ miles (4km). Turn right to Ardwell Farm, and park just before the farm entrance. Turn left to a farm track and proceed to another gate. Take the right turn just beyond and walk to the edge of the woodland. Ascend through the forest to a stile at the edge of the plantation. Head diagonally left, and climb up on a clear path to the summit. Walk north for 1 mile (2km) to Knockendoch, and descend steeply south-east to the forestry fence. Return to the starting point. The walk covers a distance of 4 miles (6km).

The Jubilee Path which links Kippford and Rockcliffe provides a good walk. Turn left at the post office in Kippford, climb steeply uphill and follow the signposted path to Rockcliffe. For the return journey there is an alternative route past Barons Craig into the forested area. Take the left fork, and descend down the steep path back to the post office. The distance there and back is 3¹/₂ miles (6km).

A walk worth trying is that from **Sandyhills**. Walk down the lane to the sands, cross the stream, and head up to a path along the cliff edge to Portling. Continue above the high cliffs with plentiful birdlife and a wide variety of wild flowers to keep you company. Descend to a monument, and then climb up to Castlehill Point overlooking the Urr Estuary. Walk round the headland, down to the site of a Bronze Age fort and along to Rockcliffe. The distance of the cliff path walk, travelling in one direction is 4¹/₂ miles (7km).

Another walk begins at **Bengairn**, ¹/₂ mile (1km) north of Auchencairn, near Dundrennan. Take the minor road on the left, and then second right, to ascend up through a forest to a gate. The track bears sharp right to a fork. Take the route on the left and continue past the ruins of Foresthill, through gates in the fences of sheep pastures, to the summit. The distance, returning by the same route, is 5 miles (8km). A longer, circular walk taking in Screel Hill, 1,128ft (343m), descends to the main road. Finally, there is a short walk of 1¹/₂ miles (2km) along the A711 back to the start. The total distance of the circular walk is 7 miles (11km).

A recommended walk is that from **Trusty's Hill**. Just west of Gatehouse of Fleet, turn north on a minor road to Anwoth. Take the footpath from the old church climbing to a wooded ridge. The tree cover clears, and the summit of Trusty's Hill can be seen south-east beyond a little glen. The remains of an Iron Age fort lie on the top of the hill, and near the southern gateway are a number of Pictish symbols incised on a rocky slab. They comprise a Z-rod, a double disc, a beast, and a circle containing a human face with curved horns. The distance covered is 1 mile (2km).

Galloway Forest Park

The park can be reached by travelling from Stranraer and the A75 to Newton Stewart and then via the A714 Girvan road, approaching from the east, via the A75 from Gatehouse of Fleet to Newton Stewart on the A712 from New Galloway. From Stranraer proceed along the A75 and turn right $^1/_2$ mile (1km) beyond the turning off the A75. This brings you to the Meadowsweet Herb Garden. The house is situated on a tongue of land in Soulseat Loch, and the gardens contain over a hundred types of herbs in individual beds.

Return to the A75 and turn right. Proceed for $^1/_2$ mile (1km) and bear left. The Castle Kennedy Gardens lie in an attractive wooded setting on an isthmus between Black Loch (Loch Crindil) and White Loch (Loch of Inch). The high ruined walls of the old castle stand close to the entrance to the gardens. The landscaped grounds, inspired by the gardens at Versailles, are formal in style, with avenues which converge on a giant lily pond.

From Castle Kennedy continue eastwards down the A75 to Glenwhan Garden at Dunragit. This is an interesting hilltop garden with varieties of trees, shrubs, rhododendrons and azaleas around two small lochans. Just before Glenluce, an access track turns sharp left and ascends to the Castle of Park. This restored, sixteenth century laird's house has crow-stepped gables and an inscribed panel just above the entrance door.

Around Stranraer, rocks of the Carboniferous and Permian systems overlie the older rocks. The former consist of interbedded pale-brown or grey sandstones, conglomerates and dark mudstones. The Permian rocks are red sandstones, mudstones and conglomerates.

North of the Machars, in the old county of **Wigtown**, the land rises, and the countryside becomes wild and bare. This remote landscape forms a canvas of heather moors, afforestation, rough bent grasses, lively burns and rushing rivers. The area is criss-crossed by ancient tracks and paths, and only two minor roads, the B7027, Barrhill-Challoch, and the unclassified route, Glenluce — Tarf Bridge — Glassoch, cross its lonely interior. It was not always so, as indicated by much evidence of human impact on the landscape. During Neolithic and Bronze Age times, when the climate was warmer, this upland region was colonised by people who found the area drier than the valleys. In medieval times, pilgrims en-route to Whithorn would tramp the ancient cross-country paths. They would pass the Wells of the Rees, three domed drystone structures, each with a recess for the statue of the saint or Virgin, and visit the Laggangairn Standing Stones. The latter are an example of a pagan holy place re-used for Christian purposes. The two prehistoric monoliths were inscribed with a cross, together with four small crosses at the angles.

This sparsely populated area is a challenge for hill walkers. The open, bleak terrain, devoid of clear landmarks, with afforestation and very wet sections, demands good map and compass skills. Walkers may strike off across the moorland from the Southern Upland Way to visit Linn's Tomb, a remote, well maintained covenanting monument.

From Barrhill the B7027 twists up and down to Newton Stewart and passes several lochs containing numerous islands — Lochs Drumlamford, Nahinie, Dornal, Maberry, Fyntalloch and Ochiltree. The two larger islands on the latter may be crannog and castle sites. Alexander Murray Monument, and Wild Goat Park is situated on the hillside opposite the Talnotry campsite, some 6$^1/_2$ miles (10km) from Newton Stewart on the A712.

Just beyond the monument is the Wild Goat Park, where a number of shaggy, long-haired feral goats roam free in a prepared enclosure. The isolated hamlet of Knowe is a welcome stopping place for Southern Upland Way walkers on the long section of 17$^1/_2$ miles (28km) from New Luce to Bargrennan. The stretch of the B7027 between Glassoch and Challoch is the area for the Penninghame Forest Walks. The Forestry Commission own a number of lochs in this part of the country. Three of them, Loch Eldrig, and the neighbouring Garwachie and Spectacle Lochs, can be fished for pike, perch, tench, roach and rudd. Day permits may be obtained from the Caldons Campsite, Glen Trool. On the minor road to Straiton from Glentrool village is Palgowan Farm. This working hill farm offers guided tours showing sheep handling, horncraft, stone walling and skin curing.

The granite hills of high Galloway are a surprise, and one does not expect a combination of the Trossachs and the Cairngorms in South-West Scotland. The geology of the region is rather interesting, with the major hill areas mainly composed of Silurian sedimentary rocks. These consist of thick beds and shales, slates, greywackes (a kind of sandstone), grits and conglomerates, which were intruded by igneous material causing metamorphism in the surrounding rocks.

The mountain heartland contains the **Merrick**, at 2,770ft (844m), the highest summit in the Southern Uplands. There are three other peaks over 2,500ft (762m), and this remote area has the wildest scenery and roughest walking in Scotland south of the Highlands. The granite mass forms the Dungeon Range — the hills of Mullwharchar, Dungeon Hill, Craignaw and the isolated range of Cairnsmore of Fleet.

Extensive afforestation, often very tightly packed, covers the lower slopes of many of the higher Galloway hills. Much more forestry has been introduced on these wet peaty soils than on the more easterly rolling hills of the southern uplands. The **Galloway Forest Park** is the second largest forest in Scotland; in fact forests now cover some 24 per cent of the land area of Dumfries and Galloway. Although conifers rule the lower slopes of the hills, many of the native broadleaved woodlands have survived in the valleys alongside the rivers and lochs.

The narrow road along Glen Trool, which continues all the way up to the loch, provides a journey of sheer delight. The long narrow loch is overlooked by craggy hillsides, and the road is fringed by deciduous woodlands which soften the impact of the surrounding blanket of larch and spruce. A beautifully-sited caravan and camping site has been established at Caldons by the Forestry Commission at the south-west end of Loch Trool.

Although the **Galloway Hills** lack the rugged nature of the Highlands, they are still wild and fairly remote. For the walker, the area represents a scene of hills, rocky bracken-strewn slopes, forests, lochs and numerous rivers and burns. Clear paths in the district are few and far between, and it cannot be stressed too strongly that care should be taken in the preparation for the hill walk and the equipment needed. It is a good idea to leave details of your intended route with another person or appropriate authority.

During the summer months, the Raiders' Road Forest Drive is open on payment of a small admission charge. From the A712, opposite the Clatteringshaws Loch Dam, the track enters the forest alongside the Black Water of Dee. The old drove road passes through the forest where the Sitka spruce is king, although copses of broadleaved trees have been planted to enhance the surroundings. The route follows the river with picnic spots and regular stopping places, such as the picturesque otter pool, and points where short walks can be undertaken. The way swings round Stroan Loch, and continues on up to the A762 Tongland Bridge to New Galloway road. This is an excellent opportunity of experiencing a remote area, and being able to view its animal, plant and birdlife. The distance from Clatteringshaws to the A762 is 10 miles (16km).

The **Galloway Deer Museum** overlooks Clatteringshaws Loch, where the waters of the Black Water of Dee were impounded to create a storage reservoir for the Galloway Hydro-Electric Scheme. The museum contains interesting and informative displays relating to forest management, archaeology, geology and wildlife.

A journey down the A713 through the Glenkens, brings the visitor to **Threave Castle**, just outside the town of Castle Douglas. Impressively situated on an island in the River Dee, the fortress includes a well preserved medieval riverside harbour. A small boat ferries visitors to the island, access is from the A75 2 miles (3km) west of Castle Douglas.

A walk worth trying is that from Caldons Camp Site, Glen Trool. This is a way-marked trail established by the Forestry Commission of $4^1/_2$ miles (7km) around Loch Trool. The route passes through conifer plantations, and climbs across the lower slopes of Mulldonoch, with fine views over Loch Trool to Benyellery and Merrick. The path crosses the Glenhead Burn and swings round to climb up to the Bruce Stone. From the car park the way crosses Kenmure Moss back to the campsite.

A walk to **Merrick** is recommended. From the higher car park north of the Bruce Stone in Glen Trool, follow the Buchan Burn to Culsharg. Bear left up to a forestry track, cross the bridge, turn left and ascend on a clear path to the slopes of Benyellery. Bear right, and head for the summit, 2,360ft (719m). Follow the wall for a short distance, then aim for the cairn and trig point on the summit of Merrick. A tremendous all-round view of the magnificent scenery is the reward.

A descent can be made via the same route, or alternatively, descend to the south-east, to the south-west corner of Loch Enoch. Follow the fence past the Grey Man of Merrick or, if it is wet, follow the wall to the gate in the forestry fence. Continue along the forest ride crossing the Gloon Burn, and proceed through the woodland to a track and on to the bridge. Turn left down the path to Culsharg and return to the starting point. The distance covered is 9 miles (15km)

A walk worth trying is one which includes **Lamachan** and **Curlywee**. From the Caldons campsite, follow the Caldons Burn. A short distance beyond a forest ride, cross the Mulmein Burn and follow a wall for a short distance. Cross a fence, negotiate a way over the burn and head up the slopes of Cambrick Hill to the top. Walk towards the large cairn on the summit of Lamachan. Head eastwards, following the line of old iron fence posts to Bennanbrack; turn right and follow the posts down to the Nick of Curlywee. Cross the wall and climb steeply to the summit of Curlywee. Descend to the White Laggan bothy keeping to the left of the Well Burn.

The return is along the track past Loch Dee, bearing right on the path alongside Glenhead Burn. At the next stile and marker post, follow the path through the forest to a track. Bear right, and keep to the forest trail back to the camp site. The walk covers a distance of 11 miles (18km).

Carrick

This region covers the coast and inland area north of Stranraer reached by the A77 and A714 to Girvan. From the east by the A713, Castle Douglas to Ayr road.

From Stranraer, the A77 hugs the shore of Loch Ryan until it reaches Finnarts Bay, crossing over the Galloway Burn, and into the Carrick District of southern Ayrshire. The road then slants inland along the narrow wooded valley of Glen App, following the line of the Southern Upland Fault and climbs over the heather moors down to the valley of the River Stinchar. On the moorlands north-east of Pinwherry is **Gleit Stone**. This solitary, tall pointed slab of stone contains strange, bowl-shaped indentations on both faces.

The gaunt ruins of Ardstinchar Castle dominate the river crossing and the town of **Ballantrae**. The attractive eighteenth-century bridge is now superseded by a more modern structure. At the mouth of the river a shingle spit has become a nature reserve cared for by the Scottish Wildlife Trust. It is a breeding ground for arctic, common and little terns, and is open to visitors, although access is limited during the summer.

The main road heads north on the raised beach platform, with the former sea cliffs lying well back from the sea, until it approaches **Bennane Head**. Here, it is forced to cling precariously to the rocks as it inches round the headland. From the lay-by at Bennane Head a gully gives access to the shore; climb over fallen rocks to reach the cave.

The A77, travelling northwards, stays close to the sea, and ultimately passes between the cliffs and a large standing outcrop of rock at Kennedy's Pass. Here, the presence of Old Red Sandstone sedimentary rocks is reflected in the tumbled debris and sea stacks of the raised beach platform.

Fishing boats in the harbour at Girvan

The seaside town of **Girvan** extends along a bay with a good sandy beach, free of dangerous currents. The resort is bordered by hills to the south and east; it faces west over the Firth of Clyde to the commanding, dome-like shape of the Island of Ailsa. This rises to a height of 1,108ft (338m), and is thought to be the basal remains of a volcanic vent, which created towering cliffs most of the way round. The red granite became famous for its use in top quality curling stones. Ailsa Craig is also well known for its vast and varied bird population. The lighthouse, which has operated since 1886, is situated on a boulder strand on the eastern side.

It is worth attempting the clear path that zig-zags up to the ruins of a castle bearing the coat of arms of the Hamilton family. The path proceeds below crags to tiny Garra Loch, and continues its airy way across great rock slabs to the summit. A boat can be hired from Girvan, and there are regular day trips during the summer months. North of Girvan, near Pennyglen, is Culzean Castle. This was formerly a medieval tower house that was transformed into an elegant mansion in the late eighteenth century. It contains fine furniture, plasterwork, and a superb oval staircase. There is a country park, a ranger service, woodland and cliff-top walks.

A little further north is **Dunure Castle**, a cliff-top tower, which has a sixteenth-century beehive-shaped dovecote. South of Dunure Castle, near Maybole, is **Crossraguel Abbey**. This is a small Cluniac monastery which dates from the thirteenth to sixteenth centuries.

From Girvan, the B734 travels inland along the valley of the Water of Girvan to Old Dailly. Just before Old Dailly is the fifteenth-century **Penkill Castle**. It houses a splendid collection of tapestries and paintings. The road then climbs on a twisting route called 'The Screws', past Penwhapple

Reservoir, and descends to the attractive village of Barr. Continue on the unclassified road following the River Stinchar before turning right at the T-junction beyond South Balloch. The road ascends through the forest and becomes a narrow and exciting way through the Nick of Balloch to Rowantree junction.

There is a picnic site close by, and a cairn with a plaque commemorating David Bell, who wrote weekly cycling articles under the pseudonym 'The Highwayman' in the *Ayrshire Post*. The little hill road to Straiton is a leisurely way through forest and across wild moorland to visit the remote vastness of Loch Doon. The alternative from the south is a colourful route along the A713 from New Galloway, through the glorious lochs and river scenery of the Glenkens towards Dalmellington.

From the attractive environs of Stinchar Bridge the road winds through Carrick Forest and descends to the Water of Girvan. A side road travels east to Fairlaw, and follows the river round the base of the tree-clad hills of Glenthraig and Cairn Craig Dhu to the dam holding back the waters of Loch Bradan. The isolated knoll, Doon of Waterhead, gives a good view of the reservoir and the neighbouring lochs of Derclach and Finlas.

Straiton is a pleasant village with an inn, the Black Bull, which dates from 1766. The church has some interesting memorial stones in the churchyard. Blairquhan House is another place of interest in Straiton. A Regency-style mansion designed by Robert Burn, the house contains a good collection of furniture and paintings, and is open to visitors during the summer months.

Minnivey, near Dalmellington, has a former colliery which is now the home of the Scottish Industrial Railways Centre. Regular 'open days' are held with locomotives in steam.

A minor road leaves the A713 south of Dalmellington, and runs along the whole length of the western shore of Loch Doon. This massive sheet of water extends for nearly $6^1/_2$ miles (10km), and forms the border between Dumfries and Galloway and Strathclyde Region. It became a key part of the Galloway Hydro-Electric Scheme, which became fully operational in 1936. Stone tools and weapons found along the shores of Loch Doon show that early people were living by the loch side as early as 6000BC.

Loch Doon Castle, until 1935, stood on an island in the loch. Due to the raising of the water level, the structure was dismantled, stone by stone, and carefully rebuilt on the shore. It is a thirteenth-century fortress of unusual polygonal shape.

For anglers, Loch Doon can prove rather a daunting prospect, considering its vast size and remote surroundings. Nevertheless, the fishing is free, brown trout and char grow well and provide good sport. The best areas for fishing seem to be close to where the many small streams enter the loch. It is a fine area for hill walkers, but the forested slopes and rugged terrain make it a difficult prospect and walkers should be well prepared and equipped.

A linear walk of 5 miles (8km) climbs from just outside the village of Straiton over Sclenteuch Moor towards Loch Spallander Reservoir. Beyond, the route heads along rough forest rides to an unclassified road at

Whitehill, and down to Patna on the A713.

A walk from **Ballantrae** is recommended. Cross the bridge over the River Stinchar, and take the minor road climbing gradually for nearly 2 miles (3km) to a point where the road turns sharp left. Proceed straight on past Currarie Farm. A little further along, the path descends to a tiny cove at Currarie Port. For the return journey climb up from the Currarie Glen and head north-east along the cliff tops, past Dove Cove, and keeping to the right of Downan Hill, to a building and a farm track. Continue past Downan on the farm road back to Garleffin and Ballantrae. The distance covered is 8 miles (13km).

A linear walk from **Girvan** starts from the junction of the A77 and the A714 to the south of the town. Walk east to the track, passing over the railway, and proceed up the little valley to the north of Dow Hill. A little extra effort to reach the ancient fort on the summit, 517ft (158m), will be rewarded with fine views.

Continue up the valley past Laggan Loch and descend to Barbae and Tormitchell in the Water of Assel Valley. Take the road past the quarry, bear right and cross the stream to Dupin, and then climb steadily to meet a track coming up from Auchensoul. Descend to cross the stream, and walk uphill over the southern shoulder of Auchensoul Hill, and down to Barr. The walk covers $7^1/_2$ miles (12km).

The Isle of Arran

The island lies some 15 miles (24km) from the Ayrshire coastline in the Firth of Clyde. A frequent roll-on, roll-off ferry service links Ardrossan with Brodick on Arran. There is also a seasonal service from Lochranza on Arran to Claonaig in Kintyre for vehicles and passengers.

Arran is an island of many attractions and great scenic contrasts. It dominates the approaches to the Firth of Clyde and the entrance to Loch Fyne, and sheltered to the west by Kintyre, from which it is separated by the Kilbrannan Sound. The landscape of the northern part of the island is in marked contrast to the southern part, principally due to the underlying geological structures which give Arran a character of its own.

The island is 19 miles (31km) long, from the Cock of Arran in the north to Bennan Head in the south, and 10 miles (16km) wide, from Machrie Bay in the west to Corrygills Point in the east. It is split almost equally by the Highland Boundary Fault, giving rise to geology and scenery similar to the Highlands in the north, and to the Lowlands of Scotland in the south.

Because of its size, the whole of the inhabited part of the island can be viewed by the motorist in a single day. The A841 runs round the island, only leaving the coast in the north and south on its 56 miles (90km) round journey. Two minor roads also cross the island from east to west. The one across its waist is the B880 String road planned by Thomas Telford, and further south is the unclassified Ross road. In the far south, a short loop road leads to the seaside village of Kildonan.

The fine array of granite peaks in north-east Arran form the magnificent

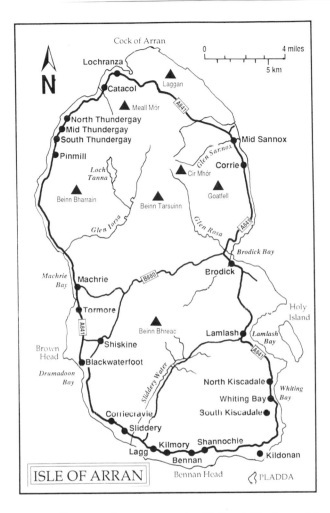

ISLE OF ARRAN

skyline that travellers see from across the Firth of Clyde, and in greater detail when approaching the island. The grey mountains are clustered around the highest point, Goatfell, 2,866ft (874m), and the serrated intervening ridges run out in all directions forming a splendid group of rugged summits. An evening sunset creates a wonderful silhouette of exciting dark outlines. The convenient composition of these mountains allows walkers to complete circuits of varying lengths, and the great glens of Rosa and Sannox effectively split them into two halves, which allows easy access to the heart of the group.

Brodick is the island's main settlement, where local bus services connect with the boat, although in winter these services are limited. The tourist information centre at the Pierhead, Brodick, is open throughout the year. The entrance to Brodick Castle and Gardens (National Trust for Scotland) lies just $2^1/_2$ miles (4km) north of Brodick Pier. The castle which overlooks

Brodick Bay is backed by Goatfell, and surrounded by woodlands and fine gardens. The building belongs to three main periods from the sixteenth to the nineteenth centuries, although the earliest remains date from the thirteenth century. The interior of the house contains rich decorations, furnishings and large collection of Beckford's treasures. The gardens are outstanding.

Arran Heritage Centre is situated at **Rosaburn**, on the north side of Brodick Bay. The museum contains the old smithy, harness room, and an archaeological and mineral collection. Amongst the fourteen villages on the island, the communities of Corrie and Sannox lie to the north of Brodick. **Corrie** is a charming little seaside spot; it has a row of neat, colour-washed cottages with attractive dormer windows gazing out to sea. Above Corrie there is a Neolithic Age chambered tomb; a Bronze Age cairn and standing stones in Sannox, and Iron Age forts at North Glen Sannox and Mid Glen Sannox.

Lochranza, in the north of the island, is spread along the shore on both sides of the sea loch. The ruined thirteenth or fourteenth century castle or fortified manor house, stands guard over the entrance to the loch. The building was heightened in the sixteenth century to become a tower house. Caledonian MacBrayne operate a vehicle and passenger service, summer season only, across Kilbrannan Sound to **Claonaig in Kintyre**. The village is an excellent centre for walks inland or north to the Cock of Arran.

From Coillemore Point the road hugs the coastline very closely down the west coast of the island to Machrie Bay. At the hamlet of **Catacol**, the 'Twelve Apostles' line the side of the road. This description is given to an attractive row of cottages built in the time of the eleventh Duke of Hamilton, to rehouse people displaced by later clearances in the north-west of the island. Throughout the island there is a wide range of birdlife, with the occasional sighting of a golden eagle.

Once over the Iorsa Water, the land becomes lower in relief as one passes into the farming area of Machrie, Shiskine and Blackwaterfoot. The fields are now a mixture of improved grassland and arable land, bordered by distant low hills with slopes planted by the Forestry Commission. The area was well favoured for settlement by early humans in the form of chambered cairns, stone circles, hut circles and standing stones. A little further south, a sign directs the visitor to the Machine Moor Stone Circles. The most spectacular of the Moss Farm stone circles is the one where three surviving uprights stand to a maximum height of nearly 18ft (5m).

The village of **Blackwaterfoot** was the port of Shiskine, a community which lies 1 mile (2km) away. At one time a sailing packet boat operated from here to Campbeltown. There is a tiny, attractive harbour where a boat can be hired for sea angling trips. North of the village, the coastline swings out to Drumadoon Point. It is worthwhile making the walk to the King's Cave. The cave was reputed to be the hiding place of Robert the Bruce before he returned to the mainland. It contains some ancient, though now faint, rock carvings, thought to date back to early Christian or Viking times.

Beyond Brown Head, the road climbs away from the coast and links

The paddle steamer Waverley, *Brodick*

several hamlets, such as Sliddery and Kilmory. The southern coastline is of interest to geographers and geologists, who come to study the extensive sections of raised beaches. Above the cliffs are the remains of duns and chambered cairns. The shoreline is an interesting mixture of rock, dykes, boulders, caves, slabs, shingle and sand. Just past Corriecrauce, a track leads south of the road to Torr á Chaisteil Dun. This typical Iron Age fort consists of a single rampart wall encircling a mound 46ft (14m) in diameter.

East of Bennan Head, a loop road climbs down to the sea at **Kildonan**. This has a pleasant seaside strand with sandy sections between the rocky dykes running out to sea. Close by are the ivy-covered ruins of Kildonan Castle, given to John the bastard son of Robert III in 1406, and out to sea is the Island of Pladda.

The area around **Whiting Bay** has been inhabited since ancient times, with the chambered tombs of the Giant's Graves in forest clearings south of Glenashdale Burn. There is a lovely walk through Forestry Commission woodlands alongside the fast-flowing Glenashdale Burn to view the spectacular waterfalls, reached by a track alongside the golf course and a turning right at South Kiscadale. The main waterfall has two impressive drops, and from a railed area there is an excellent view of the cascades.

Lamlash Bay is dominated by Holy Island, called 'Eilean Molaise' after the Irish Saint who preached there in about AD680.

Just south of the entrance to Brodick Castle is the start of the walk up Goatfell, 2,866ft (874m). The path climbs gradually to reach the open hillside. On reaching the east ridge at 2,070ft (630m), bear left up the boulder and scree slope to the summit. Return by the same route.

Another walk includes **Goatfell** east ridge, **Meall Breac** and **High Corrie**.

Take the same route as described above, but bear right on reaching the east ridge. Continue over Meall Breac, and descend left down the slope to the Corrie Burn. Cross over and follow the burn until the path leads left to the dwellings at High Corrie, and down the track to the road. The distance of this walk is nearly $5^1/_2$ miles (9km).

A walk which includes **Glen Rosa, The Saddle** and **Glen Sannox** is recommended. Start from the String road and continue past Glen Rosa Farm. Follow the clear path up the valley with magnificent views of Cir Mhor in front, the surrounding ridges of Goatfell and Stacach on the right, and Beinn á Chliabhain and A'Chir on the left. Climb up to The Saddle, and descend via an eroded dyke in a north-western direction for a short distance, before veering to the right on a north-east heading. Continue down Glen Sannox following the burn, and cross over to the remains of a former barytes mine. Follow the track to the main road. The distance covered is nearly 8 miles (13km).

From Mid Thundergay a signposted path points the way for a walk to **Coire Lochan**. Beyond the buildings pass through a kissing gate, and then to an access gate through the deer fence. Cross over the Lenimore Burn using the stepping stones, and bear right upstream. The route crosses and recrosses the burn, but keep alongside the southern bank as it cascades over ledges of rock. Soon the path reaches two cairns. The Fhionn Lochan lies in a deep hollow, a typical glacial corrie — an idyllic spot with a great deal of atmosphere. The distance, via the same route, is 3 miles (5km).

A recommended walk includes **Glen Catacol** and **Beinn Tarsuinn**. Walk up Glen Catacol and bear left to ascend Glen Diomhan on an indistinct path on the left of the burn. Higher up you will pass a nature conservancy area, where two rare species of rowan are protected. Bear right at the head of the valley, and walk westwards to the north summit of Beinn Tarsuinn, 1,819ft (554m). Continue south-west to the southern summit of Beinn Tarsuinn. Head west north-west to the head of Glen Catacol, and proceed down this very attractive valley back to the starting point. The walk covers a distance of 8 miles (13km).

Other suggested hill walks in the Goatfell area include Goatfell summit, along north ridge to North Goatfell. Descend the north-west ridge to The Saddle, some scrambling is required. Return down Glen Rosa. The distance is $10^1/_2$ miles (17km).

Another suggested hill walk is one from Sannox which includes Glen Sannox, The Saddle, and a steep climb through rocky outcrops to the summit of Cir Mhór, 2,618ft (798m). Return by the same route. The walk covers $6^1/_2$ miles (10km).

Further Information
— South-West Scotland —

Places of Interest

Arbigland Gardens
A710 Solway Coast road between
Kirkbean and Southerness
Open: May to September inclusive,
Sunday, Tuesday, Thursday, 2-6pm;
House and garden open last week in
May and last week in August. Admission
charge.

Bladnoch Distillery Visitor Centre
Just south of Wigtown on the A714
Open: 10am-4pm Monday to Friday,
tours or by appointment.
☎ (09884) 2235

Brodick Castle and Country Park
(National Trust for Scotland)
North end of Brodick Bay, A841, 2 miles
(3km) from Brodick Pier.
Open: Easter, daily 1-5pm; end April to
beginning October, daily 1-5pm; end
Easter to end April and beginning to
mid-October, Monday, Wednesday,
Saturday, 1-5pm. Admission charge.
Garden, country park, open all year daily
9.30am-sunset.

Broughton House
High Street, Kirkcudbright
Open: Easter to mid-October 11am-1pm,
2-5pm. Closed Sunday morning and
Tuesday. Admission charge.

Caerlaverock Castle
Off B725, 8 miles (13km) east of Dumfries
Open: April to end September, weekdays
9.30am-7pm, Sunday 2-7pm; beginning
October to March, weekdays 9.30am-
4pm, Sunday 2-4pm.

Cardoness Castle
A75, 1 mile (2km), south-west of Gate-
house-of-Fleet
Open: Easter to end September, weekdays 9.30am-7pm, Sunday 2-7pm;
beginning October to March, weekdays
9.30am-4pm, Sunday 2-4pm.

Castle Kennedy Gardens
3 miles (5km) east of Stranraer, off A75
Open: daily, Easter weekend to Septem
ber, 10am-5pm.
Gardens set between two lochs, famous
for rhododendrons, azaleas and magno-
lias.

Creetown Gem Rock Museum
Creetown, signposted from A75
Open: 9.30am-6pm each day (summer);
9.30am-5pm October to March.
☎ (0671) 82357

Culzean Castle and Country Park
(National Trust for Scotland)
On the coast, A77, A719
Open: castle, Easter and end April to end
August, daily, 10am-6pm; beginning to
end April and beginning September to
end October, daily, 12noon-5pm. Other
times throughout the year by appointment. Country park, all year, daily 9am-
sunset. Visitor centre and shop open:
Easter, and beginning September to end
October, daily 10am-6pm; end April to
end August, daily 10am-6pm.

Deer Museum
Clatteringshaws
A712, 6 miles (10km) west of New
Galloway
Open: daily, 10am-5pm Easter to mid-
October.

Dundrennan Abbey
A711, Dalbeattie to Kirkcudbright
Open: late March to end September,
Sunday, 2-5pm, weekdays, 9.30am-7pm;
beginning October to late March, Sunday
2-4pm, weekdays, 9.30am-4pm.

Galloway Farm Museum
The Queen's Way, New Galloway
Opening times, contact Tourist Informa-
tion Centres.
Admission charge.
☎ (06443) 317

Galloway House Gardens
South of Wigtown, A746 then B7004 to
Garlieston
Open: daily throughout the year.
Admission charge.

Glenluce Abbey
1¹/₂ miles (2km) north of Glenluce, off
A75
Open: late March to end September,
Sunday, 2-7pm, weekdays, 9.30am-7pm;
beginning October to late March, Sunday, 2-4pm, weekdays, 9.30am-4pm.

Glenluce Motor Museum
Glenluce
Open: daily, beginning March to end
October 10am-7pm; beginning Novem-
ber to end February, 11am-4pm, but
closed Monday, Tuesday.
Admission charge.

Isle of Arran Heritage Museum
Rosaburn, Brodick
Open: May to end September, Monday to
Saturday. (October by arrangement).
Admission charge.
☎ (0770) 2636

Loch Doon Castle
A713, 1¹/₂ miles (2km) south of
Dalmellington on minor road to Loch
Doon. No restricted access.

MacLellan's Castle
In centre of Kirkcudbright
Open: April to September, weekdays
9.30am-7pm, Sunday 2-7pm; winter,
weekends only.

Maxwelton House
Moniaive
Off the B729 near Kirkland
Open: house, July and August, Monday
to Thursday 2-5pm. At other times, by
appointment only.
Garden, April to end September, Mon-
day-Thursday 2-5pm. Chapel, April to
September, daily 10am-6pm.
Admission charge.

Meadowsweet Herb Garden
Soulseat Loch, Stranraer, off A75

Open: daily except Wednesday, beginning May to beginning September
12noon-6pm. Admission charge.

Museum of Scottish Lead Mining
Wanlockhead Off A74 at Abington
(B797) or Elvanfoot (A702)
Open: visitor centre, daily 11am. Last
entry 4pm. Lead mine (guided tours),
daily 11am-3pm. Period cottages
(guided), daily 11.30am-4.30pm. Open
Air Museum, 1¹/₂ miles (2km) walkway.
Admission charge.

New Abbey Corn Mill
A710 south of Dumfries
Open: late March to end September,
weekdays 9.30am-7pm, Sunday 2-7pm;
beginning October to late March, week-
days 9.30am-4pm, Sunday 2-4pm. Closed
Wednesday afternoon and all day
Thursday.

Newton Stewart Museum
Open: end March 2-5.30pm, beginning
May to end September, Monday to
Saturday 2-5.30pm; July and August,
10am-12.30pm, 2-5.30pm. Sunday
opening July to end September 2-5pm.
Admission charge.

Orchardton Castle
A711, south of Palnackie
Open: April to end September, weekdays
9.30am-7pm, Sunday 2-7pm; beginning
October to March, weekdays 9.30am-
4pm, Sunday 2-4pm.

Power Station Museum
Kirkcudbright
Tongland Power Station and Salmon
Ladder
Open: beginning April to end August,
Monday to Saturday.
Guided tours, four a day. To book,
☎ (0557) 30114, or contact Tourist
Information Centre, Kirkcudbright.

**Shambellie House, Museum
of Costume**
New Abbey, A710 from Dumfries
Open: mid-May to mid-September 10am-
5.30pm, Sunday 12noon-5.30pm.
Admission free.

Sweetheart Abbey
A710 south of Dumfries
Opening times as for Glenluce Abbey.

Threave Castle
Signposted on A75 west of Castle Douglas. Car park at Kelton Mains Farm, small boat to island.
Open: April to September, weekdays 9.30am-7pm, Sunday 2-7pm; beginning October to March, weekdays 9.30am-4pm, Sunday 2-4pm.

Whithorn Excavation
Centre of Whithorn, south of Newton Stewart A714, A746
Open: Easter to end October 10am-5.30pm daily.

Wildlife and Wetlands Centre
Caerlaverock, 8 miles (13km) south of Dumfries. Signposted from A75 at Dumfries. From Carlisle and Annan follow Solway Coast Heritage Trail (B724 and B725).
Open: daily from mid-September to end April 9.30am-5pm. No dogs allowed in the refuge. Admission charge. Limited access for disabled visitors. Special rates for parties booked in advance.
☎ (038777) 200

Wood of Cree, RSPB Reserve
4 miles (6km), north of Newton Stewart, on minor road from Minnigaff
Access at all times. Marked walks, impressive waterfalls. Warden.
☎ (0671) 2861

Tourist Information Centres

Abington
Little Chef Service Area, A74 northbound
☎ (08642) 436

Ayr
39 Sandgate
☎ (0292) 284196

Brodick
Isle of Arran
☎ (0556) 2611

Gatehouse of Fleet
Car park
☎ (05574) 212

Girvan
Bridge Street
☎ (0465) 4950

Hawick
Common Haugh
☎ (0450) 72547

Kirkcudbright
Harbour Square
☎ (0557) 30494

Lanark
Horsemarket
☎ (0555) 61661

Maybole
Culzean Castle and Country Park
☎ (06556) 293

Newton Stewart
Dashwood Square
☎ (0671) 2431

Sanquhar
Tolbooth
☎ (0659) 50185

Stranraer
Port Rodie car park
☎ (0776) 2595
All centres are open for the Easter weekend and then from May to October, except for Lanark, Ayr and Brodick which are open all year.

Useful Addresses

Scottish National Tourist Board
23 Ravelston Terrace
Edinburgh
☎ (031 332) 2433

Dumfries and Galloway Tourist Board
Whitesands
Dumfries
☎ (0387) 53862

15 • The Cairngorms
and The Grampians

The Cairngorm mountains form one of the last great wilderness areas in Britain. Four of the five highest summits in the country lie within this vast mountain range. It is the home of Arctic birds such as the dotterel, ptarmigan and snow bunting and contains remnants of the ancient Caledonian forest. As long ago as 1864, the writer John Hill Burton said that the Cairngorms were 'full of such associations of awe and grandeur and mystery as no other scenery in Britain is capable of arousing.' This still remains true today.

The Grampians are less well known, despite the fact that Grampian Regional Council adopted the name in 1975. This well marked mountain range runs across Scotland from west to east, although the limits of the range have been as elastic as the whims of cartographers. Some experts have argued that the designation 'Grampians' should include the Cairngorms.

While the Cairngorms lie between the Dee and the Spey, the most clearly defined part of the Grampians is on the southern watershed of the River Dee. The mountain mass was originally known as the Mounth, and it was through the Mounth passes that travellers made their way north in the days before General Wade's road-builders hacked out new routes across this desolate terrain. Today, only hill-walkers and deer-hunters tread these old trails.

The communities bordering the Cairngorms have flourished as outdoor activities like climbing, walking and skiing have developed. Aviemore, with its £3 million Aviemore Centre, its shops, restaurants, swimming pool, skating rink, theatre and cinema, has mushroomed from an insignificant village to a booming holiday town. Yet it is easy enough to get away from the tourist centres, off the beaten track and into the remoter areas by car or on foot. There are more than lofty mountains to be seen in the Cairngorms and the Grampians, for here you can wander through lovely valleys and past peaceful lochs, over moors purple with heather and along the banks of gurgling Highland burns.

The principal approaches to the Cairngorms are in the Spey Valley, but on the eastern side of the range access can be gained from Tomintoul and Braemar. Royal Deeside is the backdoor to the Cairngorms, and the gate-

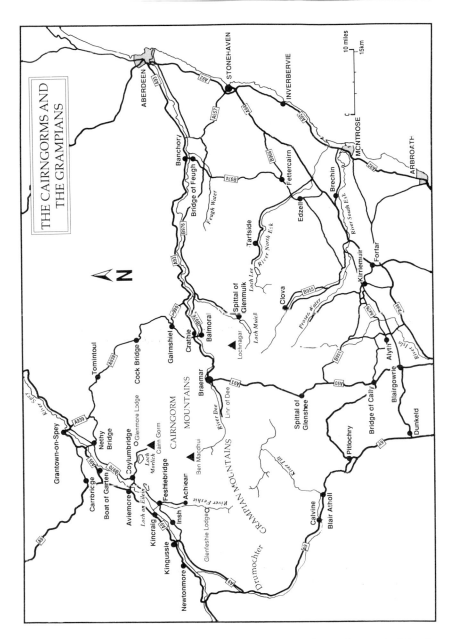

way to the Grampians. From Aberdeen, two roads — the main North Deeside road (A93) and the South Deeside road (B9077 and B976) — run west through a valley steeped in history. They call it castle country, and the first castle to loom up on the North Deeside road is at Crathes, 2 miles (3km) east of Banchory. **Crathes Castle**, dating back to the sixteenth century, is said to be one of the finest of the north-east castles owned by the National Trust for Scotland. There is also a magnificent eighteenth-century garden enclosed by massive Irish yew hedges, more than 250 years old.

The South Deeside road goes to **Banchory** by the Bridge of Feugh, where so many passing motorists stop to watch salmon leaping the Feugh falls that the authorities have had to lay out a car park near the bridge. Banchory itself has become a commuter town for Aberdeen, but a few miles further west there is a taste of the Highlands at **Aboyne**, where the village green is the setting each year for the Aboyne Highland Games.

At the Bridge of Ess, about 1 mile (2km) from Aboyne on the south road (B976), is the entrance to the estate of **Glentanar**, where there is a visitors' centre and marked paths for walkers. One of the paths passes the Chapel of St Lesmo, built last century by an eccentric laird called Sir William Cunliffe Brooks, who stamped the initials 'WCB' on stones, wells and monuments all over the estate. Old tracks probe into the Grampian hills from Glentanar, stretching south to the Braes of Angus.

From the Bridge of Ess the road runs on to Ballater, passing Pannanich Inn, which was built in the eighteenth century when the discovery of healing wells turned it into a spa. **Ballater** is a village where Deeside begins to live up to its Royal tag; there are more 'By Appointment' signs above its shops than in any other town in Scotland. Balmoral Castle is about 7 miles (11km) away. The route by the south road over the Bridge of Muick ends at the gates of Balmoral Castle, linking up with the north road across the River Dee at Crathie.

At the Bridge of Muick a road branches up Glenmuick, pushing south to the lap of Byron's 'dark Lochnagar'. Byron was not the only famous person to climb this Deeside mountain. Queen Victoria made it to the top and Gladstone, at the age of 57, pounded up its 3,789ft (1,155m) to the summit and returned 'fresh as a lark.'

A large part of the Balmoral estate, including Loch Muick, is a wildlife reserve, managed by the Scottish Wildlife Trust. There is a visitors' centre almost on the site of an ancient hospice at the Spittal of Glenmuick, where drovers once rested on their way over the Capel Mounth to Glen Clova and the south. Those who leave their cars at the Spittal car park and walk round Loch Muick are able to see an imposing Royal shiel, or shelter, the Glas-allt Shiel, built by Queen Victoria after Prince Albert's death. The more adventurous can tramp along some of the dusty paths that trace their patterns on Glenmuick, including a well trodden path to Lochnagar.

The route by the B976 from the Bridge of Muick passes Abergeldie Castle and the Royal Lochnagar Distillery and ends up at the gates of Balmoral Castle, while an alternative route is by the main North Deeside road (A93) from Ballater to Crathie. When the Royal Family are in residence at the castle, thousands of people gather at Crathie Church on a Sunday to watch them going to the morning service.

The entrance to **Balmoral Castle** is on the opposite side of the River Dee from Crathie, where the Muick road ends. Visitors are only allowed access to the ballroom, which houses an exhibition every summer of paintings,

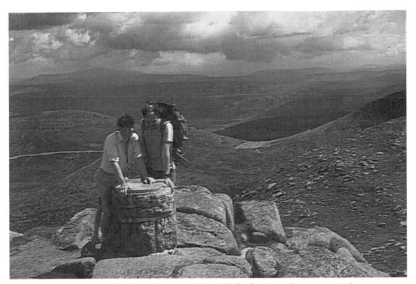

The summit of Lochnagar, Deeside's dominating mountain

sculptures and other memorabilia from Queen Victoria's time. There is plenty to see in the castle grounds and gardens, including a statue of the controversial John Brown, who has been relegated to a corner of the estate. There are two souvenir shops and a restaurant in the grounds.

West of Crathie is some of Deeside's most magnificent scenery, for **Braemar** is where the Grampian and Cairngorm hills reach out to each other. There is an old saying that people 'come over the hills to the Braemar Gathering', every September, when the hills are purple with heather and the sound of bagpipes can be heard echoing through the glens. There is nothing more stirring than the skirl of pipes as massed pipe bands march into the Gathering arena to salute the Queen.

From Braemar, where Robert Louis Stevenson spent the summer of 1881 writing *Treasure Island*, roads stretch away to the mountains in the west and south over the ancient Cairnwell pass to Glenshee. The narrow, twisting road to the west leads to the spectacular **Linn of Dee**, where the River Dee boils angrily through an awesome gorge. Here, at the Linn, you are on the edge of the wilderness. From the bridge over the Linn a track goes by Glen Dee to the heart of the Cairngorms, where the Lairig Ghru, the Gloomy Pass, links Deeside with Speyside.

East of the Linn another track goes through the hills to Derry Lodge, once a Royal shooting lodge but now a ruin. From here, other paths trail away to the Lairig Ghru and the Lairig an Laoigh, the Pass of the Cattle. These old passes are best left to the hardened hillwalker, for they can be dangerous places in bad weather. However, even a walk to Derry Lodge can give you a satisfying taste of the great Cairngorm mountains.

Going south from Braemar by the A93, the hills continue to close in on the traveller. The route by the Cairnwell (a major ski centre during the winter) passes the Devil's Elbow, or what is left of it. The Elbow was a 1 in 5 double hairpin bend that once struck terror into the hearts of motorists. It has long since been straightened out, although it is still a hard pull to the top coming from the south. Look out for fragments of it alongside the modern road, and down in the valley you can still find some of the old Wade bridges that were built as part of the military road more than two centuries ago.

Follow the A93 south to the Spittal of Glenshee and the Bridge of Cally, and from there to **Blairgowrie**, which can be a useful base for exploring the Grampian hills from the vale of Strathmore. Here, quiet and lovely glens reach into the mountains that separate Deeside from the Braes of Angus. Most of these glen roads come to a dead end, petering out against the hill barrier. When the road ends, the only way ahead is by old, forgotton tracks crossing what was known as the Mouth to the Dee Valley. The alternative approach to these Grampian glens from Strathmore is by the A92 from Aberdeen, branching off to Fettercairn, Edzell and Kirriemuir.

From Blairgowrie, taking the A926, the first glen is **Glen Isla**. This most western Angus glen, reached from either Alyth or Kirriemuir, is not a dead-end, for the B951 swings away from the Isla and runs round the foot of Mount Blair to join the Glenshee road. A minor road continues up the Isla, past ruined Forter Castle, which the Earl of Airlie 'brake down and de-stroyed' during the Covenanting Wars. The glen ends at Tulchan Lodge, but a footpath goes on to **Caenlochan**, a 9,000 acre nature reserve regarded as a botanist's paradise.

East of the Isla, two other glens run north-west, parallel to each other, from Dykehead of Cortachy, north of Kirriemuir. The first is **Glen Prosen**, which is about 12 miles (19km) long. There are motor roads on either side of the Prosen Water, as there are on a long stretch of the South Esk in Glen Clova. **Glen Clova** is said to be the loveliest of the Angus glens. Dame Maria Ogilvy, a Victorian poet called it 'the sweetest strath in a' my fatherland.' Braedownie, where the road ends, sends tracks out across the hills to Glen Doll and over the Capel Mounth to Loch Muick on Deeside. 'I daur ye gang yer lane till dark Glen Doll,' wrote Dame Maria. Few people would go alone into Glen Doll, which leads to the curiously-named Jock's Road and over a windy plateau to Loch Gallater. The landscape here is uncompromising, yet it holds its own savage beauty.

If Clova is the loveliest glen, **Glen Esk** is the longest, probing 16 miles (26km) into the Grampian massif from Gannochy Bridge, near Edzell. At the head of the glen, the tall tower of Invermark Castle looks over the 1 mile-long (1km) Loch Lee. From here a track goes through Glen Mark and over Mount Keen to Glentanar on Deeside. The Queen's Well in **Glen Mark** is a reminder that Queen Victoria came this way. At Tarfside, 4 miles (6km) to the east, more tracks go north to Deeside by the Firmounth and Fungle roads.

Halfway up the glen is **The Retreat**, a former shooting box near Millden, but now the Angus Folk Museum. It has a fascinating collection of local relics, books and photographs, arms, tools, household goods, and rooms

The River Dee at the mouth of the Lairig Ghru Pass

furnished in the style of various periods in the glen's history. There is even a whisky still, for Glen Esk, like many of the Angus glens, had its share of illicit whisky-making and smuggling in the past.

Leaving the old hill roads to the heather, return to Blairgowrie for the start of a journey on the modern A9 road, carving its way north from Atholl to Badenoch. The route from Blairgowrie is by Dunkeld and Pitlochry, both good centres from which to explore the countryside. The A9, busy though it is, opens up a magnificent and little-known area of Scotland. From this traffic-ridden highway, tracks spin away into the hills towards the Spey Valley, following routes taken by drovers, soldiers and missionaries in the days before there were proper roads.

Blair Atholl marks the southern fringe of the Cairngorms. From here, Glen Tilt runs north almost to the mouth of the Lairig Ghru, where it meets up with Glen Dee and goes east to the Linn of Dee. Queen Victoria did this journey on pony on her way home from Atholl after one of her Great Expeditions. Thomas Pennant called it 'horrible' Glen Tilt, but it is, in fact, a mixture of harshness and breathtaking beauty. Last century, after a party of botanists had been stopped by the Duke of Atholl from going through the glen, a legal battle was fought to make it a right-of-way, so now, according to an old verse, 'the road's as free to you and me as to his Grace himself, man.'

The hardy traveller will walk up Glen Tilt to Forest Lodge, or even farther, but for the less energetic a visit to **Old Blair** is an attractive alternative. This is a picturesque cluster of houses that lie north of Blair Castle. General George Wade, whose soldiers cut out the great road over Drumochter, stayed at the Inn at Old Blair. He could never have dreamed that his 'new road' would one day be swept away and replaced by a twentieth-century motorway. Look for Diana's Grove at Old Blair. It has nothing to do with Princess Diana; it was erected when the second Duke of Atholl turned part of the land around Blair Castle into an arboretum in the eighteenth century.

Old Blair, a peaceful oasis well away from its successor, Blair Atholl, and from tourist-tormented Blair Castle, was at one time a gateway to General Wade's road and also to the ancient Minigaig Pass going through the hills to Ruthven Barracks, near Kingussie. The Minigaig, an important road, went by Bruar Lodge, where another path, once used by drovers going to the Falkirk Tryst, comes up from Calvine on the A9.

The Clan Donnachaidh Museum (Clan Robertson Centre) which has exhibits from the Jacobite Risings of 1715 and 1745, is at **Calvine**. About a mile (2km) east of Calvine, and 4 miles (6km) west of Blair Atholl, there is a walk to the Bruar Falls, which Scotland's poet, Robert Burns, put on the map when he visited them in 1787. He was impressed by the falls, but felt that some trees were needed, and he wrote a poetic petition to the fourth Duke of Atholl asking him to 'shade my banks wi' tow'ring trees.' The duke took the bard's advice and planted them.

Off the A9, there are still stretches of the old Wade road on which you can walk. A mile (2km) from Calvine there is a magnificent Wade bridge called Drochaid na h'Uinneige — the Eye of the Window. Dalnacardoch was where the General had a *hutt* which he used as a base during his road-building. From here a track goes up the Edendon Water to Gaick Lodge and on to Kingussie.

Atholl's boundary with Badenoch is straddled by two conical hills called the Sow of Atholl and the Boar of Badenoch. Here you are on the spine of Scotland; beyond them, the Drumochter Pass pitches you into Badenoch, or, in its Gaelic form, *Baideanach* (the drowned land), a name that says much about the Spey, a turbulent river prone to spates and flooding.

When the hills of Drumochter give way to the distant peaks of the Cairngorms, there are plenty of opportunities to get off the beaten track. There are a number of routes by which to explore the forests and lochs along the Spey Valley, and to penetrate, even by car, parts of this vast mountainous area. One route, taking in the communities that live on the edge of the Cairngorms, is to leave the main highway by the B9150 to Newtonmore and follow the B9152 through Kingussie and Aviemore to Carrbridge.

Newtonmore is a village that has become a crossroads for traffic going south by Drumochter, west to Spean Bridge and Fort William by the A86, and north-east to Aviemore. The Clan Macpherson Museum is on the main street, its exhibits including a fiddle played by the outlaw James Macpherson when he went to the scaffold in 1700. The Newtonmore Highland Games are held on the first Saturday in August.

Kingussie, 4 miles (6km) away, is home to the Highland Folk Museum, where you can heat your hands at a peat fire in a Lewis 'Black House,' watch lacemaking and wool spinning, and look at Highland furniture and costume from the past. The Sow of Atholl and the Boar of Badenoch were reminders of a time when wild boars roamed this corner of Scotland. There are still wild animals in Badenoch, but now they are safely behind the walls of the Highland Wildlife Park near Kincraig. Red deer and European bison and wolves can be seen in the park, and there are aviaries with eagles and capercaillies.

There are more birds across the Spey on the Insh marshes, but there are no aviaries holding them in check. Insh, which holds the largest area of inland marsh in Scotland, is an RSPB (Royal Society For the Protection of Birds) nature reserve and it is said that you can spot as many as 200 different species of birds there. Seventeen species of butterfly have also been recorded on the marshes.

It is on the Insh road, the B970, that you can really get off the beaten track. It can be reached from Kingussie by a bridge crossing the river just below Ruthven Barracks, whose ruins sit spectacularly on a high mound in the Spey haughs. A striking landmark, seen from a long way off, it stands on a site which once housed a fortress built by the infamous Wolf of Badenoch — Alexander Stewart, Earl of Buchan, son of Robert the Second. The present structure incorporates something of a sixteenth-century ruined castle of the Gordons.

The B970 back-road to Rothiemurchus is a happy contrast to the frenzy of the A9. Here, where other minor roads trail away through the hills, you feel that you are being drawn into the arms of the Cairngorms — the Monadh Ruadh (Red Mountains), which is the proper name of the greatest mountain range in Scotland. Not far from Ruthven Barracks, Glen Tromie strikes south to Gaick.

The village of **Insh** is full of charm. Its tiny church is popular with visitors. It seats about thirty people and is said to have been a place of worship since the sixth century. It has only one window, formed in the shape of a Celtic cross. There is a 1,000-year-old Celtic bell on display.

Kincraig, at the head of Loch Insh, was known until the end of last century as the Boat of Insh because it boasted a large ferry boat. Queen Victoria thought the loch was lovely and wishes she could have sketched it, but she didn't think much of the ferry — 'a very rude affair,' she said. The ferry has long since gone, and now craft from a canoeing school sail between the loch's birch-lined banks.

Beyond Insh, still on the B970, the road crosses Feshie Bridge, where the River Feshie comes tumbling out of the wilderness to join the Spey. Just over the bridge, on the east bank of the river, a motor road runs up the glen by Lagganlia, where the Lagganlia Centre for Outdoor Education is sited. The public road ends 5 miles (8km) up the glen at **Achlean**, where a stalker's track zig-zagging up Carn Ban More opens up magnificent views of Glen Feshie, while from the Sgorans — Sgoran Dubh and Sgoran Gaoith, both over 3,500ft (1,067m) — you can look down breathtaking precipices with sheer drops of 2,000ft (610m) to Loch Einich.

It is well worth leaving your car at Achlean and tramping on to Glenfeshie Lodge, just over 1 mile (2km) away. Here, in what has been called 'Glen Feshie of storm blasts,' a lonely track winds its way through bare moorland to Glen Geldie and Deeside. There was a proposal a number of years ago to build a motor road linking Kingussie with Braemar, but nothing came of it.

Among the junipers and pines on the right or east bank of the Feshie, opposite Glenfeshie Lodge, is an area called Ruigh-aiteachain. This was known at one time as 'The Huts,' for it was here, early last century, that the Duchess of Bedford built a collection of rough bothies to house shooting parties. One of the guests was Edwin Landseer, who painted many of his Highland pictures in Glen Feshie. There is a hill-walkers' bothy in Ruigh-aiteachain, but nothing to recall those romantic days of long ago.

Five miles (8km) north of Feshiebridge a road branches off to **Loch an Eilein**. It is not the biggest loch in the Cairngorms, but it is certainly one of the most attractive, its woodland setting overlooked by the heights of Ord Ban, Kennapole Hill and Cadha Mor. A ruined castle, said to have been built by the Wolf of Badenoch, stands on a small island in the middle of the loch. There is a nature trail around the loch, and walks galore on other tracks, and there is an information centre for visitors. Ospreys once nested on the ruined castle, but were driven away by egg collectors. A number of years ago they returned, but not to Loch an Eilean; instead, they nested at Loch Garten, near Nethy Bridge. Their treetop eyrie is closely guarded by volunteer watchers so that the birds are kept safe from thieving egg collectors.

Loch an Eilean and Loch Garten, attractive though they are, seem insignificant compared to Loch Morlich. There are other lochs that are no less majestic — Loch Einich and Loch Avon, for example — but they are hidden away in remote corners of the Cairngorms and seen only by hill-walkers and deer hunters. **Loch Morlich** lays its beauty before the whole world. It is the largest stretch of water in the Cairngorms, although Loch Muick in the Grampians beats it for size. The road to Loch Morlich is by Glenmore, leaving the B9152 at Aviemore if you have taken the old A9, or turning on to it from the B970 if you have travelled north by the Loch an Eilean road. It passes Coylumbridge, where there is a smart modern hotel, and runs along the shore of Loch Morlich. A series of tree-shaded parking places have been laid out on the water's edge which provide good views of the mountain landscape across the loch.

The view of Cairn Gorm from Loch Morlich is said to be one of the finest in Scotland. The distant corries are softened by a green curtain of forest running down to the loch, while Morlich itself is crowned by a golden stretch of sand at the head of the loch. It has become a playground for watersports enthusiasts, but its waters can be icily cold even during the summer.

The road goes past Glenmore Lodge, an outdoor centre that provides courses in sailing, canoeing, mountaineering and skiing, and turns uphill towards the car park at Coire Cas. For those who want to reach the summit of **Cairn Gorm**, the 4,084ft (1,245m) mountain that gives its name to the whole mountain range, there are two ways up — on foot or by chairlift. In winter, this is where skiers gather, and so great is the demand for skiing facilities that there has been a long-running demand that new ski slopes be

Deer roam freely across Scotland's hills and glens

opened, a move hotly resisted by climbers and conservationists. In summer, a chairlift whisks visitors up to the White Lady Shieling at 2,500ft
(762m) and then on to the top terminus at 3,600ft (1,097m). Here you can
have refreshments at what must be one of the country's highest eating
places, before tackling the last stretch on foot. Stone steps have been cut out
of the mountain to help visitors to the weather station on the summit. From
here, looking out over the great peaks of the Cairngorms, you feel on top of
the world. From the plateau, only a short distance from the summit, there
is an impressive view of Loch Avon, one of the most inaccessible spots in
the Cairngorms, but also one of the loveliest. At the head of the Loch is the
Shelter Stone, where some famous people have spent the night over the
years.

Ben Macdhui can be reached from Cairn Gorm, but this is only for
experienced hill-walkers. It must never be forgotten that, even in midsummer, conditions on the Cairngorm tops can be treacherous (in winter,
the weather is arctic). Nevertheless, it is on top of Cairn Gorm that you begin
to sense the scale and immensity of this vast mountain range. Sir Henry
Alexander, who wrote the classic book on the range, *The Cairngorms*, spoke
about how 'the Cairngorms cast their spell over the spirit.'

There are many minor tracks into Glenmore, including two that were
once well trodden, but today are seldom used. One is by the Pass of Ryvoan,
which was part of the old Rathad nam Mearlach (Thieves' Road), the route
taken by reivers going from Rothiemurchus to Tomintoul and Strath Avon.
It is worth walking a small stretch of it from Glenmore Lodge to Lochan
Uaine. The loch is better known as the Green Loch, for its water is a
translucent greenish-blue. They say it is green because the fairies once
washed their clothes in it. The other pass is the Slugan, which runs north
from Loch Morlich, passing between two hills, Creag a' Ghreusaiche and
Craiggowrie, and comes out on the Coylumbridge to Nethy Bridge road a
little south of Kincardine Church. This little white-washed church was

burned during a clan feud and was restored in 1897. Take a look at the leper's squint, which was built into the church wall so that lepers could watch mass from outside without passing on the disease to the congregation.

The Coylumbridge-Nethy Bridge road is a continuation of the B970. It is a fairly narrow road, but a pleasant one, and it opens up interesting views of Speyside. About 5 miles (8km) from Coylumbridge a road crosses the Spey to Boat of Garten. There was a ferry here at one time, as the name suggests, but the 'boat' offers a different kind of travel — by steam train. This is the home of the Strathspey Railway whose old engines, most of them dating from the 1940s and 1950s, go puffing down the line to Aviemore. The village really owes its existence to the coming of the railway in 1863, and now it cashes in on tourists' nostalgia for the age of steam. There is a railway museum in the former barrow room.

The road from Boat of Garten joins the A95 and goes east to Dulnain Bridge and Grantown-on-Spey and west to the Aviemore-Carrbridge road. **Carrbridge**, a winter sports resort, takes its name from the picturesque single-arched eighteenth-century bridge which crosses the River Dulnain in the centre of the village. One of the main attractions at Carrbridge is the Landmark Centre, with its book and craft shop, restaurant, and multi-screen theatre. Here, through computer-controlled projectors and stereo sound, visitors are taken on a journey back through time on Speyside. Outside the centre there is an adventure playground, a treetop trail, a nature centre and a 65ft (20m) viewing tower. There is also a forestry heritage park, which boasts Britain's only steam-powered sawmill.

The great forests of Rothiemurchus and Abernethy are a reminder of how important timber has always been to this part of the country. Two centuries ago as many as 20,000 pine logs were floated down to the shipyards of Garmouth and Kingston upon Spey on a spring spate. Large rafts of sawn timber were also taken to the mouth of the Spey by raftsmen, or floaters, who were as tough and skilled as the loggers of Canada and America.

Carrbridge is where two main roads branch east and west. To the east is the A938 to Grantown-on-Spey, while to the west, starting off as a continuation of the A938 and joining the modern A9, the road goes through the once-infamous Slochd pass to Inverness. Grantown is a trim and tidy holiday town, and from it the A95 crosses the Spey and meets up with the A939 to Tomintoul.

The more pleasant route to Tomintoul from the Aviemore area is by the B970, still skirting the Cairngorms, but avoiding the busier roads to Carrbridge and Grantown. Not more than $^1/_2$ mile (1km) from the turn-off to Boat of Garten on the B970 is a side road to Loch Garten, home of the osprey. This fascinating bird has been Speyside's biggest tourist attraction; more than a million people have visited the RSPB observation post, which is equipped with binoculars and visual aids.

Nethy Bridge is about 3 miles (5km) on. The River Nethy rises deep in the eastern flank of Cairn Gorm, springing into life as the Garbh Allt in a rocky col known as The Saddle. The Lairig Ghru, from Coylumbridge to Derry

Lodge, is the best known Cairngorm pass, but another ancient pass, the Lairig an Laoigh, runs from Nethy Bridge to Derry. Only the hardened hill-walker tackles such a trek, but there are plenty of less demanding walks around Nethy Bridge.

Nethy Bridge is a quiet little place, with a large hotel, an outdoor centre, and a nine-hole golf course, but none of the commercialism of the main Strathspey centres. The road running east from the village to join the A939, the old military road to Tomintoul, passes through pleasant countryside and moorland, with the Cairngorms silhouetted dramatically against the skyline. It dips down to the Bridge of Brown and crosses the River Avon about 1 mile (2km) from Tomintoul.

Tomintoul (it is pronounced Tomin-towl) claims to be the highest village in the Highlands. It is on the edge of whisky country — an eighteenth-century cleric, the Reverend John Grant, said that of the thirty-seven fami-lies living in the village in 1795, 'all of them sell whisky and all of them drink it.' From Tomintoul, you can explore many of the whisky glens, including, perhaps, the most famous — Glenlivet.

Glenlivet estate, as well as Tomintoul itself, belongs to the Crown and plans have been drawn up to develop the economy of the area. Peat mosses spread across much of the land around the village and one moss, Fae Mussach, is still worked commercially. The old days of peat-cutting are recalled in an award-winning museum in the centre of the village.

On the approaches to Tomintoul, and particularly as you come to the village by the A939 from Grantown-on-Spey, the distant Cairngorm massif is seldom out of sight. The tors of Ben Avon have a curious wart-like appearance. Tomintoul belongs to the old parish of Kirkmichael, which lies in the basin of the Upper Avon. From below the village, Glenavon pushes deep into the heart of the Cairngorms, where the mighty River Ann has its cource in Loch Avon, or Loch A'an as it is called.

There are no easy ways into the Cairngorms from this eastern fringe. Ben A'an beckons you, but you have to approach it on foot. From the south end of the village a signposted road goes up Glenavon to Delnabo, past the Queen's View which Queen Victoria saw on her way to Inchrory in 1860. The road crosses the Spey and turns back by the east bank to Tomintoul, completing the circuit.

There is, however, a pedestrian right-of-way to the shooting lodge at Inchrory, where the River Avon meets the Builg Burn. The A'an waters were once said to be 'the clearest and purest waters of all our kingdom.' At the Linn of Avon, near Inchrory House, the river comes in from the west after its long journey from Loch A'an. An old drovers' track from Inchrory goes east to Cock Bridge, passing the Royal lodge at Delnadamph, which was bought for Prince Charles. He seldom uses it, although he shoots on the surrounding moors.

Queen Victoria passed Inchrory and followed the Builg Burn path when returning to Balmoral. Loch Builg, just over 2 miles (3km) south of Inchrory, is a gloomy stretch of water where the Bealach Dearg, the old route from Braemar, meets with a track from Gairnshiel.

These are the old hill roads from Glenavon and Tomintoul to Deeside. The motorist travels by more conventional routes, going south from the Highland's highest village by the Lecht road (A939), the second highest motoring road in the country (the Cairnwell is the highest). This is still the old military road, built by General George Wade's successors. At the Well of Lecht there is an inscription on the well, dated 1754, which says that 'Five Companies, the 33rd Regiment, Right Hon. Lord Charles Hay, Colonel, made the road from here to the Spey.'

During winter, the notorious Lecht struck terror into the hearts of travellers. It was often blocked by snow for weeks, and sometimes months, on end. Nowadays, with modern snow-clearing equipment, it is less of a problem, but motorists still think twice about crossing the Lecht when its roller-coaster road is covered in snow.

At the south end of the Lecht is the Allargue Arms Hotel, which has sheltered many a stranded traveller over the years. Across the Don is Corgarff Castle, built in 1537, burned down in 1571, burned again in 1607, and put to flames a third time in 1689. The castle, which was restored by the Ministry of Works, was used at one time as a watch-post against whisky smugglers, while in the eighteenth century government troops were quartered there to combat cattle-lifting. It is best-known as the setting for *Edom o' Gordon'*, a tragic ballad about a laird's wife, family and servants who perished there in 1571.

From Cock Bridge, the A939 mostly follows the line of the old military road to Deeside. Part of the original road, however, cuts across moorland by Delachuper and Delavine. Along this old track there are a number of Wade bridges, most of them in a ruinous condition. Nevertheless, they show how sturdy these bridges were when they were built to carry traffic across the desolate moorlands of the north-east. Queen Victoria went by what she called 'Dal Choupar' and 'Dal Vown' — she was never good at getting the names right. The Delachuper track, which is signposted, joins the A939 after it turns south on its way to Gairnshiel.

At the scattered hamlet of **Gairnshiel** there is a bridge of a different kind, dwarfing the Wade structures at Delachuper. Here, the bridge over the Gairn was built with a huge arch to avoid the floods that often plagued the Deeside rivers. Crossing the hump-backed bridge by car is a tricky business, but coaches have an even more difficult time, usually dropping their passengers to take pictures of the old bridge while they manoeuvre over its massive hump. On the other side of the Gairn is Gairnshiel Lodge, a former shooting lodge but now a hotel.

Glengairn was a busy community in earlier years. Amy Stewart Fraser, whose father was minister there at the end of last century, wrote about her childhood in the glen in *The Hills of Home*, a book that was described by one reviewer as 'a rich feast of social history, tinged with the sadness that must be felt for a human society that has vanished beyond recall.' That sadness can be felt when you wander down some of the old paths and come upon the ruins of the crofts that once flourished on Gairnside.

Dominating this corner of Deeside between the Gairn and the Dee is

Geallaig Hill where King Edward VII used to shoot. From Gairnshiel, a road runs round the base of the hill on each side. The one on the west comes out opposite Balmoral Castle, near Crathie Church, passing a farm called the Bush, where John Brown spent his childhood. The road on the east comes out at the Bridge of Gairn.

From the 'Fit o' Gairn,' as local folk call it, the way home is by the Pass of Ballater, avoiding busy Ballater, and down through Deeside by the A93 to Aberdeen, the 'Granite City'.

Further Information

— The Cairngorms and The Grampians —

Places of Interest

Atholl Country Collection
Off A9 at Blair Atholl
☎ 079 681 232
Open: daily in afternoons, Easter to September, also weekday mornings during July and August.

Aviemore Centre
☎ 0479 810624
Open: daily.

Balmoral Castle
Entrance on A93, near Crathie
☎ 033 97 42334
Open: May, June and July, daily except Sundays. May be closed when members of the Royal Family are in residence.

Blair Castle
Off A9 at Blair Atholl
☎ 079 681 207
Open: daily March to October.

Braeloine Interpretative Centre
On Glen Tanar estate, near Aboyne
☎ 033 98 86072
Open: April to September, daily.

Braemar Castle
On outskirts of Braemar
☎ 03397 41 219
Open: daily May to October except Friday.

Cairngorm Chairlift
Approach by Glenmore from Aviemore
☎ 0479 86 261
Open: daily.

Clan Donnachaidh Museum
At Calvine on A9, 4 miles (6km) west of Blair Atholl
☎ 079 683 264
Open: daily (except Tuesdays) mid-April to mid-October.

Clan Macpherson Museum
At Newtonmore, ☎ 05403 332
Open: daily May to September.

Corgarff Castle
☎ 097 56 51460
Open: Easter till end September.

Corgarff Rural Exhibition
☎ 097 56 51423
Open: Tuesday to Sunday in summer.

Crathes Castle
Off A93, 2 miles (3km) east of Banchory
☎ 033 044 525
Open: Easter and weekends April and October, 1 May to 30 September, daily. Gardens and grounds open all year, 9.30am-sunset.

Crathie Church
8 miles (13km) west of Ballater
☎ 033 97 42208
Open: 1 April to 31 October, daily, Sunday afternoons.

Glenshee Chairlift
South of Braemar, ☎ 033 83 320
Operates daily when weather suitable.

Highland Folk Museum
Kingussie
☎ 0540 661307/661631
Open: all year.

Highland Wildlife Park
On B99152 south of Kincraig
☎ 054 04 270
Open: daily except for winter season.

Insh Marshes
On B979, 2 miles (3km) from Kingussie
Warden at Ivy Cottage, Insh.

Linn of Tummel
$2^1/_2$ miles (4km) north of Pitlochry
National Trust for Scotland.
Open: daily April to October.

Loch Garten
Off B970
☎ 0479 83 694
Access to bird sanctuary forbidden April
to August, but unrestricted access to rest
of reserve all year.

Pass of Killiecranke
Off A9, 3 miles (5km) north of Pitlochry
☎ 0796 3233
National Trust for Scotland visitors'
centre and ranger service.
Open: daily April to October.

Pitlochry Power Station and Dam
☎ 0796 3152
Open: daily March to October.

Queen's View
On B8019, off A9
☎ 0796 3123
Forestry Commission visitor centre.

The Retreat
About 1 mile (2km) east of Tarfside
☎ 035 67 236
Open: June to end September.

Royal Lochnagar Distillery
Off A93 at Crathie
☎ 033 97 42 273
Open: April to October daily, November
to March, Monday to Friday.

Strathspey Railway
At Boat-of-Garten
☎ 0479 83 692
Train services Easter till end October.

Tomintoul Museum
The Square
☎ 080 74 285
Open: Easter till end October.

Tourist Information Centres

Aviemore Tourist Information Centre
The Main Road, Aviemore
☎ 0479 810 363

Grantown-on-Spey ☎ 0479 2773

Carrbridge ☎ 0479 84630

Kingussie ☎ 054 02 297

Ballater Tourist Information Centre
Station Square
Ballater
☎ 033 97 55306

Dunkeld Tourist Information Centre
Dunkeld and Birnam Tourist Association
The Cross, Dunkeld
☎ 035 02 688

Kincardine and Deeside Tourist Board
45 Station Road
Banchory
☎ 033 02 2066

Pitlochry Information Centre
22 Atholl Road, Pitlochry
Perthshire
☎ 0796 2215

Information can also be obtained from:
Scottish Tourist Board
23 Ravelston Terrace
Edinburgh
☎ 031 332 2433

16 • The Highlands
and Inner Islands

The Highlands of Scotland present to the visitor, within a relatively
small area, some of the most dramatic and beautiful scenery to be found
anywhere in Europe. The land has been shaped by successive periods of
warming and cooling, the action of glacial ice being particularly important
in scouring out the fjord-like sea lochs that penetrate deep into the west of
the country.

The mountains are not especially high, only a few being over 4,000ft
(1,219m). However, they more than compensate for their lack of height in
their shapeliness and variety, from the unmistakable humpback of Ben
Nevis, highest of them all, to the sharp gabbro teeth of the Skye Cuillin and
the magnificence of the giants of Torridon, formed from some of the oldest
rock to be found anywhere in the world.

The many offshore islands add to the area's character. They also offer a
variety: you could hardly find two places more different than Tiree — flat
and fertile, with an outstandingly beautiful Atlantic seaboard — and Skye,
dramatic and mountainous, with high cliffs plunging into the sea. The
mainland includes large and remote peninsulas such as Ardnamurchan
and Knoydart which themselves have almost the feel of islands.

Like the landscape, the climate of the Highlands is full of surprises, and
it is possible to experience all four seasons in a single day. Winters tend to
be wet and windy rather than excessively cold, especially in recent years,
and summers are unpredictable. When settled weather comes it shows the
land and sea at its best and brings the bonus of unrivalled sunsets.

It is believed that the first settlers arrived by sea in the Oban area, and also
on the island of Rum, some 8,000 years ago. They and their descendants left
few clues to their life apart from mysterious standing stones and burial
cairns. At that time settlement was largely confined to the coast — the
hinterland was mostly marsh and peat bog in the glens and dense forest or
scrub on the hills.

The Romans made virtually no impact on this area, though they were
active elsewhere in Scotland, and the principal influences came, again by
sea, from the north and west. The original Scotti came from Ireland, and
many followed them, including St Columba, who spread the Christian
message through the area from his base on Iona.

From the north came the Vikings, who already held sway in Orkney and Shetland, to take many other islands. Sutherland and Caithness abound in names with Viking roots and others are to be found down the west coast. During your travels in the Highlands you will encounter many fortifications, for the area had a turbulent history until recent times. Hillforts, duns, brochs and towers gave way to splendid castles which themselves suffered frequent siege. As recently as the mid-eighteenth century, the Jacobite Risings brought unrest and bloodshed to the area, and the last battle on British soil was fought at Culloden, near Inverness, in 1746.

Gaelic was the language of the area until recent times, and is still spoken in the islands. It has been enjoying something of a revival with more resources being put into Gaelic education, broadcasting, arts and culture. Even the most basic understanding of Gaelic placenames adds enormously to the visitor's understanding and pleasure.

Industry included iron smelting, using the abundance of oak woodland, and weaving. Fishing has long been a vital provider of both work and food, and farming has also left its mark. All these things depended on transport, and the history of the area is very much bound up with the development of transport links. Until very recent times, roads were of much less importance than sea routes, and today the ferries play a vital role in supplying the islands with basic commodities.

Railways penetrated the Highlands 100 years ago, and the lines to Oban, Fort William, Mallaig and Kyle of Lochalsh are among the most scenic to be found anywhere in the world. Before that, two canals were completed, both exceptional engineering achievements. The Crinan Canal saved the 100 mile (161km) sea journey round Kintyre, and the Caledonian Canal cut out the hazardous waters of the Pentland Firth by linking Fort William and Inverness.

There is a great deal for the discerning visitor to see, do and enjoy in the Highlands and Islands today. The scope for the more active in walking, riding, sailing and other pursuits is literally boundless and there are also many hundreds of places for the car- or coach-borne visitor to see.

'The Highlands' is a term open to various interpretation as far as geographical boundaries go. For the purposes of this section, it is taken to mean the Great Glen (Fort William to Inverness) plus all the land west and north of it and the area of Argyll to the south as far as the Crinan Canal. Mull, Coll, Tiree, the Small Isles and Skye are also included.

Excursions From Oban

Oban is a very convenient place to start a tour of the Highlands and Islands. It has a history as long as anywhere in the area and is a good base for many of the islands. Ferries sail to Mull, Colonsay, Coll, Tiree, Islay, Barra and South Uist from Oban.

The first excursion starts by heading south on the A816. At Kilninver, a diversion west on the B844 brings you across the Bridge over the Atlantic to the island of Seil and to **Easdale**. In former times slate was quarried here

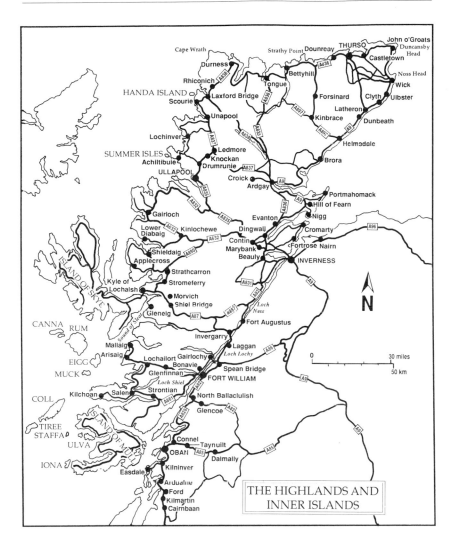

THE HIGHLANDS AND
INNER ISLANDS

on a huge scale and an exhibition displays reminders of that industry.

Returning to the A816, you pass Arduaine Gardens (open in summer) and reach **Kilmartin** with its extraordinary collection of standing stones and chambered cairns, now all scheduled Ancient Monuments; by wandering among them you will gain a sense of prehistory. A little further on, west of the road, is **Dunadd**, a hillfort which was the first 'capital' of the people of Dalriada who united this area into a single kingdom.

Three miles (5km) past Dunadd is Cairnbaan, on the **Crinan Canal**. Only 9 miles (14km) long, the canal, constructed between 1793 and 1801, cut out a difficult 100 mile (161km) sail round the peninsula of Kintyre. From Cairnbaan an easy and very pleasant walk of 4 miles (6km) leads to Crinan, at the western end of the canal.

Returning north along the A816, turn right at Ford and take the B840 along beautiful **Loch Awe**, at 27 miles (43km) the longest inland loch in Scotland. In past times, cattle were regularly swum across the loch between Taychreggan and Portsonachan, and a passenger ferry also operated here. At the northern end of the loch are the impressive ruins of Kilchurn Castle (Ancient Monument), a fifteenth-century Campbell stronghold.

At Dalmally, turn left onto the A85 to return to Oban, passing below mighty Ben Cruachan, which now houses a major hydro-power scheme. The **Cruachan Visitor Centre** explains the scheme and offers minibus rides along a tunnel to the turbine room deep inside the mountain — a most unusual experience.

At Connel you pass **Dunstaffnage Castle**, another Campbell stronghold with a superb little Gothic chapel, and in 5 miles (8km) return to Oban. Two shorter excursions from Oban are also recommended. From the south end of the town take the unclassified road through Glen Lonan to **Taynuilt** on the A85. The village boasts the earliest known monument to Lord Nelson, its own brewery, an award-winning tearoom at Shore Cottage and also the fascinating Bonawe Furnace (Ancient Monument), where iron was smelted in the eighteenth and nineteenth centuries. From the pier at Taynuilt there are twice-daily boat trips up lovely Loch Etive in summer. The name Taynuilt derives from the Gaelic *tigh an allt* meaning the house on the stream. It is also well worth taking the short trip in the small ferryboat to the island of **Kerrera** in Oban Bay. It is a beautiful island with enjoyable walks, and at its south end is Gylen Castle in a most dramatic setting.

The last excursion takes you up to the next area to be visited, along the A828 to Fort William. Crossing the Connel Bridge (formerly used by the railway) the road passes the **Sea Life Centre**, where marine life is explained in an excellent series of displays and tanks, and winds round Loch Creran to pass **Castle Stalker**, on an offshore islet and one of the most photographed places in Scotland. It is a Stewart castle and is maintained as a private residence.

At Ballachulish divert right along A82 to **Glencoe** (National Trust for Scotland) and the National Trust for Scotland visitor centre. Return to the A82 and continue north to Fort William.

Excursions From Fort William

Fort William, at the north end of Loch Linnhe, was one of a number of places which gained military and strategic importance as a result of the Jacobite Risings in the eighteenth century; it is now a holiday centre. In the town you will find the West Highland Museum, with many interesting exhibits including Jacobite relics, and the Ben Nevis Exhibition, which includes a scale model of the Ben and relates some of the stories associated with our highest mountain and the Observatory which was open at its summit from 1883 to 1904.

A short excursion into **Glen Nevis** gives a feel for the dramatic landscape of the area. To the right as you drive up the glen are the shapely Mamores, while the left side is closed off by the massive bulk of Ben Nevis itself. From the road-end there is a superb short walk through the Glen Nevis gorge to the meadows at Steall — almost an Alpine setting with a fine waterfall.

Returning to Fort William, turn right on the A82 to Torlundy, where another right turn brings you to Scotland's newest ski resort at **Aonach Mor**. The gondola — the only one of its kind in Scotland — operates all year round and takes you up to a restaurant and viewpoint at 2,000ft (610m) with superb views westward in particular.

Continue north on the A82 and turn left at Spean Bridge to view the **Commando Memorial**, erected to mark the fact that thousands of troops trained in this area during World War II. From the Memorial, take the B8004 to Gairlochy, cross the Caledonian Canal, and take the minor road to Achnacarry, the Commandos' base from 1942 to 1945. It is the home of the chief of the Clan Cameron, and a very good Clan Cameron Museum has recently opened here; it is well worth a visit. Return to Fort William along B8004 to Banavie, where you can see the start of the Caledonian Canal and Neptune's Staircase, an impressive series of locks. You may be fortunate enough to see ships passing through. When they do, the main road is closed as a swing bridge operates to allow the vessels into Loch Linnhe.

The other excursion from Fort William is a longer one. Take the A82 south for 8 miles (13km) and then use the Corran Ferry to cross Loch Linnhe. Once across, turn left on the A861 through Glen Tarbert, with the mountains of Ardgour to the north. *Tarbert* is a Gaelic word meaning an isthmus or narrow neck of land, and you will find it in a number of places in the Highlands and Islands.

Strontian is where the rare element Strontium was discovered; it also has fine oakwoods in the Ariundle Nature Reserve where marked walks are laid out. At Salen, turn left on the B8007 for the drive along the Ardnamurchan Peninsula. In 9 miles (14km), at **Glenmore**, there is a small visitor centre with excellent displays on the wildlife and landscape of the area, featuring the outstanding photography of Michael MacGregor, who runs the centre with his wife Karen.

The road continues around Ben Hiant to Kilchoan and in a further 5 miles (8km) a left turn leads to the **Point of Ardnamurchan**, the most westerly point on the mainland of Scotland. It is a supremely wild and dramatic place, especially when one of the frequent gales is raging. It used to be possible to climb the stairs in the lighthouse and sign the visitors' book, but unfortunately the light is now automatic.

Return to Salen and turn left on the A861 to Acharacle. A short diversion here leads to **Castle Tioram**. *Tioram* means 'dry' in Gaelic and the name indicates that the castle is on an islet which can be reached at low tide across a sandbar. The ancient seat of the MacDonalds of Clanranald, the castle was sacked by the chief of the clan in 1715 to prevent the Campbells taking it. It is an unusual and very beautiful spot and well worth the diversion.

Continue on the A861 to Glenuig and Lochailort. Turn right onto the A830 for **Glenfinnan** and another National Trust for Scotland visitor centre. This is the point where Bonnie Prince Charlie raised his standard to rally the clans at the start of the 1745 Rising, the most successful but also the most tragic, culminating as it did in the debacle of Culloden. The story is told in the centre and the impressive monument at the head of Loch Shiel can be visited on foot. Return to Fort William by the A830 along Loch Eil.

Another excursion from Fort William well worth taking in summer months is the steam train ride to **Mallaig**, a busy fishing port. The line passes through superb scenery, reaching the coast at Arisaig; here and at Morar are lovely sandy beaches. Loch Morar is said to be the deepest in Scotland and to house a monster called 'Morag', a sister to the more famous 'Nessie' in Loch Ness.

The Road To The Isles

This short section links the southern part of the area to the far north-west, leading us towards ever more spectacular scenery. From Fort William take the A82 north, passing Spean Bridge and the Commando Memorial and continuing along the shores of Loch Lochy. At Laggan is the **Great Glen Water Park**, where you can practise a variety of activities from windsurfing and hillwalking to clay pigeon shooting. Before turning left at Invergarry, a short diversion further along the A82 brings you to the **Well of the Seven Heads**, a monument with an inscription in English and Gaelic marking the murder of seven brothers for their slaying of two sons of the chief of Keppoch in the seventeenth century.

From Invergarry take the A87 — the modern 'Road to the Isles'. In 5 miles (8km) a minor road leads away left down Glen Garry. This is the longest no through road in Britain, ending 26 miles (42km) later at Kinloch Hourn, from where it is possible to walk into **Knoydart**, a vast peninsula with no road access which is loved by walkers and naturalists. The old road went this way to Tomdoun and across Glen Loyne to Cluanie. Part of its course is now under the waters of Loch Loyne, a reservoir formed as part of a vast hydro-power scheme. In very dry summers the old road sometimes reappears and the loch can be crossed on foot.

The A87 rises high above Loch Loyne and then drops down to Glen Moriston, where it turns left to run alongside Loch Cluanie, also dammed, and then down **Glen Shiel**, with superb mountain scenery to either side. Partway down the glen, on the lower slopes of the Five Sisters of Kintail (National Trust for Scotland), is a memorial to a curious skirmish that occurred here in 1719 when a party of Spaniards supporting the Jacobite cause sailed up Loch Duich. A brief battle ensued, and the invaders fled. The battle is still recalled on OS maps by the name *Coirean nan Spainteach* (coire of the Spaniards) indicating the place where they met their match.

At Shiel Bridge there is a worthwhile diversion along the minor road to **Glenelg**. The road twists up and over the Mam Ratagan pass. At the summit, stop in the lay-by to admire the famous view of the Five Sisters seen across Loch Duich, then continue to Glenelg. To the right of the road as you near the village is the ruin of **Bernera Barracks**, built by the government after the 1715 Rising and manned from then until 1790.

A typical Highland scene, Glen Shiel

Glenelg is a pretty spot looking across the Sound of Sleat to the hills of Skye. South of the village, a left turn along Glen Beag (this means little glen in Gaelic) leads to two magnificent stone brochs, **Dun Telve** and **Dun Troddan** (Ancient Monument). Dating from the Iron Age, these impressive fortified dwellings still stand to a height of 30ft (9m).

Returning to the A87 and heading north, a minor road from Morvich leads to Dorusduain from where the adventurous can take the 8 mile (13km) round walk to the **Falls of Glomach**, among Scotland's highest and finest with their 370ft (113m) drop. Another few miles along the main road brings you to **Eilean Donan Castle**. Severely damaged during the 1719 skirmish, the castle was superbly well restored in 1912. It includes a war memorial to the Clan Macrae and a museum with clan relics.

The road continues to Kyle of Lochalsh, separated from Skye by a narrow strait, though there are long-term plans to provide a bridge here. However, before Kyle of Lochalsh is reached, you should turn off to the north onto the A890 for the next part of the journey.

Exploring Wester Ross

The area between Kyle of Lochalsh and Ullapool is known as Wester Ross. A glance at the map will show relatively few roads or settlements and a plenitude of glorious lochs and mountains. It is a wonderful area for the walker, climber, sailor and naturalist, but there is plenty to see whatever your mode of travel.

Take the A890 to Stromeferry — where there was indeed once a ferry across Loch Carron — and continue to Strathcarron, alongside another spectacular stretch of railway line. Turn left onto the A896 as far as Tornapress. If you are bold you can make a detour here to visit **Applecross**, another large peninsula. The road twists sharply up through hairpin bends to the **Bealach-na-Bo** (Pass of the Cattle) at over 2,000ft (610m), before dropping equally sharply to Applecross village and continuing round the peninsula to rejoin the A896 at Shieldaig.

The road runs along the south side of Upper Loch Torridon. Across the loch are the mighty Torridon Mountains (National Trust for Scotland), with Beinn Alligin and Liathach (the grey one) prominent. The Torridonian sandstone of which these superb hills are made is among the oldest rock to be found anywhere in the world. A walk into **Coire Mhic Nobuil** from the car park on the north side of the loch gives a flavour of the area; you can if you wish continue over the **Bealach na Gaoithe** (Pass of the Wind) to the small village of Lower Diabaig, where the seaward views are magnificent.

Returning to the main road, continue to Kinlochewe on Loch Maree and turn left on to the A832. Two miles (3km) north of the village is the visitor centre for the **Beinn Eighe National Nature Reserve**, run by the Nature Conservancy Council. Displays tell you about the hills and the wildlife, which includes eagles, otters and pine martens, and there are walks you can follow through old pinewoods or partway up the mountain.

Another 20 miles (32km) brings you to **Gairloch**. The village has an award-winning museum which shows life in Gairloch through the ages, with a room furnished in the style of an old croft. From Gairloch Pier you can walk to **Flowerdale Falls** (3 miles, 5km). Six miles (10km) north of Gairloch is one of the West Highland's most renowned, and most unusual, attractions. **Inverewe Gardens** (National Trust for Scotland) were established in the nineteenth century by Osgood Mackenzie. Starting with bare ground, and importing all the soil, he created a wonderful woodland garden with temperate and sub-tropical plants, including many specimens from South America and the Himalayas.

The road continues to Gruinard Bay with its offshore island, which was infected with anthrax spores as an experiment during World War II. It has only very recently been declared safe again. The stretch past Dundonnell provides fine views of **An Teallach** (The Forge), a magnificent sandstone mountain.

Fish farming has become an important industry in the Highlands and Islands in recent years and you can visit **Ardessie Fisheries** at Dundonnell to see how it is done. Both trout and salmon are farmed here and products are for sale. Carry on to Braemore Junction and turn left onto the A835.

Almost at the junction is the **Corrieshalloch Gorge** (National Trust for Scotland), a spectacular box canyon including the Falls of Measach, which can be viewed from a suspension bridge built by John Fowler (who also engineered the Forth Rail Bridge), and from an observation platform. The road continues beside Loch Broom for 12 miles (19km) to reach **Ullapool**, one of the planned villages created in the late eighteenth century by the British Fisheries Society to try to encourage fishery in the area. The ferry to Stornoway in the Outer Hebrides leaves from here. At the rear of a book-

Eilean Donan Castle in its beautiful setting beside Loch Duich

shop in Quay Street, you will find the Lochbroom Highland Museum, run by the local community association, with displays relating to the landscape and scenery of the area. Up one of the side streets is a Roman Catholic chapel dedicated to St Martin. It is not an ecclesiastical building but a normal cottage used for religious purposes. What makes it unusual is that the notices in the window are likely to be in Russian or Polish, for the benefit of mariners on the large 'klondikers' which regularly visit the area to fish.

From Ullapool you can take easy walks, all giving superb views, to **Loch Achall**, **Rhue Lighthouse**, and **Glastullich** — all around 5 miles (8km) in length on good paths; guidebooks are available locally. From Ullapool take the A835 north and after 10 miles (16km) turn left at Drumrunie. The road passes Loch Lurgainn, from where the fine little mountain **Stac Pollaidh** can be climbed, and continues to Achiltibuie in its glorious setting.

The Hydroponicum at **Achiltibuie** is unique. This is space-age horticulture, with no soil being used, and the produce including bananas, figs, grapefruit, and a variety of vegetables. It is truly an extraordinary venture in such a location. Achiltibuie also has a purpose-built smokehouse by the sea where you can have the traditional process of curing fish by smoking explained and can buy the resultant delicious products. Offshore are the **Summer Isles**, which can be visited by boat from Ullapool.

The Far North-West

Take the A835 north from Ullapool again. Three miles (5km) north of the Achiltibuie turn-off is the **Knockan Cliff Information Centre**, which describes the vast Inverpolly National Nature Reserve and the geological fault known as the Mhoine Thrust, which can also be seen on a walk from the centre. The mountains here are extraordinary, rising abruptly from a flat, watery landscape. Cul Beg and Cul Mor are prominent.

The road joins the A837 at Ledmore and runs on to Loch Assynt, on the shore of which is the dramatic ruin of **Ardvreck Castle**, a MacLeod stronghold dating from the late fifteenth century and still standing to three storeys in height. The A837 then diverts westwards, as if anxious to rejoin the sea, and reaches the pretty village of Lochinver, from where a tortuous 20 mile (32km) loop on the B869 passes through dramatic coastal scenery before rejoining the main road at Newton, near Unapool. A diversion can be made to walk to the **Point of Stoer**, with its remarkable rock stack known as the Old Man of Stoer.

From Unapool the road (now the A894) crosses the Kylesku Bridge, a fine sweeping structure opened in 1984, and goes on to Scourie. From here, and from Tarbet a little to the north, a boat can be taken to **Handa Island** (Royal Society for the Protection of Birds), a bird reserve with an information centre and walks.

The road joins the A838 at Laxford Bridge and, once past Rhiconich, leaves the west coast and makes for the north. In 5 miles (8km) it passes a small well erected by the surveyor of the road, Peter Lawson, in gratitude for the kindness shown to him by local people — a kindness that today's visitors will find in equal measure. The road runs alongside the Kyle of Durness — a beautiful inlet — to the town of that name, from which a diversion should be made to **Balnakeil**, 1 mile (2km) to the north-west. Here you will find a Craft Village open in summer with a number of different crafts being practised, and high quality goods on sale. Balnakiel Old Church dates from the early seventeenth century and is on the site of an even earlier building. A monument marks the grave of Rob Donn, a famous Celtic bard.

From Keoldale, near Durness, a ferry can be taken to join the minibus trip to **Cape Wrath**, the most north-westerly point of the Scottish mainland. The name — though often apt — actually derives from a Norse word *hvarf*, meaning a point of turning for mariners. The views are extensive, across to Orkney and west to the distant Butt of Lewis. The Cape Wrath lighthouse was built in 1828; the area is sometimes used by the Navy for bombing practice.

From Durness the road runs around **Loch Eriboll**, where Allied convoys sheltered during World War II and where, much earlier, Viking galleys lay before sailing south to defeat at the Battle of Largs. The road continues along the north coast to Tongue and (now as the A836) leaves Sutherland and enters Caithness to reach Thurso, the centre for the next two excursions.

Excursions From Thurso

Thurso (Norse for Thor's River) is a pleasant town of some 9,000 inhabitants. It was once an important port linking the north of Scotland with Scandinavia. The Thurso Heritage Museum has much information on the area. St Peter's Church, near the harbour, dates from the thirteenth century,

Dramatic winter scenery in the Highlands, Kintail

and Harald's Tower is said to mark the grave of Harald, Earl of Caithness, killed here in 1196.

Take the A836 west. In 5 miles (8km) at Bridge of Forss is the ruin of **St Mary's Chapel**, probably dating from the twelfth century and with an unusual and very low doorway. The next point of interest could hardly be a greater contrast. Before long the domes and other buildings of the **Dounreay Nuclear Power Establishment** come into view. A good display informs visitors about Dounreay's work and nuclear power. Dounreay has brought much employment to the area but it is now being reduced in capacity and there are fears that its function will alter to that of a waste-processing plant and storage repository.

Continuing west, a diversion can be made to **Strathy Point**, where there is magnificent cliff scenery, before continuing to **Bettyhill**. The village was named after Elizabeth, First Duchess of Sutherland. The former church has been converted into a most interesting museum run by volunteers which tells the story of the Clearances, when many hundreds of people were forced to leave the area and their homes and emigrate to distant lands such as Canada and the United States.

To appreciate the full impact of those times, a diversion is recommended down Strath Naver and east on B871 to Kinbrace and then north again on A897 up Strath Halladale. These long glens, now almost empty, once held sizeable populations of crofting people. The diversion also enables you to see something of the **Flow Country**, the patterned landscape of lochans and low hills where the conservation of the peatbogs has aroused tremendous controversy in recent years. Attempts are being made to provide an interpretative centre at Forsinard. Return by A836 past Dounreay to Thurso.

The second tour takes in both the false and real claimants to the title of Scotland's most northerly point. From Thurso take A882 to **Wick** (this stems from the Norse word *vik*, meaning a bay), which vies with Thurso to be the principal town of **Caithness**. The Wick Heritage Centre in Bank Row has special displays on the maritime life of the town. Old photographs show Wick Harbour crammed full of fishing boats. These photographs are part of the extraordinary Johnston Collection of 70,000 plates dating back to the 1860s. In Harrowhill is the factory of Caithness Glass, with an exhibition and shop; glassblowers can be seen working.

From Wick turn north again on the A9. A diversion can be made to Noss Head, where a short walk leads to the twin ruins of Castles **Girnigoe** and **Sinclair**, both former strongholds of the Earls of Caithness; Girnigoe is the older. Ten miles (16km) north of Wick, at **Auckengill**, is the John Nicolson Museum, telling the story of this local antiquarian and his discoveries about the brochs and other relics in the area.

Another 6 miles (10km) brings you to **John o'Groats**. This is not the northern tip of Scotland, though it is a common misconception. The hotel has recently been bought by the entrepreneur Peter de Savary, who also owns Land's End in Cornwall, and he has ambitious plans for a 'heritage centre' here. The name derives from a Dutchman, John de Groot, who lived here many years ago.

From John o'Groats you should certainly take the short diversion east along the minor road to **Duncansby Head**, the true north-eastern tip of Scotland. A walk down the coast to the south soon brings fine views of the Duncansby Stacks, looking like giant teeth sticking up from the sea. Return to John o'Groats and continue west on the A836. In 6 miles (10km) you reach the **Castle of Mey**, a sixteenth-century seat of the Earls of Caithness now owned by Queen Elizabeth the Queen Mother. It is not normally open to the public.

In another 2 miles (3km) a right turn on the B855 leads to **Dunnet Head**, and here you really are at the northern tip of mainland Scotland. It has other claims to fame — the fine 400ft (122m) sandstone cliffs, and the fact that it may well be the Cape Oreas mentioned by the Roman writer Diodorus (circa 50BC), in which case it is the first place in Scotland to be recorded in writing. Returning to the A836, pass Castletown, where the Caithness flagstone industry was founded in 1824, and reach Thurso at the end of a most interesting tour.

It is time now to turn south. Return to Wick and turn onto the A9. One mile (2km) south of the town is the spectacular ruin of the **Castle of Old Wick** (Ancient Monument), a Norse tower set on a spine of rock jutting out over the sea. It should be approached with caution due to the exposed nature of the site. Between Ulbster and Clyth are two ancient sites. The **Hill o' Many Stanes** is just that — 200 stones set out in a fan-like pattern, whose significance is still unknown; not far away are the **Grey Cairns** of **Camster** (both Ancient Monuments), a chambered burial place from Neolithic times. Both are highly evocative sites.

In the former church at Latheron is the **Clan Gunn Heritage Centre**, where the story of the clan and their area is told. Above the road junction is an unusual hilltop belfry, placed here so that people in this scattered parish would all hear the call to worship. Just north of Dunbeath is the **Lhaidhay Croft Museum**, built and furnished in the style of the eighteenth century and with a special display for the blind. There is also a small exhibition in Dunbeath village itself.

Caithness is generally less mountainous than Sutherland, with more fertile land along the coastal strip, but the scene is not without its moments of drama. In 15 miles (24km) the road crosses the Ord of Caithness and plunges down a series of hairpin bends to reach **Helmsdale**, a fishing village where you will find Timespan, an award-winning visitor centre which uses modern techniques to describe the history, landscape and wildlife of the area. Its riverside garden includes rare medicinal plants.

There are two brochs at Brora, but the next major point of interest is **Dunrobin Castle**, seat of the Dukes of Sutherland, which over the centuries has changed from a square basic keep with turrets to the great Baronial fantasy seen today. Parts were reconstructed in the 1920s by Sir Robert Lorimer following fire damage. The extensive grounds and gardens overlooking the sea are well worth exploring. From Dunrobin the road crosses Loch Fleet and takes you into Easter Ross and towards Inverness

Excursions From Inverness

Inverness, the 'Capital of the Highlands', is a good centre for touring. With a population of around 40,000, it is easily the largest town in the Highlands, and is attractively sited astride the River Ness. The imposing Inverness Castle dates from 1834, previous buildings having been destroyed during the Jacobite Risings. St Andrew's Cathedral is also nineteenth century, and there is a good museum. Inverness has all the facilities you would expect from a town of this size.

The first tour takes in the Dornoch and Cromarty Firths and the Black Isle. Leave Inverness by the A9 and the Kessock Bridge, opened in 1980, and cross the Black Isle and the Cromarty Firth, branching left after Evanton onto the A836. This climbs to give good views of the Dornoch Firth, where another new bridge is under construction.

Before starting the return loop, you may wish to continue to Ardgay and take the minor road up lovely Strathcarron to **Croick Church**. This glen was the scene of numerous forced evictions. In 1845 some of the people tried to take refuge in their little church, and you can still see the poignant messages they scratched on the glass, such as 'This house is needy refuge'.

Return to Fearn and take the A9 on to **Tain**. The name derives from the Norse word *thing*, meaning a council. The Tolbooth dates from the sixteenth century; St Duthus Chapel is much older, being originally an eleventh-century structure, though little is left from that period. St Duthus is the town's patron saint. Alongside the chapel is the fourteenth-century Collegiate Church and close by is the Tain Museum and Clan Ross Centre, with a fine collection of silver.

A worthwhile diversion can be taken east on the B9165 to Hill of Fearn and **Fearn Abbey**, a thirteenth-century Premonstratensian foundation which has been restored. **Portmahomack** is an attractive, quiet village with a good harbour which was re-designed by Thomas Telford. Nearby are the ruins of Ballone Abbey, a sixteenth-century Z-plan tower. The road ends at **Tarbat Ness**, with its imposing lighthouse and superb views across the firth.

Retrace the outward route across the Cromarty Firth, but then turn left on the B9163 alongside the Cromarty Firth to Cromarty itself. The higher points of the road give excellent views across the firth, and you will often see oil platforms 'parked' there: Nigg has a major construction base.

The Black Isle, wooded and fertile, has an atmosphere and charm all its own. In **Cromarty** is Hugh Miller's Cottage (National Trust for Scotland), a thatched building of 1711 which was the birthplace of the noted geologist and writer Hugh Miller (1802-1856) and is now a museum of his life and work. A new museum is being created in Cromarty Courthouse telling the story of the town and the area; it should be open in spring 1991.

Take the A832 back to **Rosemarkie**, which can trace its origins as far back as the sixth century. Groam House Museum specialises in Pictish stones and other relics of those shadowy people. It is worth making a detour to **Chanonry Point** with its fine views across the Moray Firth to Fort George. This is one of the few places in Britain where you can see dolphins offshore.

Return to **Fortrose**. The last witch in Scotland is said to have been burnt here. Fortrose Cathedral (Ancient Monument), a red sandstone ruin, dates from the late fifteenth century. The Mackenzies of Seaforth have their burial place here. Alongside the cathedral is the thirteenth-century Chapter House, and Fortrose Town Hall contains a small museum including portraits of the Seaforth family. Rejoin the A9 at Tore and return to Inverness.

The next tour again takes the A9 to Tore but then turns left on the A835 to **Dingwall**, the administrative centre of Easter Ross. The name is again Norse, meaning a place of council, and this was the birthplace of Macbeth. The eighteenth-century Town House has a good small museum including mementoes of the distinguished soldier Sir Hector MacDonald, who is also commemorated by a large monument on Mitchell Hill above the town.

Take the A834 to **Strathpeffer**, a village which grew in Victorian times as a spa when the fashion for such places was at its height. Railway excursions from London were arranged, and visitors were encouraged to take the waters, which have a sulphurous element in them. The Pump Room in the Square is now a museum to those times, with splendid old photographs; and in Spa Cottage is a charming private collection of dolls, toys and Victoriana. The former Strathpeffer Station has been well restored as a visitor centre with audio-visual displays on the landscape and wildlife of the area, notably that of Ben Wyvis, which dominates the scene to the north.

Return by Contin and Marybank on the A832 and turn onto the A862 to **Beauly**, a name derived from the French *beau lieu* (beautiful place). Beauly Priory (Ancient Monument) is a thirteenth-century Valliscaulian foundation with unusual triangular windows, containing in its north transept the burial place of the Mackenzies of Kintail. Continue on the A862 along the south side of Beauly Firth to Inverness, crossing the Caledonian Canal by the locks at **Clachnaharry**. The name means the Watchman's Stone, indicating that here on the outskirts of the town a watch was kept for possible invaders.

You should not leave Inverness without making the short trip to **Culloden** (National Trust for Scotland), on the B9006 4 miles (6km) east of the town. The story of the 1746 battle which effectively ended the Jacobite Risings is well told, and you can wander around the battlefield site with its many memorials to fallen clansmen. It is a highly evocative place, marking a sad end to an extraordinary campaign which reached as far south as Derby.

After seeing Culloden you might like to take the B9039 and then the B9006 out to **Fort George** (Ancient Monument), a most impressive place which owes its existence to the Risings. It was completed in 1769 and is virtually unaltered, a vast and solid indication of the military presence and the determination of the English government to have no more rebellion in the troublesome Highlands. There is a good visitor centre.

Near Culloden are the **Clava Cairns** (Ancient Monument), set in a small valley and almost hidden, so discreetly are they signposted; but they too should not be missed. These three large burial mounds, with stone pavements and with many marked stones, form an impressive and powerful group and are a reminder of a people of whom little is known. They date from around 2000BC.

Our final excursion from Inverness takes us down the length of Loch Ness to another fortification — and the possibility of seeing the Monster. From Inverness take the A82 south and in 16 miles (26km) reach Drumnadrochit, the name meaning bridge on a ridge or possibly the back bridge. Here you are truly in Monster country, and you will find not only the **Official Loch Ness Monster Exhibition** but also the rival **Original Loch Ness Visitor Centre** almost next door. They both have interesting displays including photographs of 'Nessie'.

It is worth taking the A831 up Glen Urquhart for 8 miles (13km) to see the **Corrimony Chambered Cairn** (Ancient Monument) and its standing stones, which must be nearly as old as the Loch Ness Monster and are just about as mysterious. Return to the A82 and stop at the next headland to view **Urquhart Castle** (Ancient Monument), a noted Monster-watching point. Most of what remains today dates from the sixteenth century, when the castle was in the hands of the Grant family.

Continue south beside **Loch Ness**, which is 24 miles (39km) long and in places 900ft (274m) deep; it never freezes. Loch cruises are run from both Inverness and **Fort Augustus**, which was built by General Wade, of road-building fame, in 1729, and named after the Duke of Cumberland, victor at Culloden. What remained was incorporated into Fort Augustus Abbey and School later in the nineteenth century. The abbey, a Benedictine foundation, can be visited.

Fort Augustus, on the Caledonian Canal, provides pleasant walks, and is the western terminus of Wade's Corrieyairack Pass road, a magnificent piece of engineering and now a superb walk rising to 2,500ft (762m) before dropping down again to Strathspey.

Island Excursions

The exploration of the Highlands starts in Oban, and it is from there that the ferry takes its short and frequent 40 minute crossing to the beautiful island of **Mull**. Two visits (at least) are recommended as a day can easily be spent in the vicinity of Craignure, where the ferry arrives.

A short walk leads to the small station for the **Mull and West Highland Railway**. The delightful miniature trains make a 2 mile (3km) run to **Torosay Castle**, a nineteenth-century building containing much of interest and with fine gardens which include an unusual 'statue walk' with 19 lifesize figures by the Italian sculptor Bonazza.

Across the bay is **Duart Castle**, ancestral home of the chiefs of the Clan Maclean. It was badly damaged in 1691 but was restored earlier this century by Sir Fitzroy Maclean. Much of the building dates from the thirteenth century and it commands superb views across the Firth of Lorn to the mainland.

Heading north from Craignure on the A849, you will find that the ruined chapel at **Pennygown** is worth a visit to see the Celtic cross-shaft inscribed with a ship, Madonna and a griffon. The road becomes the A848 single-track after Salen and runs on to **Tobermory**. This is famous for its harbour, the legend (sadly without foundation) of the Spanish Armada treasure-ship, and the houses painted in a myriad of bright colours. The Mull and Iona Folk Museum is worth a visit as is Aros Park, south of the town, where there are pleasant woodland walks. Tobermory means the well of Mary.

Turn west on the B8073 to **Dervaig**. In this attractive village you will find The Old Byre, a crofting museum, and the Mull Little Theatre, Britain's smallest professional company. The road continues to reach the coast at the superb beach of **Calgary** — the Canadian city was named after this lovely spot by emigrants. The gardens of Treshnish House can be visited.

The road continues on its tortuous way and in a further 12 miles (19km) reaches **Ulva Ferry**, from where boat trips to the island of **Staffa** (National Trust for Scotland), can be arranged. Here the basaltic pillars of Fingal's Cave were made famous by the composer Mendelssohn. Do not return to Salen but turn right on the B8035 beside Loch na Keal and cross the east end of the Ardmeanach Peninsula, much of which (the part known as **Burg**) has been in National Trust for Scotland hands for over 50 years. To the east is Ben More, the highest hill on Mull. The summit rock is of a type which makes a compass unreliable, so care is needed in conditions of poor visibility. Otherwise the mountain is a straightforward ascent and has superb views in all directions.

Join the A849 and drive alongside Loch Scridain to Pennyghael, where a memorial honours the Beatons, physicians to the Macleans of Duart for three centuries. A diversion here to Carsaig and a fairly strenuous walk

leads to the amazing cliff formations called **Carsaig Arches**, eroded basalt pillars and stacks.

The main road continues to Fionnphort, from where you catch the ferry for the short crossing to **Iona** (National Trust for Scotland). St Columba came here in the sixth century to spread the Christian word across Scotland. The path from the ferry passes the Nunnery Church (thirteenth-century) and the Church of St Ronan, used as a museum for historic stones, to reach the **Reilig Orain**, the great royal burial ground. It is said that forty-eight Scottish kings and fourteen of other nationalities are laid to rest here.

Iona Cathedral has been extensively restored this century and is strongly associated with Lord Macleod of Fiunary, who founded the Iona Community in 1938. The buildings are impressive in themselves and the place has its own wonderfully peaceful atmosphere which seems to affect all those who visit it. Outside are the remains of the tenth-century St Martin's Cross; its larger companion, St John's Cross is to be imaginatively displayed in a glass fibre support nearby when restoration is complete. Iona is certainly worthy of its own excursion, and the return to Craignure along Loch Scridain and through Glen More offers much of the best of the scenery of the lovely island of Mull.

Coll and **Tiree** provide a complete contrast. Much flatter and less rugged, they have superb western seaboards with wonderful beaches and the machair flowers unique to the Western Isles. Tiree stages major windsurfing events each year. On Coll you can visit Breachachadh Castle, much of which dates from the fifteenth century. Regular ferries run to these islands from Oban.

The Small Isles are served from Mallaig and are all of interest. **Canna** (National Trust for Scotland), the most northerly, is flat and relatively fertile. It is the home of Dr John Lorne Campbell and his wife, noted Gaelic scholars. The largest of the four is **Rum**, which is a National Nature Reserve owned by the Nature Conservancy Council and famous as the island where sea eagles were reintroduced to Scotland, Kinloch Castle on Rum is an elaborate fantasy built in pink Arran sandstone by Sir George Bullough, a Lancashire cotton magnate who owned the island in late Victorian times. It includes many extraordinary items of furniture, antiques and a working orchestreon. The smaller islands of **Eigg** with its unmistakeable Sgurr (a sharply pointed hill), and **Muck** (which means Isle of Pigs), make up the group.

Rum has superb hills, all with Norse names like Hallival and Askival, home to thousands of nesting Manx shearwaters, and from them you look north to the higher and equally superb Cuillin of Skye. **Skye** is usually reached by the short ferry crossing from Kyle of Lochalsh; there is an alternative service from Mallaig to Armadale. There is also a ferry (summer only) from Glenelg to Kylerhea.

The Kyle of Lochalsh crossing brings into view the gaunt ruin of **Castle Moil** (this means roofless castle, an appropriate name) at Kyleakin, where the fine gardens of **Kyle House** can also be visited. Take the A850 to Broadford, and then divert via the A881 and a minor road to Elgol, a very scenic drive leading to a stunning viewpoint from where the heart of the Cuillin can be seen across Loch Scavaig. Before this the road passes below Bla Bheinn, a lovely mountain detached from the main group.

Skye; The Storr's rocks overlooking a wild and rugged landscape

Return to Broadford and continue to **Luib**, where the Luib Folk Museum is housed in a traditional 'black house' of the type which formerly made up the common habitations of the island people. The road winds around below Glamaig to **Sligachan**, with superb views of Sgurr nan Gillean. Continue north to Portree, the largest town on Skye. Five miles (8km) north of Portree are the weirdly eroded rocks of **The Storr**, easily reached on foot, and the start of the Trotternish Peninsula. Just south of Staffin is the **Kilt Rock**, a 300ft (91m) cliff named because it is shaped like the pleats of a kilt.

North of Staffin are the even more weirdly eroded rocks of **The Quiraing**, again easily reached on foot. The A855 bends west at the northern tip of the island and passes **Duntulm Castle**, one of many MacDonald strongholds in this area. A little further on, at **Kilmuir**, is the Skye Museum of Island Life which includes a weaver's house and a smithy. Uig is the start of the ferry service for North Uist and Harris. The road continues around Loch Snizort Beag, where it joins the A850, all the while with magnificent views, and heads westwards across to Dunvegan and its wonderful castle, the seat of the Macleods.

Dunvegan Castle exhibits a variety of styles ranging from the fifteenth to the nineteenth century. Its contents include the Fairy Flag, dated to between the fifth and seventh centuries, of Middle Eastern origin, and said to possess the magical property of saving the Clan Macleod from danger. There is also the Dunvegan Cup, a tenth-century Irish drinking vessel, and much else, as well as fine gardens outside.

From Dunvegan take the A863 back to Sligachan and rejoin the A850 through Broadford to Skulamus, from where an excursion to **Sleat**, the south-western part of Skye, is recommended. This is also MacDonald country and the present clan chief, Lord Godfrey MacDonald, lives at Kilmore. At **Isleornsay** a small gallery runs exhibitions of art during the summer and not far away is **Knock Castle**, another ruined MacDonald stronghold.

Sleat is much more fertile than the rest of Skye and offers a quite different landscape from the harsh rock architecture of the Cuillin. It is also home to Sabhal Mor Ostaig, the Gaelic college which has done such outstanding work in promoting the language in recent years. The **Clan Donald Centre** at Armadale is also worth visiting. Extensively restored and added to over the years, the funding coming in large part from the United States, it is now a very impressive complex with excellent displays and exhibitions, a museum, and extensive gardens with ranger-led walks. The return journey can be varied by taking the loop to Tarskavaig on the north side of Sleat, passing **Dunscaith Castle**, another MacDonald fortification.

Skye is a large — 600sq miles (1,555sq km) — and very varied island and warrants more than this brief description. It has a lot to offer and it provides links between the mainland Highland area and the further islands of the Hebrides, which can often be seen from the north-west of Skye. It is a good place at which to end our tours of the Highlands and Inner Islands. The region has many interesting and unusual places, and once you have been here and seen for yourself just how much the area has to offer, you will be back, not once but many times.

Further Information

— The Highlands and Inner Islands —

Places of Interest

Places marked Ancient Monument in the text are generally open at the following times:
April to September: Monday to Saturday 9.30am-7pm, Sunday 2-7pm. October to March: Monday to Saturday 9.30am-4pm, Sunday 2-4pm.

Opening times for some of the more significant places are given below. For other places see tourist information guides or enquire locally. Houses, gardens, castles etc are generally open from Easter to October.

Beinn Eighe Visitor Centre
☎ 044 584 258 for details.

Clan Donald Centre
Open: April to October, Monday to Saturday 10am-5.30pm, Sunday 12noon-5.30pm.
Gardens open at all times.

Clan Gunn Heritage Centre
Open: June to September, Monday to Saturday 11am-6pm.

Cruachan Visitor Centre
Open: Easter to October, daily 9am-4.30pm.

Dounreay
Visitor Centre
Open: Easter to September, daily 9am-4.30pm. Free tours of plant by arrangement. ☎ 0847 62121 extn 656.

Duart Castle
Open: May to September, daily 10.30am-6pm.

Dunrobin Castle
Open: June to mid September, Monday to Saturday 10am-5.30pm. Sunday 1-5.30pm.

Dunvegan Castle
Open: Easter to mid-May and October 2-5pm, mid-May to September 10.30am-5pm.

Eilean Donan Castle
Open: Easter to end September, daily 10am-12.30pm, 2-6pm.

Glencoe Visitor Centre
Open: April, May, September, October, daily 10am 5.30pm. June to August, daily 9am-6.30pm.

Glenfinnan Visitor Centre
Open: April, May, September, October, daily 10am-5.30pm. June to August, daily 9.30-6.30pm.

Great Glen Exhibition
Open: April to October, daily 9.30-5pm.

Groam House Museum, Rosemarkie
Open: May to September, Monday to Saturday 11am-5pm, Sunday 2.30-4.30pm.

Handa Island
Boat trips from Tarbet, April to mid September, Monday to Saturday 10am-5pm.
Further information from Royal Society for the Protection of Birds ☎ 031 556 5624

Hugh Miller's Cottage, Cromarty
Open: April to September, Monday to Saturday 10am-12noon, 1-5pm, plus June to August, Sunday 2-5pm.

Hydroponicum, Achiltibuie
Open: April to October, tours daily at 11am, 12noon, 2 and 5pm.

Inverewe Gardens
Open: all year, daily 9.30am-sunset. Shop and visitor centre: April, Monday to Saturday 10am-5pm. September to October, Monday to Saturday 10am-5pm, Sunday 12noon-5pm. May to August, Monday to Saturday 10am-6.30pm, Sunday 12noon-6.30pm.

Iona
Inclusive trips available daily from Oban in the summer.

John Nicolson Museum, Auckengill
Open: June to August, Monday to Saturday 10am-12noon, 2-4pm.

Knockan Cliff
Open: May to September, Monday to Friday 10am-5.30pm.

Lhaidhay Croft Museum
Open: Easter to September, daily 9am-6pm.

Luib Folk Museum
Open: Easter to October daily 9am-6pm.

Mull and West Highland Railway
Open: Easter and May to September, daily — timetables available locally.

Sea Life Centre
Open: March to November, daily 10am-6pm.

Skye Museum of Island Life, Kilmuir
Open: April to October, Monday to Saturday 9am-5.30pm.

Smokehouse, Achiltibuie
Open: all year, Monday to Friday 9am-5.30pm, plus Saturdays 9am-5.30pm from Easter to October.

Timespan, Helmsdale
Open: Easter to mid October, Monday to Saturday 10am-5pm, Sunday 2-5pm.

Torosay Castle
Open: mid-April to mid October, daily 10.30am-5pm, gardens open sunrise to sunset.

Area Tourist Boards

Caithness Tourist Board
Whitechapel Road
Wick
Caithness KW1 4EA
☎ 0955 2596

Fort William and Lochaber Tourist Board
Cameron Square
Fort William PH33 6AJ
☎ 0397 3781

Inverness, Loch Ness and Nairn Tourist Board
23 Church Street
Inverness IV1 1EZ
☎ 0463 234353

Isle of Skye and South West Ross Tourist Board
Tourist Information Centre
Portree
Isle of Skye IV51 9BZ
☎ 0478 2137

Oban, Mull and District Tourist Board
Information Centre
Argyll Square
Oban PA34 4AN
☎ 0631 63122

Ross and Cromarty Tourist Board
Gairloch
Ross-shire IV21 2DN
☎ 0463 73505

Sutherland Tourist Board
The Square
Dornoch
Sutherland IV25 3SD
☎ 0862 810400

Useful Addresses

Highlands and Islands Development Board
Bridge House
Inverness IV1 1QR

The **Hi-Line** information service answers all tourist enquiries and is available 24 hours a day on ☎ 0349 63434.

Historic Scotland
20 Brandon Street
Edinburgh EH3 5RA
☎ 031 556 8400

National Trust for Scotland
5 Charlotte Square
Edinburgh EH2 4DU
☎ 031 226 5922

Scottish Tourist Board
23 Ravelston Terrace
Edinburgh EH4 3EE
☎ 031 332 2433

Getting Around the Highlands and Islands
An annual guide, published by FHG Publications in association with the Highlands and Islands Development Board, is an invaluable listing of all transport services in the area with timetables for air, sea, rail, bus and postbus routes.

Index